Mother Tongues of the High Andes

Mother Tongues of the High Andes

MOTHER TONGUES of the HIGH ANDES

GENDER, LANGUAGE, AND INDIGENOUS DIFFERENCE IN PERU

SANDHYA KRITTIKA NARAYANAN

THE UNIVERSITY OF ARIZONA PRESS
TUCSON

The University of Arizona Press
www.uapress.arizona.edu

We respectfully acknowledge the University of Arizona is on the land and territories of Indigenous peoples. Today, Arizona is home to twenty-two federally recognized tribes, with Tucson being home to the O'odham and the Yaqui. The University strives to build sustainable relationships with sovereign Native Nations and Indigenous communities through education offerings, partnerships, and community service.

© 2025 by The Arizona Board of Regents
All rights reserved. Published 2025

ISBN-13: 978-0-8165-5563-5 (hardcover)
ISBN-13: 978-0-8165-5311-2 (paperback)
ISBN-13: 978-0-8165-5312-9 (ebook)

Cover design by Leigh McDonald
Cover photo of textile by Max Maximov/AdobeStock
Typeset by Sara Thaxton in 10.5/14 Warnock Pro with Good Headline Pro and Epsom WF

Publication of this book is made possible in part by support from the College of Liberal Arts Dean's Office and the Office of the Vice President of Research and Innovation at the University of Nevada, Reno.

Library of Congress Control Number: 2024060724

Printed in the United States of America
♾ This paper meets the requirements of ANSI/NISO Z39.48-1992 (Permanence of Paper).

Contents

List of Illustrations		*vii*
Preface		*ix*
Acknowledgments		*xv*
Note on Languages and Transcripts		*xix*
	Introduction: Mother Tongues and Indigenous Difference	3
1.	Indigenous Wives and Mothers' Tongues: Gendered Transitions Between Language, Kinship, and Land	47
2.	Brokering Across Boundaries: The Lives and Language of Market Women in Puno	81
3.	Institutionalizing Inter-Indigenous Differences: Formalizing Ethnolinguistic Boundaries in the Altiplano	135
4.	Mythical Mothers and the Reinvention of Indigenous Contact	177
5.	Fairest in the Land: The Pageantry of Linguistic Variation and Diverse Female Bodies	219
	Conclusion: The Gendered Indigenous Voice in a Global World	265
Notes		*287*
Bibliography		*303*
Index		*319*

Illustrations

Figures
1. Indigenous puneñas waiting to perform in La Morenada   29
2. View of small farm plots and Lake Titicaca from the hills outside of Chucuito   37
3. Mercado de San Ignacio after everyone has closed the market stalls early for the day   91
4. Cover of Quechua and Aymara phrase booklet   92
5. The front façade of the municipal building in Puno   136
6. Page from *Willakuy-Yatiyawinaka*   142
7. Excerpt of activity from Quechua worksheet   152
8. The arrival of Manqu Qhapaq and Mama Uqllu   179
9. The *Ayarachis de Cuyo-Cuyo*, the traditional danza autoctóna for the community of Cuyo-Cuyo   221
10. A beauty pageant contestant performing the traditional dance of her community   226

Tables
1. Lexican Purisms in Manqu Qhapaq's Speeches   199
2. Directives in Manqu Qhapaq's Speeches   199
3. Errors and Commentaries on Mama Uqllu's Speech   207

Preface

"*Qué quieres saber de mi lengua materna?*" From the day I first arrived in Puno till my last, I was frequently asked versions of this question, asking me, the researcher, what I wanted to know about the Indigenous languages of Puno. Over time I slowly understood that this rejoinder to my requests to interview Indigenous *puneños* about their linguistic background was made in reference to the two Indigenous languages of the Peruvian *altiplano*: Quechua and Aymara. Even as I would grow accustomed to other aspects of living and being in Puno, the phrasing of this invitation to discuss, explore, and compare different communicative social worlds would still catch me off guard. After all, I had come to Puno to see how Indigenous puneños spoke Quechua and Aymara—Indigenous languages that were widely regarded as "languages" in the formal grammatical and sociopolitical sense by academics and the general public. But the Indigenous Quechua- and Aymara-speaking puneños I spoke with rarely would refer to Quechua or Aymara as an *idioma*, the most direct Spanish translation for a named, grammatically distinct "language." Instead, my interlocutors more frequently would describe their native linguistic backgrounds through the phrase *lengua materna*—"mother tongue."

This book has been shaped and framed around what it means to be recognized as a speaker of an Indigenous language in multilingual Puno. But this book is also about the personal affective connections that speakers have with the ways that they communicate and interact with each other across social and linguistic differences. In this way, calling one's native language a lengua materna draws our focus away from thinking about these modes of communication as strictly defined by socially recognized named languages like Quechua or Aymara. Instead, thinking about talk in this region as shaped by different lenguas maternas emphasizes ways of speaking, and the role that they play in building social worlds and nurturing bonds and connections within and across different Indigenous communities in Puno and the Peruvian altiplano. The gendering of the phrase aligns these ways of speaking with mothers and motherhood. It evokes these connections by emplacing these ways of talking within spaces we might typically associate with mothers, such as the home and hearth, which foster talk and other social activities central to creating social relations and bonds. But these activities can also occur outside of the home, transporting these practices to create new connections with people and communities. In these situations, using one's lengua materna also becomes a vehicle to form new bonds that bridge social differences and relationships between individuals across different communities.

In many ways, the frequent use of lengua materna by puneños to describe their communicative practices felt similar to my own experiences with minoritized languages and multilingualism. I was born in Toronto, a first-generation South Asian immigrant living in Canada as part of the large wave of immigration that came to the nation in the late '70s through the '80s. At that time, Toronto and its surrounding neighborhoods transformed to a multilingual hub, with enclaves and boroughs slowly coalescing around distinct diasporic nations and ethnic identities. My early childhood memories include playing primarily with other children of South Indian and Sri Lankan Tamil descent; having to answer to various aunties and uncles when we got caught causing some kind of mischief; and being surrounded by the love that came from these other adults and families in our community, some of whom were connected by blood and others through a shared sense of being foreigners and minorities in Canada. But this sense of community was also made through the commonalities in how the adults in our lives spoke to us in a mixture of their respective mother tongues and English. As a child, I knew that there were differences in how many of those families spoke, and especially the ones who would label what they spoke as "Tamil." My brother and I would pick up these differences and novelties and sometimes reproduce them at home, only to be corrected by our mother or grandmother as not being how "we spoke." "Well don't we speak Tamil too?" I would ask, not always knowing what these terms meant. "Yes, and no," my mother would respond, and she would end the discussion decisively by saying, "That is not how we speak in our home." The significance of what my mother and grandmother told me did not make sense till I got older, when I slowly came to learn about the history of my mother's and grandmother's mother tongue—a product of contact and multilingualism from the highlands of Kerala. Did that mean that we still spoke Tamil? Or did we speak Malayalam? To this day, I still do not have any straight answers to those questions from my mother, grandmother, or maternal kin. Instead, our mother tongue, a mixed variety that is a testament to both our Tamil and Malayalam linguistic heritages, is used proudly in extended family WhatsApp group chats. Jokingly named "the clan," the group of extended family members are spread across three continents and frequently post in our mother tongue, discussing family recipes such as the correct way to make *aviyyal* and *puliakuthi* (traditional South Indian vegetable dishes) and sharing pictures of all the "clan" women donning their best traditional *kasava* or *mundu* saree for festivals like Onam and Trissur Pooram.

By the time I was a preteen, we had moved to Boston and into yet another South Asian community that was very different than the one I originally grew up among in Canada. Frequent visits back to Canada helped make those differences apparent, where the ways that we spoke at home were more recognized by our original immigrant community than by those in our new home in Boston. Many of my peers from the same South Asian community were primarily from families who came from the northern parts of the subcontinent and spoke Gujarati, Hindi, and Marathi. Like other South Asian youth at the time, we recognized each other as different and as coming from homes with not only different mother tongues but different foods, music, and broader communities. Those differences were never acknowledged by our peers or teachers. And in the wake of 9/11, those differences were treated and regarded as threats that intensified the existing undercurrents of xenophobia, Islamophobia, and racism in Boston.

These histories in no way should be thought of as equivalent to the kinds of experiences faced by Indigenous Quechua- and Aymara-speaking communities in the Peruvian altiplano. Nor can I ever claim that the varied experiences of exploitation, discrimination, or deployment of a kind of colonial romanticism that has targeted Indigenous populations in Puno and Peru are an exact replica for the kinds of colonial and racist legacies that I and my family have experienced. But connections did emerge over the course of my fieldwork in Puno, which were also shaped by my positionality as a first-generation South Asian immigrant and a woman and scholar of color who was largely raised within a diverse, multilingual community, whose internal linguistic and social differences were often overlooked by others around us. My decision to first go to the Andes, and do work in Peru, was inspired by my aunt Rosa, who was from Bolivia and raised in La Paz. Rosa would tell me and my brother stories of her childhood in La Paz and about the traditions and languages of Indigenous communities across the Andes. I decided that in college I would find a way to spend a summer or semester abroad in either Peru or Bolivia in order to get a better understanding of the world my aunt came from prior to moving to the United States and marrying my uncle.

After spending one summer abroad in Peru, I chose to pursue graduate work in Puno because of its Indigenous multilingual history and how that appeared to be similar to the multilingual milieu I was raised in. Because of how I looked, I was often able to pass for other young Indigenous *puneña* women of my peer group. These factors shaped my fieldwork experience and influenced my decision to spend most of my time with Indigenous puneña women. It was through these women, particularly middle-aged women, that I found a sense of safety, security, and comfort that mirrored my own upbringing of being raised and cared for by a wide network of aunties and fictive older sisters within two different South Asian diasporic communities. In these circles, and especially among Indigenous market women (see chapter 2), I was often treated much like another daughter, sister, or niece. These connections helped place me within these families and kin networks and granted me access to the conversations, stories, and personal life histories that shaped these women's lives and their relationship with their lenguas maternas. I was also encouraged and expected to participate in many of their activities that included helping out in the fields or *chakras,* providing assistance in the markets, and utilizing the slower moments of the day to catch up on knitting or crocheting projects. Soon these activities were complemented by conversational lessons in Quechua and Aymara and, eventually, formal interviews on their lives and linguistic biographies.

My focus on women in this book largely derives from having spent most of my time with women in general. But by spending time with these women, I was able to get a closer glimpse of how their lives, and in particular their gendered positions and backgrounds, intersected with the significance of referring to Quechua and Aymara as lenguas maternas. I was also able to see how the gendering of Indigenous language use and the gendered backgrounds of Indigenous Quechua- and Aymara-speaking women were important in shaping and transforming Indigenous multilingual praxis and competing visions of inter-Indigenous difference. Lengua materna did not necessarily refer to Quechua or Aymara as languages. Instead, it referred to the specific ways that you spoke, and how those communicative practices connected you to a place, a home, and a community that you could call kin. Knowing your lengua materna meant knowing how to speak in ways that reflect the relationships that shape and define an individual's identity. And it was also about sharing those forms of communication to create new bonds of solidarity and intimacy across boundaries of social difference. Everyone has a lengua materna. However, my point of access through the lives, stories, and communicative lengua materna practices of women provided a specific vantage to understand the unique role that women play in managing how Indigenous puneños think about, evaluate, and reconsider how these Indigenous lenguas maternas should be spoken in relation to ongoing negotiations around their histories of Indigenous multilingualism and the recognition of inter-Indigenous differences in Puno.

Discourses and discussions about multilingual practices and histories are never static. They are ever changing with the times and shaped by larger political and social processes. This has certainly been true in my own life experiences, where my extended family's understanding and conceptualization of our multilingual histories have taken different routes and detours that have been influenced by our communities and social networks and the ways those intersect with broader political discussions. The same is true for Indigenous puneños, whose relationship to their lenguas maternas and their multilingual history is still undergoing new kinds of ideological transformations that affect perceptions of Indigenous language speakerhood and linguistic knowledge and expertise. These shifts directly impact how these lenguas maternas will be spoken in the future. But they also have consequences on how Indigenous puneños understand their own social differences and negotiate these understandings with competing modes of inter-Indigenous identification and differentiation that are more readily recognized by audiences outside of Puno and the altiplano. By centering on the lives, practices, and linguistic idealizations associated with Indigenous puneña women, this ethnography pulls into focus the centrality of Indigenous women in mediating these discourses and contradictory perspectives.

Acknowledgments

This book is the product of over a decade of research, writing, and introspection. Over that time, my life has been touched by so many people whose love, support, kindness, and friendship have made this study and this book possible. There are not enough words and pages to fully thank them and capture the many ways that these individuals have helped me intellectually and emotionally. But know that I am forever indebted to all of the support, guidance, and insights that I have received from all of you over the years. Without it, this book would still be a vague pipe dream, yet to be fully materialized.

This project was first conceived during my graduate doctoral studies at the University of Michigan. During those years, I was fortunate to work very closely with Bruce Mannheim, Barbra Meek, and Judith Irvine. I am so grateful for all of their insights and unending pools of patience as they helped me formulate this project as part of my doctoral dissertation research, and later to rethink some of my main arguments once more as preparation for the book. I was also so fortunate to be in conversation with other scholars whose generosity, creativity, and intellectual curiosity provided me other perspectives to enhance my own understanding of this research. Marlyse Baptista and Robin Queen gave me additional invaluable mentorship and guidance, which to this day shapes how I think about my scholarship and the stakes that it has on describing multilingual communities. Gillian Feely-Harnik and

Tom Trautmann continue to inspire how I think about my research in relation to larger anthropological questions and how I bring those lessons into my teaching as well. Adela Urpi Carlos Rios, thank you so much for your friendship and caring spirit. I am forever indebted to you for teaching me and so many others Quechua prior to starting fieldwork. And I am even more fortunate to continue to have had a conversation partner in the language when I returned from the field. So much of this book would not have been possible at all without your endless amounts of energy and commitment to sharing your lengua materna. *Urpillay sunqullay ñañachay*!

Funding for this research was generously provided through the Rackham International Research Grant, the NSF Doctoral Dissertation Improvement Grant, a Fulbright-Hayes Doctoral Dissertation Research Award, and research awards from the Institute for the Research of Women and Gender at the University of Michigan. Preliminary fieldwork funding for this project was provided by a National Geographic Society Young Explorer's Grant, Tinker Field Research Grant, and an International Institute Research Grant at the University of Michigan. Pre-field language training in Quechua was supported through a FLAS fellowship. Writing support was provided through generous startup funds through the CLA Dean's Office and the Office of the Vice President for Research and Innovation at the University of Nevada, Reno. This financial support was matched by the emotional support provided by close friends. In particular, I would like to thank Adrienne Lagman, Annemarie Creighton, Warren Thompson, Nick Emlen, Josh Shapero, Geoffrey Hughes, Courtney Cottrell, Cheryl Yin, Ariana Bancu, Elspeth Geiger, Aaron Michka, Jose Enrique Solano, and Jenny Larios. More than surviving our seminars and writing our term papers together, you all provided me the friendships and encouragement to persevere through the highs and lows of graduate school. This book would not be here if it weren't for your support during those years, and continued friendship since then.

I am so thankful to everyone in Puno and Peru who also facilitated this research and made this work possible. Victor Maqque and his family, thank you for opening the doors of your home to me and getting me situated in Puno. To Mama Justina, my stay in Puno would never have felt like home without your warmth and love. So much of this book was only possible because of you and the company you provided, whether it was knitting together while watching Spanish-dubs of Turkish telenovelas or enjoying a nice *vino caliente* together spiked with a shot of *pisco*. My days in Puno were never complete without Grober Cutipa, with whom conversations were always the highlight of my day, whether it was discussing political events in Puno, or sitting in discomfort and sometimes horror over the political and social developments taking place in the United States while I was in Puno. Thank you so much for the generosity of your friendship. To Cathy and Guernot, thank you so much for a warm meal whenever I was feeling down or sick. Your soups kept me nourished throughout my time in Puno. Thank you Rozaluz and Paula for opening your homes to me in Lima and Arequipa anytime I needed to visit those cities as I was accompanying my interlocutors on their extended travels. Most importantly, thank you to all of my friends and interlocutors who are featured in this book. Although you are named in these pages with pseudonyms, I still remember all of you and think of you to this day. None of this would have been possible without you and how you all welcomed me into your homes and lives. I hope that this book does justice in capturing the complexity and beauty of your lives and life histories in Puno.

Since completing the primary research that informs this book, I have come in contact with other people whose enthusiasm for this project has helped get this book to this final stage. Thank you to Domnica Radulescu at Washington and Lee University, where I did a one-year visiting assistant professorship. Weekly dinners at your house over a bottle of wine were so instrumental in helping me develop my voice as a scholar and a writer. To my colleagues at the University of Nevada, Reno: Erin Stiles, Sarah Cowie, Mikaela Rogozen-Soltar, Debbie Boehm, Chris Morgan, Michael Aguirre, Nasia Anam, Prisca Gayles, Vadricka Etienne, Daniel Enrique Perez, Lydia Huerta, and Ruthie Meadows. And a special thank-you to Annamaria Pazienza, who was my constant writing, swimming, and Friday-night-taco buddy. You all helped me stay grounded and motivated during the writing and rewriting process. A very special thank-you to Chris Morgan and Erin Stiles, who were both department chair while I was writing this book, for always being so supportive in reassuring me about this process. To Ashlee Dauphinais and Anna Babel, you made sure that this project moved across the finish line during the final revisions. Ashlee, thank you for always being my sounding board during this entire process. Finally, to Kathleen Kelly, of Grey Bevins Editorial, for helping me structure the book and get it ready for review.

Needless to say this book would not have happened were it not for the University of Arizona Press. To Allyson Carter, my editor, thank you so much for shepherding this entire project. Your reassurance and constant compassion for the trials associated with writing one's first book kept me going. A big shout-out to Alana Enriquez, who helped with streamlining the process of getting the final manuscript ready for production and publication. And thank you to the various anonymous reviewers who read and commented on this book at its various stages. Without all their comments and dedicated insights, this ethnography would not be what it is today.

Lastly, this book, and even my own entry into the field of linguistic anthropology, would never have happened if it were not for my family, their love and support, and also how their linguistic biographies and life experiences nurtured my own interest in the relationship between language and social life from an early age. I dedicate this book to my *amma*, Mallika Narayanan, and my *ammamma*, Bala Narasimhan, who first taught me the importance of our mother tongue. To my *appa*, Srinivasan Narayanan, brother, Siddhartha Narayanan, and sister-in-law, Lauren, for their encouragement and support. This book is in memory of my late maternal uncle (*mama*), Sudarshan Narasimhan, who passed away too soon while I was in the field. I come from a very large family, where extended connections are treated as close family relationships. To my Anandhi chitthi and Sethu chitthappa, my cousin brothers, Ananth, Madhavan, and my sister-in-law (*mani*), Madhuvanthi. To my Padmini athai and O.S. athimber, and to my Chander chittappa and Rosa chitthi, who loved to compare my research experiences in Puno with her own memories of growing up in La Paz, Bolivia. She passed away while this book was in press. Last but not least, thank you, Solomon. Your daily love, encouragement, and humor always gave me the little bit of extra energy I needed to get in my hour of daily writing, even after a full day of teaching. Thank you!

Note on Languages and Transcripts

As the two main Indigenous languages of the *altiplano*, Quechua and Aymara have been spoken prior to Spanish colonial contact in the Andes. The shared histories between speakers of both languages have contributed to several grammatical similarities across both languages (Adelaar and Muysken 2004). Both languages have very similar phonemic inventories, with a three-way voiceless consonant distinction between a voiceless stop, voiceless aspirated stop, and voiceless ejective (e.g., [k], [kh], and [k']). Today voiceless consonant series are written using the symbols employed by the IPA (International Phonetic Alphabet), with the exception of the post-alveolar/palatal voiceless consonants, which are written as [ch], [chh], and [ch'] accordingly. Both languages share the voiceless alveolar fricative [s]. And both languages share the same set of nasals (the bilabial [m], the alveolar [n], and the palatal [ñ], which is similar to the Spanish *ñ* as pronounced in the word *niña*). Lastly, Quechua and Aymara have the same liquids and glides, with the bilabial [w] and palatal [y] glides and the alveolar [l] and palatal liquids [ll]. The palatal liquid for both languages will be written as [ll] in order to match standard orthographic practices for Quechua and Aymara. However, it is also important to note that this palatal liquid is not the same phoneme represented by the Spanish [ll], which is pronounced like a palatal glide.

Their vowel inventory consists of three cardinal vowels [i], [a], and [u]. Similarly, both languages have vowel lowering when sharing the same environment with the voiceless uvular stop or ejective, resulting in the phonetic realization of [i] and [u] as [e] and [o], respectively. Additionally, Aymara also differentiates between its vowels for length, which is usually spelled on the vowel as [ä], [ï], and [ü].

Their phonemic inventory also differs in a few ways. Aymara has a voiceless velar fricative, which will be written as [x], and a voiceless uvular fricative, which will be written as [j] following standard Aymara spelling practices in Peru and Bolivia today (Coler 2014). Quechua does not have the voiceless velar or uvular fricative. Instead, Quechua has the voiceless glottal fricative, which, following standard orthographic practices in Quechua, is written as [h]. Quechua also has the voiceless post-alveolar/palatal fricative, written as [sh].

Quechua and Aymara also have similar agglutinative, suffixing morphology and a system of evidentials that mark knowledge source vis-à-vis speaker positionality. The standard syntactic structure for both languages is subject-object-verb (SOV), with verb finality being the most commonly occurring syntactic paradigm in spoken Quechua and Aymara. Lastly, both languages also share about 15–30 percent of their lexical roots (Cerrón-Palomino 1994). Considering all these similarities, some scholars have proposed that Quechua and Aymara are part of the same genetic language family (Campbell 1995). However, other scholars have effectively argued against this view. For instance, focusing on such similarities overlooks the even larger number of dissimilar grammatical and lexical features (i.e., the 70–85 percent of non-shared lexical roots) between the languages (Emlen 2017). These scholars also argue that these similarities emerged from close connections between speakers of these languages and their proto-varieties over time (Adelaar 2012). This means that the similarities found between both languages are a result of contact and interactions between speakers rather than from sharing a common linguistic genetic ancestor (Mannheim 1991).

Across the Andes, Indigenous linguistic contact and interactions with Spanish (*castellano*) have also led to contact-induced changes in Spanish. These changes are broadly categorized as Andean Spanish (*castellano andino*) and typically involve the raising of the vowels [e] and [o] to [i] and [u], respectively, as well as the prevalence of SOV syntactic structures (Escobar 2011). These changes mirror similar kinds of grammatical features and characteristics present in both Quechua and Aymara.

NOTE ON LANGUAGES AND TRANSCRIPTS

Given that this study is focused on the linguistic practices in Puno, all instances of spoken puneño Andean Spanish will be transcribed and spelled to include features associated with Andean Spanish. Thus, vowels like [e] and [o] may be transcribed as [i] and [u] depending on if the speaker produced those vowels in their recordings. Lastly, transcripts of spoken Quechua and Aymar are transcribed to capture how these varieties are spoken in Puno. As such, the ways that lexical items will be transcribed in this book, especially in transcripts from interviews and conversations, will deviate from standardized or institutionally recognized ways of spelling and writing Quechua and Aymara in other parts of Peru and Bolivia.

Transcripts in this book will follow the spelling conventions outlined above. And with the exception of vowel changes, transcriptions of Spanish will also follow the language's standard orthographic conventions. Transcripts of conversations and dialogues across this book freely move across and incorporate elements from Quechua, Aymara, and Spanish. As such, language distinctions in the transcripts throughout this book will adhere to the following conventions:

Regular Font	Spanish
<u>Underline</u>	Quechua
Italics	Aymara

In addition to these font changes, the following transcription conventions will be employed to convey additional information about communicative and conversational practices in Puno:

- .   Period; used to indicate the end of a phrase or utterance.
- ,   Comma; used for a short pause, such as the short pauses that appear between clauses.
- —   Dash; used to indicate a break in the flow of speech, either appearing in moments of correction, a slightly longer pause of under three seconds, or a break in the flow of talk accompanied by a change in topic.
- ...   Three-dot ellipsis; used for speech pauses longer than three seconds.
- = X =   Overlapping speech; used to indicate moments when speakers are talking over each other.

Mother Tongues of the High Andes

Mother Tongues of the High Andes

Introduction

Mother Tongues and Indigenous Difference

On a cold morning in the middle of the Andean winter, where morning temperatures easily drop below freezing, I bundled up in my warmest layers of long underwear, vest, hat, and mittens to help my friend Señora Estela open up her market stall in Puno. Despite the cold, I was looking forward to meeting Señora Estela early in the day. As a devout *evangelista* (Evangelical Protestant Christian), Señora Estela would go to the local Maranatha church every day to attend the midday service. Being the first to open her market stall meant that she could get a head start on her competition and complete the majority of her sales early in the day. As a clothing vendor with a particularly large inventory of school uniforms, she always tried to be ready for her target clientele—frantic mothers and schoolchildren in desperate need of an extra sock, tie, or brand-new skirt to complete their uniform before going to school.

I knew that mornings were the best time to chat with Señora Estela. That day I tried to take advantage of the lull that followed the morning rush to have an informal interview with her. After Señora Estela had the chance to properly nourish herself with her breakfast *salteña* (beef empanada) and *ponche de habas* (hot drink of fava beans) that she purchased from her friend and longtime co-vendor, she sat down to tell me her life story. Born to an Aymara-speaking family in the provinces south of Puno, Señora Estela moved to the city to become a market vendor in her early twenties. Upon moving to the city, she learned Spanish. But her move to the city also put her in contact with Quechua-speaking vendors. Soon, Señora Estela learned enough Quechua to form relationships with other Quechua-speaking vendors and friends, eventually meeting and marrying a Quechua-speaking man who attended the same church. As she spoke, I scribbled down these details as quickly as I could, in spite of the cold seeping into my fingers through my fingerless gloves. Once Señora Estela felt satisfied with her account, we continued to chat the rest of the morning, gossiping about Peruvian celebrity news, politics, and the affairs of some of her market associates.

Before I knew it, it was noon. Quickly, Señora Estela covered her stalls with some blankets, a tarp, and a long wooden pole—signs that were widely recognized across Puno that the vendor was going to return later that day. After letting her fellow market vendors know that she was off to church, she quickly bundled her *artesanía* handiwork into her *awayu* (shawl), slung it over her back, and hurried off. I too had to hurry off to another appointment, a long-overdue lunch with a professor at the local university. This professor was an Aymara-speaking professional born and raised in the southernmost Aymara-speaking districts in the Department of Puno. Despite living primarily in the regional capital of Puno, he proudly identified himself as an Indigenous Aymara man and would often remind me whenever we met, "*Soy aymara nativo*" ("I am native Aymara"). After inquiring about my health and complaining about the cold (a very real pastime in Puno any time of the year), he asked me how I spent my morning. I told him about Señora Estela, sharing with him some of the basic details of her life and that she was an Aymara-speaking woman who also learned to speak Quechua and Spanish. Before I could go any further, he very politely interrupted me, saying, "Señorita, why are you spending time with this *casera* [homemaker]. If you want, I can help you find a proper *awicha* [grandmother] in the countryside who can speak good Quechua or Aymara for you."

This was neither the first nor the last time I heard a statement like this. During my time in Puno, I became accustomed to hearing similar comments from other local professors, municipal government employees, teachers, and other professionals. Often these judgments would come from men who also strongly identified with being Indigenous, ethnic Quechua or Aymara, who perhaps felt that they were showing their care and concern by giving me this advice. Even more surprising were the times that I received the same advice from Quechua- and Aymara-speaking women, like those who I had become acquainted with in the markets. These women would often say that I should instead consult with their husbands, brothers, or fathers—men in their lives who they felt were better speakers of Quechua or Aymara and therefore more suitable participants for a research project being conducted by a U.S.-based academic researcher. I would deflect these suggestions, highlighting the multilingual virtuosity of my female interlocutors, while also encouraging my female participants to value their own linguistic knowledge as a form of expertise. And yet with every suggestion I received, I would nonetheless wonder what it meant to be a good or proper speaker of Quechua and Aymara. And if there was such a thing, who spoke it?

This ethnography centers on these questions, focusing on how Indigenous Quechua-Aymara speaking *puneños* negotiate what speaking Quechua and Aymara mean in relation to defining Indigenous identities and inter-Indigenous ethnic difference in Puno, Peru. Specifically, this ethnography is about how knowing Quechua and Aymara—and the ways these forms of expertise contribute to conceptions around being an authentic Indigenous Quechua and Aymara citizen—are inseparable from ideologies around Indigenous differences and gender identities in Puno. Through the various chapters in this book, I illustrate how the different indexical values and qualities associated with Indigenous Quechua- and Aymara-speaking women and men are at the center of shifting ideologies around Indigenous linguistic knowledge, authority, and authentic Indigenous identities in Puno and the Peruvian *altiplano*. On the surface, these questions seem to align with other kinds of ideologized associations between language, gender, and indigeneity that have been attested within and across the Andes and in Latin America. The relationship between gender and indigeneity, for instance, has been central in defining and shaping racial hierarchies, racialized identities, and racial categories in Peru and across the Andes since the colonial period (Cadena 2000; Poole 1997; Rappaport 2014). Throughout this history, language, and specifically the salience of Indigenous linguistic knowledge and practices, has been instrumental in mediating the alignment between gendered bodies and Indigenous racio-ethnic subjectivities (Babel 2018; Swinehart 2018). Yet what makes these questions unique (and more complex to answer) in Puno is how these processes and the semiotic alignments between gender, indigeneity, and language play out in a zone of language contact, multilingualism, and Indigenous linguistic and social diversity. It is these histories of multilingualism and language contact that complicate not only linguistic and Indigenous ethnic categories like "Quechua" and "Aymara" but also the relationship that they have with gender differences.

Running throughout this ethnography is a larger tension about what Quechua and Aymara are as languages, identities, and mediums of communication, and how those categories may be less apparent or straightforward to answer in a region known for Indigenous multilingualism and inter-Indigenous contact. Typically, in Puno Quechua- and Aymara-speaking puneños, men and women alike describe their linguistic backgrounds and linguistic knowledge as *"lenguas maternas."* Translated as "mother tongues," this term has a wide range of meanings. In public discourses, particularly in socially and hegemonically dominant or privileged spaces and mediums, lenguas maternas often only refers to Indigenous languages from the Peruvian Andes and Amazon. On national television stations and on talk shows, for instance, Quechua and Aymara are labeled as lenguas maternas, contrasting these languages from Peru's official and hegemonically dominant "language," Spanish. This also extends colloquially among puneños and non-Indigenous Peruvians, who use the label "lenguas maternas" to refer to non-Spanish languages that are linked to an individual's heritage and ancestry. But when Quechua- and Aymara-speaking puneños use the term, it is not always entirely clear if lengua materna refers to Quechua and Aymara as two distinct Indigenous languages or as general ways of speaking that reflect an individual's linguistic heritage and background. The term "lengua materna" is also not gender neutral. It is gender specific, explicitly linking non-Spanish, Indigenous linguistic practices and linguistic heritage with mothers, the maternal line, and the practices, spaces, and domains associated with motherly figures and maternal kin. The ways that lenguas maternas are discursively used across Puno to identify Indigenous linguistic practices genders those ancestries and practices, aligning Indigenous language use and linguistic histories with Indigenous women. Yet these gendered associations highlight how local conceptions and growing debates around Indigenous language speakerhood, Indigenous identity, and inter-Indigenous differences cannot be neatly separated from the lives, practices, and ideological perceptions surrounding Indigenous women in Puno.

In this sense, gender differences and, more specifically, closer attention to the place of women and Indigenous femininity in Puno complicate how we need to think about the semiotic and ideological relationships between language, gender, and Indigenous ethnicity in the Andes. The chapters that follow will highlight the diverse roles that Quechua- and Aymara-speaking women play in managing and negotiating the boundaries between languages and their associations with inter-Indigenous differences. Yet in turn new constellations of gendered subjectivities also emerge as Indigenous puneños adopt contemporary discourses to define their Indigenous languages and to grapple with what it means to be Indigenous within Puno and beyond.

Documenting Indigenous Ethnic Difference

The Peruvian national census was scheduled to be conducted at the end of October 2017. As a technocratic practice using the science of statistics to document the changing demographics of a nation, the Peruvian census, run through INEI (Instituto Nacional de Estadística e Informática; National Institute of Statistics and Information Technology) ideologically reflects the specific politics around the documentation of race, ethnicity, and language, while also excluding other categories and forms of identification from national rhetoric. One category that has long been the subject of exclusion was the question of Indigenous identity, and specifically Indigenous ethnicity and ethnic differences. These categories were systematically omitted from earlier versions of the census as part of a longer historical legacy of erasing indigeneity, Indigenous ethnic diversity, and alternate forms of identification that depart from the national racial rhetoric of *mestizaje* (Arispe-Bazán 2023).[1] This historical exclusion is made more stark by the fact that Indigenous languages like Quechua and Aymara have been counted on previous censuses, listed as lenguas maternas along with a select number of Amazonian Indigenous languages like Ashaninka and Shipibo. But 2017 was different, marking the first time in recent history that separate categories documenting Indigenous ethnic and racial difference were included on the national census form, creating a space for individuals to self-identify as a member of a racialized or Indigenous ethnic group, regardless of whether they lived in rural areas or urban spaces, or if they spoke only Spanish. For the first time in modern Peruvian history, Quechua and Aymara were included as two distinct Indigenous ethnic categories, making it a landmark moment for these distinct Indigenous ethnic populations to be counted on official government documents. On the surface, the inclusion of these terms might appear as a kind of neoliberal, multicultural victory, officially placing Indigenous ethnic differences as distinct categories of identification for all citizens, and was regarded as the next logical step within the longer politics around the formation and recognition of "Indigenous citizens" in Peru (García 2005; Poole 2016). However, the decision to acknowledge inter-Indigenous differences according to categories like "Quechua" and "Aymara" is also complicated by the state's role in recognizing and denying the presence of Indigenous populations and Indigenous alterity and diversity (Cox Hall, Alcalde, and Babb 2022; Alcalde 2022).

In many ways, the historical significance of the 2017 census were accompanied by a distinct set of ideological challenges that complicated the relationship between Indigenous linguistic knowledge and Indigenous ethnic identity. Similar to past censuses, the 2017 census allowed individuals to list which languages they speak. But identifying which language one spoke did not have to match how individuals could identify in terms of their racial and ethnic heritage. More than opening the door to asking what linguistic and communicative characteristics qualify an individual to count as a speaker of Quechua or Aymara, the 2017 census also set the stage for new discussions of how individuals could go about identifying as an Indigenous, ethnic Quechua or Aymara (Narayanan 2023a). Prior to 2017, whether or not someone could claim to be Indigenous, ethnic Quechua or Aymara was evaluated through Quechua or Aymara linguistic knowledge or fluency and residency. Descendants of Indigenous migrants living in larger urban areas such as Cusco, Arequipa, and the national capital of Lima in the past may have been hesitant (or prohibited) to self-identify as Indigenous Quechua or Aymara because they lived in cities and primarily communicated in Spanish. Instead, identifying as Indigenous ethnic Quechua or Aymara were categorical choices only reserved for individuals who lived in rural areas, tended to their fields and flocks, and primarily spoke in Quechua or Aymara. The 2017 census invited citizens, and especially urbanized Indigenous migrants living in larger cosmopolitan cities like Arequipa and Lima, to rethink these alignments and encouraged them to openly identify as Indigenous, ethnic Quechua and Aymara, even if they did not know these languages or actively use them in their daily interactions or communicative practices.

Openly identifying as Indigenous in Peru has always been a contradictory process in which Indigenous identification was long seen as a potential threat to the state's hegemonic national identity. This was despite the fact that the celebration of a pre-Hispanic Indigenous heritage was central to establishing and legitimizing a distinct national cultural and racial identity (García 2008; Weismantel and Eisenman 1998). This tenuous relationship not only was present during the colonial period (MacCormack 1991) but also became prominent soon after the Wars of Independence, where an Andean Indigenous cultural heritage and racialized identity based on a pre-Columbian, Inkaic past was important to cultivating Peru's national identity after its independence from Spain. As Cecilia Mendez (1996) notes, post-independence national discourses and rhetorics that promoted Peru's cultural and historic proximity and a shared kinship with Indigenous elements was summed up by the phrase *Inkas sí, indios no*[2] ("Inkas yes, not indians") — a phrase that emphasized Peru's national and cultural legitimacy through embracing the grandeur of pre-Hispanic civilizations of the past while also denying this same recognition to contemporary (colonized) Indigenous populations.[3]

The erasures embedded in this statement are also reproduced in other kinds of racializing discourses that celebrate and highlight the racial, ethnic, and cultural diversity found within Peru. Today in major urban cities like Lima or Arequipa, one can hear the common phrase *el que no tiene de inga, tiene del Mandinga* (If one does not have Inkan [ancestry], then they have Mandinka [ancestry]),[4] which, when uttered in these spaces equalizes the pervasiveness of non-European ancestry in Peru without attending to the inherent racism still leveled against Indigenous and

Afro-Peruvian populations today (Zavala and Zariquiey 2009). More commonly heard is the statement that Peru is divided into three distinct regions: *La costa, sierra, y selva*. *La costa* (the coast) is home to the largest cities in the country, including the national capital of Lima. It is also heavily identified with non-Indigenous, *criollo* or white populations, and is interpreted as a non-Indigenous space. *La sierra* (the mountains) refers to the high mountains of the Andes, whose populations are not referred to as Indigenous but instead as *serranos* (from the mountains) or *campesinos* (peasants). To a certain degree, the altiplano contains many of the features that, for Peruvians living on the coast, epitomize the sierra with its rugged, harsh landscape, high-plateau plains filled with tall grasses, and a background studded with snowcapped peaks. The sierra is also home to Quechua- and Aymara-speaking populations, who are largely regarded by coastal *limeños* as an undifferentiated group of Indigenous Andean communities who are essentially the same people directly linked to the Inka empire and its downfall. Lastly, *la selva* (the jungle) refers to the Amazonian lowlands of Peru, a place populated by Indigenous groups who are characterized as representing a truly primal, untouched, pre-modern form of indigeneity. The Amazon is typically celebrated for its biodiversity, where the national television station of Peru, TVPerú, will often televise footage from the region that showcases bright and colorful animals like parrots and macaws, beautiful flowers, and the production of delicious agricultural products for export like papayas and cacao. The selva is also home to Indigenous populations who speak languages like Ashaninka, Matsigenka, and Shipibo and who are typically depicted as living pristine, pre-modern traditional lives, disconnected from capitalist societies that characterize the cosmopolitan cities of la costa.

Despite such overtures in acknowledging cultural and racial diversity in the nation, all these discourses fundamentally also erase those differences, such as the continued presence of diverse Indigenous and Afro-Peruvian populations by being overshadowed by the dominant national racial discourses of mestizaje[5] (Wade 2008) or racial and cultural mixture and miscegenation. Positioning the nation as a land of *mestizos* completes this racialized erasure of other, non-criollo populations and groups through either portraying them as archaic elements of the distant past, framing them as incompatible with visions of a modern nation-state (Drinot 2014; Quijano 2007), or completely denying their presence and existence in urban spaces and areas that are marked as criollo or white (Cusicanqui 2010). These kinds of ideological moves that erase racial and ethnic difference, which lie at the heart of discourses that declare Peru's national identity as a mestizo nation, have been noted by scholars like Marisol de la Cadena (1998) as a primarily modern project, linked to the political, social, and cultural discussions around the relationships between race, culture, and citizenship that emerged at the turn of the twentieth century among scholars and non-Indigenous elites from Cuzco and the highlands. Yet this management of social, racial, and cultural diversity has long been part of Peru's history since the colonial period, where the active marginalization and control over the boundaries and qualifications for nondominant Indigenous and Afro-Peruvian populations nonetheless continue today and are often decided and enacted by non-Indigenous individuals in positions of power. The rootedness of these practices to the power imbalances that emerged at the moment of colonial contact reflects what Peruvian scholar Anibal Quijano (2000) has termed the "coloniality of power," which calls attention to the many ways that systems and practices of social inequality, especially between Indigenous and non-Indigenous populations, is an ongoing legacy of Spanish colonialism. The coloniality of power, for instance, can contextualize how discourses around mestizaje and the glorification of racial and cultural mixture as the nation's racial and ethnic identity can only exist through a kind of distancing away from non-criollo, and non-mestizo, histories and cultural practices such as those that are explicitly Indigenous or Afro-Peruvian. It also provides insight into how everyday forms of discrimination and racism persist in Peruvian society, which for Indigenous Andeans are largely fueled by and through language (Back and Zavala 2018).

Considering this history, the inclusion of Quechua and Aymara as distinct ethnic Indigenous categories opens up broader questions about what these linguistic names and labels really mean in relation to histories of settler-colonial and Indigenous interactions. Furthermore, asking what Quechuas and Aymaras are, how their differences are accounted for, and what the metrics and standards for deciding who is counted as each, becomes even more complicated in multilingual and multiethnic Puno. The Quechua- and Aymara-speaking puneños featured in this book continue to grapple with these questions concerning the definitions and boundaries that make and constitute an Indigenous, ethnic Quechua and Aymara citizen. Such discussions are rooted in not only what Quechua and Aymara are as languages but also what these terms mean in relation to being Indigenous within Puno, highlighting the importance of understanding Indigenous ethnic identity as grounded in processes of understanding inter-Indigenous difference and diversity.

Indigenous Identity, Difference, and Recognition: A View from the Andes

Pueblos originarios. Comunidades indígenas. Comunidades nativas. Today the discourses around identifying and labeling Indigenous communities in Peru are as vast and varied as Indigenous diversity within the nation-state. The differences between each of these labels speak to the inconsistency on the part of the state to recognize Indigenous difference and identity within Peru. The continued presence of such terms also reflects the increasing recognition of the rights and sovereignty of Indigenous populations across Latin America (Warren and Jackson 2002). This is especially true of the Andean republics, where the fight for Indigenous recognition has ranged from pan-Indigenous mobilizations in Ecuador (Lucero 2008) to the renaming of the now pluri-ethnic, plurilingual Republic of Bolivia (Gustafson 2009; Postero 2017; Villarreal 2017). The rise and presence of such movements share grassroots origins, stemming from the ways that Indigenous actors from different backgrounds and geographic regions build solidarity and networks with other groups to voice their histories and demonstrate their collective resistance toward Western hegemonic settler-colonial practices that erase, exclude, or exploit their status as racialized, internal "others" (Portocarrero 1993). Yet amid this promotion and mobilization lingers a larger assumption and problem: To what degree are terms such as "Indigenous," "*indígena*," "*nativo/a*," and other politicized racio-ethnic categories universally understood and embraced by all Indigenous individuals and communities?

In his ethnography of Wila Kjarka, Bolivia, Andrew Canessa (2012a) highlights these questions and tensions in the years following the election of Evo Morales, the first Bolivian president of Indigenous ancestry. At the time, the election of Morales was widely touted as a victory, and to some as the long-awaited moment of *pachakuti* (lit. "turning of the earth," or the entry of a new era) toward the advancement of Indigenous rights and the valorization of Indigenous identities within Bolivia, and exemplified how global discourses of indigeneity were recruited to reframe discussions around citizenship, history, and politics within the state. Such moves, however, are contrasted by the intimate lives and local histories of Wila Kjarka's Aymara-speaking residents, who Canessa argues do not resonate with the term "Indigenous," or the politics of a globalized discourse around indigeneity. The Indigenous/non-Indigenous binary, as Canessa argues, is much more mutable, shaped by dress, occupation, and language, each of whose trajectories are as changeable and fluid as the historical discourses of discussing and recognizing Indigenous citizens within Bolivia. More importantly, being Indigenous for the residents of Wila Kjarka, or identifying as *jaqi*—Aymara for "people"—is a specific kind of racialized subjectivity that emerges from histories of exploitation, marginalization, and violence associated with settler-colonial contact (Canessa 2012b).

Part of being indígena, jaqi, or a recognized member of Wila Kjarka is, therefore, having one's everyday lived praxis of engaging in relationships with others contrast with the actions and practices of non-Indigenous individuals and groups. Often labeled as *"q'ara,"* meaning "bare" or "naked" in both Quechua and Aymara, the term when applied to identify non-Indigenous individuals signals their overall lack of humanity through their acts of violence and exploitation. Positioning Indigenous populations as the antithesis of those who would be seen as q'ara also resonates across the Peruvian highlands, which have also experienced similar histories of exploitation and marginalization. Detailed ethnographic analysis of Indigenous lifeways throughout the Andes also emphasize how being seen as a member of an Indigenous community, and being recognized as *runa* (Quechua) or jaqi (Aymara), is borne out of long-term relationships of reciprocity and obligation, aligning indigeneity with a broader framework of being a person and human who is a product of a complex set of kinship relationships with the landscape and with other human and nonhuman entities and beings (Cadena 2015; Canessa 2006; Salas Carreño 2019). As Catherine Allen (2002) beautifully notes, identifying oneself as runa is not derived from a political stance. Instead, being runa means being a full human being, whose life and subsistence is intertwined with the ability to sustain, and be sustained by, relationships with other human and nonhuman entities.

Such studies thus frame local modes of Indigenous identification as emergent from other kinds of practices of relationality and relation making, situating kinship and personhood at the forefront of such processes and departing from categorical and institutional modes of defining Indigenous identity and indigeneity. Yet the disjuncture between localized practices of understanding and inhabiting indigenousness and more politicized formulations of Indigenous identity also lays the groundwork to question where and how inter-Indigenous difference is defined, lived, and recognized. When approached ethnographically, understanding the boundaries that differentiate between Indigenous individuals, groups, or collectivities also becomes equally complex. Such an approach foregrounds the semiotic parameters that guide and negotiate inter-Indigenous differentiation and highlights how those signs intersect with other modalities of defining indigenousness.

Understanding inter-Indigenous difference, in other words, requires shifting our analytic gaze toward the sociality of such differences as they emerge from the interactions between various Indigenous (and non-Indigenous) social actors. Within Peru and across Latin America, however, any approach to inter-Indigenous difference through contact and interaction must consider the overlay of colonial and settler-colonial histories in shaping these interactions, which in turn produce new kinds of practices and competing regimes of recognizing inter-Indigenous difference. This view fundamentally questions the assumed existence of ethnic categories and the boundaries that divide them. At the same time it can also uncover other kinds of practices and demonstrate how competing metrics and ideological standards of inter-Indigenous differentiation might coexist together, leading to a more complex understanding of the persistence of Indigenous practices of maintaining their own forms of identification and differentiation.

Within this scope, thinking about inter-Indigenous difference through the lens of language contact becomes a particularly useful avenue to explore and disentangle how inter-Indigenous difference is negotiated. However, taking a language contact approach can encompass a range of potential foci. From a more language-oriented focus, language contact within zones of inter-Indigenous contact can highlight the kinds of linguistic changes and innovations that occur through the interfacing of different grammatical systems (Mufwene 2014; Thomason 2001). Investigations into inter-Indigenous language contact in South America have been particularly insightful in this regard, where notable case studies include the grammatical convergences present in the Uaupés and Rio Negro regions of the Brazilian Amazon (Aikhenvald 2010; Epps 2009; Epps and Stenzel 2013), and more recently the emergence of a mixed-linguistic variety called Guaraché from the lowlands of Paraguay (Hauck 2022). But language contact also entails specific moments, spaces, and periods of time when speakers of different linguistic varieties interact with each other, creating a chronotope that draws into focus how different linguistic resources are used across those interactions and the long-term pragmatic and social effects that they produce (Narayanan 2022a). This view highlights how linguistic differences are recognized and recruited into other social practices and semiotic systems of negotiating, talking about, and maintaining social differences (Agha 2006; Ball 2014; Gal and Irvine 2019). In other words, linguistic differences not only influence how speakers construct the semiotic configurations that generate social difference, but also are the primary medium from which these differences emerge and are maintained over time through talk and the basic metalinguistic reflexivity that is inherent to language (Lucy 1993).

Approaching language contact in this way takes on additional significance when analyzing inter-Indigenous interactions, histories, and social relationships as a kind of ongoing phenomenon that is simultaneously interacting with colonial social structures, the languages of settler-colonial hegemony, and settler-colonial language ideologies (Mannheim 2018). Across the Andes, and Latin America more generally, the consequences of settler-colonial contact are present through the hegemonic dominance of European languages like Spanish and Portuguese. But in addition to the dominance of these languages, colonial powers also introduced their own language ideologies into Indigenous, and later multiethnic and multiracial, landscapes of their American colonies, which further affected the relationships between Indigenous linguistic varieties and their speakers. One especially important consequence of this contact can be seen in the selected elevation of specific Indigenous languages to be used in the colonial project (Errington 2008). These decisions introduced new sets of structural relationships between Indigenous languages and their speakers, which led to the leveling of Indigenous linguistic diversity in the region through prioritizing these Indigenous linguistic mediums over others and initiating a process of language shift away from other de-privileged linguistic varieties. For instance, the widespread use and presence of Quechua across the Andes can be attributed to this history, where the maintenance of Quechua over other Indigenous languages can be traced back to the language's selection and association as the language of colonial administration and Catholic conversion (Mannheim 1991; Durston 2007). Over time, the spread and elevation of Quechua as the most privileged linguistic vehicle of colonial rule and control came at the detriment of other Indigenous languages. With the exception of the maintenance of Aymara in Puno and the altiplano (Heath and Laprade 1982), there was a widescale language shift across the Andes away from other Indigenous languages and toward Quechua. This practice has also been reproduced to similar effect in the Uaupés River region through the elevation of Nheengatú as the primary Indigenous lingua franca at the expense of other Indigenous languages in the region (Shulist 2018), and in the Yucatán Peninsula through the elevation and transformation of Yucatec Maya (Hanks 2010). Yet what is important to remember is that these colonial linguistic practices, and the colonial linguistic project more generally, did not erase other kinds of thriving inter-Indigenous interactions or relationships across the Americas (Kroskrity 1993; Yannakakis 2012), for which the Andes are no exception. However, such histories also have had profound consequences that have not only shaped how language is thought of and conceptualized among Indigenous populations but also affected the role that language plays in mediating interactions between various Indigenous actors.

Today, as calls for decolonization among Indigenous populations become more prominent in academic and public discussions around Indigenous identity, knowing and understanding the processes behind inter-Indigenous differentiation from a non-colonialist perspective becomes necessary to informing such discussions. While ethnolinguistic labels and categories are part of this story, they too are a product of settler-colonial histories and today are modern artifacts of neoliberal states. Thus, names like "Quechua" and "Aymara" for linguistic varieties that scholars and even lay audiences might colloquially call languages are ideologized objects that emerged out of the colonial encounter and control over Indigenous populations and their speaking practices in the Andes. Moreover, names like "Quechua" and "Aymara" carry additional connotations, not simply referring to a linguistic and communicative variety but also referring specifically to two different bounded abstract grammatical systems. The colonial roots behind how these languages are thus named and defined echoes what Veronelli (2015) has called the "coloniality of language." Here the ideological process of naming and bounding Indigenous linguistic and communicative repertoires cannot be separated from how those practices were first introduced during the colonial encounter to control and subjugate the linguistic practices of multilingual colonial subjects. Yet those processes continue today, extending the coloniality of language through ongoing modern practices that reify and uphold the distinctiveness of Quechua and Aymara as bounded, distinct, abstract grammatical systems that prohibit any kind of commensurability or overlap.

Such discourses and ideologized positions do not necessarily correlate with how Quechua and Aymara as languages and their variations are practiced and spoken in communities like Puno, where different kinds of multilingual practices across both linguistic varieties have long been the default and norm shaping everyday communicative practices for Indigenous puneños. Yet more pertinent to this book are the contrasting and sometimes conflicting accounts of the role that language, communicative practices, and ideas of speakerhood correlate with processes of social identification and the creation of inter-Indigenous difference. This means that language, what it is, and what it signifies have diverging and sometimes contradictory roles to play in shaping local forms of Indigenous identity and regulating and managing competing regimes of understanding inter-Indigenous difference. This also means that indigeneity, Indigenous identity, and being Indigenous are not necessarily based on language and linguistic differences. Instead, Indigenous identity in Puno is something that is also undergoing different discursive and institutional forms of contestation and negotiation that reveals a larger misalignment between how Indigenous identity might be broadly conceived and the ways that puneños enact their indigeneity through their most quotidian and everyday communicative and cultural practices.

This book is not aimed at dismantling the use of ethnolinguistic categories and labels like "Quechua" or "Aymara," whose use today is entrenched in academic discourses and are also actively used by Quechua- and Aymara-speaking puneños. Instead, one of my main goals in this book is to situate what those labels are, who uses them, when are they invoked, and who they encompass from the perspective of Quechua- and Aymara-speaking puneños who have long negotiated other forms of inter-Indigenous difference before the adoption of these labels. Moreover, my continued use of the term "Indigenous" to describe the individuals and communities mentioned and described in the following pages is to highlight the myriad ways that these individuals do not see themselves as white, criollo, or unmarked within the racio-ethnic landscape of Peru and the Andes. Discussing their experiences and lives in relation to the language of indigeneity emphasizes how these individuals and communities continue to struggle with having their specific experiences, histories, and ways of communicating recognized and legitimized in Peru. This suggests that the negotiation of Quechua and Aymara also occurs alongside competing discussions around Indigenous identity and indigeneity within Puno, reflecting the social histories and demographic shifts that have largely defined and differentiated the Peruvian altiplano from other places in Peru and the Andes.

As such, this ethnography will explore how the maintenance of these alternative modes of Indigenous identification and inter-Indigenous differentiation clash and coexist with more modern discursive and language ideological modes of categorizing and evaluating inter-Indigenous difference that has divided groups by language with a corresponding distinct ethnicity. As the following chapters will show, language and linguistic difference are only part of this story, highlighting alternate ways that language intersects with the construction of Indigenous personhood, identity, and difference. Yet those modes of understanding the relationship between linguistic difference and social difference continue in a world where the question of who and what is Quechua or Aymara is part of hegemonically dominant discourses that make inter-Indigenous differences legible within Peru and on the global stage. This pushes Indigenous puneños to balance between localized practices of differentiation and identification with institutionalized discourses of Indigenous difference, all through the diverse linguistic mediums that have shaped the linguistic and social landscape of the altiplano since European colonial contact.

Puno: The Consequences of Inter-Indigenous Contact in the Peruvian Altiplano

The Andean altiplano (lit. "high plains") spans two countries, beginning in southern Peru around the Lake Titicaca Basin and extending into Bolivia to include the Departments of Bautista Saavedra and Norte de Potosí. The region includes major capital cities like La Paz, Potosí, and Oruro in Bolivia. But in Peru, the altiplano is primarily contained around one political division, known as the Department of Puno, which bears the same name as the Department's regional, political, and social capital, Puno. At almost four thousand meters above sea level, the Peruvian altiplano is marked by high peaks, flat plains, and Lake Titicaca—the highest navigable lake in the world. Its location in the tropics would suggest a temperate year-round climate, with lush rains, high moisture, humidity, and dense tropical vegetation. However, because of its elevation that forms a high plateau, otherwise more temperate and tropical temperatures are replaced with more extreme climatic features. At these higher altitudes, the warmer weather of the tropics is replaced with drier and colder temperatures. The UV index in the region is also higher, requiring you to be fully covered to block out the sun's strong rays. Even on a cloudy day you can still get a sunburn, as I painfully learned the first time that I carelessly forgot to wear my typical wide-brim hat that shielded my face during the intense, bright, sunny days that characterize most of the year there. Yet once the sun sets, the intense warmth from the midday sun is soon replaced by cold, dry winds, blowing hard and fast across the plains from Lake Titicaca. Although the region is separated into its dry (or winter) and rainy (or spring) season, it is an area with cold temperatures that plummet below freezing nearly year-round. The high altitude has enabled the easy cultivation of certain crops, like quinoa, *kiwicha* (amaranth), and potatoes, while the cold, arid climate makes it the ideal place to herd sheep and camelids like alpacas.

The average non-puneño Peruvian often views the altiplano as a cold hinterland, where life and living are harder and tougher when compared to the more temperate and warmer regions of Peru. In order to get to Puno, I had to take a connecting flight from Lima to Juliaca, the other major urban center in the Department of Puno and the closest airport to the regional capital. During these flights, I would often meet Peruvians from other larger cities like Lima, Arequipa, and Trujillo while sitting in Lima's international airport waiting for our flights to be called. These individuals, who were often the same age as my parents, would curiously inquire where I was going. "Puno," I would respond, only to immediately receive looks of amazement, revulsion, and sincere concern. "*Señorita, por qué?*" (Young lady, why?), they would ask me, wondering what on earth would ever possess me to willingly want to go to Puno and the altiplano. Didn't I know that Puno was *frio, triste,* and *feo* (cold, sad, and ugly)? This general attitude toward Puno that I heard from these concerned adults, worried how I was going to survive in the region by myself, was not only because of Puno's location in the high Andes. While the Andean region in general is treated as a peripheral place in relation to the more centralized, cultural capitals along the coast, Puno and the Peruvian altiplano are often perceived as a more peripheral, marginal space within the nation, and is largely considered to be more rustic and less developed than the more recognizably historic Cusco, the quainter and prettier Ayacucho, or the more criollo-influenced Arequipa.

Yet unlike these other cities and the regions that they hail from, Puno, as the Departmental designation, regional capital, and stand-in name for the entire altiplano, is also home to long-standing Quechua and Aymara language contact and multilingualism—a fact that distinguished the region from other areas in the Andes that were home to Spanish bilingualism with one other Indigenous language. It was this multilingualism that first interested me in going to the altiplano during my graduate research, to see not only how Quechua and Aymara were spoken in this region but how they continued to be maintained such that Puno stood out as one specific example across the Andes where some kind of inter-Indigenous multilingualism remained a cornerstone of everyday life. In this way, conducting my research in Puno provided the opportunity to understand the communicative and cultural practices that contribute to the maintenance of inter-Indigenous multilingualism and to see how these practices were shifting in relation to new discourses and sensibilities around Indigenous linguistic praxis and their connection with Indigenous speakerhood and Indigenous authenticity.

This is not to say that inter-Indigenous contact and multilingualism is absent from other parts of the Andes, or that such multilingualism has only existed between Quechua- and Aymara-speaking communities. Although Quechua and Aymara are the main Indigenous languages spoken today in the altiplano, historically the region was also home to speakers of Puquina, Uru, and Chipaya, with evidence of Uru and Chipaya still being spoken sparsely by a handful of adults in the region through the end of the twentieth century (Adelaar and Muysken 2004).[6] Over the past fifty years, newer zones of language contact have also emerged in the Andean lowlands through increased migration of highland Indigenous Andean populations to the fertile grounds of the lowland Amazon to set up plantations and cultivate crops like coffee and chocolate as well as illegally traffic coca, all for a global market (Emlen 2016). Through this movement, highland Andean populations come into contact with lowland groups, thus making these lowland areas fertile for the cultivation of crops and the negotiation of new kinds of inter-Indigenous multilingual dynamics. Nicholas Emlen's (2015, 2020) research in the lowland communities of La Convención, outside of Quillabamba, documents this recent epicenter of contact and interactions between highland Quechua-speaking populations, who are associated with the cultivation of coffee, and lowland Matsigenka speakers. Yet this kind of contact also exists in Puno in the very small Amazonian regions on the periphery of the Department, where highland Aymara-speaking communities have also established coffee and cacao plantations in the lowland communities of San Juan del Oro and Putinapunco, which are located deeper in the Amazon and within close proximity to the historically older, lowland Quechua-speaking communities of Sandia.

Nevertheless, what makes Puno special is its history of maintaining contact and multilingualism between Indigenous linguistic varieties—a history that spans several centuries and includes various sociopolitical shifts that have also changed the nature of inter-Indigenous language contact and multilingualism in the region. The presence of multilingualism can be dated back to the emergence of the first civilizations and states, with the most notable being the Tiwanaku empire that was concentrated around the Lake Titicaca Basin (Stanish 2003). Like other pre-Hispanic states and polities, Tiwanaku was multilingual, with populations speaking proto versions of Quechua, Aymara, and Puquina[7] (Goldstein 2005; Janusek 2004). Following the fall of the Tiwanaku, the altiplano became home to several polities, each identified by what Andean ethnohistorians term as distinct ethnicities (Bouysse-Cassagne 1986).

Although these polities primarily spoke Aymara and Puquina varieties, that did not mean that communities in what is now known as the Peruvian altiplano did not have contact or interactions with Quechua-speaking communities. This became even more true following the incorporation of the altiplano into the Inka Empire in the fifteenth century, forming the province of Qullasuyu within the larger Inka Empire known as Tawantinsuyu (Sillar 2012). As such, Aymara- and Puquina-speaking altiplano communities engaged in economic and social exchanges with Quechua-speaking communities, largely enabled through the maintenance of different roads and routes that connected and facilitated trade and interactions between communities in the altiplano with other communities across the Inka Empire (Murra 1995). These connections also fostered Indigenous multilingualism across the region, creating a linguistic landscape and ecology that Mannheim (1991) describes as mosaic multilingualism. Mosaic multilingualism highlights the extent to which different communities spoke their own linguistic varieties while also being home to individuals who were multilingual and could therefore interact and communicate with speakers of different linguistic varieties from other communities. This kind of multilingualism was so pervasive at the time of Spanish colonial contact that colonial records note how bewildered Spanish colonial officials were to find that the varieties that people spoke radically changed from community to community. This did not mean that each community was necessarily monolingual; colonial records and accounts also highlight how this multilingualism was also present at the community level, creating a complex set of repertoires for each local speech community that was shaped and defined through the intersection and management of different linguistic mediums.

The Spanish conquest, and subsequent forms of colonial administrative practices over Indigenous populations across the Andes, significantly altered both the social and linguistic landscape of the altiplano, and the Andes more generally. Many of these changes were based in the large-scale movement and displacement of Indigenous communities, uprooting whole communities and peoples from one part of the Andes to other regions, which were all attempts to disconnect families and communities from their native lands. Through this displacement, uprooted communities were often moved to work on lands assigned to colonial *haciendas* (feudal estates) (Vázquez 1961) or sent to labor in the colonial mines such as the silver mines of Potosi (Mangan 2005). Yet even communities that were not displaced experienced other forms of colonial regulation known as the *repartimiento*, which reorganized the basic structural principles of Indigenous communal life, and which ultimately conflicted with how Indigenous Andean communities interpreted the boundaries around their communities and the ways they could move around and utilize their landscape (Mumford 2012). These social changes were also accompanied by sociolinguistic shifts, where, in the altiplano specifically, Quechua-speaking communities from other parts of the Andes were brought over to settle in the region as *forasteros*, or "foreigners" (Heath and Laprade 1982). The movement of speakers across the landscape today has been cited as one significant cause for widespread language shift and eventual loss of the vast array of multilingual communicative practices and varieties that once characterized the Andean multilingual mosaic ecology. And although the altiplano did experience similar kinds of eventual language shift and leveling of linguistic diversity over time, the region also saw the maintenance of Aymara spoken alongside Quechua, forming one bastion of inter-Indigenous multilingualism that was sustained despite colonial-era linguistic policies that privileged Quechua as the Indigenous linguistic tool of colonial and religious administration (Durston 2007; Mannheim 1992).

This maintenance of Indigenous multilingualism is not just the subject of academic discourse but also something that puneños note and comment on when discussing the region's core linguistic and cultural identity and heritage. As several puneños would proudly tell me, "In Puno, there are three languages spoken. Everywhere else in Peru, they only speak one or two." Such metalinguistic statements reflect the degree to which identifying as puneño, and claiming roots and residency with the region, comes with the recognition and celebration of the persistence of inter-Indigenous linguistic complexity and social multiplicity. While such discourses showcase a broader social awareness and recognition by puneños of their own linguistic multiplicity, there is nonetheless an implicit projection of this multilingualism as existing in the region through the existence of two bounded Indigenous linguistic codes, which indexically map onto two distinct sets of Indigenous speakers and populations. Yet although the existence of defined and bounded languages (Quechua and Aymara) and speaker populations (i.e., "Quechuas" and "Aymaras") are assumed to exist, the articulation or awareness of this boundedness is more indeterminate from the perspective of Quechua- and Aymara-speaking puneños. Instead, asking Indigenous puneños what Quechua and Aymara refer to and signify in Puno and the altiplano often becomes a difficult task for them to define, answer, or elaborate on. And the challenges that arise from defining these terms is telling, because they also lead to other kinds of conflicting and contradictory perspectives about how Quechua and Aymara as linguistic varieties are differentiated by speakers, and the extent to which these differences also contribute to the construction and maintenance of inter-Indigenous social and cultural difference more generally.

The indeterminacy of these labels draws attention to the socially contingent nature of naming languages and also the ways in which these differences could be linked to social differences, groups, and social categories. Linguistic anthropologists have long noted the language ideological processes of boundary regimentation and management underlying the politics and histories of language naming (Kroskrity 2000c; Woolard 1998), emphasizing how the assumed boundedness for any named language is the result of ideological processes that emerge out of specific social and historical moments. These kinds of ideological processes, which purify and harden boundaries between named languages, are also semiotic processes (Irvine and Gal 2000) that highlight how the association between linguistic and social differences emerge through the rhematization of linguistic differences, creating a contrast that makes an axis of differentiation, which then shapes how these differences are indexically scaled through fractal recursivity to reproduce the contrast between these linguistic differences onto larger scales and levels of analysis (Gal and Irvine 2019). Thus, the differences between named languages can be seen as one level of fractal recursive projection, where the axis of differentiation created by the contrast between different rhematized grammatical features are then indexically projected onto different languages, which are then extended onto a distinct set of social or cultural practices and eventually projected onto the differences that separate speakers, ethnic groups, and even geographic regions. These semiotic processes of ideologizing contrast between linguistic elements and semiotically connecting signs of linguistic difference to the differences between languages and populations enables the symbolic emergence of linguistic and social boundaries. Yet those boundaries and the ways that they are projected and maintained across different analytic scales have to also be regimented through processes of semiotic erasure, which elides or obscures signs, practices, or entities that complicate the naturalization of semiotic linkages and contrasts that maintain those differences.

Since the inception of the broader theoretical field of language ideologies, other commentaries concerning its explanatory power and analytic breadth have also emerged. In particular, recent conversations emerging in tandem with the ontological turn have argued to rethink ideologized named and bounded languages and ontological inventions (Makoni and Pennycook 2005, 2006). In identifying and locating the "invention of language" within specific historical moments, Makoni and Pennycook interrogate the ontological nature of language, suggesting the importance of critically investigating what kind of ontological object language is for speakers, and what qualities and features define its essence (Ferguson 2019; Hauck 2023). They also argue that the invention of language as a bounded abstract, grammatical object cannot be separated from histories of colonialism and the ways that linguistics was an important tool in the colonial project (Pennycook and Makoni 2020), especially in the creation and maintenance of racial hierarchies and racializing speaker subjectivities whose legitimacy and authenticity are evaluated and framed in relation to a colonial listening subject (Reyes 2021; Rosa and Flores 2017). While these discussions have certainly enhanced many theoretical discussions and approaches to language ideologies and their role in shaping ideas and conceptions of what a language is (and is not), language ideologies are still important to unpacking the practices that are central to understanding the relationship between linguistic differences in the generation and maintenance of social differences. Language ideologies and language ideological research, in other words, emphasizes the ways that language and linguistic differences are inseparable from the semiotic generation of social difference. Thinking about the relationship between the identification and naming of linguistic varieties and how they become aligned with social differences also foregrounds the need to consider how these processes are partial and subject to specific perspectives and positionalities (Gal and Irvine 2019). Work around language ideologies, in other words, calls attention to the moments and situations when linguistic differences become salient, to the point that they become the locus for ongoing forms of rationalization such that they are semioticized into other kinds of boundaries, linguistic and social alike. Moreover, language ideologies are never singular nor uniform, highlighting the social meaningfulness of their multiplicity and the ways that they may contradict each other within any ethnographic setting (Gal 1993). Their co-occurrence within any social context can be understood as its own kind of language ideological assemblage (Kroskrity 2018), which helps us understand how competing ideological perspectives, compounded by histories of contact and colonialism, come to bear on speakers' communicative practices and the ways that they continuously shape and negotiate local understandings of their own speakerhood in relation to these diverse social influences.

These insights and approaches are important to understanding how Spanish colonial linguistic policies have shaped inter-Indigenous multilingualism in the altiplano and highlight the significance of why linguistic and social categories like "Quechua" and "Aymara" are more complicated to answer and define for Quechua- and Aymara-speaking puneños. Part of this comes from the history of how Quechua and Aymara were named. Prior to the Spanish conquest, Indigenous linguistic varieties were neither named nor necessarily talked about in ways that mirrored modern ideological constructions of a named language. Names like "Quechua" and "Aymara" are all inventions and artifacts of the Spanish colonial enterprise,[8] selected and implemented through the colonial linguistic project to name and control the linguistic and social complexity of their Indigenous, Andean, multilingual subjects. Yet more than imposing boundaries around a subset of complex Indigenous multilingual repertoires, these policies also are part of a "coloniality of language" (Veronelli 2015). Selecting and naming specific communicative practices are only part of the colonial linguistic project; the effects and ongoing coloniality also comes from how Indigenous language speakers and their communicative practices and repertoires are characterized or described, which include the ways the Quechua and Aymara are ideologized to be spoken, and what kinds of characteristics and features qualify and legitimize Indigenous Quechua and Aymara speakerhood, thereby positioning Indigenous multilingualism and Indigenous linguistic knowledge in relation to colonial linguistic ideological frameworks.

The coloniality of these named categories also extends to how puneños nonetheless use and incorporate terms like "Quechua" and "Aymara" in their everyday metalinguistic practices. However, a key argument in this book is to interrogate the use of these terms, and to not assume that the metalinguistic use of "Quechua" and "Aymara" by Indigenous puneños necessarily represents the same set of ideas and referents that can be traced back to the colonial naming of these linguistic varieties, speakers, and populations. This difference is important, because it also emphasizes how Indigenous puneños' understandings of what Quechua and Aymara are is also intimately connected with how Indigenous puneños situate linguistic differences in relation to other practices and conceptual modes of recognizing inter-Indigenous difference more generally across the altiplano. The question of what it means to speak and be Quechua and Aymara will be explored and discussed in a multitude of ways over the following chapters. My use of these terms is a kind of shorthand to refer broadly to two distinct Indigenous linguistic varieties. However, my main point in this study is to question what these terms mean in relation to linguistic and social differences for puneños, emphasizing how these linguistic varieties—and how they are named—are employed in everyday talk and communication. While some examples will focus on the ways that Quechua- and Aymara-speaking puneños align themselves and their ideas about Quechua and Aymara as linguistic varieties according to how such terms are discursively created and reproduced across elite and institutional spaces, such examples will also be countered with other accounts that highlight how most puneños in their daily lives speak Quechua and Aymara in ways that blur the boundaries between these languages and the social and cultural categories they are ideologized and projected onto. As the following chapters of this book will show, Indigenous puneños' communicative practices and repertoires have not always neatly matched the same kinds of ideologized boundaries that map Quechua and Aymara onto two distinct ethnolinguistic groups. But these perspectives and discourses are also subject to ideological shifts (Errington 1998), creating an ideological landscape where Indigenous puneños are thinking about their native Indigenous languages in new ways and using these novel ideological perspectives to reframe the parameters and ideological regimes that evaluate and recognize inter-Indigenous difference in the region.

Women, Language, and Indigeneity in the Andes: A History of Contradictions

The complex terrain concerning Indigenous linguistic practices and indigeneity highlight the varied and sometimes contradictory linkages between language, race, and ethnicity across the altiplano, and the Andes more generally, since the Spanish colonial conquest. However, it is also important to consider the ways that these processes are not necessarily applied to all Indigenous individuals or communities, where Indigenous speakerhood or Indigenous identity is not evaluated equally. In this regard, gender differences have been one salient site that complicates both discourses around indigeneity, Indigenous identity, and Indigenous linguistic practices historically across the Andes. Specifically, the ideologization of Indigenous femininity, and the ways that Indigenous women (figure 1) have been discursively presented, imagined, and historically treated, have been at the center of shaping the social histories of Indigenous populations and managing and evaluating their linguistic practices since the colonial conquest. Yet within this history, the practices and ideologized perspectives on Indigenous femininity and gender differences do not produce a uniform historical narrative, mirroring the equally fraught discursive and political landscape associated with the construction of Indigenous identity in the Andes. Instead, this gendered and racialized history coalesces around two main ideological and discursive threads. While these two perspectives might appear to contradict each other, the contrasts between them speak to the marginal space that Indigenous populations and their linguistic repertoires continue to occupy within Peru and the additional forms of marginalization that Indigenous women experience within and across Indigenous and non-Indigenous spaces.

The first significant ideological thread comes from how Indigenous women are often closely correlated with the consequences of Spanish colonial contact and conquest, aligning women and their sexuality with colonialism and portraying Indigenous women as the objects of conquest. Such an objectification can be found in the personification of the Americas in the form of a woman (MacCormack 1991; Silverblatt 1987), as well as the sexualized positioning of Indigenous women as significant interactants strategically managing their own agency with colonial forces and colonial powers (Mangan 2016; Rappaport 2014). Indigenous Andean women's history and role as sexualized partners in colonial regimes, however, also illuminate the dynamic and flexible positioning of Indigenous women that was achieved both through their gender and their racio-ethnic background and classification (Harris 1995; Weismantel 2001). Historically such flexibility has been noted for women of Indigenous heritage or ancestry who negotiated their racio-ethnic

FIGURE 1 Indigenous puneña women dressed in festive attire. Credit: Sandhya Krittika Narayanan (author).

affiliation through dress, occupation, residency, and spouse or partner. This flexibility to a certain degree allowed women to gain some degree of economic autonomy, and also some—albeit restricted—freedom and ability to inhabit rural spaces and more racially restricted urban spaces (Mangan 2005; Paulson 2002). At times, this flexibility seeps into Indigenous women's history of being the object of sexual desire, and especially their sexualization for non-Indigenous white, criollo, or European-descended individuals (Canessa 2012a). Yet their social flexibility also demonstrates the porousness of racio-ethnic categories, placing Indigenous women as the mediators of ever-shifting social boundaries over time through participating in practices and activities that both question and uphold the recognition of these boundaries and categorical divisions.

The discursive construction and enfigurement of Indigenous femininity and Indigenous womanhood found across these discussions frame Indigenous women and Indigenous femininity as a specific kind of social personhood that straddles social boundaries and social differences. Whether it comes from the nonrestrictive sexuality of Indigenous women or their presence and labor across Indigenous and non-Indigenous spaces, Indigenous femininity emphasizes the fluidity that emerges from Indigenous women's role as arbiters and mediators of colonial-Indigenous contact. Yet this particular enfigurement of Indigenous womanhood contrasts with a second set of ideological perspectives and discursive threads, which instead equate indigeneity with Indigenous women. This history is also varied, complicating the interdiscursive links and connections between indigeneity with Indigenous women and Indigenous womanhood. During the colonial period, fictionalized accounts and travel narratives about the Andes represented Indigenous populations through women's bodies (Poole 1997), which in many ways complemented colonial depictions of conquest and coloniality through the figure of an Indigenous woman. The codification, however, of indigeneity with Indigenous female bodies entered a new period of ideologization during the early half of the twentieth century. This period saw the emergence of the *indigenista* and *neoindigenista* intellectual and political movements across the Andes, ushering in over half a century of anthropological, folkloric, and political discussions on the relationship between indigeneity, past and contemporary Indigenous populations, and Peru's racial heritage and identity, which also cemented the former Inka capital of Cusco as the primary epicenter for those cultural and political discussions and activities (Cadena 2000).⁹ One main legacy from these projects is the entrenchment of a mestizo racial and cultural identity as the default racial identity for Peru—a legacy that makes the inclusion of other racial and ethnic categories on the 2017 census more striking and significant. But these movements also sought to reframe Indigenous identity in the Andes, creating a pathway that attempted to ideologically promote ideas around Indigenous racial purity, thus establishing the parameters by which Indigenous authenticity and legitimacy is still evaluated today. This was especially the case during the indigenista period of the early twentieth century, which privileged and selectively celebrated Andean indigeneity if it maintained specific signs that were thought to represent the maintenance of pre-contact cultural forms and practices. These signs included rural residence, maintaining traditional labor practices such as farming and herding, adherence to pre-contact religious and cosmological practices and worldviews, and being monolingual in a pure, pre-contact Indigenous language. These qualities, moreover, were also gendered, where indigenista, and later neoindigenista, intellectuals saw Indigenous women as the embodiment of these values and practices and the representation of all things Indigenous. Such discussions continue to shape more recent portrayals and understandings of indigeneity and Indigenous womanhood, where Indigenous Andean women are often considered to be "more Indigenous" than men (Cadena 1995). Yet the social and ideological consequences of these discussions are also far reaching and can be seen in both public perceptions and interpersonal interactions that racialize and treat Indigenous Andean women as subjects who are incongruent with modernity or socioeconomic development (Huayhua 2018) and in political and artistic projects in which they are often related to the role of a domestic servant (Barrig 2001).

Andean Indigenous women, therefore, have been both the paragons of Indigenous identity and the primary transgressors of racio-ethnic categorical boundaries, allowing them to inhabit a protean state where they move between two poles that measure and evaluate the quintessential Indigenous subject. And in this history of racial and gender-based evaluations and the recognition of Andean indigeneity, Indigenous language use has also played a role in shaping these competing discourses. In some contexts, the ability to speak an Indigenous Andean language, and often the status of being a monolingual Indigenous language speaker, is assumed to be the primary linguistic background for an Indigenous Andean woman (Babel 2018; Spedding 1994). However, other studies have also highlighted how bilingualism, or being identified as *la bilingüe*, is also iconic of an Indigenous Andean woman, reflecting the long-standing history of these woman being able to enter into and share spaces that are linguistically and culturally marked as non-Indigenous (Swinehart 2018). As such, Indigenous women are both at home in urban spaces and restricted to, and legitimized within, rural spaces and communities (Babb 1998). Despite these contradictions, both approaches, interpretations, and treatment of Indigenous Andean women have been mediated primarily by and through a non-Indigenous gaze, largely defined by the positions and perspectives of non-Indigenous settler-colonial men. Viewing Indigenous women as hyper-Indigenous while also seeing them as social, cultural, and linguistic interlopers reflects two contrasting interpretations that emerge from being compared with non-Indigenous spaces, populations, positionalities, and perspectives, which ultimately reveal an underlying anxiety and need for control over Indigenous populations and, through that, legitimize the presence of Indigenous female bodies. Through this, both kinds of discursive constructions and projections about Andean female indigeneity are framed in response to colonial interactions with Indigenous populations and the ways that such relations and perspectives shape the Indigenous/non-Indigenous divide (Harris 2008).

It is not surprising, therefore, that many of the challenges that continue to plague descriptions of Indigenous populations also extend to discussions around Indigenous women and their representation as well. As Silvia Rivera Cusicanqui (2010) notes, any attempt at decolonizing Andean indigeneity must also take into account the ways in which Andean women have been recruited in settler-colonial projects that manage and prescribe the category of Indigenous while also attending to how they have been actively erased from modernizing projects and discourses (Cusicanqui 2012). Or, to put it differently, a fuller, and perhaps truly decolonial, grasp of the politicization of Indigenous Andean identities needs to seriously center the role that gender, and specifically the role of Andean Indigenous women, has within these projects, considering both their objectification and their agency as social actors in these spaces (Babb 2018; Valdivia 2020). Making sense of the varied history around the formalization of Andean indigeneity that includes the essentialization of Indigenous alterity to the erasure of alternate forms of Indigenous expression is a task that requires greater attention to the lives, practices, and subsequent treatment of Indigenous Andean women. Additionally, deconstructing the ways in which Andean Indigenous populations are denied their contemporaneity and projected as antithetical to modernizing projects or incompatible with a present-day neoliberal social order[10] can be more clearly illustrated through recognizing how Andean Indigenous women have been at the center of such ideological projects and the object of commentary in related discursive practices.

Perhaps now more than ever there is a growing imperative to address the lasting legacies of colonialism on Indigenous populations in the Andes and across the world. Yet often such calls to action do not fully explore how the "politics of ethnicity" can also include the practices and politics of negotiating and defining alterity, difference, and inequality between Indigenous groups, extending beyond the recognition of Indigenous identities in relation to state (Canessa 2014; Maybury-Lewis 2002). Understanding inter-Indigenous difference and relationships through language contact and Indigenous multilingual repertoires can offer one path to avoid some of the analytic pitfalls long associated with previous approaches to Indigenous identity. But in the same vein, it is also important to recognize that these processes that define and recognize indigeneity are not necessarily applied to all Indigenous individuals or speakers—a fact that can be traced back to the unequal treatment, interpretation, and ideologization of Indigenous men and women since the colonial encounter. As I have discussed in this section, gender differences have been central and instrumental in shaping discussions around race, indigeneity, and Indigenous linguistic practices. Yet these discursive projects are not simply intellectual. They also go on to shape and inform how Indigenous Andean women have been and continue to be heard, interpreted, and treated today by Indigenous and non-Indigenous individuals alike. Centering Indigenous puneña women in an analysis of inter-

Indigenous linguistic and social difference thus highlights how women in areas of Indigenous linguistic and social multiplicity must contend with not only how they have been ideologized and discursively enfigured and constructed from non-Indigenous perspectives but also how these perspectives coexist and interact with local puneño and Indigenous views of gender differences and the social and linguistic practices assumed by women in the management of inter-Indigenous linguistic and social contact. To put it simply, understanding inter-Indigenous relationships and the linguistic and communicative practices that have shaped these histories and interactions must include the gendered dimensions of these practices and processes. Centering gender differences, and in particular the lives and practices of Indigenous Andean women, highlights the degree to which any account of inter-Indigenous histories and relationships cannot be fully delinked or separated from how Indigenous puneño communities continue to experience the ongoing effects of Spanish colonial histories. Furthermore, focusing on the lives and practices of Indigenous puneñas reinforces how gender differences and their ensuing social and linguistic inequalities influence the linguistic and social positioning of Indigenous women, which in turn informs the ideologization of a legitimate and authentic Indigenous speaker in a zone of Indigenous multilingualism and contact.

Spaces, Places, and Practices: Understanding Inter-Indigenous Multilingualism and Gender in Puno

This book unpacks the practices and dynamics that characterize inter-Indigenous contact in Puno and, in doing so, focuses on how the linguistic and cultural practices of Indigenous puneña women shape competing understandings of inter-Indigenous linguistic and social difference. Yet how does one go about understanding inter-Indigenous language contact? And how would one navigate a space and terrain as large as the Department of Puno and the altiplano, such that you can select the most representative spaces to answer these core goals? Between initial visits in 2014 and 2015, I traveled across the Department of Puno, trying to get a sense of the overall linguistic landscape and local linguistic ecology in order to see where inter-Indigenous language contact was occurring. Based on these visits, I decided to focus my research on the regional capital of Puno,[11] a city that not only sits at the junction of Quechua- and Aymara-speaking provinces and rural municipalities but also has a wide spectrum of Quechua and Aymara speakers evenly distributed across the small urban capital (Narayanan 2023a). From 2016 to 2018, I immersed myself in the everyday activities that constituted daily life in Puno. Spending time in the city provided me the chance to see how Quechua- and Aymara-speaking puneños understood their spaces and used their different linguistic resources to navigate within and across the Department of Puno, interacting with a wide range of speakers from Quechua, Aymara, and Spanish-speaking-dominant backgrounds. Considering my focus on inter-Indigenous contact, situating my research primarily within Puno allowed me to compare the multilingual Indigenous repertoires of Quechua- and Aymara-speaking puneños with burgeoning ideological discussions around Quechua and Aymara language use. Whether it was observing the kinds of multilingual fluencies that were on full display within the market spaces, being immersed in the politics of Indigenous language use at the radio stations, or attending public performances of indigeneity, it was important that I was in a place where I could see and hear both Indigenous languages being used along with Spanish. More rural areas, as I would come to learn through my initial visits to Puno and through accompanying many of my interlocutors back to their rural communities and provinces across the altiplano, proved to be primarily home to one Indigenous language. But the regional capital of Puno was home to both Quechua and Aymara, along with Spanish. Puno, therefore, provided the space to see how Quechua- and Aymara-speaking puneños shared their spaces with each other. And as the region's political and cultural capital, it also provided the opportunity to compare these practices with more institutional and politicized discourses around Quechua and Aymara ethnolinguistic differences and the specific practices, spaces, and institutions that were promoting these newer ideologized discourses.

While my research focused on inter-Indigenous contact within Puno, I was also interested in how urban life within the regional capital compared with more rural spaces, especially considering that such spaces are linguistically identified with one Indigenous language. At the time, the relationship between rural communities and small provinces and villages and the regional capital was especially important considering that most Indigenous puneños living in Puno were born and raised in rural Indigenous communities across the Department. Indigenous puneños who lived in the city were not disconnected from their rural communities and instead returned frequently and often back to their natal communities. These visits were often done for the purpose of helping with the harvest, attending important family events such as weddings and funerals, and participating in patron saint festivals. Being able to travel freely and easily across the region also provided the opportunity for puneños of different generations, such as younger teens and youths, to stay connected with their extended family and rural community. In addition to this movement, recent regional infrastructural projects that have resulted in the construction of paved roads that connect rural and otherwise distant provinces and communities to Puno have also increased public transportation options to and from the city, making it possible and much easier for individuals and families living in more rural areas to commute to the city every day on one of several affordable *combi* busses and vans. The increased presence of these combis has not only made it more convenient for recent Indigenous migrants in Puno to make frequent visits back to their natal rural communities, but it has also made it easier for individuals from these communities to travel into Puno to buy and sell their goods in the local markets. Moreover, the general ease in accessing the city has also made it possible for children living in these rural spaces to attend school within the city. Together, these changes highlight another dimension of movement and contact not only between rural and urban worlds but also between Quechua and Aymara speakers from different provinces to converge and interact with each other in the city.

To understand the complex relationship between rural and urban spaces as well as the effects that it had on shaping inter-Indigenous linguistic practices and language ideologies around linguistic and Indigenous difference, I chose to live about eighteen kilometers south of Puno, in a village outside of Chucuito—a rural town with deep historical roots associated with Aymara-speaking communities and populations (see figure 2; Tschopik 1951; Hickman and Stuart 1977). In addition to being close enough to Puno that I could observe the comings and goings of

FIGURE 2 View of small farm plots and Lake Titicaca from the hills outside of Chucuito. Credit: Sandhya Krittika Narayanan (author).

people taking the local combi into Puno and back, my choice to live in this community was also motivated by my desire to improve my conversational proficiency in Aymara, having already had extensive training in Quechua conversation and grammar as a postgraduate. Through living near Chucuito, I was able to learn more about the linguistic practices and social histories that typically shape life in these rural spaces. But I also saw how these rural speakers, practices, and worlds intersected with the regional capital of Puno, where I would ride on these combis every day, sharing a seat with older men and women traveling to Puno to sell their harvest, or with school-aged children and youth clad in their school uniforms. Through this daily travel, I was also able to see how Indigenous linguistic practices in these rural spaces compared to Indigenous linguistic practices in the city, as well as the ways that urban and rural perspectives and metalinguistic discourses about Indigenous linguistic praxis and inter-Indigenous differences aligned and diverged. Although most of my daily ethnographic interactions and focus was on the Quechua and Aymara linguistic and communicative practices found within the regional capital, insights that I gained from living outside of the city, and traveling frequently to the city with these adults and youths, helped me understand the kinds of ideological shifts that were taking place in Puno, and the influence and impact these changes had for puneños living in the city of Puno and across the rural altiplano landscape.

Certain details and data presented in this book came from attending specific spaces or events that explicitly focused on inter-Indigenous language use and overt expressions of Indigenous identity and inter-Indigenous difference in Puno. These include, for instance, spending time at Pachamama Radio station, attending and observing Indigenous language classes at one of the secondary schools in Puno, and attending public events and performances such as ritual reenactments and beauty pageants. Yet the observations made in these institutionalized spaces and during institutional and ritual performances were complemented by the observations of everyday life and Indigenous linguistic practices. On days that I did not venture into the city, I would spend time in the company of my neighbors, helping them in the fields and learning about their lives and the history of their community. But most days I did spend in the city, and I dedicated most of that time to observing and interacting with Indigenous market women. While I would come to spend time in different markets across Puno, with some markets having a different proportion of Quechua- and Aymara-speaking Indigenous market vendors, most of my time was spent in the centrally located Mercado de San Ignacio, which I selected due to its almost even representation of Quechua- and Aymara-speaking Indigenous market women.

My first introduction to the world of market cooperatives and associations came through a chance meeting of a handicraft cooperative and association meeting in the UNCA building in Puno.[12] The women of that cooperative, who together would knit and crochet woolens made from natural alpaca and sheep wool to sell wholesale in tourist markets across Peru, were also all market women who worked across the different market cooperatives in Puno. The association was also a mixed one, with membership evenly split between Quechua- and Aymara-speaking women. Luckily I was already familiar with the basics of knitting and crocheting, having been taught by both my mother and my grandmother, who, when I was younger, would knit sweaters for my brother and me.

After having demonstrated my own basic abilities in knitting and crocheting, I was allowed into the handicraft association's weekly knitting circles, getting to know women who would eventually become my closest interlocutors and friends, like Señora Marcela and Señora Fidelia, while also gaining some new knitting skills. Soon I was invited to spend time with these women outside of the knitting circles, to help them with their shopping errands or spend time with them in their market stalls. These connections led me to spend much of my fieldwork within the market spaces and especially within the stalls of Mercado de San Ignacio.

Between the day-to-day hustle of market life and the peaceful tranquility that characterized living near Chucuito, I came to understand a different side of the relationship between language and social life that was not present or represented in how Quechua and Aymara were talked about, discussed, or spoken in institutional spaces and public performances. I slowly realized the sometimes-vast gulf that exists between how Quechua and Aymara are spoken, how they are thought of relative to histories of inter-Indigenous contact and relationships, and how these more personal stories and experiences contrasted so sharply with the more ideologized discourses and influenced performances of Quechua and Aymara linguistic expertise and Indigenous identity that came from institutional spaces and public performances. Formal linguistic life history interviews,[13] complemented by the intimacy that would come with more casual conversations, made apparent the kinds of ideological shifts and transformations that were underway in Puno and the extent to which all puneños were rationalizing and internalizing these competing ideological perspectives in their own day-to-day lives, shaping not only how they spoke their lengua materna but the extent to which they used their lengua materna with other speakers and taught it to their children. Moreover, these more casual interactions also helped make some of the gendered inequalities associated with Indigenous linguistic praxis more salient. Yet this perspective also clarified the extent to which certain domains of social life remain segregated along gendered lines in the altiplano.

My focus on Indigenous puneña women in this monograph is an outcome of my own circumstances in the field. And in this way this ethnographic account is a partial view of Indigenous linguistic and communicative practices within Puno and the altiplano. However, it is my hope that the narratives, stories, and analyses presented in this book, focused on the lives, stories, and talk of Indigenous Quechua- and Aymara-speaking puneña women, draw attention to the critical role that Indigenous puneñas play in past practices and ongoing ideologization of Indigenous linguistic praxis and inter-Indigenous differentiation in Puno. Moreover, in centering this ethnography around the lives of Indigenous puneñas and the diverse ways that they practice and embody their lenguas maternas, this ethnography complicates the semiotic processes that are assumed to underly the generation and reproduction of linguistic boundaries and ethnolinguistic categories, drawing attention to the ways that gender identity and the lives and positionality of Indigenous puneña women and femininity are significant in both upholding and disrupting these processes and the ideologized borders that they create.

Structure of the Book

This book frames the practices and politics central to negotiating inter-Indigenous linguistic, cultural, and social difference through focusing on the lives, practices, and attention around Quechua- and Aymara-speaking women in Puno and the Peruvian altiplano. A focus on Andean Indigenous women, however, also entails a wide ethnographic and analytic landscape to understand the role of gender in relation to the ideologization of Indigenous language use and the mobilization of inter-Indigenous difference more generally. This suggests that an analytic focus on gender at the intersection of Indigenous linguistic praxis and forms of Indigenous ethnic identification is not a unified process confined to any single ethnographic site of analysis. Instead, understanding the relationship between gender, language, and Indigenous identification is a multiscalar process that occurs across various ethnographic and interactional contexts. In order to better capture this reality, I approach Indigenous puneña womanhood and femininity through the lens of figures of personhood. For figures of personhood, I follow Agha's definition: "Contingent, performable behaviors effectively linked to social personae for some determinate population" (Agha 2011, 172). In other words, Indigenous puneña womanhood, as a kind of figure of personhood, is evaluated and understood through certain kinds of practices and behaviors that involve the incorporation and alignment of linguistic and communicative practices and behaviors with other kinds of social and cultural practices. Important to this definition are that such figures are the product of ideological and discursive processes, such that "to speak of the existence of 'figures of personhood' is to speak of forms of perceivable and performable behavior that undergo such semiotic processes, and of actual persons oriented to them through such processes over specific demographic and sociotemporal scales" (Agha 2011, 173).

In this way, Andean Indigenous puneña womanhood is an example of a figure of personhood—a social persona and social category that sits at the boundaries of linguistic and Indigenous social difference in Puno and the altiplano. In the altiplano, Indigenous women and their speech and communicative practices historically can be taken as a form of metacommentary on the legitimacy and authenticity of Indigenous puneña women, not only as speakers of Quechua and Aymara but also as representatives of an Indigenous Quechua or Aymara identity and inter-Indigenous difference. But these discourses and metacommentaries also become the base to generate alternative narratives of the role of Indigenous women in shaping Indigenous linguistic and social differences in the altiplano, leading to other instances and cases where alternate idealized models of puneña indigeneity are celebrated and privileged. The interdiscursive links that connect these diverging and sometimes contradictory views on Indigenous women with respect to Indigenous linguistic legitimacy, authenticity, and ethnolinguistic identity and difference demonstrate how the construction of a figure personhood is not from a homogenous worldview but rather from the intersection of these different perspectives as they appear in communicative practices and metalinguistic and metadiscursive commentaries across different social scales. This suggests that the cultivation of the figure of Indigenous puneña personhood emerges through interscalar linkages (Carr and Fisher 2016), where the practices, values, and metacommentaries on certain kinds of female bodies, practices, and lifestyles that may be the subject of talk and discussion in intimate spaces become the semiotic ground for additional kinds of commentary and idealization within institutional spaces and discourses that circulate regionally. More pertinent to this ethnography is that the existence of these diverging views on Indigenous puneña personhood are also important in revealing the shifting perspectives on inter-Indigenous linguistic and social difference, placing Indigenous puneñas and their personhood at the center of negotiating these ideological transformations.

Given that the figure of Indigenous puneña personhood is not created through a unified field of discourses and the ideologized interpretations of their communicative practices, this book is structured around four subfigures of Indigenous puneña personhood and the communicative practices and ideologized expectations that are associated with each subfigure: traditional Indigenous brides and wives, female market vendors, the mythical Indigenous mother, and Indigenous beauty pageant contestants. Each subfigure will be the subject of her own chapter, highlighting the ethnographic contingencies and linguistic practices that shape the recognition and mobilization of that subfigure in relation to broader debates around Indigenous puneña personhood and ideas about Indigenous linguistic praxis and inter-Indigenous difference. Through this centering of a specific subfigure of Indigenous puneña personhood, each chapter will also highlight a different perspective on the relationship between Indigenous language use and negotiation of inter-Indigenous difference in Puno. Together, these highlighted aspects provide a broader ethnographic picture of the linguistic ecology of Puno and its shifting language ideological landscape.

Chapter 1 focuses on the subfigure of the traditional Indigenous wife and the kinds of linguistic and social symbolic transformations that Indigenous women as brides, then wives, typically experience across rural, Indigenous communities in the altiplano. This analysis, moreover, situates women in relation to local perspectives of understanding and negotiating inter-Indigenous differences as a product of kinship practices. Language and linguistic difference are an important indexical sign within these kinship practices, which are embodied and realized through the role that women inhabit as brides and wives. Women's embodiment of signs of their difference, which includes linguistic differences, thus marks them as the arbiters of kin and community-based forms of alterity. Through this, Indigenous wives become marked for their embodiment of the boundaries of inter-Indigenous social and linguistic difference across the altiplano as well as their ability to maintain those boundaries through their symbolic transformations. Chapter 2 focuses on market women, who are emblematic of the ways that Quechua-Aymara language contact is also shaped by the political economy of the region. While Quechua-Aymara language contact does emerge in different labor sectors across the altiplano, markets are one historical site par excellence of highlighting how socioeconomic factors shape the interfacing of linguistic varieties and speakers from different linguistic backgrounds. Markets are also one of the few economic domains that are predominantly run by Indigenous women, making market vendors one kind of iconic figure of Indigenous femininity across the Andes. Part of her significance and iconic status derives from the market vendor's ability to live between social and economic worlds that have been largely thought antithetical to each other. In Puno, her iconic status becomes more marked because of her ability to also work in spaces that require cross-linguistic knowledge of Quechua and Aymara. The linguistic knowledge, proficiencies, and backgrounds of market women highlight the ways that language is, and to a large extent has been, used as a medium to cross and blur social boundaries. Furthermore, this linguistic flexibility allows these women to inhabit other kinds of identities that are defined and shaped through their social networks within the market economy.

Chapter 3 introduces the shifting language ideological landscape in Puno and the effect that it has on privileging discourses of Indigenous ethnic difference and authentic Indigenous identities as derived from the ideologization of Quechua and Aymara as distinct, bounded linguistic objects. In this way, this chapter examines the rise of distinct ethnolinguistic categories that have emerged with globalized discourses around Indigenous recognition and autochthony, and new neoliberal modes of recognizing diversity in the state. This focus on the rise of a new ideological, discursive landscape around ethnolinguistic authenticity, which presents a bounded view of inter-Indigenous difference that conflicts with histories of cross-linguistic networks and interactions, is largely promoted in the region through the work of institutions. Here I will focus on the work of three specific institutions and their role in promoting and naturalizing the language of inter-Indigenous difference around mobilization of ethnolinguistic categories like "Quechua" and "Aymara": literacy practices in a locally run newspaper; teaching practices in an intercultural, bilingual education program; and the activities surrounding the production and management of multilingual difference at an Indigenous-based radio station.

Chapters 4 and 5 center on how specific subfigures of Andean Indigenous puneña personhood are invoked to negotiate the relationship between language contact and Indigenous difference in relation to this new ideological landscape of bounded ethnolinguistic difference. Chapter 4 addresses the reinvention and annual performance of the founding myth of Puno, and the discursive attention and construction of Mama Uqllu, the region's mythical founding mother. As a product of newer forms of Indigenous cultural and political revitalization, Mama Uqllu and Manqu Qhapaq, her male counterpart, are venerated annually in Puno as the founding figures of Andean Indigenous heritage. Yet both characters have also been refashioned to capture and reflect the histories of inter-Indigenous difference and contact, with Mama Uqllu being celebrated as the founder of Indigenous diversity and difference. Through the festival's annual reenactment, and the tensions, anxieties, and expectations that come from replaying this important moment that defines the cultural and linguistic heritage of Puno, this chapter traces the ways that Mama Uqllu's performance is often the greater topic of conversation and scrutiny for puneños, resulting in a discursive repositioning of Andean indigeneity as captured and epitomized by the reinvention of the mythical, founding female figure.

While chapter 4 focuses on the role of a single Andean Indigenous puneña in the remote, mythical past, chapter 5 highlights the future aspirations of Indigenous puneña identity and language use as embodied through young women who compete and perform in local Indigenous beauty pageants. As the newest generation of young Indigenous adults, and the ones who have lived primarily in a discursive space that describes Indigenous identity through the discourses of ethnolinguistic authenticity, pageant competitors represent what the future of this new discourse might look like, reproducing and embodying a new kind of ideal Indigenous woman of the altiplano. But this idealized indígena woman is also an ideological composite of competing visions of Indigenous puneña femininity in the region. Through language, beauty pageant competitors present and uphold a new kind of Andean Indigenous femaleness that must conform to growing ideals of Andean ethnolinguistic authenticity that also echoes idealizations of a settler-colonial Andean Indigenous femininity. At the same time competitors must balance these expectations with locally specific modes of defining inter-Indigenous differences as they have been regarded and valued within Puno, thus becoming a mini site of seeing these competing discourses at play. The concluding chapter argues for a more nuanced look at multilingualism and language contact for our world today. It also makes the case for future discussions regarding the role of inter-Indigenous difference and gender's place within it.

CHAPTER 1

Indigenous Wives and Mothers' Tongues

Gendered Transitions Between Language, Kinship, and Land

Señora Florencia was one of my neighbors, and during my time living in the altiplano, she became one of my closest interlocutors through her relaxed demeanor and her subtle sense of humor. Much of that humor was directed toward me and my ineptness at speaking Aymara or being able to herd sheep without losing them (a frequent enough occurrence where two or three sheep would always wander away in a different direction). But through our time together, I was able to learn some Aymara through our mixed Aymara-Spanish conversations—a practice that mirrored her conversational interactions with her family. One day she asked me about my research and why I had come to Puno. I responded that Quechua and Aymara were both spoken in Puno and I wanted to see how people spoke these languages. I then told her that I needed to go to town later in the day to potentially interview some Quechua speakers. To that she responded, *"Tú puedes entrevistarme"* (you can interview me).

Surprised by this statement, I asked her if she knew Quechua, and if so, how she learned. Instead of directly answering my question, Señora Florencia slowly and casually recounted her life story, a narrative she would thereafter informally retell to me several more times before I could finally get the chance to conduct a formal sociolinguistic interview with her. She told me that as a child she was sent to live with her maternal aunt and godmother, who spoke both Quechua and Aymara. This aunt, her mother's sister and an Aymara speaker by birth, married and started a family with a Quechua speaker. Their family lived just north of Puno, in the Quechua-speaking communities near the peninsula of Capachica. But after she married her husband, an Aymara speaker, and returned to live in the Aymara-speaking provinces on the southern shores of Lake Titicaca, there was never a need to speak Quechua again on a regular basis. Señora Florencia's linguistic life history provides important insights into how Indigenous puneños perceive the relationship between language and land, where certain areas and regions in Puno are considered either Quechua- or Aymara-speaking. Indeed, in our conversation, Señora Florencia would describe where her aunt lived as the *lado Quechua* (Quechua side) and the Aymara-speaking community she returned to after her marriage as *lado Aymara* (Aymara side). Her use of the Spanish term *"lado"* points to her own frame of reference for understanding and describing places located along the shores of Lake Titicaca, where certain parts were home to Quechua speakers and other parts home to Aymara speakers. Her life biography also sheds light on how knowing, speaking, and practicing a language was rooted in and shaped by an individual's history of residence, history of household membership, and who was included within her broader kin network. Being able to identify as a speaker of any particular language is not just a statement about linguistic knowledge or competence. These statements, instead, serve as commentaries about an individual's relationship with a specific community and kinship network, and how those become the semiotic ground for determining inter-Indigenous difference in the altiplano.

In a region of long-term inter-Indigenous language contact, what defines knowing Quechua or Aymara, or even defining who is a speaker of a language, cannot be easily determined through a simple declarative statement. One of the major arguments that I make in this book focuses on how ideas around Quechua or Aymara as linguistic objects, and by extension forms of linguistic expertise, are made more indeterminate due to histories of contact, borrowing, code-switching, and multilingualism. These kinds of linguistic practices not only blur the linguistic boundaries that distinguish Quechua from Aymara but also question whether or not recognizing these linguistic boundaries figured into how Indigenous puneños thought of their daily communicative practices. In not focusing on the supposed linguistic lines that differentiate Quechua and Aymara, and by extension Quechua speakers from Aymara speakers, other kinds of relationships become more salient. For Señora Florencia, her discussion of her life mentioned specific moments, places, and people that were characterized by and through a named language like Quechua or Aymara. But her linguistic life history also highlights how the appearance or presence of these named linguistic entities in her story are only meaningful when understood through more complicated relationships and interactions between individuals, their extended families, and places and communities in the altiplano.[1]

Commentaries about linguistic knowledge in Puno are inseparable from the kinds of connections that speakers have with their families and affines, and with specific communities in the region. This chapter unpacks those relationships and connections, explored through linguistic life history conversations and interviews with primarily middle-age and older Quechua- and Aymara-speaking puneños. Together, analysis of these conversations and life histories highlight how being able to communicate and know Quechua or Aymara are forms of linguistic knowledge that are intimately connected with speakers' connections with people and places. In this way, communicative competence and linguistic knowledge cannot be understood independently from understanding the significance of kinship in shaping a speaker's linguistic background over their lifespan. In connecting linguistic and communicative practices with kinship, language and linguistic knowledge become linked with other kinds of knowledge and modes of cultural transmission and reproduction, which inform structures and networks of relatedness across the altiplano. Yet like other kinds of kinship practices, processes of linguistic transmission and reproduction are also gendered, revealing unique divergences in how language and conceptions of relatedness differ between men and women, and what effects those differences have in shaping linguistic practices within families and kin networks and extending those practices to shape and define inter-Indigenous linguistic and social differences across the altiplano.

Andean Kinship in the Altiplano

Kinship is about the forms of relationality that individuals have with broader social networks (Carsten 2000). It includes practices that include reckoning kin members through descent and common ancestry and the creation of new alliances through marriage (Needham 1971). But kinship, and the processes that determine who is kin and who is not, is also shaped through practices like co-residence and commensuration through the sharing of substances (Carsten 2004). The combination of these discussions has helped complicate scholarly debates around Andean kinship (Mayer and Bolton 1977). Pre-Hispanic accounts of Inkaic kinship, for instance, stressed the importance of bilateral descent, where individuals claimed ancestry from both the paternal side and maternal side of their family (Zuidema 1977). These accounts framed Andean kinship with the significance of gender complementarity found in idealizations of husband-wife relationships known as *qhari-warmi* (Quechua) or *chacha-warmixa* (Aymara), and how these notions intersect with the exchange practices between wife-givers and wife-takers and other kinds of economic changes.

Over time, closer ethnographic analysis of Andean kinship has fleshed out these findings, providing deeper insight into the processual aspects that are pivotal to creating and expanding kin networks. Studies on trial marriages (Carter 1977), prevalent across different communities in the Andes, provide an alternative picture of marriage and alliance making, drawing attention to ideas around companionate partnerships and how those inform relationships of reciprocity and obligation. Equally important is the centrality of relationships through *compadrazgo*—making non-kin into godparents or co-parents—where the addition of *compadres* broadens one's kin network and increases the number of people who can provide support to an individual or family over the course of their lifetime (Mintz and Wolf 1950). The critical inclusion of discussions on compadrazgo as a fundamental part of understanding Andean kinship and processes of relatedness highlights how individuals and communities actively seek out means to expand their kin networks, acknowledging the benefits that accompany finding ways to include individuals who are not related by blood or through marriage. Additionally, these practices are not abstract formations, but rather they are mediated and made through material processes. More recent ethnographic analysis of Andean kinship elaborate on the materiality of these processes, focusing on the household as the central unit of social reproduction in the

Andes (Collins 1986; Maxwell 2011; Mayer 2002), and the materiality of the house in forging and strengthening these connections (Leinaweaver 2009; Narayanan 2023b).

In spite of what may seem on the surface as competing observations and analyses of what kinship is in the Andes, taking stock of these differences together coalesces around two core features that unite diverging practices and ways of calibrating relatedness in the region (Leinaweaver 2019). The first is the preference for horizontal kinship networks as a structural principle for Indigenous Andean communities. "Horizontal relationships" refers to the emphasis and privileging of connections that represent an individual network's social breadth over the course of their lifetime. Horizontality, in other words, highlights the importance of the relationships that one acquires and accumulates over a lifespan, drawing attention to the lifelong work that kinship and kin-making involves. This preference for horizontal relationships also deprivileges relationships that go back in time, such as practices that emphasize the maintenance of deep ancestral lineages. Marriage, for instance, enables this horizontal expansion through creating networks of affines (i.e., in-laws) that are maintained over the course of a lifetime. Compadrazgo similarly also extends those boundaries by extending the bonds of kinship to individuals outside the parameters of shared descent (or blood) or marriage.

In Puno, for instance, honoring deceased family members rarely extends further back than a great-grandparent's generation. This lack of deep ancestral depth becomes most salient during the annual *Todos Los Santos* celebration on November 1 and 2 every year.[2] Similar to *Día de Muertos* celebrations in Mexico, Todos Los Santos also involves creating altars with offerings for the dead that typically include cookies and decorative loaves of bread known as *t'ant'a wawa* (bread babies). While these celebrations honor the dead, they primarily celebrate the recently deceased; most Todos Los Santos celebrations I attended did not honor anyone older than a grandparent. Instead, the annual celebration is more focused on individuals who had passed away within the past decade, which could include brother, sisters, and even individuals from the younger generations such as young adults who may have passed away due to sickness or accidents. Celebrating and honoring the recently deceased reflects this horizontality by not invoking ancestors of previous generations. And, although older ancestors may not have been honored, celebrations were always offered to *compadres* (co-parents), *padrinos* (godfathers), and *madrinas* (godmothers) of the family who had also recently died within the last few years. Including and honoring recently deceased kin through compadrazgo reflects the horizontal nature of kin relations in the altiplano, thus including ritual kin as part of the broader set of kin relationships who have played important roles within the single lifespan of an individual, couple, or household.

The preference for horizontal kin relationships is complemented with the second core feature of Andean kinship, which is a recognition that kin are made (and unmade) through processes of commensuration and differentiation. Notably demonstrated in Janet Carsten's analysis of kinship processes in Malay fishing villages (Carsten 1995, 1997), understanding kinship through commensurate practices are commonly linked to ideas around personhood and highlight how living in the same space and engaging in shared communal practices around feeding and eating cultivates a sense of sameness that is also central to feelings of belonging together as kin. Importantly, viewing kin-making through the lens of commensurate processes highlights both the mutable nature of identity and personhood formation, emphasizing how the recognition of and care put into making kin is not limited to procreation or kinship through shared descent. In this vein, commensurate practices in the Andes are largely defined through shared residence, cohabitation, and the sharing of things like food and drink. Additionally, these processes are intimately linked to the significance and importance given to the house such that individuals living under the same roof and sharing the same space will also spend time sharing food, drink, and other resources together that create and maintain the bonds of kinship (Alderman 2021; Narayanan 2023b). Spending time in a shared residence, where different forms of sharing occur, strengthens the bonds of kinship between parents and their children. But these practices are also extended to newer individuals introduced into the kin network, symbolically smoothing the process by which non-kin can eventually be transformed into kin (Weismantel 1995). This process of transition and transformation, what Jessaca Leinaweaver (2007) in her analysis of child fostering and child-circulation practices in Ayacucho identifies through the term *"acostumbrarse"* is a period where individuals become accustomed to the practices of a particular group, highlighting how kinship is reckoned through some kind of shared essence that can only be cultivated and maintained through cohabitation, food sharing, and participating in the daily practices that hold individuals living together under the same roof. Such processes are central to the transformations that are expected of new brides to become part of their husband's family (Van Vleet 2008) and of children who become kin through adoption and fostering (Leinaweaver 2008). However, these processes are not only limited to the kinship between humans. They also extend to the forging of relationships with nonhuman entities like mountains, houses, and land (Salas Carreño 2016). Such relationships are also made and maintained through shared residence, and food-sharing through *pagos*, or ritual payments of food and drink to the land (Cadena 2015), which are done periodically during planting and harvesting seasons and to honor the start of the Andean New Year during the winter solstice (June 21). Together, such practices of ritual payment with the land reinforce an individual's connection with a place and community and illustrate how their identity and personhood is rooted and shaped through their connections with named locations. As such, networks of relatedness also include named places and promontory sites that contribute to the making of kinship networks and the formation of individuals in the region.

Together, these practices and processes highlight how kinship, both in the making of new kin relationships and the maintenance of kin bonds, are lifelong processes that individuals and households undertake for their entire lives. Being a full social person in the region is defined through a lifetime of making and maintaining kin relationships, accumulating bonds that represent the spectrum of connections that can exist between both human and nonhuman entities. The breadth of relationships that one can include in their network therefore are important in shaping individual identity. But these processes are not continuous and are filled with moments of disruption where the connections that an individual may be born into are broken as individuals move and are raised and nurtured under other roofs, in other homes, and among other human and nonhuman kin. Attention to the processual nature of kinship and personhood in the Andes, therefore, highlights how identities are fluid and can change over time through practices of commensuration. Moreover, they also draw attention to the ways that identities are not fixed at birth but are fluid and can be dynamically shaped by the individuals that are included within one's network and residence and household. Just as kinship is a lifelong project of creating and broadening one's social network, so too are processes associated with social personhood, which are also made and unmade over an individual's lifespan.

Locating Identity and Difference in the Local Landscape

Social personhood and social identity are shaped and characterized by the relationships that individuals cultivate over a lifetime with human and nonhuman entities. Thus, the people and nonhuman beings that one engages in reciprocal exchanges with over a lifespan, or commensurate practices such as cofeeding and shared residence, help to strengthen the connections between those individuals. They also contribute to the formation of social identities, where who one engages in these commensurate practices with shapes their social identity. This also means that the specific relationships an individual has and maintains with human and nonhuman beings also set the limits to understand social difference across the altiplano. Here, the reciprocal relationships of feeding and sharing of substances with named places and geographic landmarks fosters a sense of understanding social personhood and the creation of social identities as derived from a named community or place in the landscape (Salas Carreño 2016). Social identity, in other words, is defined by the named place or community where an individual was raised or where they live and engage in ritual sharing of food and drink. This also means that social differences are understood to be defined by the boundaries that differentiate between the communities, where individuals from different communities have different essences and identities derived from the unique aspects of their specific named place and shaped by specific and particular relationships with named areas in the landscape.

Absent from this understanding of social difference among Indigenous puneños, therefore, is an understanding of social difference as defined through language or linguistic differences. Equally absent is also an articulation of Indigenous identity and inter-Indigenous differences along ethnolinguistic lines. Although inter-Indigenous identity and difference in the altiplano may increasingly be discursively reproduced using ethnolinguistic categories like Quechua and Aymara, it is important to note that many puneños, especially those who are middle-age and older, do not self-identify or recognize inter-Indigenous differences through these ethnolinguistic labels.[3] Instead, these individuals tend to articulate who they are as something that cannot be separated from the land that they live in or were raised in. For instance, if an individual was from the Quechua-speaking provincial district of Ayaviri, they would say *Ayaviri kani* (I am Ayaviri). Or if they were from the Aymara-speaking provincial district of Acora, they would say *Acora satatwa* (I am Acora). Note that in each of these utterances, the meaning is not simply that an individual is "from" these places, but rather that they "are" these places, emphasizing more of a continuous link between place and self rather than acknowledging any of these places as simply locations where one resides in or travels from. Even if translated into Spanish, these meanings are also calqued, thus producing commonly heard phrases like *soy puneño, soy ayavireño*, or *soy acoreño* to mean "I am Puno," "I am Ayaviri," or "I am Acora." Just like their Quechua and Aymara antecedents, these phrases highlight how social personhood, identity, and social difference are defined and shaped by the boundaries that separate distinct communities in the landscape. It is a connection that has been maintained and fostered through ritual feeding practices to the earth, *apus*, and the community. And it's a connection that has been reciprocated through eating the crops and livestock that are cultivated on these lands, thus directly taking in those shared substances with those named places.

When these practices are scaled outward, these means of identification and defining personhood also extend to others within the same community. Community boundaries, and the boundaries that are recognized and understood through named places, form the basis by which all individuals who are connected to those lands through practices of commensuration form their identities and cultivate their personhood. This also means that all of these individuals are also kin with each other, whose connections to each other are mediated through ritual feeding practices and long-term histories of cohabitation and shared residence on the land and with nonhuman entities within their landscape. Belonging to the same place, which allows for a sharing of similar essences, is the symbolic grounds for similarity. Processes of acostumbrarse within the houses and homes of individuals within these spaces and places ensure that this sharing of similarities and commensuration is maintained with the addition of newcomers to a community and within a kin network. And within the Peruvian altiplano, folks within any community are also related to each other through shared descent or marriage. However, some of those connections may be generations deep, and community members may not necessarily remember how or why that connection is there. Nonetheless, the kinship connections are recognized because these same distant kin relations maintain their relatedness to each other through continuing to participate and engage in forms of communal work and reciprocity with their land and community, and with others who share those same connections in the same place.

I noticed this within my community outside of Chucuito, which was composed of around fifteen interrelated households. As was common across the altiplano, elderly individuals were addressed as *tiu*, the Aymaracized version of the Spanish *tio*, or "uncle," and *tia*, or "aunt." These were used as terms of respect, and I especially heard them used by Señora Florencia's daughters and granddaughters when addressing the different elderly men and women within their community. After noticing how these elders were addressed early in my fieldwork, I one day asked Señora Florencia's daughter and granddaughters who these various tius and tias were. Were they actual kin? If so, how were they kin? Señora Florencia's granddaughters gave me what I thought was a typical answer for teenagers at the time: Yes, those people were family. But how? I don't know, you should ask my mother or grandmother, they would know. I got slightly more precise answers from Señora Florencia and her daughter, who were able to confirm that these various tius and tias were kin of Señora Florencia's husband, Señor Pedro. But how exactly they were related, they were not sure, only that they were all distant family. To which Señora Florencia quickly added in her Aymaracized Spanish, "*Aqui tudus sumus familia*" (Here, we are all family). Eventually I got to know these various tius and tias, and I would hear similar statements where everyone was related to each other. The specifics of how everyone was related was rarely provided. At the same time, they all regarded each other as kin, which for them meant that they were present for every significant community event from weddings and funerals to participating in ritual pagos for the earth at the start of the harvest and planting seasons each year.

These responses for who is kin and how they are related reflect the horizontality of Andean kinship, where deep ancestral ties between individuals and families are not prioritized or recorded. My own questions inquiring how households were related to each other was instead countered with vague responses of how everyone, and particularly the men, were related to each other through some kind of distant cousin or uncle or great-granduncle relationship. Yet the lack of those details did not seem to matter, nor did they prohibit these families from recognizing each other as kin and coming to each other's aid and mutual support on communal issues. Instead, these recognized bonds of kinship were founded on the fact that everyone in that community was a lifelong member who had cultivated equally long relationships with everyone else. Their relatedness, and on a deeper level their sameness, was mediated and formed through everyone's ongoing commitment to each other and their shared place and space.

While their shared relationship with the same community made them all kin, these connections also made them different from individuals from other communities. Because identity, personhood, and broader relatedness is primarily defined by being from the same community, difference comes from the boundaries that separate communities and their associated kin groups and networks across the landscape. In this way, inter-Indigenous difference is defined by the boundaries that distinguish and differentiate one community from another and also separate distinct sets of kin-making practices that cultivate and maintain the bonds of relatedness across each of these spaces. This means that inter-Indigenous difference is based on the differences that one can claim by belonging to a specific place—a feature that shapes practices involving the transmission of linguistic heritage along community lines.

The Gender of Andean Kinship

The cultivation of personhood in the Andes parallels lifelong processes of kinship curation in the Andes. Yet it is important to remember that these processes are also gendered, and they reinforce the differences between men and women. These differences, for instance, run through more traditional tropes of Indigenous Andean kinship, such as the gendered differences described in bilateral descent and parallel inheritance (Silverblatt 1987), as well as the cosmological vision of gender complementarity in the world captured through notions of qhari-warmi and chacha-warmixa in gender complementarity (Harris 2000). However, such gender divisions in kinship relationships and the basic foundations of households and families are not predetermined. Instead, these differences are symbolically shaped, emergent through differences within kinship relationships and kinship practices. In other words, differences between men and women, or male and female gender identities, are influenced by the differences in their associated domains of kinship practices and their symbolic significance in cultivating networks of relatedness. As such, gender differences within kinship in the Andes rely on some recognition of alterity as a broader principle of determining the boundaries and limits of one's horizontal network of kith and kin (Harris 2008; Vilaça 2016).

Thinking about gender identity and difference as shaped by the sociosymbolic significance of alterities between different kinds of individuals also complicates long-standing assumptions around gender equality within Andean kinship that are sometimes embedded in ideas like gender complementarity. Instead, approaching gender differences as another socially significant form of alterity can draw attention to the kinds of social asymmetries and inequalities associated with each gendered role and set of responsibilities. One such example of gender asymmetry are marriage preferences in the altiplano, with the dominant preference for patrilocal, exogamous unions. This preference means first that marriages must be exogamous, strongly preferring that men and women come from different communities. The preference for patrilocality also means that, after marriage, women are expected to move into their husband's and in-laws' community. Because of this movement for women, and the lack of movement for men in the altiplano after marriage, patterns of inheritance also tend to favor men and paternal lands. This is especially true for the maintenance and inheritance of traditional lands within each community, where they are inherited, cultivated, and maintained with each subsequent generation of sons, resulting in the maintenance of ancestral landholdings within the paternal line. While brides typically bring with them flocks of sheep or alpacas, and in some cases still have access to crops grown on their fathers' traditional lands, movement out and away from their natal communities result in women beginning a process of separation away from their natal communities and kin networks associated there, eventually losing their access to these lands for themselves and their descendants.

This process of separation that begins when a young bride moves away from her natal community and kin continues through the early years into her marriage as she begins to embark on the process of acostumbrarse to become a member of her husband's family, community, and kinship network. But this process is not a straightforward transition, bringing with it additional social expectations that heighten gender differences between men and their exogamous brides. Van Vleet's work on gender and kinship in the Bolivian highlands (2002, 2008), for instance, draws attention to the kinds of emotional stress and violence that young brides experience after marriage, connecting the realities of embarking on this journey alone without the support of your extended family to similar concerns voiced by the mothers and older female kin of brides, who also remember the emotional and sometimes physical hardships they endured during their early marital years. These accounts would align with my own observations of what older puneña women would talk about too, sharing similar kinds of concerns and stories with their friends and peers about their daughters, nieces, or granddaughters.

Yet these fears and concerns for the challenges that a young bride faces alone in her husband's community and without her kin are also compounded by the other kinds of symbolic transformations that are expected in the process of acostumbrarse. In my conversations with older puneña women, they talked about how they had to relearn how to perform basic chores and household tasks according to the standard practices of their husband's family. Not only were they expected to learn how to cook and typically act like their husband's family but they were also expected to change their dress and learn the ritual songs and dances that shaped and defined belonging within their husband's community. Over the course of being separated from their natal community, young brides are transformed into members of their husband's kin network and community through learning and engaging in practices that accustom them to their in-laws' families. But this process of learning is also a sociosymbolic transformation, making these women into kin and community members within their husband's kinship network, and while also unmaking the connections and bonds that they had with their premarital kith and kin in their natal communities.

Through this, women as brides and wives shed their signs of otherness that mark them as outsiders and non-kin for their husband's family and community. Yet in becoming kin within their in-laws' household and community, they also become separated from their natal kin, losing the signs, connections, and commensurate practices that reinforce their connections and belonging within their natal community. Key to these processes, however, is how these transformative processes are specific to women. Marriage practices and preferences, and the ensuing processes that contribute to their transformation into their in-laws' community, are only focused on women. Moreover, these practices are often reproduced between women, as mothers-in-law from the previous generation socialize their younger daughters-in-law in similar transformative practices that they experienced when they were young brides. These practices, however, are not expected of men. Just as women and femaleness are shaped and constructed through years of sociosymbolic transformations to kin members, men and maleness is equally defined by the absence of these transformative kinship processes. Yet in this way women are equally important to maintaining the boundaries between communities. Through their symbolic transformations, women also uphold the boundaries between communities, limiting to the horizontal breadth that can exist within kinship networks.

Indigenous Wives and Transitions in Linguistic Genealogies

Thus far, practices involving kinship, the construction of social personhood, and the maintenance of inter-Indigenous differences have been largely analyzed as being grounded in the differences between distinct communities and the role that gender differences play in maintaining those differences. Less prominent in this discussion is the role that language and linguistic differences play in shaping distinct social identities and mediating the recognition of inter-Indigenous differences. Although identity is primarily recognized through community-based kinship connections and relationships, this does not mean that language or linguistic practices are not important in creation of Indigenous social differences. Instead, language is viewed as a set of practices that are important in the cultivation and maintenance of inter-Indigenous differences across the altiplano. This view of language does not limit communicative practices to a bounded denotational object like a named "language" (e.g., Quechua or Aymara) but instead focuses on how speech can be seen as a set of community-defined practices. In this way, language and linguistic differences are central to creating a very specific speech community that is associated for each distinct community and its kinship networks (Mannheim 2022). Community-specific speech practices also become one component of broader constellation of practices that also define a community, making these practices part of a very local community of practice (Eckert and McConnell-Ginet 1992) that is formed and maintained through speech and other customs that include dress, agricultural and animal husbandry practices, cooking, and specialized ritual and cultural knowledge that encompasses knowing place-specific songs and how one should speak and communicate with the earth for ritual practices and offerings.

The distinctness of each speech community, or rather, knowing how to speak in a way that is indexical of being part of a specific named place, contributes to a hyperlocal form of autochthony in the region, where each named community and its boundaries contributes to the creation and cultivation of a distinct set of identities that are differentiated from each other (Mannheim 2022). More importantly, this view of language in terms of locally specific speech and communicative practices embedded within a local community of practice also emphasizes how language differences along the lines of Quechua and Aymara traditionally have not been the arbiters of understanding and recognizing inter-Indigenous differences in the region. Instead, each community speaks differently, even if they technically speak the same Indigenous language (whether it be Quechua or Aymara). While in some cases those differences may be specific to a region or community,[4] the significance of these differences here does not just lie in whether a community is speaking some variation of Quechua or Aymara. Communicative difference is also about knowing how to communicate in a way that makes one intelligible to the human and nonhuman entities within their community-specific kinship networks, and to maintain reciprocal relationships with nonhuman entities who are central to mediating kinship, social personhood, and inter-Indigenous difference in the region (Mannheim 2022).

Speech-community-specific practices, in other words, are habitually cultivated and maintained practices that have to be embodied over longer periods of time. And once that embodiment has been achieved, it becomes another set of signs that marks the individual as being part of a distinct place and its associated kinship networks. This means that social identity, and by extension inter-Indigenous difference, is shaped by differences in speech and communicative practices. What this does not necessarily entail, however, is the degree to which social identity is grounded in language as a distinct, bounded object.

Given the gendered asymmetries associated with the exogamous brides and wives, the maintenance of communicative practices specific to a local speech community is also a gendered process that accentuates the symbolic transformations and the strengthening and weakening of kinship bonds and networks that Indigenous women experience. As noted earlier, the first few years of marriage are a time when young brides are expected to undergo a symbolic transformation to shed all signs of their difference. Learning how to speak like those in your husband's community and broader kin network is included in this process, where young brides are expected to learn to speak like their in-laws and communicate in ways that align them with the communicative practices that define that community. In my conversations with Señora Florencia, for instance, she would sometimes tell me that even though she could speak Aymara since she was a child, she still felt self-conscious about how different her Aymara was from her husband's and his family's. In her efforts to change this, she worked hard to ensure that her Aymara sounded just like his and everyone else's in the community. A similar theme emerged while conversing with one of my longtime friends from the market, Señora Fidelia. In discussing her linguistic life history and family tree, she said that her mother spoke Quechua differently than her maternal uncles. She reasoned that the difference probably came from the long marriage that her parents enjoyed and the fact that, after getting married, her mother was busy tending to the children and maintaining the household. But she also noted that it was a different time, when marriage meant you had to follow your husband and his family, eat how they eat, dress how they dress, and act how they do as well. Señora Fidelia's account of her mother suggests that being socialized to speak like one's husband's family accompanies other forms of socialization that Indigenous brides are expected to follow.

Through this process of communicative socialization, women also tended to interact less with their kin in their natal community. The consequences of these infrequent interactions contribute not only to the differentiation in communicative practices between brides and wives and their natal kin but also to a slow weakening of connections with their communities, kin, and birth identity. It is important to note that after marriage, neither wives nor their children are prevented from ever returning to visit a woman's natal community. The Indigenous women that I knew and spoke with noted that either they or their elderly or deceased mothers would return back to their maternal community to attend ritual celebrations like patron saint festivals, attend family events like funerals, or help with the harvest and bring their share of the crops grown on their natal lands. But over time these visits and connections fade, with a woman's children and eventually her grandchildren and great-grandchildren having less of a connection with their maternal ancestral community, lands, and kin. Some detachment and separation of kinship is accomplished by communal lands being traditionally held and maintained by men through the paternal line, thus passing lands to each successive generation of men. But it is also reinforced by the fact that women, through their separation from their natal community at marriage, also begin the process of losing their connections and kinship with their community and natal kin. It is a process that begins with women marrying out of their community and continues with each successive generation of children. Yet through this, community boundaries are also maintained over time such that women neither inherit nor pass on their ancestral lands to children and descendants in other communities.

This kind of symbolic regulation of differences between communities extends down to the practices that are specific for each community, including language and communicative practices. Yet this regimentation of practices is also gendered, where in addition to being expected to learn the practices of their husbands and in-laws, women also bear the responsibility to teach and socialize these practices for the next generation. Like other Indigenous communities across South America, women are also tasked with being the primary caretakers responsible for the linguistic and cultural socialization of children (Ochs and Schieffelin 1984). In Puno and in the Andes (Bolin 2006), once children are deemed old enough to participate in household labor activities, they are split up according to their gender roles, with young girls staying with their mother and older female kin and young boys working with their fathers and older male kin. Yet, prior to this age, children of both genders are primarily socialized by their mothers and older female kin, with additional support and socialization provided by an older sister or two. However, mothers do not socialize their children in the practices that they learned for their own community. Instead, mothers socialize their children as members of their husband's community, down to the communicative practices and languages used in those interactions.

This aspect is saliently marked in cases and situations where the wives and brides come from a speech community where a completely different language is spoken, resulting in the union between a Quechua speaker and an Aymara speaker. Cross-linguistic marriages, like in the case of Señora Florencia's Aymara-speaking maternal aunt marrying a Quechua speaker, are not uncommon across the altiplano. From casual conversations with people on combis, to being told about the marriages of friends' parents or of other friends, I soon came to learn that regardless of the linguistic background of the individual—Quechua or Aymara speaking—many families had at least one case of a cross-linguistic marriage in their extended family tree.[5]

One example was told to me by an older Quechua-speaking woman in her early sixties named Susana, who married an Aymara-speaking man. After marriage, she moved in with her husband, and she remembered that the years immediately after her wedding were a trying time. During this period she was very lonely, after being told that she was not allowed to go back and visit her natal family as often as she would like. Instead, she lived under the watchful supervision of her mother- and father-in-law in the Aymara provinces near Laraqueri outside of Puno. To this day, she admits that these years were difficult, and she was only able to survive because her husband was kind to her. But because her interactions with her natal family were limited, she had no other alternative but to become a full member of her husband's Aymara-speaking community. As a result of this intense transformative process, she learned how to speak fluent Aymara and was eventually regarded and loved by her in-laws as a natural daughter of the family. When I asked why she never returned to her native community in the province of Azángaro after the death of her in-laws and after her children had grown up, she dryly remarked that years of being married to an Aymara speaker made her forget her Quechua. Though she thought she could never forget her natal language, she realized during one of the few post-marriage visits to see a sick uncle that she noticed some difficulty in communicating in Quechua with her family. This bothered her enough to feel that although she was a Quechua speaker at birth, she had become too accustomed to speaking Aymara to be able to go back and maintain connections in her natal village and community.

These dynamics also shape the linguistic practices around child language socialization, where children of interlinguistic marriages often only grew up learning and speaking one language at home despite the multilingual capabilities of their mothers.[6] One close friend of mine, Lidia, who at the time was an Aymara-speaking woman in her late forties, told me that she always knew that her mother was originally a Quechua speaker who fell in love and married Lidia's father, an Aymara-speaking man. But her knowing this did not come from her mother speaking Quechua at home, nor from interactions with her mother's Quechua-speaking kinsmen. Instead, the issue was raised primarily because her father would tease her mother about the fact that she spoke another language that he could not. During one of our conversations, she brought up these linguistic tensions between her father and mother, saying:

> My father while we were eating dinner would try and say things in Quechua, and then ask her in Aymara, "How do you say this." My mother did not like to teach him how to say things in Quechua and felt that it was not right to teach something to him and us if we were not going to speak it properly. So instead, he would imitate how he thought she spoke Quechua. I know that this bothered her. I know it bothered her that she could not speak Quechua at home. But she never said anything either.

When Lidia told me her story, I asked how she would describe the linguistic heritage and identity of herself and her mother. She said that she sometimes thinks that she is both a Quechua speaker and an Aymara speaker by heritage, a statement that allows her to honor the linguistic heritage of her late mother. But more often than not, she felt more comfortable saying that Aymara was her primary linguistic heritage and that she was an Aymara speaker. Even though she knew her mother also spoke Quechua, she herself grew up in an Aymara-speaking home, and lived in an Aymara-speaking community and on lands that were largely recognized as being a home to Aymara speakers. Most importantly, her father was an Aymara speaker, which for her was the most important factor in determining whether or not someone could claim Quechua or Aymara as part of their linguistic heritage.

Lidia's story mirrors that of many other puneños for whom the knowledge of their mothers' linguistic difference from their fathers was a topic of conversation that was openly discussed within family circles. But this knowledge never translated into any kind of sustained effort to cultivate either a linguistic knowledge or connection with their mothers' linguistic heritage and natal community and kin. Thus, in spite of knowing that their mothers were linguistically different from their fathers, they nevertheless self-aligned with the linguistic heritage and background of their paternal line. Yet for other women and Indigenous puneñas I spoke with, their family history of linguistic exogamy was something that was not typically talked about or discussed openly. This is not to say that these conversations were secretive, taboo topics to be avoided but rather that these histories were not necessarily important points of discussion in relation to broader ways of talking about Indigenous identities, peoples, places, and the ways that they spoke across the altiplano. This fact was certainly the case for one of my Quechua-speaking friends, Silvia. At the time of my fieldwork, Silvia was in her early forties. When we were discussing her family, she said that she knew her mother was originally an Aymara speaker prior to her marriage to Silvia's father. But she also noted that this was something that her mother never told her directly herself, nor was it something that the family ever discussed openly. Instead, she learned about her mother's linguistic heritage during her preteen years. At that time, Silvia's maternal grandparents got really sick, and her mother made the decision to go help take care of them with Silvia and her sister. Had it not been for this one incident, she would have never really known that her mother was an Aymara speaker, nor would she have had any contact with that side of the family or their customs at all.

A similar and more pronounced example of how little linguistic difference is discussed comes from Marianna's linguistic life history. An Aymara-speaking woman, also in her early forties during my fieldwork, Marianna was born and raised in the southern provinces in the Aymara-speaking region in the southern part of the Department of Puno. Marianna said that until she was a teenager she never really thought about her parents or her extended family. As far as she was concerned, both her parents were Aymara speakers maintaining her father's traditional lands in the southern provinces of the altiplano. All that changed when she was as teenager, when her mother got really sick one winter and died. It was in the midst of that mourning that she learned that her mother was a Quechua speaker by birth. At the funeral, her mother's Quechua-speaking kinsmen arrived to pay respects to their deceased sister and cousin. After the funeral, she never heard from those maternal family members again for the rest of her childhood, leaving her to once again remain in her Aymara-speaking community, to be raised by her father. A few years after her mother's passing, her father remarried, to another Aymara-speaking widow, maintaining her contact with Aymara for the duration of her childhood and young adulthood.

In talking with Marianna, I asked how she thinks about the linguistic heritage of her mother—was she only an Aymara speaker or was she also a Quechua speaker? Marianna said that at this point deciding how to identify or describe her mother's linguistic heritage did not really matter. True, her mother was first born into a Quechua-speaking family and community. But she married an Aymara speaker, learned Aymara, and went on to raise all of her children to only speak and communicate in Aymara. Her mother lived her life like any other Aymara-speaking woman, mother, and wife within Marianna's community. And for her own part, she noted that she was not raised like a Quechua speaker; she was raised in an Aymara-speaking home, where she ate the same food as her neighbors and friends, wore the same clothes as others in her community, and spoke Aymara like both her parents. Therefore, she is and always will be an Aymara speaker. Her mother's linguistic heritage had no role in changing that otherwise. And although her mother's early death precipitated a visit from her Quechua-speaking kin, her mother died as an Aymara speaker and was buried in the earth within the bounds of her Aymara-speaking community.

Together, these various stories reflect something that one Quechua-speaking acquaintance said to me early in the course of fieldwork when discussing my interest in seeing how Quechua and Aymara were spoken and maintained in multilingual families: "Quechuas and Aymaras have always married each other. But when the woman gets married, no one ever sees or hears from her again." On the surface, such a statement might seem like a warning or a form of admonishment, highlighting the threat of complete separation and alienation that occurs when cross-linguistic marriages occur. At the same time, this statement also echoed similar kinds of warnings and stories that women would share in passing about other young women who were foolish enough to marry across linguistic lines. Within the broader context of how these stories and warnings were told to me, their significance as warnings and cautionary tales were also based on my own positionality as a young, unmarried woman.[7] But these conversations, moreover, reinforce the core fact that marriage is filled with challenges and difficulties that all brides and wives must face, regardless of if they speak the same language as their husbands. Although these transformative challenges are more salient for women in interlinguistic marriages, they are the same kinds of formative processes that all young brides and wives experience as they negotiate their signs and communicative practices of belonging within their husbands' and in-laws' community and kin networks. In this sense, marriage in the altiplano has always been a marriage of differences, with women transforming from Indigenous brides to Indigenous wives, all the while mediating inter-Indigenous difference across the region.

Inverting the Linguistic Order: Urban Kinship and the Reversal of Gendered Linguistic Genealogies

Since the early 2000s, the demographic landscape of the altiplano has been rapidly changing, largely due to increased migration to urban and commercial centers like Puno, Juliaca, and other larger cities like Arequipa and Cusco (Paerregaard 1998; Ødegaard 2010). These changes have also influenced how families come to negotiate and make sense of their Indigenous linguistic genealogies. As younger couples increasingly seek to live in more urbanized centers to earn more money and provide better access to educational and economic opportunities for their children, they are not necessarily faced with the same expectations in terms of social commitments associated with lands and communities. This not only has an impact on child language socialization and the transmission or maintenance of Indigenous linguistic heritages but also affects the expectations of Indigenous wives.

This kind of negotiation of gendered expectations and the maintenance of their lengua materna and linguistic heritage is most noticeable in the newer, younger generations of cross-linguistic marriages and couples who live in these urbanized centers.[8] Because cities like Puno are not recognized as belonging to any one specific kin group, nor do they hold any predefined set of kinship relationships, building a house and starting a family in these cities can be accomplished without the necessary transformative processes that are normally expected in rural communities. The absence of these processes can be seen in how couples start their families as an independent unit away from other kin relationships. Unlike their grandparents' or even parents' generations, who built their houses on ancestral lands and through the support of kin and community members, these urban houses are built and constructed through wages and earnings often accumulated through working in professional jobs or working in the mines, markets, and local transportation services. Increasingly, these sources of income are augmented through small loans from the local bank, which are often used to finance the purchasing of materials to build a house. With these two financial sources, couples are able to purchase a plot of land within the urban perimeter (instead of inheriting an ancestral plot from the husband's father's family) and construct their house using materials that they purchased on their own. Typically, these newer houses tend to be built using more modern materials like concrete and steel, which also speeds up the time to completing a house for the young family (Narayanan 2023b). All of these practices reduce or completely eliminate the need for young couples to be supported by their broader kin network while establishing their household. And in doing so, it also bypasses the kinds of personhood-making processes that are accomplished through practices of cohabitation and sharing of food, drink, and other things. Furthermore, building a house and starting a life in urbanized centers also removes the symbolic transformation of brides from the social life cycle of homes and households. Because cities like the regional capital of Puno are not associated with any one kin group or set of kin-making practices, young brides and wives within the city are exempt from practices of commensuration that would have transformed them into members of their husbands' kin network and community.

This lack of established links between kinship networks and urban areas like Puno provide these younger families with new ways to think about their own linguistic genealogies and how this will be transmitted and maintained through the next generation. Often younger couples inevitably choose Spanish as the primary language of communication within their home, especially once they have children. The young couples and friends that I knew in Puno, who at the time were in their late twenties to mid-thirties, were either recently married or perhaps had one or two young children under the age of five. While both members of these couples were fiercely proud of their Indigenous linguistic heritage, they often opted to only speak Spanish within their household. Part of the decision to speak Spanish was motivated by socioeconomic pressures, where ensuring that children learned Spanish as their first language without any Indigenous linguistic influence or interference might guarantee more opportunities for socioeconomic advancement later in life. However, in some cases, parents also saw socializing their children in Spanish as a way to socialize their children as puneños—a kind of uniform identity that is not defined by any one language, nor by any connection to a specific community or kinship network.

This sentiment was shared by many younger puneño couples who saw a puneño identity as a way to embrace an individual's altiplano roots without being explicitly marked as any specific Indigenous, ethnic background, which might predispose their children to experience a lifetime of racial prejudice and discrimination if they decided to one day leave the altiplano to explore economic opportunities in the national capital or abroad. But embracing a generic puneño identity also took on different connotations and significances for cross-linguistic couples. Marianna's life, for instance, highlighted the possibilities of how raising her children as puneños might benefit her personally and emotionally. After reaching adulthood Marianna moved to the city to eventually work in the artesanía markets close to the docks that take tourists to visit the Uros (the floating islands). After moving to the city, she fell in love with a Quechua-speaking man that she met through a friend of a friend who also worked with her in the tourist artesanía markets. As a young migrant to the city, she got to know him first in the company of other friends and eventually on more intimate dates. Soon after, they fell in love, moved in together, and eventually started their family with the birth of their daughter. As an Aymara-speaking migrant with a Quechua-speaking husband, Marianna had no intention of moving to her husband's community and living her life as a traditional Indigenous wife, complete with working the fields and learning how to speak Quechua under the watchful eye of her mother-in-law. She also had no wish to return to her community, seeing the socioeconomic advantages that came from living in Puno.

Building a house and raising her family in Puno offered Marianna the chance to live her life and raise her family on her own terms. In Puno, her daughter had access to schools that could help her become an educated professional one day. And Marianna felt that in the city, she and her husband actually had an equal partnership—a relationship ideal that was strengthened by the fact that they primarily spoke to each other in Spanish and not the language of either of their Indigenous linguistic backgrounds. Given that Marianna felt very strong and sure about her decision to put down roots in Puno, I asked if she or her husband had taught their daughter either one of their heritage Indigenous languages, Quechua or Aymara. Confidently, she responded that neither her husband nor she feels any pressure to teach their daughter either of their lenguas maternas. Marianna did note that if their daughter showed any interest in learning either Quechua or Aymara, then they would think about sending her to a certificate program or *instituto* (institute) to properly learn those languages. But in the meantime, they decided to socialize their daughter as a puneña, ensuring that Spanish is her primary language, and guaranteeing that she grows up feeling free to be a child and away from the responsibilities and demands that come from being directly tied to a specific community.

One characteristic that stands out in Marianna's narrative of her own cross-linguistic marriage is how she does not have to learn her husband's heritage Indigenous language. The lack of social pressure to thus learn the language of one's husband figured in other narratives and linguistic life histories from other Indigenous puneña women in cross-linguistic marriages and was also used to demonstrate the success not only of their marriages but also of the decisions that they made in raising their children within the urban perimeter of Puno. This was certainly the case for one of my closest friends, Sumaq Ruray. Sumaq Ruray was a Quechua-speaking woman in her late thirties with a bright smile and a bubbly personality, who also worked in the tourist markets close to the docks by Lake Titicaca. Her husband was an Aymara speaker. Like other cross-linguistic couples in Puno, she and her husband primarily spoke with each other, and their children, in Spanish. When I learned that her husband was an Aymara speaker, I asked Sumaq Ruray how she managed those differences and if she felt pressured to conform to the needs or demands of her husband's family. She acknowledged the factual part of my question, highlighting how those pressures are real and something that women in previous generations had to experience and suffer through. But she was an exception. Her marriage and family life were happy and strong. Some of her sense of security was partly attributed to the fact that she, her husband, and her three boys were living in Puno, away from either her or her husband's natal community. But this feeling was also supported by the fact that her mother-in-law was like her, a Quechua speaker by birth who had to learn and only speak Aymara after marrying an Aymara-speaking man. As such, Sumaq Ruray considered herself lucky to have a really supportive mother-in-law with whom she could speak Quechua. While she also added that her mother-in-law's Quechua did sound *medio raro* (a little bit odd), sharing this linguistic background provided a kind of emotional support, knowing that there was someone like her among her in-laws that she could count on. Even though Sumaq Ruray technically married into an Aymara-speaking family, she never really had to learn Aymara because of the Quechua proficiencies of her mother-in-law and because she could choose to live and work in Puno.

However, Sumaq Ruray also admitted that being free of some of the linguistic and kin-based obligations while living in the city had its downsides. For instance, living in Puno meant that she and her family were still far from the supportive network of kin that she and her husband enjoyed as children. Her boys would grow up not fully understanding who they are and how this understanding is shaped by the relationships that they have with their kin and community. And because they were raised in Puno, her boys were also growing up without much knowledge of either Quechua or Aymara, moving through this world as primarily Spanish speakers. But, because Sumaq Ruray was living in Puno, she was also free to be flexible in her language socialization practices with her children, thus giving her boys the freedom to potentially choose which lenguas maternas they wanted to learn and which linguistic heritage they wished to identify with in the future. This stance toward how one's lengua materna aligns with their linguistic genealogy was something that fluctuated and evolved over the course of our friendship. One day while helping Sumaq babysit her middle son, who was not feeling well enough to go to school, I asked her how her children might talk about themselves when they are adults and, if they so choose, what linguistic heritage they would identify with. Sumaq Ruray went back and forth, wondering aloud if her sons and their descendants should say that they are from an Aymara-speaking family, or Quechua-speaking family. Perhaps they should identify as both, she concluded, and say that they have a Quechua-speaking mother and an Aymara-speaking father.

As time went on, I would continue to ask Sumaq Ruray this question. And each time she would change her answer, providing a different rationale. Once she said that her boys can only identify as Aymara-speakers and should only learn Aymara because that is the language of their father. Other times, she felt that her boys should at some point learn Quechua, but only after they had learned Aymara, which is the language of their father. By the time I was finishing fieldwork and getting ready to leave Puno, she had decided that it was important that her boys learned at least one Indigenous language or lengua materna. Since her husband was not going to teach them Aymara and, as the mother, it was technically her responsibility to teach the lengua materna to her sons, she started to slowly socialize her boys into Quechua through only communicating directives in the language.

Sumaq Ruray's various linguistic decisions over time highlights how urban cross-linguistic couples negotiate a blending of maternal and paternal linguistic heritages into their family narratives. They also demonstrate a gendered inversion between the transmission of linguistic and cultural heritage and their alignment with the communities, kin networks, and practices associated with the maternal line. For instance, for many young urban Indigenous couples, it was not uncommon to find the wives' kin spending time within the house to help provide support. This is a shift from traditional Indigenous brides and wives found across rural communities, where support from extended kinsmen primarily came through the husband's extended kin network. Urban Indigenous puneño households instead often relied on the help of the wife's family, and often came from a woman's mother or younger sibling (either male or female), spending long periods of time in the home to help raise children and manage the household. Having the wife's younger siblings around to help raise the child and complete daily household tasks would end up becoming a mutually beneficial arrangement; young mothers and wives could enjoy all the benefits of free in-house childcare from kin that they knew and trusted, while the younger siblings could attend school or college-preparatory programs that could only be found in the regional capital. These newer household structures also meant that children were primarily being socialized in the linguistic and communicative practices of their mother's kin and community and not having the same kind of daily exposure to the practices that shape and define their father's kin network and social identity. And in the case of cross-linguistic marriages, this also meant that children were often being socialized in the maternal lengua materna, often at the expense of their father's heritage Indigenous language and place-based communicative and social practices.

These changes also coincide with the ideological restructuring around the revitalization and maintenance of Indigenous lenguas maternas. Discourses promoting the need for and importance of Indigenous language maintenance and literacy are explicitly presented through the name *lenguas maternas*. Labeling Indigenous languages through the phrase "lengua materna" helps to reinforce the idea that women as wives and mothers are primarily responsible for maintaining heritage Indigenous language use in the region. But for younger, urban families that are composed of cross-linguistic marriages, these politicized projects around Indigenous language maintenance and revitalization through the language of lengua materna take on new meaning, publicly signaling that, regardless of traditional kinship practices and expectations, Indigenous wives and mothers are the main transmitters of Indigenous linguistic knowledge and competence. This emphasis, however, does not specify whose lengua materna should be taught and reproduced in the younger generation of babies and children, creating the opportunity for the maternal lengua materna to take precedence over the paternal lengua materna. This is perhaps most clearly illustrated in the following two examples.

The first example comes from my friend Señor Aldo, a Quechua speaker in his late forties from the border between the altiplano and the Department of Cusco. Señor Aldo lives and works in Puno as a tour guide during the height of the tourism season, which runs from late May through late September. His wife is also an Aymara speaker, and together the couple have a teenage son. His wife's parents and sisters often stay in their house for large portions of the year and can easily come and visit since they are not too far from their natal community in Platería, about an hour south of Puno. During their long, extended stays, Aymara was the primary linguistic medium of communication for everyone, including Señor Aldo's teenage son, who was also comfortable conversing in Aymara. Spanish was only used whenever his wife's family wanted to include Señor Aldo in their family discussions and conversations. Señor Aldo over time has come to understand Aymara from listening to the conversations between his wife and her kinsmen when they are at home. He has also visited her natal community frequently over the course of their almost twenty-five-year marriage for various special occasions and events, thus improving and building on his conversational knowledge of Aymara. In spite of the dominant presence of Aymara-speaking individuals in their domestic life, Señor Aldo also mentioned that he tries to maintain some Quechua in their household through occasionally speaking the language with his son.

One day I asked him if his son could hold a conversation in both Quechua and Aymara. Proudly, he said that his son could understand Quechua, and had no issues understanding his Quechua-speaking extended family whenever they would go back to his natal community for special events and holidays. However, he sheepishly admitted that his son was much more comfortable with Aymara and was practically bilingual in Aymara and Spanish. I asked if it bothered him that his son was not as proficient in Quechua, the language of his father and his paternal family.

Carefully considering my question, he replied with an emphatic "no." Instead, he reasoned that it was more important for children to learn their lengua materna—the mother's language—and that it was the mother's responsibility to teach her language to her children. Because of this, his son's dominance in Aymara was to be expected, because that is the language of his wife and her family. If this was so, then how would his son describe or characterize his Indigenous linguistic heritage and genealogy, especially in light of the 2017 census that was asking all puneños to identify themselves using the ethnolinguistic categories of "Quechua" and "Aymara"? Surprisingly, Señor Aldo replied that his son would always be Quechua because that identity comes from him as the father. But, after hearing his own response, he paused, and then with a small chuckle clarified his response saying, "Yes, my son is a Quechua with an Aymara mother. That is it."

A similar type of situation is also illustrated through the life of my friend Katarina, a Quechua-speaking woman in her mid-thirties who grew up in the high-altitude provinces of Carabaya. After living and working in Puno for many years, she met and married an Aymara-speaking man, from the southern provinces that bordered Bolivia, who was a classmate of one of her friends and colleagues who worked with her at one of the local newspapers in Puno. During my fieldwork, the two were in the middle of building their house in the northern outskirts of Puno and shared their home with Katarina's mother, younger brother, and younger sister for much of the year. Because of her marriage to an Aymara-speaking man, she and her husband christened their children with an Aymara-Quechua compound name—a dual representation that reflects their joint, cross-linguistic union. Although she wants her children's linguistic repertoires to match the multilingualism that is exhibited in their names, she admitted that her children really don't know Aymara and that they primarily seem to respond to directives and conversations in Quechua. This is because at home the only Indigenous language that is spoken is Quechua. Moreover, she noted that only she and her mother, brother, and sister have all agreed (explicitly and implicitly) to only speak to her children in Quechua. Her husband only rarely speaks Aymara at home. And his family rarely visits, thus limiting her children's exposure to being socialized in Aymara. I asked her how her husband felt about their home's linguistic environment, where he as the sole Aymara speaker had limited influence in how his children were being socialized. She was not worried at all about that and said that husband felt much closer to her family than his own Aymara-speaking family, and she also said that her mother loved him as if he were her own son. Slyly smiling, she also added "Instead of the woman becoming Aymara, we instead made my husband into a Quechua." Although she found it funny that her husband had become a full member of her own natal family, she was a little bit bothered that his comfort with her family excused him from taking more responsibility in speaking more Aymara at home, and teaching Aymara to their children. Like Señor Aldo, I also asked Katarina if her children would identify as ethnolinguistic Quechuas or Aymaras when they grew up. She just smiled and replied that they will identify as *qullasuyeños*—children of a true mixed, Quechua-Aymara-speaking family from Qullasuyu, the original name for the Department of Puno under the Inka empire.

These two examples show how the movement of cross-linguistic couples to the city are providing new avenues for the negotiation of kinship, identity, linguistic heritage, and the role of women in those processes. Based on the idea of lengua materna, children in these families are growing up much closer to the language, identity, and practices of their "mother's tongue." Husbands in these cases have become more incorporated into their wives' families, resulting in some admitting that they feel out of touch with their own natal family. In such cases, couples claim that they are the new face of what it means to be from Qullasuyu, bringing about a new compromise of Quechua-Aymara language contact and relations in the region. Fully acknowledging how marriage, kinship, and the transmission of linguistic heritage occurred in the past, these couples are optimistic that their marriages in today's context can bring about a new understanding of Puno as being a mix of Quechua- and Aymara speakers, where such a mix is not only exhibited in the diversity of linguistic practices of their children but also in their mode of identification as simply qullasuyeño or puneño. These couples, therefore, highlight the need to question discussions around language maintenance and lengua materna, requiring one to ask the clarifying question, "Whose mother's language?"

Señora Florencia's Epilogue: The Ideal Indigenous Woman as the Traditional Indigenous Wife

I want to end this chapter by returning to Señora Florencia's life story, and how her biography exemplifies the various nuances that shape the lives of multilingual kin networks and how those multilingual lineages and connections are managed to maintain specific linguistic genealogies and the landscape of inter-Indigenous differences in the region. Señora Florencia's mother's sister, born as an Aymara speaker, married a Quechua-speaking man and lived in the Quechua-speaking communities on the Capachica peninsula. This aunt and her children and grandchildren have very little interaction with Señora Florencia or her own family and children after she got married to Señor Pedro and became a wife and mother. Yet this general outline of Señora Florencia's biography overlooks the more intense, lived experiences that complicate her kinship and linguistic and communicative formalization. For instance, Señora Florencia did not only have a Quechua-speaking uncle or cousins; she also lived with them for several years as a child, where she helped her aunt sell fish from Lake Titicaca in the markets of Puno. During these years, she had to learn Quechua to play with her cousins, and she fondly recalled having once learned all of the songs, games, and jokes that her Quechua-speaking cousins knew. She returned to her Aymara-speaking community as a teenager, quicky reimmersing herself in the specific Aymara communicative practices that make up her speech community, only to soon be married to Señor Pedro from the neighboring community, whose father had visited her mother and uncle asking for her hand in marriage to their son. After she was married, Señora Florencia became the traditional rural, Indigenous wife, having six children and socializing all of them in Aymara and later in Spanish. Her children have limited contact with her Quechua-speaking cousins. And yet, Señora Florencia has managed to maintain these connections, quietly taking time each year to visit those cousins and see their children. And during these visits, Señora Florencia not only reconnects with her extended kin, but also has the chance to reconnect with them in Quechua, sharing in the same linguistic practices that define membership within her cousins' community.

These broader cross-linguistic connections and genealogies are topics that Señora Florencia never really talks about. She never discusses her knowledge of Quechua while her husband is present, nor does she ever speak Quechua around her family or in public more generally. It was not that Señora Florencia was scared or ashamed to talk about these details. Rather, she never thought that they were important and always dismissed the need to recount details of her life. Additionally, it was not that no one knew about Señora Florencia's Quechua-speaking connections. Everyone in the community knew about it, including her children. To the point where, during one wedding, while everyone was a little bit tipsy on beer, pisco, and whiskey that I was always tasked with bringing, and amid rounds of jokes, her eldest daughter exclaimed, "Look at my mother. You wouldn't know it, but she is really a Quechuista!" Everyone laughed, including Señora Florencia. While not everyone present knew all of the details regarding Señora Florencia's extended Quechua-speaking connections, the statement did not threaten Señora Florencia's belonging within the community. Irrespective of her extended family or past experiences, Señora Florencia was like them, another Aymara speaker from the community.

Señora Florencia's story, linguistic biography, and life history are as complicated as the ways that her family and community understand and recognize those details. Yet, her history and background were generally treated as matter-of-fact, unremarkable, and a non-topic of conversation for everyone other than me, the anthropologist. Similarly, Señora Florencia's own multilingual fluencies were considered to be a boring topic of conversation. Even after she told me that she could speak Quechua and Aymara, she did not feel comfortable elaborating further on her linguistic knowledge or reveling in how she was fluent in both Indigenous languages. For her, these were practices that corresponded to specific moments of her life. She learned Quechua when she was fostered by her aunt and her aunt's Quechua-speaking husband. She went back to speaking Aymara after returning to Aymara-speaking lands and got married. To a certain degree, the contours of her linguistic life history reflect these important milestones in her life. But her matter-of-factness about these details also reinforced a fundamental principle in her life—that Señora Florencia is an Aymara-speaking wife to an Aymara-speaking husband, with Aymara-speaking children and of an Aymara-speaking community.

Señora Florencia fits the mold of a traditional Indigenous wife of Puno and the altiplano—a woman who transformed herself for each community she lived in, with the final transformation coming after marriage when she erased all the signs that coded her as different. Included in this erasure are the essences that are also carried by her linguistic difference, making her transition a multifaceted one through embodying a different set of linguistic practices and set of signs that are grounded in her husband's community. Traditional Indigenous wives like Señora Florencia, however, stand out when compared with the more modern, urbanized Indigenous wives. These younger women appear on the surface as almost radical for not undergoing the same kinds of transformations that were expected of their more "traditional" mothers and grandmothers. This freedom is even more palpable for cross-linguistic wives, who have the flexibility to maintain their lengua materna with their children at the expense of their husbands'. Nonetheless, whether traditional or modern, all these Indigenous puneña wives do share one thing in common: their primary role and responsibility in transmitting the lengua materna, the heritage Indigenous language, to the next generation. Regardless of if the Indigenous wife undergoes a linguistic transformation or not, she is still responsible for maintaining their Indigenous linguistic repertoire for future generations.

As I will describe in later chapters, many of these symbolic aspects of lengua materna are taken literally as the language of mothers, lending to other ideologized discourses that locate and place the emphasis of language learning and the maintenance of Indigenous language transmission and the formalization of inter-Indigenous ethnolinguistic differences on the shoulders of women in their roles as wives and mothers. Yet this shift also has a role in changing the linguistic ecology of the altiplano, not only by altering the linguistic ideological landscape of understanding inter-Indigenous difference but also reframing the role of women in mediating what those differences signify today in relation to newer discourses that focus on the ethnolinguistic labels of "Quechua" and "Aymara."

CHAPTER 2

Brokering Across Boundaries

The Lives and Language of Market Women in Puno

In the middle of the Andean winter, the members of the Mercado de San Ignacio (Saint Ignatius Market) convened for one of their quarterly meetings to discuss issues with the market. Typically, these meetings involved discussions around establishing new codes of conduct for market associates and collecting dues from its members. As a linguistically mixed space, the market was evenly divided between Quechua- and Aymara-speakers who originally came from different parts of the Department of Puno. These individuals settled within the urban periphery of the city and earned their livelihoods through owning a stall and selling goods within the city's various market spaces. Like most meetings, the main points of business were discussed in Spanish, the shared language and medium of communication among vendors within the regional capital of Puno. Most of the speeches were presented by the market president and secretary, who, as elected members, were responsible for conveying important information to their other associates regarding new fees, taxes, and how the markets might be affected by local municipal policies.

Even though the meeting might have been technically conducted in Spanish, it was in fact a multilingual meeting. While the president and secretary carefully went through all of their announcements, back-channel conversations abounded across the markets. Vendors grouped together with other co-vendors and long-time friends, huddled under blankets to stay warm while also gossiping and commenting on the content of that day's meetings. These conversational sidebars—some in hushed tones, others loud enough to perhaps be distracting to the market association's president or secretary—were done in a mix of Spanish, Quechua, and Aymara. During these meetings, I tended to sit in the back with the two market women I had come to know the best in Puno: Señora Fidelia, a Quechua speaker, and Señora Marcela, an Aymara speaker. Even though I tried to listen to the main points of the meeting, I was inevitably more interested in the different conversations that Señora Fidelia and Señora Marcela were having between themselves and with others. At one moment, I would turn to see Señora Fidelia talking seriously about her friend's niece's surprise pregnancy in Quechua with another Quechua-speaking vendor. Then Señora Marcela would be chatting away with another Aymara-speaking vendor, complaining about how boring these market meetings are. And just when I would think I could follow the meeting, I would be drawn back to Señora Fidelia, cracking jokes at everything that the association president said, with Señora Marcela valiantly trying to stifle her giggles.

I eventually became more engrossed in these interactions and conversational asides than the ongoing discussions and debates about how large stalls should be, timetables for when older market stalls should be renovated or remodeled, or whether or not the vendors dedicated to selling hardware items like screws, nails, and tools were upcharging their customers and clients more than other markets (which they were). But, like other meetings that I attended, I knew that I had to save my energy and listen to the portion that was dedicated to the open forum, turning the floor over to market members to discuss the agenda that was shared in that meeting. Unlike the sidebar conversations across Quechua, Aymara, and Spanish, when members spoke at the open forum, they only spoke in Spanish. Members who volunteered to speak decided to continue discussing the different violations that vendors responsible for selling hardware items were committing. The open forum soon devolved into a public airing of grievances, with other members joining in to complain about the questionable pricing practices of the hardware vendors and accusing those vendors of un-collegial actions such as directing potential customers looking to buy other products such as shoes, clothes, and kitchen goods away from their colleagues within the market. Each complaint launched an even louder onslaught of comments and conversations from the audience, as everyone was discussing in Quechua, Aymara, and Spanish the serious problems that they had within their market ecosystem.

In the midst of these discussions, and in some cases loud uproars of accusations and complaints, one of the few male market vendors, Señor Mario, an elderly man in his mid-sixties, got up to speak. Recovering from a nasty head cold and case of bronchitis, as many older puneños tended to have during the bitingly cold Andean winter months, Señor Mario had a hard time trying to command the attention of his fellow market associates, who at that point were more involved in debating and arguing among themselves. In listening to my recording of the event with Señora Fidelia and Señora Marcela in the weeks after the eventful meeting, we too had a difficult time making out what Señor Mario was actually saying in his unsuccessful attempt to bring some order and stability to the market meeting. Yet from what little we could hear and make out, something interesting happened in his speech.

Like other public speeches, Señor Mario started to address the crowd in Spanish. Then at one point, Señora Fidelia and I could make out some Quechua, with Señora Mario saying, *"Rimamuychis, quechuamanta allinta"* (let's speak with each other, and in Quechua, which is good). The fact that Señor Mario had attempted to use some Quechua made sense to Señora Fidelia. As the son of Quechua-speaking parents, and part of the first wave of migrants to Puno to work in the markets, he should know some Quechua. What he might have been trying to say in that moment did not make sense, but the fact that he used some Quechua did in relation to his background and history. But as he continued to try to reconnect with the already rowdy market, Señor Mario did another thing that was interesting. He switched to Aymara, with Señora Marcela being able to discern through the shouting and raised voices that dominated the recording, *"Kawkita lurjañana?"* which, in that context, Señora Marcela interpreted as Señor Mario trying to ask everyone, "Where would we go to work?" Was Señor Mario's use of Aymara expected in this context? Unlike my surprise to hear Señor Mario's use of Aymara, Señora Marcela did not find the use remarkable at all. Although she might not consider Señor Mario's Aymara performance at that moment to be grammatically correct or felicitous, the fact that he knew enough Aymara to attempt to include some while trying to address his market associates seemed normal given that he had spent his life working in the multilingual markets in Puno.

Señor Mario's multilingual attempt to build consensus and regain some semblance of order and civility within the market meeting, along with Señora Fidelia and Señora Marcela's response to his use of Quechua and Aymara, highlight an important fundamental characteristic about market life in Puno and the altiplano: Working in the markets requires vendors to have some kind of multilingual knowledge and proficiency. By extension, this also means that market life and the interactions that facilitate the buying and selling of goods are multilingual, where the specific linguistic backgrounds of clients and customers are accommodated through the varying multilingual fluencies and practices of market vendors. In this way the multilingualism of market life can be seen as representative of the multilingualism found across the Department of Puno, drawing into focus the multilingual backgrounds of market vendors, who adjust and adapt their own fluencies to meet the linguistic and communicative needs of their customers. Market life across the altiplano stand as a testament to the long histories of inter-Indigenous contact and multilingualism in the region and how linguistic differences are not seen as distinct languages but, rather, communicative resources that facilitate the buying and selling of goods, and sustain the livelihoods of vendors who engage with a diverse clientele on a daily basis. But like their clientele, and multilingual praxis more generally across the altiplano, the multilingual backgrounds and proficiencies of market vendors do not mean that each vendor speaks Quechua, Aymara, and Spanish as three distinct, bounded, and complete codes. Rather, these multilingual proficiencies are flexibly defined and understood, where the need to engage and interact is accomplished through mutual accommodation and receptivity to multilingual communication and practices. Puneños regard these kinds of performances in linguistic multiplicity as a hallmark of Puno's cultural and linguistic heritage, positioning Puno as uniquely different than other regions in the Peruvian Andes. Yet this understanding of the range of repertoires that are encompassed by market vendors' multilingual practices also complicates the parameters that define speakerhood for Quechua, Aymara, and Spanish.

The communicative continuities that flow through otherwise assumed boundaries between Quechua, Aymara, and Spanish are additionally made more complex through these practices' intersection with the gendered backgrounds of market vendors and the gendering of market spaces. Across the Andes, market vendors are predominantly women, gendering the profession and these spaces as female (Babb 1998; Seligmann 1993; Weismantel 2001). The Indigenous femininity of market women in Puno, therefore, reflects how aspects of Indigenous femininity in the region are also reproduced through women's presence and labor in the markets. But this also means that in Puno, the gendering of market spaces and market labor as female also indexically feminizes the communicative practices that characterize social life and interactions within the altiplano's markets. In other words, the complex multilingual repertoires that characterize market life constitute a broader indexical and semiotic field (Babel 2018; Eckert 2008) that informs specific ideologized evaluations of indigeneity and femininity within the high Andes, both within and beyond the market.

This chapter explores this set of semiotic relationships, drawing on the ways that the life histories, livelihoods, and everyday social practices of Indigenous market women are intimately intertwined with complex multilingual repertoires that capture both the linguistic fluidity and creativity that lies at the heart of being multilingual Puno. Here, interactions between market vendors and their clients demonstrate the ways in which these practices reflect the emergence of different kinds of translinguistic practices that are neither constrained nor limited by the grammatical boundaries that separate Quechua, Aymara, and Spanish in the region. Yet the success of these translinguistic practices is also enabled through different forms of receptive multilingualism, which are equally significant in shaping intersubjective interactions that enable and prioritize the ability to accommodate varying and diverse forms of multilingual knowledge and communicative expertise. In this way, understanding the repertoires and practices that constitute communicative and listening competence within the markets can provide a lens to how Indigenous multilingual praxis has been sustained in the altiplano in the past. Moreover, this chapter highlights how these forms of multilingual communication are also important for female market vendors in creating networks of solidarity and unity within the market spaces, where one's ability to improvise and creatively play with the various linguistic and communicative resources that they have is also important to building friendships and lifelong connections of support, mutual aid, and care among market women of differing social and linguistic backgrounds. Market women, through their labor, dress, social histories, and social networks, come to embody a specific aspect of Indigenous multilingual praxis that has been central to mediating social life in the altiplano. Yet through their engagement and embodiment of a diverse range of communicative repertoires, these women also become a site to interrogate the range of practices and the linguistic and communicative limits of a legitimate or authentic Indigenous language speaker.

Market Multilingualism in the Altiplano and Andes

Open-air markets are as much a social fixture of Andean life as they are an economic one. Similar kinds of markets predate the arrival of the Spanish, and under colonial rule were one of the few spaces where Indigenous populations could exercise some economic agency through negotiating transactions and participating in the basic buying and selling of goods (Harris 1995; Larson 1995). But this does not mean that markets across the Andes, let alone across Puno and the altiplano, all fall into a single mold. Instead, market vendors can be found in a diversity of spaces. In Puno, for instance, it is not uncommon to find a market vendor alone on a street corner, selling goods straight out of their woven *lliqlla* (Quechua) or *awayus* (Aymara), shawls that carry items ranging from medicinal herbs to *chuño* (freeze dried potatoes) and *k'ispiña* (a local fry bread made of wheat and quinoa flour), to batteries, socks, and even cheeses. The range of goods sold by these vendors, however, pale in comparison to the range of goods and prices that are found in the more elaborate networks of market associations, who sell their goods in specific spaces across the city from semipermanent stalls. Unlike the single vendor at the street corner, these larger market associations sell a wide range of goods from meats and cheeses to produce, clothes, and basic household items.[1]

Markets also hold a special place in organizing social life across the altiplano. This fact is best exemplified through the importance of regionally designated market days—specific days of the week that each community or provincial municipality has designated as the primary day to hold an open-air market. Market vendors across the altiplano keep track of the various market days that stretch across the region, planning out their travels to move across the landscape to be present for each locale's designated market day to sell their goods. On such days, large empty spaces are magically filled by the early hours of the morning with rows of *carpas*, or tarp-like tents that provide shade cover for each vendor selling their goods on the rugged high plains. Much like the organization of formal market associations, rows in these open-air markets are also organized by the kinds of goods that are sold, creating a winding labyrinth that ensures that customers slowly pass through each aisle, taking note of the wide range of goods sold by vendors and comparing the prices offered by each one. By the end of the day, these carpas disappear, taken down by their owners along with everything that was not sold, leaving behind no trace of the day's bustling market scene. Because this is a large and recognizable event that occurs once a week, market days become a time and space where people can meet and reconnect. Often when I would travel around Puno with my interlocutors to try to collect family life histories and other kinds of interviews from extended family members, I was told to plan my trip around each community's market days. Going to visit the extended family members during this day, I was told, was the best option for me since market days were the best time to generally meet and get to know local residents. As my interlocutors shared with me, during the rest of the week most people would be too busy working in the fields or watching their herds to have either the time or energy to meet and speak with me. Market days were one of the few occasions where people would take a break from their normal routines, making use of this pause in their work life to purchase the goods that were needed to last them through the following week. They also were an opportunity for smaller, sleepy villages and communities to transform into social hubs, filled with a new kind of energy and buzz as residents and locals rush from vendor to vendor to make their purchases.

As an important social and economic event across the Andean altiplano, markets and market days draw large crowds of puneños from all walks of life. This means that markets often function as a social space that invites nonlocals to travel to other communities to meet new people and inspect the specific goods that may be bought or sold in those areas. While markets do bring a diverse group of individuals from different linguistic backgrounds together, these spaces are rendered similar through the continued presence and prominence of Indigenous market women as the primary vendors. These women and their physical and aural presence take over the market, where market women along with their stalls, *mantas*, *lliqllas*, or *awayus* (shawls), filled with a myriad of goods for sale, compete with each other for the attention of potential clients and customers. These economic interactions and transactions up until the recent past were primarily conducted through the direct exchange of goods, where the main goal for a market woman was to have all of her goods exchanged with other items that she may need, such as food and textiles. As one Aymara-speaking interlocutor told me:

> I remember going to market days as a child. My mother would wake us up early and would be preparing things to take to market day that week. She would have us carry extra mantas while she would carefully wrap a few kilos of *habas* [fava beans], *papas* [potatoes], *chuño y tunta* [dehydrated potatoes], *oca* [another tuber], and quinoa to also take to the market. For everything that we needed, she would exchange some of the items that we had brought with us for the item that we needed. A small piece of meat would be exchanged for some oca, carrots or other vegetables would be exchanged with habas, eggs and cheese we would exchange for some of the quinoa that we had brought.

Today, these transactions have shifted to the buying and selling of goods through the use of modern-day national currencies. Yet even these transactions come with their own form of negotiation, down to the currency that is used. Because of the history of currency failures in Peru and ongoing practices of currency counterfeiting, every currency-based transaction has to include a detailed inspection of the monies being exchanged along with the goods. Experienced market vendors know how real money should feel, tasting coins to ensure that they are legal, and smelling and folding bills to make sure that they are not fakes or frauds. Customers are also encouraged to engage in a similar game of evaluating the realness of currency that is exchanged, affording customers the opportunity to demand different change that meets their standard of what they think is non-counterfeit money, similar to the ways that a customer may inspect and demand a better version of a squash, herb, or fruit that is free of bruises or not over-ripened.

Market days provide an important opportunity for locals and non-locals to meet and socialize, providing a space to make connections and meet new people away from the humdrum of everyday life. But these days are also important for market vendors, who also take advantage of these days to build networks, which are necessary to sustain their business efforts. On days when they are not selling goods on their own local market day, vendors will also take it upon themselves to travel and visit other markets in the region. Since the day designated for market exchanges varies from locale to locale, vendors could essentially travel across the region, selling their goods all the week. For the market women I knew, traveling to these other regional market days was an opportunity to expand their own business network. Sometimes they would sell some of their goods to another vendor, who would sell those goods to a different rural market on their behalf. Other times, the urban market vendors I knew preferred buying some of their goods in bulk from rural vendors, noting how they could get a better wholesale deal from some of these rural vendors than another middleman from cities like Puno or Juliaca. Other times, traveling to markets in other regions provided the opportunity to make new connections and expand one's business network. This could be simply accomplished through meeting new vendors and suppliers from these other regions. But it could also take place through some vendors taking advantage of the market day and finding some space to sell their goods informally outside of the main open-air market space. While the open-air markets might be the main event, market days also allow many vendors not formally connected with those spaces to sell their goods along unoccupied street corners, in the shade provided by awnings and rooftops of small local restaurants and shops.

The most formal kind of market organization, however, is the cooperative market association, which is found across urban spaces throughout Andean cities like Puno. Participation in these market associations requires market vendors to join a cooperative association and pay their annual dues to be allotted a permanent market stall in these year-round, permanent markets. Membership in these cooperative associations is often held within families, and in particular is managed by women who enroll their daughters as associates. Similarly, membership in these cooperatives can also be inherited, highlighting how access to these cooperative markets can be passed down from mothers to their daughters and even their granddaughters. In addition to selling goods to the public throughout the year, these permanently designated spaces provide cooperative members some financial and economic stability, allowing vendors to pool their resources to buy a piece of land and divide that among themselves to create individual market stalls. Unlike the makeshift carpas in the open-air markets, market stalls in permanent market cooperatives are made from concrete and tin that are firmly secured into the ground (figure 3). Each stall becomes a self-contained unit, complete with a sliding door that can be locked to prevent thieves from entering and stealing their goods. Over time, they are expanded to include additional levels, which serves either as a depository of extra goods or as a place where vendors could take a nap during the lull in business that happens during the middle of the day. Often in the small kiosk-like structures with two levels, vendors would send their children or grandchildren above to sleep or do their schoolwork while they were busy below selling their products.

In this way, markets form a self-contained intergenerational network, which contributes to the uniqueness of market life in Puno. Within each market stall, one can find a multigenerational family working together in the small family business, where vendors would often look after grandchildren within their market kiosk or older teenage grandchildren would come after school to help their parents and grandparents with their sales. At their core, markets help cultivate a special kind of kinship, where vendors collectively share connections of reciprocity and obligation that mirror those kinds of ties that are also found among close-knit kin groups and households in rural communities.

These networks and relationships extend beyond the market to include the clients, buyers, and sellers who engage in economic transactions with vendors at any particular market. And in urban centers like Puno, these networks are also mixed, where market vendors ideally seek to attract and maintain relationships with a loyal customer base across linguistic and cultural backgrounds. On any given day in the cooperative markets of Puno, it is easy to find customers from both Quechua and

FIGURE 3 Mercado de San Ignacio after everyone has closed the market stalls early for the day. Credit: Sandhya Krittika Narayanan (author).

Aymara linguistic backgrounds, making their purchases and getting the best products at the best price. Yet these transactions are also enabled by the fact that market vendors together represent both Quechua- and Aymara-speaking linguistic backgrounds. As such, markets within Puno represent a microcosm of inter-Indigenous linguistic and social contact, where networks and bonds of solidarity, trust, and friendship between vendors, buyers, and clients, are forged across linguistic lines. Having these cross-linguistic and inter-Indigenous relationships means that surviving in the market environment requires buyers and sellers to practice a kind of accommodative multilingualism that both welcomes and requires some kind of linguistic flexibility between Quechua, Aymara, and Spanish.

The multilingual and inter-Indigenous status of markets is widely recognized across Puno and is something that market vendors and customers and clients will also reflect upon. Some of this recognition can be seen through the promotion of multilingual fluencies and proficiencies for customers and market vendors through the circulation of tri-

FIGURE 4 Cover of Quechua and Aymara phrase booklet. Credit: Photo of cover taken by author.

lingual phrase books in Quechua, Aymara, and Spanish (figure 4). Although these kinds of booklets can be purchased from a small bookstall or newspaper stand, they are most commonly bought from ambulatory salesmen, who move through the market aisles advertising these little booklets and even demonstrating their efficacy by reproducing simple phrases and lexical lists across the three languages such as listing the numbers from one to ten and saying one's name.

Such phrasebooks and dictionaries contain the translations for specific words and commonly used phrases in both Quechua and Aymara, mediated through Spanish. And buying these books is extremely popular among market vendors. Every market vendor I knew had at least one copy of these booklets in their possession, with some vendors having three or four different versions and copies because they forgot that they had previously purchased a copy or two for their own reference. Yet despite their ubiquity, I never saw any market vendor actively use or refer to these booklets in their daily interactions. In fact, such phrase booklets were both so pervasive and so infrequently used that many of the market vendors I knew would often gift me one of their extra booklets, explaining that I should learn Quechua and Aymara from reading these books. Though relatively inexpensive (the average booklet costing no more than $1 USD), the presence and ownership of such booklets, and the fact that they are most often purchased within the market space itself, reinforces the fact that markets are mixed linguistic spaces, where market vendors (and, to a lesser degree, customers) must continually adjust and enhance their linguistic and listening practices to accommodate the linguistic backgrounds of other individuals.

Enfiguring the Market Woman

In addition to being mini-laboratories of inter-Indigenous linguistic and social contact, markets are also gendered spaces, dominated by the presence, and figure, of the market woman. This is not to say that men are not present in the market as vendors. During my fieldwork and survey of the various market cooperatives across Puno, which included the Mercado de San Ignacio, I did note a few men who occupied and ran stalls as part of the cooperative's list of associates. Yet men were in the minority, where the majority of vendors were women of different ages and linguistic backgrounds. Market work and market labor is a multigenerational affair, with many market stalls co-owned and operated by three or sometimes four generations of a family. And, in these multigenerational operations, the individuals participating in the market economy were, more often than not, all women.

The multigenerational presence of women, owning and operating family businesses, is not strictly unique to Puno nor exclusive to contemporary life in the Andes. As historian Jane Mangan (2005) notes, participating in the market economy was one of the few socially sanctioned places for Indigenous populations in public and urbanized spaces during the colonial era. But more than being just one of the few places for Indigenous individuals to engage in independent labor outside of rural life, the markets were also one of the few places where Indigenous women could also participate in the cash-based economy. This in turn gave Indigenous women some autonomy and independence, allowing them to make a stable living as the head of their own household without a male head. The value of female economic independence still holds true today and resonates with many of the Indigenous women I became acquainted with across the different cooperative markets in Puno. While some women were married and also operated their market businesses with their spouses and male partners, many women were single, either due to widowhood, husbands leaving them when they were young, or simply never marrying and having children by different fathers. Many women would often serve as family matriarchs, often employing and caring for their older daughters and their young children. These older daughters, many of whom were also raised within the markets, would sometimes return to the safety of the market spaces with their mothers after either separating from their husbands or escaping abusive relationships with their male partners. And in returning to the markets, this younger generation of women are still able to make a living for themselves as independent women while receiving the support and additional care from their mothers and other older market women in the same space.

The economic and social independence that market labor affords Indigenous market women distinguishes them from established gender norms in the region. Not only is the autonomy and social and economic freedoms that market women enjoy contrasted against the standards of heteronormative coupling that are promoted by the state, but they are also at odds with ideas of traditional Indigenous wives and motherhood. This social freedom and flexibility also extends into other aspects of their lives that expands expectations of what traditional Indigenous femininity may be. Residence is one arena where this is apparent, where the traditionality of Indigenous wives is rooted in recognizing indigeneity and Indigenous identity, as qualities and features that are derived from residing in a rural place and engaging in reciprocal relationships with those named places. Market women, however, are not confined to those spaces. Instead, market women travel extensively across the countryside, and often split their time between living in urban centers like Puno and their natal, rural communities.

That flexibility also extends to dress, which is an equally important facet of locating and recognizing one's Indigenous identity and provenance. Across the altiplano, dress varies by locale, becoming one of the primary material signifiers of an individual's origin. The significance of dress is more important for women, who exhibit this association more distinctly than men. Dress and clothes are important for marking where one is from and for establishing transitions in identity backgrounds, such as the change in sartorial practices that exogamous brides and wives undergo. Market women, however, normally do not wear the traditional dress associated with their natal communities. Instead, these locally specific markers of Indigenous identity are swapped for the large and flowing *pollera* (skirt), shawl, and the traditional *bolsanaro* hat or a large sun hat. This basic uniform has the ability to be dressed up or down, with some market vendors changing the colors, textiles, and even embroidery of their pollera by season and the latest fashion trends. Regardless of if their clothes are flashy or simple, this basic uniform equalizes all women, erasing them from any specific locale and thus any specific mode of Indigenous identity and social difference, and placing them all as unmarked female market vendors of Indigenous backgrounds.

This unmarked status is equally mirrored by their linguistic expertise. Many, if not all, market women in Puno self-identify with an Indigenous Quechua- or Aymara-speaking community and also identify with some aspect of puneño indigeneity. During my time in Puno, this was especially so of the older market women in their fifties and sixties, who were first born and raised in the rural countryside before moving to Puno in their late teens or early twenties to begin working as market vendors. But this was also true of the second generation, the daughters in their twenties, thirties, and forties who, despite being born in the city, nevertheless maintained connections with their mother's Quechua- or Aymara-speaking communities through frequent trips back to their natal communities, or at some point having lived several years in these places to help take care of their ancestral lands and provide care for aging relatives. Yet in spite of these histories, the linguistic practices of these women do not conform with any ideologically pure, monolingual standard for an Indigenous speaker. Instead, the communicative practices of market women reflect a diverse range of repertoires that traverse across different linguistic codes and boundaries. Regardless of if these women were born in Puno or raised in a monolingual Quechua- or Aymara-speaking community, market women across the different market spaces in Puno and the altiplano represent a wide array of linguistic proficiencies, freely experimenting and mixing across linguistic boundaries to build a solid network of buyers, sellers, and clients, and carving out their own space within the local market economy.[2]

Although these histories, practices, and linguistic proficiencies might not conflict with how Indigenous market women in Puno articulate or think about their indigeneity, it is also important to note that these signs have often been interpreted as signifying the racially and socially hybridized status of Indigenous market women in the past. Some of these evaluative practices stem from the colonial era, which regarded Indigenous market women as different than the typical Indigenous woman who tended to her chakras (fields) and lived in her Indigenous communities, which in turn positioned market women as socially salient gendered and racialized figures in the Andes that reflected the tensions between Indigenous and non-Indigenous populations (Rappaport 2014; Weismantel 2001; Van Vleet 2005). In particular, the freedom and autonomy granted to Indigenous market women in making money and owning their own property also extended to their sexual freedoms that included having relationships with men across different racial categories. These practices and their racializing implications resurfaced in Peru during the early twentieth century, amid evolving discourses around Peru's racial identity and heritage that eventually led to formalizing Peru's racial identity as one premised on mestizaje and processes of acculturation (Cadena 2000, 2002). During the neoindigenista movements in particular, criollo elites identified Indigenous market women as prime examples of what this social and cultural acculturation could look like, interpreting their social, sartorial, and linguistic practices and repertoires as signs of the racial hybridity between an Indigenous past and a not quite fully realized social and cultural mestizo identity.

These interpretations underscore the extent to which Indigenous female bodies and practices have been the object of inquiry and attention for non-Indigenous elites and intellectuals engaged in social projects around racial identity and difference in Peru. Yet these discussions highlight a stark contrast between the privileged perspectives informing ideological discourses around race and the actual experiences and life histories of Indigenous market women themselves. Market women's lives are not neatly bounded by living as an economically savvy urban entrepreneur or as an ideal Indigenous wife residing in her rural community and diligently tending to her crops, livestock, family, and community. They live within and across both worlds, navigating effectively across those boundaries to maintain both their livelihood and the complex, intersecting social networks. This ability to live across these spaces also influences their communicative practices and repertoires. Just as the lives of market women are not confined to any one social space, so too do their linguistic proficiencies and practices expand beyond any ideologized boundary around Quechua, Aymara, or Spanish fluency or expertise. Being an Indigenous market woman means that these women over time had to develop their own practices for communicating and making connections with speakers of different cultural and linguistic backgrounds. This kind of social and linguistic flexibility and fluidity is a cornerstone of life as an Indigenous market woman. However, this kind of linguistic fluidity that transcends linguistic and social boundaries can also frame market women as potentially falling short of ideological practices that are seen as critical for upholding inter-Indigenous differences and the ongoing ideologization of an idealized and authentic Indigenous language speaker.

Linguistic Flexibility and Accommodation Among Market Women

Markets are multilingual contact zones par excellence in Puno. In these spaces, Indigenous market women must have some kind of linguistic comfort across Quechua, Aymara, and Spanish in order to maintain their business and standing within the market. Yet being linguistically versatile does not necessarily mean that each individual approaches each linguistic code in their repertoire as a bounded and discrete communicative medium. Instead, market women display their linguistic competence through different forms of cross-linguistic mixing between Spanish, Quechua, and

Aymara. In this way, the code-mixing and multilingual repertoires of market women can be thought of as showcasing diverse forms of translanguaging (García and Wei 2018; Vogel and García 2022). Thinking about the multilingual practices and repertoires of Indigenous market women as an example of translanguaging highlights how these moments of mixing in interaction are not necessarily bounded by the grammar of any one code nor the ideologized differences and divisions between Quechua, Aymara, and Spanish. This is especially important in moments of mixing, where speakers may not necessarily view those practices as coming from different, bounded grammatical systems. Moreover, approaching these practices as examples of translanguaging praxis also draws into focus the creativity and adaptability of Indigenous market women, who utilize the vast range of linguistic resources at hand to create transactions and cultivate important relationships with speakers of different linguistic heritages and speaking backgrounds. As such, the multilingual repertoires of Indigenous market women present a different perspective on what it means to know a language, where multilingual knowledge and expertise is evaluated through one's comfort, creativity, and awareness of how to carefully and strategically use whatever they know from Quechua, Aymara, and Spanish in their daily interactions.

Over the course of my time in Puno, and through the various life history interviews and conversations that I had with market women of different Indigenous linguistic backgrounds, I would hear different accounts of the kinds of linguistic practices that they recognized as being important to ensuring the success of a market vendor. Across these conversations, having the ability to try and make the most of learning another language they were unfamiliar with became a salient theme that was deemed critical for all market women to possess if they wanted to survive in the markets. In some cases, this urgency to try to become familiar with another language, or at the very least pretend that they had some familiarity with a language that they did not regularly speak, was just as important as learning and developing some fluency across Aymara, Quechua, and Spanish. This was certainly true for Señora Adela, an Aymara speaker whose stall was surrounded by mostly Quechua-speaking market vendors in Mercado de San Ignacio. During my times with Señora Adela, I noticed that she would primarily communicate with customers and other vendors and clients in Aymara and Spanish, often mixing between both languages or relying primarily on Spanish if her interlocutor was a Quechua speaker. However, during the midday and early afternoon lulls, she liked to sit outside of her stall with the other vendors as they ate lunch, knitted handicrafts made of alpaca and sheep wool to sell to tourist shops, and shared the latest gossip in Quechua. During these times, Señora Adela would quietly attend to her own knitting. But she also looked engaged and seemed to actively follow everything that was being shared in these conversation circles, down to gasping in dismay when a piece of salacious gossip about an extramarital affair was told, or clucking and shaking her head along with the others when another story about one of the women's goddaughter's relationship with her philandering husband was discussed. Privately in our conversations, Señora Adela never admitted to knowing Quechua. And yet, I found her participation and engagement in these conversation circles interesting. One day, while she was helping me learn how to knit in the round, I asked her how she was able to follow the conversations around her and whether she might actually know more Quechua than she might admit to. Her response was simple, exclaiming, *"No entiendo ni una palabra. Si se dice un chiste, me rie también. No entiendo lo que se ha dicho"* (I don't understand a single word. If they tell a joke, I laugh as well. But I don't understand what they just said).

Señora Adela's remark reflects a more cautious stance toward claiming a specific kind of linguistic fluency or proficiency. Over time, I would observe Señora Adela respond to requests from customers in Quechua, asking if she had a certain item or whether she could lower the price. During these interactions, Señora Adela would mostly respond in Spanish or some combination of Spanish and Aymara. While these patterns reflected the codes that Señora Adela felt most comfortable communicating in, they also reveal how years working in the market alongside other Quechua-speaking women and interacting with many Quechua-speaking customers had shaped her listening competence in the language as well. Nonetheless, while Señora Adela was more hesitant in claiming proficiency or knowledge of Quechua, her nonnative Indigenous language, other women that I had come to know were bolder in how they counted their multilingual proficiencies and fluencies. Some women would joke about how they acquired their multilingual fluency, commenting that learning to speak the other Indigenous language was actually easier than one thought, if one knew what to listen for. For instance, women from Aymara-speaking backgrounds always found Quechua somewhat similar to Spanish. They would routinely comment that the best way to sound like a Quechua speaker was to add the Quechua diminutive *-chay* to Spanish words. And, to complete the best approximation of a Quechua speaker, you had to use this diminutive marker while fluctuating your voice and modulating your tones so that it would sound similar to how you might sing a *huayno*, the traditional folk song and music of the Andes.[3] While this singsong quality reflects perceptions of the intonational patterns of Quechua for Aymara speakers, the reliance on the diminutive morpheme *-chay*, which is primarily added to nouns, performs a phatic function that enables the speaker to create some kind of intimacy and close connection with their potential buyer. And although this intimacy is assumed for interactions between Quechua speakers, using the diminutive *-chay* in one's Spanish allows a non-Quechua speaker to also create a similar kind of intersubjective closeness in attempting to mimic those bonds of affinity without necessarily speaking Quechua like a native speaker. Quechua-speaking women likewise also had their preferred tricks when trying to "speak Aymara" and catch the attention of potential Aymara-speaking buyers. For them, it was the use of the suffix *-akanaka*, added to basically any Spanish or Quechua noun, and sometimes some verbs. *-Akanaka* is a Quechua-based interpretation of the Aymara plural suffix *-naka* and the Aymara demonstrative *akha* or "that." Both the plural suffix and the demonstrative pronoun are used so frequently in conversational Aymara (and especially within a market setting) that many of my Quechua-speaking interlocutors would joke about how easy learning Aymara was since it is just *-akanaka* all the time. The salience of akha and *-naka* was so well recognized that some of the Quechua-speaking women I knew would point to a group of Aymara-speaking women passing down the street and say, "Look at those *akanakas* go." While *-akanaka* is based on a Quechua speaker's perspective of Aymara linguistic difference, it also bears a second meaning due to akha having a close resemblance to the Quechua word *aqha*, or "feces." In this way, Quechua women play on the phonological similarities between Quechua and Aymara to also slightly insult or throw shade at their Aymara-speaking associates and friends, who in this joke are only talking about shit.[4]

Humor aside, such comments and widespread techniques of trying to learn the other Indigenous language highlight the fact that at the heart of these jokes, or even moments of pretending, connections across linguistic lines are made without the need for strict fluency in the Indigenous language. The use of *-chay* and frequently modulating intonations, and *-akanaka* productively added to the end of almost any noun, highlights how some kind of baseline knowledge or awareness of the grammatical features of the other language, no matter how minimal it may be, is all that is needed to connect with another individual from a different linguistic background and establish a relationship that could eventually be mutually beneficial for both parties. In general, market women do invest the time to learn the other Indigenous languages of their region. But this linguistic education is not realized through attending formal institutions or reading about the language in books. Instead, this knowledge and expertise is acquired through simply listening and picking up what they hear from the context around them and using it to the best of their ability to establish a wide enough network of clientele and vendors that will ultimately sustain their success as small business owners.

More importantly, multilingual knowledge and proficiency is also not strictly limited to spoken competence. As the case of Señora Adela shows us, sometimes knowing the basic cues of when to participate, even if one may not speak the language, is also enough to build that solidarity with others around her. Even though Señora Adela may not outright admit her knowledge or fluency in Quechua, she nonetheless is able to listen and respond to those around her, whether it be passively following the conversation and gossip shared by her fellow vendors who share her aisle space or her ability to respond to Quechua-speaking customers in some way when they wish to purchase something from her. Moreover, her participation and engagement in these midday conversation circles with her associates did help build solidarity between herself and these other women, who would often pitch in and help take care of Señora Adela's stall anytime she would have to leave, often returning back to her community in Platería to check in on her aging mother. These practices thus emphasize how the ability to listen is just as important and vital a skill for a market vendor as the ability to speak and communicate across Quechua, Aymara, and Spanish. This suggests that market vendors must also develop their listening competence[5] in addition to their communicative competence to survive and thrive alongside other weathered and experienced market women. The interactive and communicative practices of Señora Adela and other vendors like her who are more cautious in describing their linguistic proficiencies reflect an implicit understanding of the necessity for receptive bilingualism and multilingualism in facilitating social relationships and interactions across linguistic lines (Bilaniuk 2005; Singer 2023). Though this ability to listen effectively may not always be articulated as a component in one's multilingual repertoire, the linguistic knowledge that is reflected in both actively listening and accommodating the speech of others are critical and significant forms of linguistic expertise and knowledge that are key to success as a market vendor.

Managing Fluencies and Receptivity in Market Interactions

Through my various interviews and conversations with the market women I had grown close to, several thematic threads emerged that highlight how market women approach the multilingual landscape that defines market talk, navigate the dialectic between listening to and learning a new or unfamiliar linguistic variety, and successfully use their diverse set of linguistic and communicative resources to engage in receptive and accommodative interactions with speakers from diverging linguistic heritages and backgrounds. Across these conversations, many market vendors would point out how they learned to hone and master a few key phrases in the other Indigenous language that would position them as a viable vendor, supplementing what they did not know using Spanish and their own heritage Indigenous language. This reliance on a few strategic phrases in the other Indigenous language was central to Señora Mily's personal experiences and longevity as a market woman. An Aymara speaker, originally from the Aymara-speaking province of Huancané, Señora Mily spent her childhood primarily speaking Aymara. Because her mother was also a market woman within the province, Señora Mily became comfortable with speaking Spanish at a young age while helping her mother sell her wares across Puno. That reliance on Spanish increased after she moved to Puno as a young woman, where Spanish is treated as the unmarked code for everyone regardless of one's Indigenous background. Upon arriving to

Puno, Señora Mily went about establishing herself as a trusted purveyor of dry goods like pastas, beans, grains, and flour at competitive wholesale prices. Yet her business and stall, located in the Mercado Bellavista, which is one of the oldest cooperative markets established in Puno, was located closer to one of the predominantly Quechua-speaking neighborhoods. This meant that Señora Mily's associates were mostly Quechua-speaking vendors, and she primarily interacted with Quechua-speaking clients and customers. Over time, she began to understand some phrases in Quechua, and also picked up a few key phrases that were important to her business in a predominantly Quechua-speaking market.

[Example 1]
1. Algo (a)sí
   Something like this

2. De dónde eres, cómo eres, cuánto es ahhh . . .
   Where are you from, how are you, how much is ahhh . . .

3. tales precios.
   various prices.

4. Eso es así.
   Something like this it is.

5. Eso así no emmm . . .
   Like this no emmm . . .

6. <u>Caserita rantikuy</u> le digo no?
   Caserita please buy this I tell them no?

7. Llévate!
   Take it!

8. A veces, cuánto cuesta, cómo pregunta,
   Sometimes, how much does it cost, how does one ask,

9. <u>Haykaq</u>,
   How much,

10. le digo,
    (and) I tell them,

11. que tanto es así,
    that is it so much like this,

12. no ve?
    you see?

13. Así le digo.
    Like that I tell them.

For Señora Mily, the key phrase that establishes her as a viable vendor to her Quechua-speaking clientele is *caserita rantikuy*. A composite of both Quechua and Spanish, the meaning of the phrase is somewhat akin to a kind of greeting between vendors and particular clients. Caserita refers to a "homemaker," a term that addresses and interpolates women coming to the market as housewives who are there to purchase things for their family. But the phrase rantikuy, or "please buy something" pragmatically acts as an invitation for casual shoppers to stop by a vendor's stall and inspect their goods. In this way, caserita rantikuy changes Señora Mily's interactional footing[6] when trying to catch the attention of potential Quechua-speaking clients by communicating and performing her communicative and linguistic alignment with the linguistic background of her soon-to-be customers. Additionally, Señora Mily's reflections on how she approaches her Quechua-speaking clients also reveals her understanding of certain questions that her Quechua-speaking clients may ask, such as the quantifier question word, *haykaq* or "how much." While Señora Mily, like Señora Adela, was always more careful in discussing her Quechua knowledge, her inclusion of haykaq in her narrative illustrates that she does know how to listen to certain key phrases, which in turn directs her to respond appropriately to better serve her customers.

While being able to listen and incorporate different linguistic mediums and resources in your communicative repertoire is important, different market vendors still had varying levels of comfort and confidence in their knowledge. These differences would then correlate with how each vendor may approach using linguistic and grammatical elements that they are less familiar with in order to build relationships and secure the best deals or bargains. Señora Celia was one of these women whose narrative also showcased her ability to strategically utilize phrases and features from another Indigenous language so that she could be better aligned with her interlocutors. Additionally, her narrative also demonstrates how sustaining this kind of communicative practice with specific individuals over a lifetime is key to building close relationships between market women of different linguistic backgrounds. A Quechua speaker originally from the provinces just north of the regional capital Puno, Señora Celia made her living as a local healer and as a seller of women's clothing in Mercado de San Ignacio.[7] Perpetually cheerful with the biggest and brightest smile, Señora Celia had three great loves of her life: making friends, laughing at a good joke, and passing as many hours as she could conversing with anyone who had as good of a sense of humor and outlook on life as she did. These personality traits certainly helped her attract and maintain a dedicated female clientele who consistently purchased woolen clothing that is necessary year-round in the high and frigid altiplano. But Señora Celia's success was not only limited to her warmth and charisma. As a longtime vendor in her sixties, her success both as a market woman and as a trusted member of the broader puneña market community was also connected to her ability to strategically use some Aymara in her business transactions and to build relationships with Aymara speakers and Quechua speakers alike. In the excerpt of her interview below, Señora Celia reenacts all of the possible phrases she might use to shift her footing to invite the potential business of an Aymara-speaking customer who might stop and take a look at the items that she has for sale.

[Example 2]
1. *kunas muntale,*
   What do you want,

2. diría será-pe.[8]
   I would tell them.

3. *kunas muntale,*
   What do you want,

4. Qué quieres.
   What would you like.

5. *Kunas muntxa,*
   What do you want,

6. *Kunasa alxita,*
   What do you wish to buy,

7. Qué cosita quieres comprar diría será-pe.
   What thing do you wish to buy I would tell them.

In addition to knowing some key phrases in Aymara, Señora Celia's reflections also demonstrate how knowing Aymara does not necessarily mean that one has to know it perfectly. In asking someone what they want in Aymara, Señora Celia switches between an incorrect version of the question *kunas muntale?* (line 3) to the more acceptable but still incorrect version of the question for Aymara-speaking puneños, *kunas muntxa?* (line 5). Yet such errors within the broader puneña market landscape are still acknowledged by Aymara-speaking customers, who will accommodate different kinds of attempts at Aymara and nonetheless proceed with the interaction and potentially purchase something from the vendor. The kinds of mistakes made by Señora Celia are similar to other kinds of small mistakes and grammatical inconsistencies that many experienced market women will make when communicating in one of their nonnative languages. However, these errors do not prohibit an interaction and are not seen as a barrier to enabling an economic exchange from happening, reinforcing a broader norm around communicative receptivity and accommodation within the market space.

Markets are, to a certain degree, also a self-sustaining economy, where vendors will look out for each other and buy goods and products from one another, thus forming a network of reciprocal vendor-client relationships. Building these reciprocal vendor-client relationships, where a clothing vendor may purchase their food from another associate in their cooperative, strengthens both the cooperative market community and any single market vendor's place and legitimacy as a known colleague and friend. These kinds of relationships also encourage vendors to be able to communicate across Quechua, Aymara, and Spanish, such that their comfort and flexibility in moving across all three codes helps them build these connections of intimacy and solidarity with linguistically diverse vendors. Additionally, the pervasive recognition and acceptance of translanguaging praxis across Quechua, Aymara, and Spanish reinforce the importance that linguistic fluidity, creativity, and receptive accommodation play in mediating transactions and strengthening relationships over time. When Señora Celia discussed how she knew some basic Aymara question phrases to use when interacting with Aymara-speaking customers, she also discussed how she learned enough Aymara to establish herself as a careful and loyal buyer from other vendors in the area, such as her longtime Aymara-speaking produce vendor.

[Example 3]
1. Cuando voy a comprar las verduras así no?
   when I am going to buy vegetables like this no?

2. papa digo no?
   potato I say no?

3. *kawkach chuqmate* arroba?
   How much (are) the potatoes for the arroba?

4. *kawkach chuqmasti* digo no?
   "How much are the potatoes," I say right?

5. Entonces,
   and then,

6. ya me dijen tanto es pue no?
   then they tell me it is so much right?

7. ahh rebajame le digo yo.
   ahhh lower the price for me I tell them.

8. Ento—
   And then—

9. no así siempre es dice,
   no like this always say it,

10. o también me puede rebajar,
    or they can also lower the price,

11. uno de dos.
    one or two [soles].

12. Se dice no,
    They say this right,

13. así no más es siempre el precio,
    [or] they can say this is always the price,

14. no rebaja.
    no discount.

Like other vendors, Señora Celia had a set group of individuals from whom she bought things like produce and potatoes. Some of these individuals happened to be from Aymara-speaking backgrounds, giving Señora Celia an opportunity to establish a relationship with these vendors by using some Aymara she knew. But Señora Celia's success when interacting with her market vendors is not based on whether or not she can speak Aymara in ways that may be identical to how a native Aymara-speaking puneño might communicate. From the example above, Señora Celia changes how she would ask the question "How much are the potatoes?" so that it might align with how an Aymara speaker would make that same request. Yet regardless of how Señora Celia actually communicates that question when interacting with her produce vendor, her attempt at asking that question in Aymara is nonetheless accepted by her vendor who has an established relationship with her longtime Quechua-speaking customer. The familiarity between both women also affords Señora Celia the interactive space to potentially haggle with her vendor, and to do so in Aymara as well.

[Example 4]

1. *wak'titay* se dice-pe no?
   "reduce the cost" they say no?

2. uhuh . . . *rebajkt'titay* se dice no?
   uhuh . . . "lower the cost" they say no?

3. que me rebajepe, aha . . .
   that you give me a discount, aha . . .

4. así ya no ve?
   like this no ve?

5. allí va-pe,
   (if) you go there,

6. ehh . . . *wakt'itay* se diría creo, no?
   ehh . . . "lower the price" is what I would say I think, no?

Similar to Señora Celia narrating how she would ask her vendor "How much are the potatoes?" in Aymara, her metalinguistic conjecture of how she would haggle also reflects some ambivalence in how she has negotiated a lower price with her produce vendor in the past. Señora Celia questions if her choice of word for "to give a discount" is correct, going between *wakt'itay*, and the more Spanish-inflected version *rebajkt'itay*, which takes the Spanish verb *rebajar* or "to lower" and inflects it with Aymara morphology. In her reflexive guess of how she has asked for a discount from her vendor, Señora Celia does not mention the Aymara verb *iraqt'itay*, which means "to lower" and is typically used to ask for a discount. But whether or not these choices are correct is beside the point. Regardless of which lexical choice she makes, Señora Celia is still able to initiate a haggling session with her respective vendor. And this highlights the norms and understandings that shape customer-vendor interactions in the multilingual markets of Puno. As a speaker, Señora Celia is both encouraged and expected to utilize different translingual practices when interacting with her Aymara-speaking vendors. But her practices also have to be received and accommodated by her Aymara-speaking vendors and co-associates, who engage in her interactive alignments and respond in kind regardless of if Señora Celia's Aymara attempts are considered grammatically felicitous or not.

Being a market vendor is ultimately based on striking this particular balance between linguistic flexibility and accommodation while also being very much aware of your own linguistic limitations as they emerge through interaction. Señora Celia was a very confident woman and felt comfortable enough to carry on with whatever amount of Aymara she knew to make her transactions and maintain her relationships with buyers and other market women. At the same time, she was also very much aware of her limitations, where in the example below, she reasons that those limitations are a result of her incomplete acquisition of Aymara as an adult whose first language was Quechua.

[Example 5]
1. Es que yo casi,
   It's that I almost,

2. con ella no puedo hablar—
   with her [Aymara neighbor] I am not able to speak [Aymara]—

3. que tal mal,
   what if it's bad,

4. hablo y se- de rei—
   [or] I speak and it makes them laugh—

5. reirsere [laughing]
   Makes them laugh

6. entonces no.
   then no.

7. No, no hablo tanto.
   No, no I don't speak much.

8. Así pa(ra) mirastito no más.
   It's just like this for a small look but nothing else.

9. Correcto correcto,
   [Like] really correctly,

10. si pero,
    yes but,

11. Entiendo pero hablar hablar—
    I can understand but to really speak—

12. no, cuando—
    no, when—

13. no no no sabes sí—
    no no no you know right—

14. tú sabes el quechua también es largo.
    (well) you know that Quechua is also long.

15. Eehh no es igual,
    Eehh but it's not the same,

16. o sea,
    or rather,

17. moto le sale así como,
    a speech impediment like this will come out like,

18. uhhh no se,
    uhhh I don't know,

19. algo, algo,
    something, something,

20. distinto, entonces,
    distinct, therefore,

21. Cuando ellas saben, se rien de ti, no cierto?
    When they know (Aymara), they laugh at you, correct?

Here, Señora Celia is very much aware of her lack of knowledge, not only admitting that her ability to speak Aymara is incorrect but likening it to a *moto*, or a speech impediment that is noticeable and might make those who actually know Aymara laugh. Yet in spite of this, knowing how to speak the other Indigenous language and make oneself understood is fundamental to working in the market economy, as she makes clear in her continuing narrative below.

[**Example 6**]
1. Claro si estudia mal me está entendiendo.
   Of course (even) if I learned it badly (they are still) understanding me.

2. Ahora en el quechua, no se, ya-pe?
   Now in Quechua, I don't know, you know?

3. Hablo, como yo hablo bien el quechua,
   I speak, like how I speak Quechua well,

4. me—
   I—

5. el quechua hablaría pero,
   I would speak (always) in Quechua but,

6. para vender tienes que hablar-pe,
   but to sell you have to speak,

7. pudiendo no pudiendo,
   and even if you are able to or not,

8. tratar de entenderle,
   [you have] to try and understand [others],

9. tratar de coordinar aunque sea con mímica, ya está?
   [you have] try and coordinate even if it is through mimicry, right?

10. No ciert?
    Am I not correct?

For Señora Celia, speaking across all three languages, especially for languages that one is not familiar with, is compared to the act of mimicry. This mimicry and imitation may not be perfect, lending to mistakes or errors that a native speaker of the language or an individual who consistently communicates in that language, might not make. Nevertheless, a market vendor must always try to perform this mimicry, and through it, try to make themselves understood to as many people as possible. However, a speaker's intentions of consistently trying to make themselves understood to others must also be reciprocated by their interlocutors. Such reciprocity highlights a collective stance that flexibly accommodates a diverse range of multilingual repertoires and communicative practices.

Because linguistic knowledge is framed and understood through linguistic flexibility around different forms of receptive and accommodative multilingualisms, most market women are very careful to articulate whether or not they know each language in terms of speaking and comprehension. This was certainly the case with Señora Fidelia, who also worked in Mercado de San Ignacio. As a native Quechua speaker who also grew up in another neighboring Quechua-speaking community on the periphery of Puno, Señora Fidelia was first introduced to market work through her mother, who would take her around Puno and surrounding areas selling shoes. Traveling the region in her childhood first exposed her to hearing and learning some Aymara. This exposure increased for her as an adult, not only through owning her own market stall and business but also through supplementing her family's income by working as a cleaning lady and a teacher's aide for home economics (teaching knitting, crocheting, and sewing) in an Aymara-speaking school in Acora, a small town in the province of Acora located in the southern part of the Department of Puno. At the time I met her, she was in her mid-sixties and had retired from working in that school twenty years earlier. Another warm and strong figure within the market, Señora Fidelia was proud of her Quechua-linguistic background and liked to perform her linguistic heritage through speaking Quechua as much as possible with other Quechua-speaking vendors and her own loyal base of Quechua-speaking customers. Because she knew of my research interests in Puno, she also tended to converse with me in Quechua during formal recorded interviews, and also informally, taking every opportunity to test my Quechua knowledge and make sure that my communicative competence was up to snuff to survive and defend myself in Puno.

It was during one of these informal conversations that I asked if I could interview her on her life history and, in particular, ask about her linguistic background. Señora Fidelia said yes, and true to form defaulted to doing her interview in Quechua. It was during this interview that I learned about her history of working in a school in an Aymara-speaking community, which helped her feel comfortable in understanding Aymara. However, in describing her linguistic knowledge, she was also very aware of her limitations in speaking Aymara, and knowledge of Aymara in general.

[**Example 7**]
1. Uhmm ... palabras sueltas digan.
   Uhmm ... we can say (I know) random words.

2. <u>Mana correditotachu</u>.
   But (I'm) not fluent.

3. <u>Yacharqani correditut</u> pero <u>kuna(n) kay</u>—
   I used to know a bit more fluently but now—

4. Mira veinte <u>anosña jubilaqapuni Aymara ladomanta</u>,
   Look for twenty years I have been retired from working around the Aymara side,

5. <u>manaña parlañiyachu</u>.
   and have not really spoken (Aymara).

6. Pero <u>entiendini</u>.
   But I understand.

7. <u>Corridut man(a) parlay</u>,
   I don't speak fluently,

8. palabras <u>sueltasta yachani</u>.
    random words I know.

9. Aha,
    Yes,

10. <u>entiendini</u>.
    I understand.

11. <u>Imatachus kun(a) parlashanku uyirini</u>.
    Whatever they may speak I listen.

12. <u>Hinaspa uyirini, entiendini</u>.
    Like that as I listen, [and] I understand.

13. Ah . . . <u>radiopips parla chaykuntaps entiendini</u> . . . ah . . .
    Ah . . . like how they speak on the radio I can understand . . . ah . . .

14. Solo <u>mana—cor(ri)ditut hinata parlayta atinichu</u>.
    Only I don't—I can't speak fluently like that.

15. <u>Quechuat hina parlani</u>,
    Like how I speak Quechua,

16. <u>anchayta mana parlayta atiniñachu</u>.
    like that I cannot speak [Aymara].

17. <u>Pero entiendita entiendini</u>.
    But for comprehension, I can understand.

18. Palabras <u>sueltataps yachani</u> ah—
    Random words I know ah—

19. <u>Entiendinaykuyku</u>—
    And I can make myself understood by them [as well]—

20. ah ah . . . <u>Aymarat—parlan hamun</u> señora <u>aymaramanta</u>,
    ah ah . . . in Aymara—to say "come Señora" in Aymara,

21. <u>wakin palabrata yachani nispa parlapayani</u>.
    some words I know to say and can say them.

22. a de yats—q'imhina parlapayats [chuckles]
    [untranslatable]

23. pay parlapayawan entiendini ari . . . aha,
    And when speaking with them I understand as well right . . . aha,

24. ña allinta rimani ya.
    like that I speak well.

25. Aymarata manaña nichu.
    (But) Aymara I can't speak (like that).

26. Ya?
    Yeah?

27. Pay parlapayawan chay entiendini. Ari!
    [When] I speak with them do I understand. Yes!

28. Como por ejemplo, a vere,
    Like for example, let's see,

29. eh . . . imata munashanki?
    eh . . . what would you like?

30. sut . . . eh *kuns muntxwa casera*,
    sut . . . eh "what do you want casera,"

31. *alxasitawa*, a ver, aha . . .
    "to purchase," let's see, aha . . .

32. *suma ukha sumit*,
    "this is beautiful and pretty,"

33. *suma prendita ukhaxa*—así,
    "this brooch here is pretty"—like this,

34. palabrits sueltas, aha.
    random words, aha.

35. Ya entendita yachani, aha.
    Yes to understand (Aymara) I know, aha.

36. *Kuns muntwa, kuns muntwxa casera*?
    What do you want, what do you want casera?

37. ah . . .
    ah . . .

38. Por ejemplo colores no?
    For example colors right?

39. *Q'illu*,
    Yellow,

40. *Chupika* es rojo.
    Chupika is red.

41. *Q'illu* es amarillo, no?
    Q'illu is yellow, no?

42. Y *ch'uqniya* es verde.
    And *ch'uqniya* is green.

43. Colores <u>ahinata yachani ya</u>? Ah . . .
    Like colors I know right? Ah . . .

44. Por ejemplo *thaya* quiere decir
    For example *thaya* is to say

45. hace frío no cierto? Ah . . .
    that it is cold correct? Ah . . .

46. *Thay—thayjituwa* dice.
    "Cold—it is cold" they say.

47. Me está haciéndome frío.
    I feel cold.

48. Ah, <u>chaykuna yachani</u>, ah . . .
    Ah, those things I know, ah . . .

49. Mmm . . . <u>yachani chaykuna</u>.
    Mmm . . . I know these things.

50. <u>Aymarata yachakani hina</u>.
    I know Aymara like this.

51. <u>Hinata parlani</u>.
    I speak like this.

In her narrative, Señora Fidelia draws our attention to two main aspects of speaking and understanding Aymara in her life as a vendor.

There is first a distinction between speaking and listening competence and how both figure into constructing a broader sense of communicative competence for successful membership and belonging in the markets. For Señora Fidelia, she is good at understanding Aymara. This comprehension did not come from any formal education but rather from daily contact via travel, work, and proximity to other Aymara speakers. At the same time, while she self-evaluates herself as having good comprehension of Aymara, she also notes her limitations in producing or reproducing stretches of talk in the language. She mentions that she knows *palabras sueltas* (a few random words) that include colors or the state of the weather, and even some key phrases that she might use in market transactions. But in qualifying her knowledge of Aymara, she also does not claim to be a speaker because Aymara does not flow in the same speed or rhythm that she speaks Quechua, her first language (*mana corriditachu*). She continues her narrative, further linking her hesitancy in speaking Aymara or claiming linguistic proficiency to her not knowing how to properly conjugate verbs, which leaves her open to committing grammatical errors that might cause misunderstandings.

[Example 8]
1. Ya ves,
   Yes you see,

2. ñuqaps ahina entiendini mana allinta parlanichu, ah,
   I can understand well but I don't speak well, ah,

3. aha a veces equivoca con—o sea en la conjugación de los tiempos.
   aha sometimes I make a mistake with—or in conjugating tenses.

4. Es(e) es difícil.
   Those are difficult.

5. Ah, como de—como digamos pasado presente futuro una misma palabra,
   Ah, how—how we say past, present, future with only the same word,

6. no puedes—
   you are not able—

7. sea por decir, yo quiero decir,
   or rather to say, I want to say,

8. algo en pasado y lo digo en futuro o así,
   something in the past and I say it in the future or like,

9. o sea [laughs] me equivoco en esas conjugaciones [laughs].
   something [like this] where I mix up my conjugations.

10. Ah así es.
    Aha it is like this.

11. Es—eso justamente allí es donde me equivoco,
    Its—like in exactly this way where I make a mistake,

12. pero se rienpe.
    but they laugh [as well].

13. Les digo una cosa por otra [laughs] aha?
    I tell them one thing for another right?

14. En qué ejemplo más o menos?
    What other examples [do I have about this] more or less?

15. A ver en . . .
    Let's see in . . .

16. Quieres comer, dije, a ver,
    Would you like to eat, I said, let's see,

17. *manqasi mun . . . mun . . .*
    eat "mun . . . mun . . ."

18. *muntwxa.* A ver . . .
    "want." Let's see . . .

19. como por decir,
    like how to say,

20. Eso es lo que no puedo conjugar-pe.
    Things like this I just cannot conjugate.

21. Ah—quieres comer?
    Ah—"would you like to eat"?

22. Como se puede decir as ver?
    How would one say it let's see?

23. [Sandhya: umm ... *jumaxa manq'aña muntati*. O algo como—]
    umm ... "would you like to eat something." Or something like—

24.   = ves algo, ah =
                                = See something [like that], ah =

25. si a esas conjugaciones es lo que no puedo.
    Or these kinds of conjugations I can't do.

26. Yo por ejemplo *manq'askiti*.
    I for instance (would say) "manq'askiti."

27. Quiere decir "comer," no?
    Which is me wanting to say "eat," right?

28. Quieres, *muntxma*? O asi?
    "You want" (is) "muntxma"? Or like this?

29. Entonces,
    Therefore,

30. la conjugación en tiempos, ya no puedo ya
    conjugating tenses, yeah I can't do it yeah.

31. A ese es el problema [laughs].
    [And] this is the problem.

32. En Quechua ya más o menos si quieres.
    In Quechua, yeah I can more or less [do this] for you.

33. Se puede-pe como tú sabes cómo es tu lengua materna.
    One is able to since, you know, it is your mother tongue.

34. Antes <u>quechuamanta yachani</u>,
    Before in Quechua I knew [how to say],

35. pero—<u>mikhuyt munashankichu</u>?
    but—"would you like to eat"?

36. cómo dice, no? ah—
    It's how it is said, no? ah—

37. <u>Imay horasta mikhuwaq</u> dicen,
    "<u>Imay horast mikhuwaq</u>" they say,

38. a qué hora vas a comer, no?
    at what time are you going to eat, no?

39. Ah, así más o menos.
    Ah yes, it's like this more or less.

40. Entonces todos de estos tiempos en Aymara me confundo.
    Therefore all of these tenses in Aymara confuse me.

41. No puedo. Ah—
    I can't. Ah—

42. Pero sí en—palabras sueltas . . .
    But yes (I can) in—random words . . .

43. Normal entiendo, aha, palabras sueltas normal entiendo, aha.
    I understand fine, yes, random words I understand fine, yes.

44. Las conjugaciones de los tiempos es lo que no puedo.
    But I can't conjugate the tense.

45. Mmm . . . me equivoco.
    Mmm . . . I make mistakes.

In narrating her own perceptions of her knowledge of Aymara and comparing this with her lengua materna, Señora Fidelia focused on the mistakes that she would make, linking those metalinguistic evaluations to the fact that she did not know how to properly conjugate verbs across the different tenses. Lacking this specific piece of knowledge for her meant that she could not properly claim to know Aymara, or at least claim that she knew Aymara in the same way that she knows Quechua. Interestingly, in the process of explaining different kinds of linguistic competencies and focusing on the extent of her knowledge and the faults of her Indigenous linguistic proficiencies, Señora Fidelia eventually switched the flow of her talk from Quechua into Spanish. Even more notable was how this switch occurred right at the point of her narrative when she was most focused on the different kinds of mistakes she might make when speaking in Aymara, later extending that switch to even encompass uncertainties that she may also have in speaking Quechua. In earlier excerpts from her narrative, Señora Fidelia would often explain her linguistic knowledge and background while fluidly moving between Quechua and Spanish. This ease in freely using elements from both Quechua and Spanish to narrate her life experiences and linguistic knowledge match similar kinds of communicative competencies for many Indigenous market women in Puno, where Quechua- and Aymara-speaking women equally rely on, and deftly move across, the grammatical boundaries that separate their Indigenous language and Spanish in their daily communicative praxis. But in this last portion of her narrative, Señora Fidelia's marked switch into Spanish, with the exceptions of quoting phrases in either Quechua or Aymara, also signals a distinct shift in her narrative. This switch into Spanish could be interpreted as Señora Fidelia's attempt to shore up her own linguistic expertise by switching into another language that she felt best captured what she perceived as her own linguistic and communicative weaknesses, shifting her linguistic medium to maintain her general narrative stance that establishes her linguistic knowledge and expertise. More germane, however, is that this ability to switch the communicative medium of her narrative from Quechua to Spanish demonstrates how even in the process of narrating life histories, market women similarly utilize the full range of linguistic and communicative resources at their disposal to shape their interactional footing and alignments with their interlocutor.[9]

Regardless of their own fears or personal reservations, all these women comment on the importance of being comfortable with maneuvering across three linguistic mediums. Although each of these women qualify their knowledge in terms of listening and speaking proficiencies, both forms of linguistic knowledge and competence are supported, and to a large extent expected of vendors and customers in the market landscape. Even if some women may harbor reservations about how they speak and communicate in Quechua and Aymara in their everyday lives, such reservations become immaterial within the intersubjective scope of interactions between market women as associates and close friends. Instead, what is more important within the market economy is building a strong network of relationships that you can rely on while also separating out those who may cause you harm through envy or sabotage.[10] And in this realm, the ability to manipulate all of the linguistic resources you have is necessary not only to complete economic transactions and get the best deals but also to build and maintain close relationships of trust, reciprocity, and mutual understanding with your fellow Indigenous market women.

Mixed Repertoires: Making Sales, Maintaining Friendships

Within the markets, linguistic differences become a resource individuals use to negotiate different kinds of market interactions and relationships. In this scope, an individual's knowledge and awareness of linguistic differences between Quechua, Aymara, and Spanish becomes a kind of linguistic symbolic capital (Bourdieu 1991; Irvine 1989). This approach to linguistic knowledge in economic transactions and the local political economy aligns with the linguistic repertoires of market women in Puno. Yet going beyond basic economic needs, the ability to maneuver across different linguistic codes and mediums is an important aspect in establishing and building relationships between buyers and sellers, and more significantly, in cultivating deep friendships and bonds between market vendors.

In her detailed analysis of the linguistic practices and lives of market women in Cuzco, Linda Seligmann (2004b, 2004a) notes that the bilingual abilities of market women form a kind of protective space between them and their predominantly *criolla* (white) clientele. In Seligmann's analysis, the ability to switch between Quechua and Spanish affords market women the interactive space to insult or rebuke the selfish or self-serving actions of *criolla caseras*, thus granting a small intersubjective affordance that momentarily reverses the power inequalities that many Indigenous market women experience due to their racial and gendered backgrounds. Manipulating multiple linguistic mediums helps to socially distance the market vendor from her *casera*. To a certain degree, this kind of social distancing through switching between Quechua, Aymara, and Spanish is also at play within the multilingual markets of Puno. From the jocular naming of Aymara women as *akanakas* by Quechua women to the moments where I witnessed Aymara women explicitly refuse to accommodate the linguistic proficiencies of their Quechua-speaking clients by only speaking in Aymara, the differences between the various linguistic mediums that constitute the acoustic soundscape of the markets can create borders and boundaries, distancing vendors from other would-be buyers and sellers. But these instances of using linguistic difference as a distancing mechanism were infrequent and occurred primarily on days when the vendor was tired, was not feeling well, or did not feel like actively making sales to reach her personal quota for the day. More often than not, the market vendors that I knew and observed on a daily basis wanted to make connections with as many customers as possible, with the hope that some of these individuals would return back as loyal clients. This desire to be open to forming as many relationships and connections as possible therefore necessitated and privileged the ability to navigate and strategically incorporate elements from different linguistic mediums, which were then utilized to create connections, ranging from the most banal friendly acquaintances to more long-lasting bonds of friendship, solidarity, and intimacy. Moreover, the ability to include these moments of creative linguistic play also reflect and reinforce these women's long-standing membership and establishment within the market economy. Instead of treating linguistic differences as barriers toward creating community, how women creatively use the different linguistic sources in the marketplace in socially recognizable and felicitous ways signaled their membership within the market economy, and belonging within a community of fellow female market vendors.

Take the following interaction, which is a very common kind of interactional turn that often occurs between Aymara-speaking vendors and Quechua-speaking buyers, especially on those days when the Aymara-speaking vendor is not feeling well or is too tired to properly engage with customers in general. Señora Marcela was an older woman in her early sixties, was one of the first founding members of the Mercado de San Ignacio, and also part of the first wave of Indigenous migrants coming to the city in the late '70s and early '80s. An Aymara speaker from the southern Aymara-speaking province of Yunguyo, Señora Marcela loved to coach me on my conversational Aymara while correcting my knitting. Able to speak in Aymara and Spanish, Señora Marcela tended to speak primarily in Aymara with those she knew best such as other Aymara-speaking vendors, friends, family, and Aymara-speaking customers. She also knew some basic Quechua and would use some basic Quechua phrases such as "how much" when talking about prices with potential

Quechua-speaking customers. One day, however, Señora Marcela was not feeling well and did not feel like interacting with customers and people she did not already know. It was in the middle of the afternoon, and she started to feel her post-lunch fatigue set in. Just as she was ready to take a nap, leaving me and her daughter in charge of her stall, an older Quechua-speaking woman came up to her stall, asking how much a pair of alpaca knitted gloves were. Señora Marcela did not feel like dealing with the customer at all, and quickly shouted the following while shooing the woman to look across the aisle to instead purchase something from Señora Fidelia.

[Example 9]
1. Señora Marcela: No casera. <u>Mana entiend-ki-chu</u>.
                    No, my client/homemaker. I don't understand.

Grammatically, the phrase is a mixture of Spanish and Quechua, with the Spanish verb *entender* (to understand), inflected with Quechua morphology. Yet this kind of morphological mix is not marked for Quechua-speakers in Puno, and especially within the market scene, where such seamless blending between Spanish roots and Quechua morphology characterizes translanguaging practices among Indigenous market vendors. It is also important to note that the inflectional morphology is not entirely correct, due to the insertion of the syllable *-ki*. This *-ki*, which closely resembles second-person verbal suffix in Quechua (*-yki*), is often used by Aymara speakers, reflecting morphological aspects of Quechua that they frequently hear and apply whenever possible. Even though the insertion of *-ki* does not conform to how a Quechua speaker may say that phrase (*mana entindichu*), the message is generally understood, and usually prompts the buyer to switch into Spanish if possible, or in the case of Señora Marcela that day, move on to a different seller and hopefully a Quechua-speaking one.

At that moment, Señora Marcela's teenage daughter and I were quite happy to not deal with the sale. I was mortified, worried that I might tell the woman the wrong price for the gloves. And Señora Marcela's daughter was too engrossed in the telenovela she was watching on the tiny TV that they had within the market stall, not wanting to leave the episode to tend to a client. Nonetheless, beyond its utility within the scope of interactionally accepting or shutting down a potential sale, *mana entiendkichu* (I don't understand) is also a common joke or punchline used by and between Aymara speakers, and especially among Aymara-speaking market women. Señora Marcela was particularly adept at using this phrase as a sort of comic relief in conversations, drawing an additional layer of humor to emphasize her lack of knowledge in a particular situation when conversing in Aymara with other women. The contrast of a Quechua phrase in the middle of an Aymara conversation punctuates the conversational flow, drawing attention to a salient, non-Aymara element in the conversation. But this salience and contrast has a humorous effect. Its use and response, coupled with smiles and laughter, reinforces a closeness between speakers who understand the use of this ubiquitous Quechua phrase within an Aymara conversation as some kind of inside joke.

The use of mana entendikichu between Aymara-speaking women as a form of humor and intimacy also highlights how the creative use of linguistic elements across Quechua, Aymara, and Spanish is an important tool to maintain and perform long-term friendships and relationships within the market landscape. Consider the following interaction between Señora Fidelia and one of her longtime friends and co-vendors, Señora Maria. As part of the market ecosystem, Señora Maria made her living bringing lunch to all of the market vendors, many of whom were unable to leave their stalls to go home and eat lunch for fear of missing out on some crucial sales.

[Example 10]
1. Señora Maria: <u>Casera, chayamushankichu</u>?
    Homemaker, have you finished?

2. Señora Fidelia: [searching for plates and money and not finding them]
    Y, ahor-*asti*?
    And now?

3. Señora Maria: [laughing] ahor-*asti*!
    "And now!"

    <u>Kutimusaq</u>.
    I will come back.

4.   [both laugh]

Central to this joke is the mixing of the Spanish word *ahora* (now) with the focus suffix from Aymara, *-asti*. As Quechua-speaking market vendors, with years working in the market cooperatives of Puno, both women have some knowledge of Aymara, as Señora Fidelia noted earlier on in her interview. Yet this interaction is telling in that it highlights an aspect of Fidelia's knowledge, going beyond the individual words and phrases that she claimed to know and revealing her recognition and knowledge of specific discursive features in Aymara, such as a focus marker. Moreover, Señora Fidelia's use of the borrowed features from both Spanish and Aymara within the interaction highlights how both Señora Fidelia and Señora Maria not only recognize the non-Quechuaness of the word "*ahorasti*" but read the use of it within that interaction as funny, and reflective of the easygoing rapport that the two women shared with each other over many years of working together.

These kinds of translanguaging practices that seamlessly move across linguistic boundaries can also establish and perform close ties between women of different Indigenous linguistic backgrounds. This kind of relationship can be seen below in the interaction between Señora Filomena and Señora Nancy, one a Quechua-speaking woman and the other an Aymara-speaking woman. Both women are long-time market women and friends and members of a cooperative association for Indigenous women selling artisanal handicrafts. Through this cooperative association, these women would organize small, short-lived handicraft markets in Puno and sometimes in Arequipa and Lima through various contracts with the Ministry of Culture and Ministry of Tourism. It was on one of these days that the artisanal market in the center of Puno was rather quiet. It was the middle of August, and most locals had retreated back to their rural communities to finish preparing the chuño (freeze-dried potatoes) and harvesting the last of the barley and quinoa of the season. It was also a low point in the tourist season, as most international tourism to the area began to dwindle around the first few weeks of August. Nevertheless, the fair experienced some local foot traffic, and Señora Filomena finally got her break when some tourists from Arequipa stopped by her stall, interested in her knitwear. When they had selected what they wanted, they handed her a one-hundred-sole note, a large bill for which they hoped to receive change through the purchase. Not having enough necessary change but also not wanting to lose the sale, she quickly approached her neighbor and close friend Señora Nancy and asked her if she could lend her a fifty-sole note.

[Example 11]
1. Señora Filomena: Señora Nancy, *mayti'ita ma cincuenta solesxa*
   Señora Nancy, please give/lend me 50-soles note

2. Señora Nancy: [after searching in her purse] *ukhasti.*
   Here it is.

3. Señora Filomena: Gracias
   Thank you

More than asking to borrow a fifty-sole note, Señora Filomena's switch to Aymara when asking Nancy demonstrates her closeness with her longtime friend. This closeness goes beyond just knowing how to correctly switch into Aymara for Nancy, it also shows the implicit trust between the two women that the borrowed fifty soles will be paid back and returned. As such, the switch here publicly performs and establishes the two friends' closeness and mutual understanding, a comprehension that spans beyond just a switch into Aymara and encompasses the norms of solidarity that comprise market relations.

The examples thus far illustrated the role of creatively recruiting and using elements across Quechua and Aymara in building, maintaining, and establishing close bonds between market women. However, equally important in this linguistic ecology is the role of Spanish in mediating these relationships. The importance of Spanish can be seen in two ways. The first is the fact that Spanish is the ethnically neutral language of the altiplano, not being specifically attached to any Indigenous linguistic background or any specific province or community in the region. Despite Spanish's association with colonial and racial hegemony and hierarchy, its Indigenous ethnic neutrality in the altiplano also correlates with the ways in which Spanish is intermixed in conversation, making it an unmarked example of linguistic syncretism (Hill and Hill 1986) that is pervasive in talk found in mixed contexts like a market. Thus, within the market space, the use of Spanish is not necessarily interpreted or understood as the language of settler-colonial hegemony. Rather, Spanish is another linguistic resource, and its lack of connections with any particular Indigenous linguistic or social background makes it an available linguistic medium for all speakers, enabling its incorporation into basic communicative practices for Quechua and Aymara speakers in a way that does not compromise their understanding of the differences between Quechua, Aymara, and Spanish.

The unmarked incorporation of Spanish in basic communicative practice takes on additional salience when considering the multiple generations of women who work and maintain these small family businesses. Across any market, it is not uncommon to see older children, teenagers, and youths help their mothers and grandmothers manage the family market stalls. As children or grandchildren of Indigenous market women, these younger adults have grown up with some knowledge of either Quechua or Aymara. More often than not, these youths have grown up primarily in Puno, meaning that they predominantly use Spanish in their everyday conversations and interactions. But they also understand and use some Quechua or Aymara when interacting with their parents or older family members. While this difference in certain institutional contexts might appear as marked, within the space of the markets the flexibility of using Spanish alongside another Indigenous language is unmarked and widely accepted by market women of different ages and generations.

One individual who exemplified this was Señora Marcela's teenage daughter, Analisa. Like other teenage girls in Puno at the time, Analisa was interested in K-pop, reggaeton, and telenovelas. Over time she became more interested in learning to speak Aymara. Her mother liked to joke that she became interested because I was always hanging around the family and, as a foreigner, I had managed to learn enough Aymara to hold a very basic conversation. While Analisa showed a sincere interest in learning Aymara, part of her desire to speak Aymara more frequently occurred after Analisa turned sixteen, when Señora Marcela would often leave her in charge of their market stall while she went back to her natal rural community to care for elderly kin. From this experience and new set of responsibilities, Analisa became more comfortable with speaking an Aymara that was mixed with Spanish. Yet that accommodation was also reciprocated by older Aymara-speaking buyers and sellers at the market, who responded and recognized Analisa as a legitimate speaker of Aymara. One occasion came during the Saturday market, when I was left to "chaperone" Analisa. While she and I gossiped about her classmates at school and the unflattering haircuts they decided to get in response to the newest rage in hairstyles for teenage girls that year, an older Aymara-speaking woman came to purchase a traditional pollera (skirt) from her mother's stall. The casera knew that the stall belonged to Señora Marcela, who after many years had developed a reputation for providing the best deals on the fanciest polleras specially brought over from Bolivia. When handed a fifty-sole note, Analisa realized she did not have enough change to give her customer. Calling out from across the stall to Señora Silvia, another Aymara speaker and longtime friend of her mother, she asked the woman to provide her with the change that she needed.

[Example 12]
1. Analisa: Casera Silvia, *nayaxa* cambia*ki'ta*
   Casera Silvia, could you please give me change?

2. Señora Silvia: *Jai?* Cambio?
   What? Change?

3. Analisa: Jai! *Pa* cinco soles*anaka*. Por favor*siphja*!
   Yes! Two "cinco soles." Please!

4. Señora Silvia: *Janiw utkhiti*
   I don't have it

5. Analisa: *Utkhiw*!
   You do [have change]!

Analisa is part of the newest and youngest generation of market women. Compared to her mother, and even her older sister, she is more comfortable speaking Spanish than Aymara. Nevertheless, she does speak a mixed Aymara and is able to interact with her mother's friends and clients through combining Aymara and Spanish in her speech. And within the market space, such a combination is not only understood but also welcomed. That is because within the market, the ability to appropriately speak an Indigenous language is flexible enough to allow a wide range of communicative practices and welcomes a repertoire that appropriately mixes Spanish with Quechua or Aymara. Although Analisa did not get the change she needed, her mode of interaction and the response she received highlights how she is seen as an established and legitimate member of the market community. Furthermore, her communicative legitimacy in the space reinforces a central tenet within the linguistic practices of market women. Being a legitimate market vendor, and speaker, is not only limited by an individual's ability to conduct all of their interactions in only Quechua or Aymara. Instead, legitimacy is conferred to those who actively do this mixing across all linguistic boundaries. And in this way, belonging and membership within this community of practice is established not by any one single set of communicative repertoires. Instead, membership within the market space encompasses a wider range of communicative repertoires and practices that do not neatly match the grammatical divisions between Quechua, Aymara, and Spanish.

At the Crossroads of Language, Goods, and Inter-Indigenous Interactions

One evening I was sitting with Señora Fidelia, casually practicing my conversational Quechua while being corrected on some of my stitches on a sweater I was attempting to knit. This led to a conversation about the state of Quechua and Aymara in Puno and the fact that the younger generations are not learning to speak the languages as much. In thinking about the landscape of language use and language change in Puno, Señora Fidelia exclaimed:

[Example 13]
1. Pero <u>wakin runa kay Punopiq kay yachayku</u>,
   But some people here in Puno they know,

2. <u>quechuatay aymarat parlayta yachayku</u>.
   they know how to speak Quechua and Aymara.

3. <u>Ahina . . . puneño</u>—
   Like that . . . a puneño—

4. allin puñeñuqa ahinata kimsa idiomatata,
   to be like a good *puneno*, three languages,

5. castellano, quechua, aymara,
   Spanish, Quechua, [and] Aymara,

6. ahinata parlay yachayku.
   they know how to speak.

Señora Fidelia's comments echo similar sentiments that I heard from other market vendors and from puneños who did not work in the market economy. Namely, that Puno, as a city, a Departmental designation, and even as a general place within the altiplano is defined by the presence of Quechua, Aymara, and Spanish. Linguistically, Puno encompasses two Indigenous languages and the language of colonial domination and settler-colonial hegemony. Thus, to be puneño or puneña, and to claim that belonging and affiliation, means that one must be comfortable in speaking all three languages or idiomas, for those are the three codes that have shaped inter-Indigenous relationships and interactions historically. These three communicative mediums continue to mediate those relationships, which distinguish the unique essence of Puno from other places in the Andes. Also central to this description is the equal status and place of both Quechua and Aymara, and how knowing both languages along with Spanish is important for entering and shaping social relationships across the altiplano.

Señora Fidelia's comments highlight the significance of linguistic flexibility and accommodation in both Quechua and Aymara. What she did not elaborate on, however, is what speaking those languages looks like and how speaking all three might not correspond to ideologized expectations of how Quechua, Aymara, and Spanish as idiomas or ideologized languages should be spoken. This omission is not intentional, but rather it is telling for market women like Señoras Fidelia, Celia, Mily, Adela, Marcela, and others that I came to know. For these women, Quechua, Aymara, and Spanish are not practiced as bounded distinct codes or languages but instead as different mediums of communication that compose a wider set of communicative resources for them to select and use for different pragmatic and social needs. While one or two codes may figure more predominantly in their lives than others, all three codes are resources for them to access and use toward their efforts of establishing broad social networks to ensure their success and enable forms of mutual support within the market landscape. Knowing all three languages furthermore does not necessitate knowing all three fluently but rather knowing how to use aspects and elements of each language to build connections and form lifelong friendships of mutual support and aid.

Such an approach and orientation to language, and the porousness of linguistic boundaries, is not unique to the communicative repertoires of market women. Instead, the histories of market women, which today can now be extended to include the younger second and third generation of women working in their mothers' and grandmothers' businesses, highlight how this linguistic flexibility, receptivity, and creativity has also been central to inter-Indigenous linguistic life across the altiplano. Yet of these spaces, markets provide a unique window into how these dynamics coexist in public domains. In markets, these dynamics actively foster the formation and maintenance of social networks across diverse communicative backgrounds and repertoires. And of the kinds of speakers who participate in these flexible linguistic repertoires, market women encapsulate this flexibility the most due to their gendered positionality that has long enabled them to participate in market labor as a primary form of nondomestic labor and work.

The communicative practices of these women, however, become more salient in relation to the growing orientation toward Quechua and Aymara as bounded languages or idiomas, with specific bounded domains that present each language as incompatible with each other and prohibitive of translinguistic practices. Such views are often directed toward the differences between Quechua and Aymara as Indigenous languages that are radically different from Spanish. However, these ideologized orientations toward linguistic boundary maintenance are also increasingly directed toward perceptions and a growing awareness of the distinctiveness between Quechua and Aymara. In this light, the repertoires and life histories of market women stand as a testament to how older modes of understanding and negotiating inter-Indigenous linguistic and social difference contrast against an increasing push to view Quechua and Aymara as distinct idioms and starkly different ethnic Indigenous groups. These newer ideological regimes are not value-neutral but instead serve as a touchstone to evaluate the legitimacy of these women as ideal speakers of Quechua and Aymara, and to compare their speaker status to other more idealized figures of Indigenous femininity and Indigenous linguistic speakerhood in the altiplano more generally.

CHAPTER 3

Institutionalizing Inter-Indigenous Differences

Formalizing Ethnolinguistic Boundaries in the Altiplano

In the center of the Plaza de Armas stands the local municipal building, which includes offices for the management of the Department of Puno. With its late-twentieth-century, Brutalist style, replete with cold cement exteriors and sunlight-blocking glass windows, the building imposes itself compared to the more traditional, brightly colored colonial aesthetics of other buildings around the Plaza de Armas. But the central municipal building also distinguishes itself in another crucial way: it is the only one in the Plaza de Armas, and one of the few within the regional capital, that bears writing in Quechua, Aymara, and Spanish.

The Quechua (top) and Aymara (bottom) on the front of the municipal building are translations of the Spanish phrase *municipio provincial de Puno* (Provincial Municipality of Puno), located squarely between the other languages (figure 5). Following similar orthographic practices that are widely accepted across the Andes (Coronel-Molina 2008), both languages are represented using the Roman alphabet that was first imposed through colonial contact. The sign is also a diagrammatic icon (Mannheim 1999), spatially replicating the relationship between the different languages spoken in Puno and the distribution of its speakers. Quechua speakers, for instance, are regarded as primarily residing in the northern parts of the Department of Puno. Aymara speakers are generally regarded as residing in the southern regions. And although Puno, as the

FIGURE 5 The front façade of the municipal building in Puno. All three lines translate to "Provincial Municipality of Puno," with Quechua in the top line, Aymara at the bottom, and Spanish in the middle. Credit: Sandhya Krittika Narayanan (author).

regional capital, is a meeting space of these two language areas, its central location in the Department and urban status has resulted in the space being ideologized as a Spanish-speaking one as well.

Today, Indigenous puneños, especially younger ones, have come to identify and talk about each region as pertaining to a specific ethnolinguistic group, utilizing ethnolinguistic labels like "Quechua" and "Aymara" to identify the differences between Indigenous individuals in the region. The *zona Quechua* not only identifies the language that is spoken in those northern provinces but also labels its inhabitants as a distinct Indigenous ethnic group called Quechuas. Similarly, the *zona Aymara* designates a specific, ethnically unique group of people who not only speak Aymara but also are ethnic, Indigenous Aymaras. These divisions make the central placement of Spanish on the sign more meaningful. Although Spanish continues to bear the legacy of being associated with colonial linguistic powers and policies, its position in the center of the municipal building's sign makes it an ethnically neutral language that does not belong to any Indigenous ethnolinguistic nation. It is the language of no one group, meaning that it is the language of everyone, and the primary channel to mediate communication between ethnic Quechuas and Aymaras.

Public signage that proudly showcases written representations of Quechua and Aymara is part of a set of discourses and practices that promote Indigenous ethnolinguistic identity and reconstruct Puno and the altiplano as an Indigenous landscape defined by ethnolinguistic differences between ethnic, Indigenous Quechuas and Aymaras. These ethnolinguistic differences are at the heart of other victories for Indigenous recognition across the nation, such as the inclusion of Quechua and Aymara as distinct ethnic Indigenous categories on the 2017 National Census. However, the emergence and proliferation of ethnolinguistic terms to label and identify Indigenous difference are also newer ideological developments that contrast against more localized understanding of inter-Indigenous difference in the region. As such, the use and circulation of ethnolinguistic terms like "Quechua" or "Aymara" pose a new set of challenges for puneños, who must learn to reckon with what those terms mean, and what kinds of linguistic practices, cultural traditions, and social identities are included and excluded from these Indigenous ethnic categories and labels.

This chapter considers the challenges associated with cultivating new sensibilities around Indigenous ethnolinguistic affiliation through institutionalized language practices, which circulate ideologically privileged versions of Quechua and Aymara. Many of these practices, which reflect an ideology of language purism (Dorian 1994; Kroskrity 2000a, 2000b), focus their ideological work on regimenting the boundaries between Spanish and Quechua and Aymara, targeting lexical loans that have been imported into both Indigenous languages as a result of colonial contact with Spanish. However, this emphasis on linguistic purity also extends to the boundary between Quechua and Aymara as languages, focusing on the need to ideologically harden the divisions between those Indigenous languages, and by extension reinforce the boundaries between ethnolinguistic Quechuas and Aymaras as distinct speakers and distinct Indigenous peoples.[1] Practices that promote and privilege bounded and hyperpurified versions of Quechua and Aymara in the region contribute toward the creation of a "metadiscursive regime" (Swinehart 2012)—discourses that not only comment on the legitimacy and authenticity associated with an idealized standard for Quechua and Aymara linguistic and communicative praxis but also introduce and establish the ideological connection between idealized versions of Quechua and Aymara with ideas around Quechua and Aymara Indigenous ethnic difference, authenticity, and legitimacy. These discursive and metadiscursive practices within institutional settings, therefore, go beyond creating an awareness of the differences between Quechua and Aymara as distinct linguistic codes. Instead, the connections that are fostered through promoting and circulating a unified set of linguistic practices and ideological orientations are crucial for also mobilizing a new shared sense of indigeneity and ethnic Indigenous identity for puneños.

From Linguistic Purism to Ethnic Groups

Ethnolinguistic differences, and the generation of ethnolinguistic groups, are based on ideologized indexical links between some named "language" and its association with a defined group of speakers (Irvine and Gal 2000). While Quechua and Aymara are the two main Indigenous languages spoken in the region, the challenge of promoting and circulating the recognition of Quechua and Aymara as two distinct ethnolinguistic groups in the region includes defining what "Quechua" and "Aymara" mean as ethnolinguistic labels. This means that defining these labels is an ideological project that includes formalizing the symbolic boundary between the two categories and sorting linguistic, social, and cultural objects and practices into their ideologized group. Elsewhere across the Andes, this ideological sorting process may be easier since defining what is "Quechua" or "Aymara" is based on the contrast between these Indigenous languages and Spanish (Allen 2002; Babel 2022). But in a region that has been defined by the interactions between two Indigenous languages that have often blurred the linguistic and social boundaries associated with each ethnolinguistic label, such processes of separation and sorting are not as easy to achieve.

The blurring of linguistic boundaries, for instance, which can be traced to borrowing, code-mixing, and code-switching, is not a unique phenomenon only found in Puno. Across contexts of language contact, such mixing and multilingualism is very much the norm (Bilaniuk 2005; Minks 2010; Singer 2023; Stenzel and Williams 2021). However, such practices come into question in situations where modern, Western-influenced ideologies present a monolingual standard as the ideal form of communicative behavior for all speech communities and nations (Silverstein 2000). For many multilingual contexts today, disentangling the differences between the linguistic varieties that constitute a multilingual speech community often coincides with projects of modernity, sovereignty, and nationalism (Hauck 2018; Paugh 2012). As such, formalizing the boundaries of what is "Quechua" or "Aymara" involves practices that reflect ideologies of linguistic purism, which define what elements are included in each language (Dorian 1994; Kroskrity 1993) and set a benchmark for language standardization practices (Gal 2006; Milroy 2001), where the creation of a linguistic standard offers social and political legitimacy to a bounded linguistic object that is then used to evaluate and regiment linguistic and communicative practices.

Formalizing these processes, however, is doubly challenging within Puno. First, distinguishing the boundaries between Quechua and Aymara as distinct linguistic objects contradicts other kinds of conceptualizations and relationships between language, speech, and processes of identification that have been discussed earlier.[2] And second, histories of cross-linguistic interactional dynamics such as multilingual fluencies or translanguaging practices (such as those described in chapter 2) complicate the perceived boundedness between languages and their speakers. Both these phenomena make the process of fixing a distinct ethnolinguistic identity like Quechua and Aymara more difficult and require an ideological semiotic recalibration of Indigenous linguistic diversity that makes a bounded, named "language" the primary axis of differentiation to both separate and unite Indigenous puneños.

Much of the ideological work to promote visions and discourses of ethnolinguistic differences, therefore, lies in the purview of institutions that are often central in promoting language standards and maintaining the dominance of ideologies of linguistic purism (Jaffe 2019). However, the efficacy of these practices in promoting and privileging the use of idealized and purified versions of Quechua and Aymara has to be supported and developed. This means that in addition to promoting purified varieties of Quechua and Aymara, institutions are also tasked with modeling how such idealized versions of each language should be used. But in modeling how each idealized variety of Quechua and Aymara should be practiced, these institutions also become spaces that introduce and circulate new metadiscursive regimes about Quechua and Aymara ethnolinguistic difference, thus cultivating new sensibilities and a broader awareness of how Indigenous ethnic and cultural differences and authenticity are rooted in the differences between Quechua and Aymara as distinct languages. Although many institutions in the altiplano rely to varying degrees on shared Indigenous cultural practices and customs across the Department of Puno to address a pluralistic Indigenous puneño society, most of the linguistic practices and discourses on language and social difference promote a view of inter-Indigenous difference that is rooted in linguistic differences. Therefore, in spite of other kinds of attempts to celebrate Indigenous plurality in the altiplano, the dominant discourse that emerges from these practices is one of the divisions between ethnic, Indigenous Quechuas and Aymaras. As a result, characterizations of Indigenous linguistic and social diversity in the region are presented through the ideologized contrasts between Quechua and Aymara, which influence practices in media production, Indigenous language education, and regional politics, while slowly transforming discursive representations around social and linguistic boundaries in the altiplano and across the Department of Puno.

Literacy and Creating a Bounded Indigenous Readership

Like many other Indigenous and minoritized languages, Indigenous literacy is an ideologically laden process. Due to colonial linguistic legacies, both Quechua and Aymara orthographic practices continue to use a Roman alphabet as part of their ongoing efforts to promote Indigenous language literacy. As a result of years of increased activism to legitimize Indigenous linguistic practices across the Andes (Godenzzi [1997] 2012; Zavala 2014), being literate in one's lengua materna is increasingly seen as the primary metric by which one can claim knowledge of either Quechua or Aymara. The work done by activists to promote Indigenous language literacy was originally intended to build awareness about the importance of maintaining Indigenous linguistic knowledge for non-Indigenous audiences, which included Spanish-speaking, non-Indigenous teachers, politicians, and other policy makers residing primarily in Lima (García 2005). Yet this ideologized stance that prized Indigenous literacy as the ultimate form of Indigenous linguistic knowledge was also shared by many adult Indigenous puneños I knew. Moreover, their general acceptance of associating Indigenous language literacy with Indigenous linguistic authority and expertise was steeped in a broader politics of inequality regarding Indigenous literacy and institutionalized forms of Indigenous knowledge. Unlike the range of communicative repertoires that characterize Indigenous linguistic communicative competence in Puno, knowing how to read and write in one's lengua materna is a skill that very few Indigenous puneños possess—a discrepancy that primarily affects older puneños, who are more likely to have either Quechua or Aymara as their first, and often sole, language of communication, yet who have historically lacked access to educational programs to learn to read and write their Indigenous lengua materna. Like other forms of expertise, lengua materna literacy is a skill that has to be learned and cultivated through attending schools or programs that are taught by certified professionals. And while younger Indigenous puneño youth are increasingly seeking out these opportunities, such programs are still out of reach for the vast majority of puneños, who do not have the adequate economic or social resources to participate in them.

To address such structural problems, various local institutions implemented small programs to try to make Quechua and Aymara literacy more accessible and available to all Indigenous puneños in the region. One program that enjoyed moderate success in this arena was the local Puno-based newspaper *Los Andes*. In December of 2016, the editorial board of the newspaper decided to publish a trilingual column titled *Willakuy-Yatiyawinaka* (figure 6), translating to "stories" in Quechua (*willakuy*) and "shared knowledge" or "the news" in Aymara (*yatiyawinaka*). The column initially started as a once-a-week feature created for the sole purpose of normalizing Indigenous language literacy in public venues by making it more widely accessible for Indigenous puneños. Over time, the column's publication frequency decreased to eventually become a once-a-month novelty. However, the column's initial introduction generated a lot of buzz for many puneños. Newspaper stalls across Puno, which remain the only way that newspapers can be purchased in

FIGURE 6 Page from *Willakuy-Yatiyawinaka*. Credit: Photo taken by author.

the city, created large signs advertising the weekly feature saying *"Los Andes ¡Hoy página trilingüe!"* (*Los Andes* trilingual page today!) to market the unique editorial feature to customers. Following the column's inaugural issue, one reader wrote a letter to the editor that was published in the following week's editorial page saying, *"Felicito esta iniciativa, está en sintonía con los objetivos de valorar las lenguas originarias, y que bien que en la región de Puno tengamos un diario que informe en nuestros idiomas"* ("I commend this initiative, this is in concert with the objectives to value the native languages, and how good it is that in Puno we have a newspaper that informs us in our languages").

Although the weekly column's principal aim was to promote Quechua and Aymara literacy, the column's structure and format were shaped by ideologized practices that reinforce the boundary between Quechua- and Aymara speakers in Puno as two bounded ethnic Indigenous groups who speak purified versions of Quechua and Aymara. Like other forms of institutionally sanctioned Indigenous language practices, the column's articles were written by professionals who had received extensive training in Indigenous-language literacy from an accredited institution. Because of this, both articles were written according to the grammatical and stylistic conventions of the Quechua and Aymara that are associated with elite Indigenous-language institutions (Coronel-Molina 2008).

The only use of Spanish in these weekly articles appeared as a side translation alongside its respective article in Quechua and Aymara. Next to each Spanish translation was also a vocabulary box, which offered readers the chance to learn new and sometimes specialized vocabulary in their lengua materna. When I chatted with one of the editors at *Los Andes* about the structure and format of the column, both the Spanish translation for each article and the smaller vocabulary insert were rationalized as providing readers from different linguistic backgrounds the opportunity to learn these languages and improve their literacy in Quechua and Aymara. This meant, therefore, that the trilingual column was designed to cultivate Indigenous literacy through positioning Spanish as the central translating medium. Like the use of Spanish in the sign of the municipal building in the center of Puno, Spanish functions as a translational medium or channel to aid readers in parsing the meaning and content for each article written in Quechua or Aymara.

This division between how Quechua, Aymara, and Spanish were used in the column reveals how each language performed a specific function in cultivating an Indigenous language readership and specific Indigenous linguistic literate public. As the translating medium, Spanish's role was confined to performing a metalingual function (Jakobson 1960), thus placing Quechua and Aymara as viable linguistic mediums to communicate the news within one of Puno's most widely read newspapers. This kind of framing, however, also positioned Quechua and Aymara as linguistically and graphically incommensurable to each other, creating the effect where inter-Indigenous linguistic intelligibility could only be achieved through the presence and role of Spanish to facilitate any kind of translation. The incommensurability between Quechua and Aymara in their written and graphic representation, therefore, reinforces not only the ideological boundedness between both languages but also the boundedness between each language's set of speakers who require Spanish to create a communicative bridge to unite both Indigenous ethnolinguistic groups.

This bounded untranslatability between the Quechua and Aymara columns was also not lost on Indigenous puneños, who also approached each column as being specific to one group of Indigenous-speaking readers. These practices were in some ways influenced by existing print media consumption practices in Puno. Typically, most puneños would often look through newspapers while spending time at public locales like small restaurants or juice bars, or while reading whatever newspaper was left behind by a previous reader on public transportation combis across the city and region. In these spaces, while waiting for a meal or for the driver to take you to your desired location, most readers would casually flip through each paper's main headlines and political cartoons. Engagement with print newspapers would also occur while walking through the city, where nearly every corner housed a small newspaper and book stall. Each day, stall owners would carefully cover the exterior of their small shops with the papers and magazines that they had for sale. Local and national magazines would be hung outside within small plastic bags, similar to the plastic covers that might encase a rare and expensive comic book. Newspapers would be showcased to allow passersby a quick glance of the top headlines that each paper covered. Although articles at the center of each paper were not frequently displayed, having only the main headlines on the front page shown to the public allowed puneños with different Spanish literacy abilities to get a quick sense of the current events occurring regionally and nationally. This often produced the common sight across Puno of men (and to a lesser degree women) standing in front of the stalls and scanning the various headlines of the day. If someone was interested in a headline, they would purchase a paper. However, most of these observers would simply glance at the different papers, and slowly move about their day once they felt like they had enough of a sense of current events in Puno and in Peru.

Stalls that sold *Los Andes* would advertise when they had *Willakuy-Yatiyawinaka* every week.³ Like other papers, the inner pages, including those that had the special column, were never put on display, in the hopes of encouraging interested readers to purchase the paper. Although I was not able to track how many people purchased issues of *Los Andes*, or what they read when they purchased them, my sense of the selective readership associated with the Indigenous-language column emerged through how puneños I knew would react whenever I purchased copies of the paper for others to read. On weeks when a new *Willakuy-Yatiyawinaka* was available, I would always purchase a few extra copies to share with my friends and interlocutors during the day. For some of these friends, like my Aymara-speaking friend Señor Abelardo or my Quechua-speaking friend and market vendor Señora Celia, opening and reading the page dedicated to *Willakuy-Yatiyawinaka* was an exercise in testing one's ability to try to learn how to read in their heritage Indigenous language. I noticed that Señora Celia, for instance, would immediately go to the Quechua columns, and audibly try to voice out the passage, reading each sentence several times to see if she could understand that specific form of Quechua, relying on the Spanish translation to help her make sense of how Quechua was graphically represented and discursively presented. Señor Abelardo would try a different tack, starting with the Spanish translation of the Aymara column to then see if he could rephrase the Aymara that was written in the article so that it more closely matched how he would say the same information. In this way, both would proceed reading the columns in "their" Indigenous language. Yet once they finished with the column in their language, neither of them was interested in reading the passages written in the other Indigenous language, preferring to continue with reading the rest of the news written in Spanish.

This preference was there even during times when I offered to help read the column in the other language. Typically, my friends and interlocutors who enjoyed trying to read the paper on their own did not express any interest in hearing the column written in the other Indigenous language at all, with Señora Celia once stating that the news in the other column was not for "Quechuas" like her. This kind of response was shared by many of the other market women at Mercado de San Ignacio, who preferred for me to read the Quechua or Aymara stories out loud to them instead of them trying to slowly parse out on their own the orthographic practices associated with their language. Slowly I would read the relevant article that each woman wanted to hear, often stumbling through passages and phrases that I myself was unfamiliar with. During these moments, my steadfast listeners would slowly clarify my pronunciation while also paraphrasing what was written in each statement in a way that matched how they spoke Quechua or Aymara. But once I had finished reading the column in their particular language, the reading session just ended, with my market interlocutors having no interest in the news covered in the other language's column.

In this way the separation of languages in the weekly column also bifurcated Indigenous reading publics along ethnolinguistic lines. The focused interest in only the news written in the same language as one's Indigenous linguistic heritage suggested that, for my interlocutors, the information written in each article was only meant for speakers of that language. This approach toward the different columns written in *Willakuy-Yatiyawinaka* was further supported by the fact that the Quechua and Aymara articles were always about two different stories. This difference in the referential content of each article thus also encouraged the general interpretation that each article written in a different Indigenous language was only meant for listeners or speakers of that language. By making these choices, Quechua- and Aymara-speaking puneños were laying the groundwork for a new set of ethnolinguistic practices that maintained the boundaries between Indigenous speakers through the separation that came from the media that they consumed. Simultaneously, these decisions and metapragmatic comments also reveal how conceptions around Quechua and Aymara as linguistic codes are also in flux, no longer being seen as neutral communicative mediums but rather as specific channels that can communicate the world in ways that are specific to individuals who identify as ethnic, Indigenous Quechuas and Aymaras.

Indigenous Bilingual Education Through Spanish

The creation of *Willakuy-Yatiyawinaka* in *Los Andes* highlights how the promotion of Indigenous linguistic diversity in the region is closely tied to developing literacy in Quechua and Aymara. But this interest, and general acceptance that Indigenous literacy is important for the legitimacy of Indigenous languages like Quechua and Aymara and their speakers, is part of a longer history of Indigenous language revitalization and maintenance across Peru and the Andes. In Peru, activities promoting the importance of Indigenous language revitalization programs has been largely accomplished through the creation of IEB (*intercultural educación bilingüe*, or bilingual intercultural education)[4] programs through the national Ministry of Education, which oversees educational programming and standards for all public schools in Peru (García 2005; Hornberger 1988, [1997] 2012). IEB as national policy, and even within the altiplano and Department of Puno, has been in existence since the 1980s (Godenzzi [1997] 2012). However, histories of implementing and maintaining IEB programs have not always been consistent, with programs often losing their funding or having their trained teachers eventually being cut from schools. This history has been more fraught within the regional capital for several reasons. IEB typically has been seen as a rural program. While its location in rural areas reflects dominant ideologies that emplace Indigenous language use outside of urban contexts, such practices overlook the degree to which cities like Puno are composed of children and youth from Indigenous backgrounds whose parents recently migrated to live and work within the city. These factors are further complicated by other challenges that include cuts to regional IEB programing, teacher shortages, and disruptions to the academic calendar from political strikes, which often result in school closures that can last weeks or months.

During my time in Puno, I learned of four programs within the city's public schools that were all terminated early either because the school ran out of funding from the government to support teachers for the program or because classes (and therefore the program) were interrupted because of strikes (which during my time in Puno included one very prominent and long-lasting teacher's strike). Of these, one program that I was able to observe came from IES Maria Salesiana,[5] a public secondary school located in the center of Puno. Despite the program's short-lived run, the teaching practices at IES Maria Salesiana mirrored many of the practices that were considered to be common in other IEB programs in Puno. First, students were separated into classrooms dedicated to teaching only one Indigenous language, providing one class and teacher dedicated to teaching Quechua, and another, separate class and teacher dedicated to teaching Aymara. On the first day students were asked, *Cuál es tu lengua materna*? (what is your mother tongue?) in order to determine which classroom they went into. As young adults who had grown up most of their lives familiar with discourses around Quechua and Aymara ethnolinguistic differences, most students were able to answer the question with "Quechua" or "Aymara." The few who did not know were asked one of two follow-up questions: *Cuál es la lengua de tu papa*? (what is your father's language?) or *De dónde son tus padres*? (where are your parents from?). Based on the answers to these three questions, each student was sorted into their appropriate language classroom, ensuring that children of Quechua-speaking parents went to the Quechua classroom and children of Aymara-speaking families were placed in the Aymara classroom.

While these classes were focused on teaching the Indigenous language to students, both classes relied on Spanish to help translate or contextualize the lessons within each class. As such, learning Quechua and Aymara to different degrees was filtered and understood through the lens of Spanish, often placing each lengua materna as equivalent to some lexical or grammatical feature of Spanish. For instance, in the Aymara class, many equivalences came from explaining the grammatical nuances of Aymara in relation to Spanish grammar. Under this approach, Aymara was presented to students as a full grammatical system, with a complete set of rules that made it a language that was equal to Spanish. The value of that grammatical system was also described in relation to Spanish grammatical structures. This is shown below, where the Aymara teacher, Señor Arturo, begins his lesson by teaching the students about the person and pronominal system in Aymara, which is notable for having a single, dual pronoun—*jiwasa*. In a combination of Spanish and Aymara, Señor Arturo repeats the phrases and words as a pedagogical method to teach his Aymara-heritage language students. Furthermore, he introduces the lesson with a hyper-stylized name for pronouns in Aymara (*sutilanti arunaka*). This phrase is a calque for the word for "pronouns" in Spanish (*pronombres*). Through identifying pronouns by a specific, technical grammatical category in Aymara, he not only positions grammatical elements in Aymara as comparable to those same grammatical categories in Spanish but also performs his expertise in an ideologically purified form of Aymara.

[Example 14]

1. Arturo: *Akasa kamsisa?*
   How do you say this?

2. [writing and erasing things from the board]

3. *Akasa kamsisa?*
   How do you say this?

4. *Kamsisa?*
   How do you say?

5. "*Sutilanti arunaka*"
   Pronouns

6. [students repeat in the background softly]

7. Los pronombres—
   pronouns—

8. Ese vamos a escribir aquí en este parte [moves to a different blackboard]
   We're going to write this on this part [of the blackboard]

9. *Naya* . . . a ver?
   "I" . . . see?

10. *Kamsisa . . . naya?*
    How do you say . . . "I"?

11. *Kamsisa?*
    How do you say?

12. Students: *Naya*
    "I"

13. Arturo: *Kamsisa?* [writing on board]
    How do you say?

14. Students: *Juma*
     "you"

15. Arturo: *Juma* [pointing toward students]
     "you"

16. *Naya. Juma.* [writing on the board]
     "I." "You."

17. *Kamsisa*?
     How do you say?

18. [students mumble "jupa"]

19. *Jupa.* Ya—
     "he/she." Yes—

20. *Naya* [gesturing to himself]. *Naya.*
     "I." "I."

21. *Jum(a)* [pointing to students] Ya?
     "You." Yes?

22. *Jupa* [pointing out the window] Ya?
     "He/she." Yes?

23. [writing on the board]

24. *Kamsisa*?
     How do you say this?

25. [students mumble]

26. *Jiwasa. Jiwasa.*
     "We." "We."

27. Bien.
     Good.

28. Qué dice?
     What does it say?

29. *Naya*, ya.
     "I," yes.

30.		¡*Naya*! ¡Sí uno más!
		"I"! Yes, one more time!
31.		Tienes que hacer.
		You have to do it.
32.		¡Más fuerte! [pointing to Student 1]
		[And with] more force!
33.	Student 1:	*Naya*
		"I"
34.	Arturo:	*Naya*
		"I"
35.		A para esto también. [pointing to the next line on the board]
		And for this one too.
36.	Student 1:	*Juma*
		"you"
37.	Arturo:	aaah . . . *juma*. *Jupa*, y—
		aaah . . . "you." "He/she," and—
38.		*Juma, jupa*. Es muy importante, ya?
		"You," "he/she." This is very important, yes?
39.		Pero finalmente *juma*—es muy cercano.
		But this "you"—it's [for] someone very close.
40.		Este segundo pronombre de persona.
		This second person pronoun.
41.		Ya?
		Yes?
42.		Por eso por *juma*—
		Therefore "you"—
43.		*Naya, juma, jupa*.
		"I," "you," "he/she."
44.		*Jupa*.
		"He/she."

45. [writing on the board]

46.   *Jiwasa.* [students mumble]
        "We."

47.   Qué es? [students mumble]
        What is it?

48.   Nosotros, a ya, nosotros.
        "We," yes, "we."

In the Quechua class, establishing the grammatical and linguistic parity between Quechua and Spanish took the form of teaching students direct lexical translations between Quechua and Spanish words. Unlike the Aymara class, which taught vocabulary through grammatical concepts, the Quechua class alternatively focused on familiarizing students with Quechua translations of common lexical items that they knew in Spanish. This was not only mirrored in interactive practices between the teacher and students, which were mostly conducted in Spanish, but also through using educational materials that framed learning Quechua as secondary to Spanish as a matrix language (Meek and Messing 2007). Worksheets (such as in figure 7), for instance, were often filled with vocabulary tables and lists that helped students learn the one-to-one correspondences between Quechua and Spanish lexical items.

These correspondences would also be repeated through practices that relied primarily on mastering the meaning of individual lexical items. This can be observed through one lesson that was focused around learn-

Imataq kanman/ imasmary	¿Qué puede ser?
❖ Pillpintu	Mariposa
❖ /Ch'usiqa	Búho/lechuza
❖ Pachak chaki	Cien pies
❖ Ch'ia	Liendre
❖ Urpi	Paloma
❖ Waka	Vaca
❖ Atuq	Zorro

FIGURE 7 Excerpt of an activity from a Quechua worksheet. Credit: Photo taken by author. Worksheet by Señora Mariela.

ing kin terms in Quechua. The interaction was conducted primarily in Spanish, where the Quechua teacher, Señora Mariela, used Quechua to create direct translations with their Spanish lexical equivalents.

[Example 15]
1. Mariela: En la parte de que—
   In the part where—

2. acostado qué dice?
   along the side what does it say?

3. [students say "vocabulario"]

4. "Vocabulario"
   "Vocabulary"

5. Mamá es <u>mama</u>
   Mother is "mama"

6. En castellano se dice "mamá"
   In Spanish they say "mamá"

7. pero en Quechua se dice <u>mama</u>.
   but in Quechua they say "mama."

8. Y papá <u>tata, entiendichu</u>?
   And father (is) "tata," do you understand?

9. Hermana <u>panay</u>,
   Sister [is] "panay,"

10. Hermana a hermana, <u>panay panay</u>. [pointing to two female students]
    Sister to sister, "panay panay."

11. Porque ella es hermana.
    Because she is (her) sister.

12. Y si es a tú a tu hermano—
    And if it's you [and] for your brother—

13. <u>Turay</u>. [writing on the board] <u>Turay</u>.
    "Turay." "Turay."

14. Ya ves. Seguimos.
     Ok [lit. "you see"] Let's continue.

15. Eso es diferente.
     This is different.

16. Waqiy turay.
     "Wayqiy turay."

17. Turay wayqiy.
     "Turay wayqiy."

18. Wayqiy es varón a varón,
     "Wayqiy" is male to male,

19. Porque él es su hermano
     Because he is his brother

20. Pero cuando es ella a varón, es turay.
     But when it's her to a male, it's "turay."

21. Yá es diferente.
     It's different.

Despite being labeled as IEB, these classes and others like them nevertheless relied on Spanish to communicate and contextualize the grammatical and lexical intricacies of Quechua and Aymara to urban Indigenous puneño youth. While this reliance on Spanish might superficially betray the core ethos behind IEB education, the use of Spanish in these classes within the puneño context reproduced certain ideological shifts in thinking about inter-Indigenous ethnolinguistic differences that would have definitely made sense to Spanish- dominant puneño youth. In both these classrooms, Spanish is the translating, referential medium to communicate utterances and lessons in Quechua and Aymara. Yet elevating Spanish as the primary medium of translation also mirrors similar kinds of translational practices, such as the layout for the sign on the city's municipal building, and in the organization of Quechua, Aymara, and Spanish translation columns in *Willakuy-Yatiyawinaka*, which present the meaning of phrases written in Quechua or Aymara as only decipherable through Spanish. Teaching practices within the IEB program at IES

Maria Salesiana replicate this metalinguistic function for Spanish, casting Quechua and Aymara knowledge as achievable through either some direct comparison or translation with and through Spanish.

Yet like these other sites of translation, Spanish also symbolically hardens the linguistic and social boundaries between Quechua and Aymara. In graphic representations, this is accomplished through having a Spanish translation visible, making it a necessary linguistic medium to understand Quechua and Aymara orthographic practices. Within IEB programs, the role of Spanish in the classroom ideologically hardens the divide between Quechua and Aymara as distinct languages, reinforcing the spatial separation between Quechua- and Aymara-heritage language students by then becoming the medium to teach each class specialized forms of linguistic expertise associated with each language. This means that puneño students are not only taught that Quechua and Aymara are two discrete languages; implicitly, students are also taught to see Indigenous linguistic knowledge as being accessible through Spanish. But in doing this, teaching practices within IEB programs also erase the possibility of cross-linguistic or translanguaging practices between Spanish and either Indigenous language, or between Quechua and Aymara. This kind of semiotic differentiation between Quechua and Aymara through Spanish thus cultivates an awareness for the next generation of Indigenous puneños to think of their heritage Indigenous languages as bounded, discrete entities that can be both compared to Spanish and made comparable and understandable to each other through Spanish. However, the value of these lessons and practices is not only in promoting and privileging a specialized view of Quechua and Aymara linguistic expertise. More importantly, these programs and practices within Puno are also significant venues to cultivate a sense of ethnolinguistic "Quechuaness" and "Aymaraness" that recognizes the legitimacy of Quechua and Aymara as "languages," and the maintenance of different Quechua and Aymara identities associated with two distinct ethnic Indigenous groups.

A Radio Station for all Indigenous Puneños

A nondescript, three-story concrete building, the Pachamama Radio station is nestled off the main road in one of the newer neighborhoods in the southern part of the city of Puno. If you did not notice the small yellow sign saying "Pachamama Radio," you might mistake the building for another residential home within the neighborhood. For a stranger or newcomer to Puno, it would be hard to locate the building, resigning yourself to the mercy of locals who would know where to find the radio station through their daily practice of walking the various streets of the city. But once you find the radio station and walk through the front doors and up the first flight of stairs, you very quickly experience the energy contrast within the building. On any given day, the main lobby and foyer will have individuals and families speaking with each other in Quechua or Aymara. Some of the individuals are representatives from Quechua- or Aymara-speaking communities, coming to the radio station to be interviewed about some event that took place in their community. Other times, these community-based representatives would come to the radio station to announce a festival or large community-based celebration that they would like everyone in the altiplano to know about. Among a steady stream of individuals, journalists, producers, assistants, and interns would flutter through the hallways and stairways, ushering visitors to the interviewing rooms, volunteering to babysit small children to allow mothers and other female caretakers to be recorded for interviews and announcements, and running drafts of scripts to be finalized or vetoed between creative producers and the journalists who would read them on air. Though it was not an official government building, Pachamama Radio had the feel of a community center for the Department of Puno—a welcoming place for individuals from all Indigenous backgrounds and communities. And like market spaces across the altiplano, the building and space also became a place where one could hear conversations across the three languages of Puno happening simultaneously around you.

Pachamama Radio[6] was founded in the early 2000s on a few basic principles: to provide quality radio programming for all of Puno free of political or religious influence or affiliations, to adequately represent the needs of the people (with a special emphasis on those who live in rural communities), and to promote the pan-Indigenous Quechua-Aymara cultural, linguistic, and political roots and identity of Puno and the Southern Andes. At its core, Pachamama strove to promote Indigenous unity and worked hard to become a recognized symbol of Indigenous identity for all Indigenous communities across the altiplano. Yet like any other linguistic and cultural institution in the region, Pachamama reproduces many similar practices around language use and linguistic expertise in the creation of their programming. Writers and producers had some sort of postsecondary training in media production, with many producers being literate in their lengua materna. Writers and producers also frequently consulted with the Quechua and Aymara teachers at the local Centro de Idiomas, who also had specialized training in teaching purified and standardized versions of Quechua and Aymara. Because of this, the programs produced by Pachamama in either Quechua or Aymara adhered to ideologized preferences for Indigenous linguistic purity, where the Quechua and Aymara used on the radio avoided Spanish borrowings, and mirrored if not matched varieties that were generally perceived as the ideological standards of Indigenous linguistic purity in the area. The fact that the Quechua and Aymara used at Pachamama was thought to be better than the Quechua and Aymara typically spoken by Indigenous puneños was widely echoed by many of my interlocutors when they learned that I was also spending time studying the linguistic practices at Pachamama Radio. Señora Fidelia, for instance, once commended me when she learned that I was going to spend time doing observations at Pachamama after spending the afternoon at her stall, saying "*Sí, eso es bueno. Allá se habla el quechua y el aymara muy bien*" (Yes, this is good. They speak good Quechua and Aymara there).

In spite of being regarded as promoting the best version of Quechua and Aymara in the region, the radio station's primary aim was not necessarily language revitalization or education. Instead, Pachamama was founded as a journalistic voice to accurately capture, portray, and promote the lives and news and culture of Indigenous communities in the altiplano, for all Indigenous puneños. Because the primary objective was directed toward pan-Indigenous unification and Indigenous political activism, most of the programming was conducted in Spanish, reproducing Spanish's status as the ethnolinguistically neutral language for all Indigenous puneños. Yet because language was still seen as important in the fight for Indigenous autochthony and recognition in the region, creating and producing Indigenous language programming was a task that required special care, requiring the expertise of IEB-trained professionals in the creation of any and all language programming for the radio station. And like other versions of institutional practices in Puno, these programs maintained a separation between Quechua and Aymara language programming, which in turn maintained a separation in Quechua- and Aymara-speaking and -listening publics.

There were two main venues where Indigenous language production occurred. The first were Indigenous language radio programs for each set of ethnolinguistic publics. The Quechua program, *Pacha Illariy*, was reserved for the early morning, airing from 4:30–6:00 a.m. Monday through Friday. The Aymara program, *Markasa Layku*, was reserved for the early evening from 5:00–6:00 p.m. Monday through Friday. The second kind of programming was radio specials that were created to promote pride in Indigenous cultural and linguistic identities in the region. These projects included recordings of Andean folk tales, radio serials that included a dramatization of the famous (local) Indigenous revolutionary Pedro Vilcapaza, and another serial about a semi-fictitious community protesting an exploitative foreign mining company. In addition to airing these programs on the radio, many of these programs would be copied onto CDs that were later given out for free to local village communities when Pachamama reporters would do their interviews or reporting from the field.

Pachamama writers and producers worked carefully to ensure that there was equal linguistic representation for both Quechua and Aymara speakers in the region. However, that equal representation was also seen as necessary, where producers and writers felt that programs written and produced in each Indigenous language communicated information that was only important for that specific set of linguistic publics. For instance, one of the former hosts of *Pacha Illariy*, Gabriela, said that when she planned the shows for the upcoming week, she always thought about current events and people to interview that would be interesting for Quechua speakers and that reflected the values that were most important for them. Such topics included respect for *pachamama* (Mother Earth), respect for the sun and the moon, a love and preference for living out in the country and provincial areas, maintaining traditional religious practices with coca leaves and pago or ritual payments for pachamama and the *apus* (Mountain Deities), maintaining traditional farming and animal husbandry practices like their Inka forebears, and speaking the Quechua language and maintaining Quechua folkloric traditions.

Except for speaking Quechua, maintaining Quechua folkloric traditions, and the direct connection between Quechua speakers and their Inkaic past, I mentioned to Gabriela that similar values were also raised in my conversations with the hosts and producers for *Markasa Layku*, who, like her, also labeled these values as important Aymara values. Gabriela considered my observation and noted that while the values could superficially appear very similar, they were similarities in name only. She went on to stress that the way Quechua speakers value pachamama, nature, and traditional practices was still different from how Aymara speakers practice and understand these values. These differences were there because Quechua and Aymara speakers were ultimately different people, with different histories and relationships to the region. But they were also different because the way they spoke was radically different from each other. My conversations with the writers and producers of *Markasa Layku* also echoed many of the same things that Gabriela mentioned. They all noted that while Quechuas and Aymaras may talk about the same things, or privilege similar values, the specific ways that they spoke about these features of Aymara culture and worldview were fundamentally different than how a Quechua speaker might discursively represent these topics. These differences made having a separate Aymara-language program necessary because that was the only way to make these concepts and ideas understandable for Aymaras. As Roberto, an Aymara speaker and producer, once put it to me, "the *cosmovisión* for Aymaras is different than Quechuas."[7]

Scholars of Indigenous radio practices across the Andes have noted the different ways that Indigenous language use cultivates a broader listening public that also aligns with a broader imagined Indigenous national collective. In his analysis of Quechua language practices on Radio Quispillaccta in Ayacucho, Joshua Tucker argues that using Quechua on the radio's program plays a large role in both developing a Quechua-listening public while introducing the language of indigeneity to listeners from the community, performing what he calls "a calculated linguistic enactment of the Indigenous corporate identity"

(Tucker 2019, 150). Similarly, Gabriela Zamorano Villareal (2017) highlights how Indigenous media practices have been important in both implementing Evo Morales's new Constitution for the Plurinational State of Bolivia as well as empowering diverse Indigenous communities across Bolivia to push the government for their own various political demands. Similarly, Pachamama Radio's entire philosophy and reason for being was to both teach and develop a renewed idea and commitment toward Indigenous identities and an Andean indigeneity among all of their listeners. But the success of this kind of political education relied on communicating those lessons in the appropriate medium such that they made sense and resonated with their puneño listening public. In other words, successfully promoting a general sense of Indigenous identity for puneño listeners could only happen if listeners first actively identified as ethnic Indigenous Quechuas and Aymaras, a connection that can only be fostered through having Quechua or Aymara as one's heritage Indigenous language. As such, making Indigenous language programming only in one Indigenous language was absolutely necessary to both reach their target publics and effectively communicate the language of Indigenous identity to each set of listeners. With the exception of the Andean folktales collection, which recorded the same stories in both languages, the idea that each language was suited to communicate a specific message that resonated only with one set of speakers influenced how each Indigenous language was assigned to one radio special or another. The *Pedro Vilcapaza* radio serial, for instance, was only recorded in Quechua because of the hero's background and roots with Quechua-speaking communities. The serial about the miners' protest on the other hand was only produced in Aymara. When I asked Roberto why both programs were not made in both languages, he responded that the decision to make a program in one language or another depended on whether the given program would better serve the listening needs of Quechua or Aymara speakers. The content of the program had to match the corresponding ideology and broader worldview for each group of speakers and their language. *Pedro Vilcapaza* had to be done in Quechua because the storyline was supposed to awaken the ideology of what it means to be a "Quechua" for Quechua speakers. The story about the miners resisting the exploitation of a foreign mining company in Aymara was a story that spoke specifically to the character and political commitments of Aymara speakers and communities.

The rationalization provided by writers and program producers at Pachamama Radio echoed similar dominant discourses about ethnolinguistic difference in the region; that Quechua and Aymara are not only different grammatical structures and languages, but also correspond to distinct ethnolinguistic speaking and listening publics who differ in their ideological worldviews. Language choice was not merely for referential purposes, but also had larger social and political commitments at stake, which was to develop and awaken the consciousness of Indigenous communities across the altiplano. Yet per these metalinguistic comments, such an awakening and development could only occur along ethnolinguistic lines, thus separating listeners according to their distinct ethnolinguistic publics.

Hyper-Difference in Sharing Sound Spaces

For one short period of time, Pachamama experimented with the possibility of creating programming that featured both Quechua and Aymara simultaneously to bridge the divide between their Quechua- and Aymara-listening publics. However, finding ways to facilitate bilingual Indigenous-language programming had to be done carefully given the longer histories of having Indigenous-language programming in only one language, and the general sentiment that programming conducted in each Indigenous language only served the ideological needs of one ethnolinguistic group and listening public. Introducing these moments of shared ethnolinguistic listening publics had to happen slowly, often through the insertion of momentary "spots," or small segments of another Indigenous language, in ways that did not appear too intrusive or clash with the flow and content of the overall text. These inserted texts created a heteroglossic weaving of voices from different lenguas maternas and were done carefully to highlight some shared aspects of Quechua and Aymara cultural worldviews in spite of linguistic differences. This kind of insertion to highlight a potential site of linguistic and political commensurability first came with the inclusion of Aymara in the opening music for the Quechua radio program *Pacha Illariy*.

[Example 16]
Introduction to *Pacha Illariy*
1. [Andean music playing in the background]

2. [in man's voice] <u>Kawsachun llaqtanchiskuna</u>!
   Long live the villages of the people!

3. [in woman's voice] *Jallalla Aymaramarka*!
   Long live the Aymara nation!

4. [response from bigger crowd] *Jallalla*!
   Long live!

5. [narrated in man's voice] <u>Ñawpaq watakunaqa allunchispi</u>,
   In the times before, in the communities [ayllus],

6. <u>allin kawsaymi mast'arikurqan</u>.
   a good life was extended to all.

7. <u>Chayrayku puku-pukuq takininwan kuska chayarimunqa qamkunapaq</u>,
   Because together with the song of the puku-puku bird we bring to you,

8. [said with many voices] <u>Pacha Illariy</u>!
   Pacha Illariy!

9. [in man's voice] <u>Pachamama! Rimanawasiq sunquchamantapacha</u>!
   Pachamama! We speak to you from the heart!

10. [in woman's voice] <u>Pacha Illariy</u>.
    Pacha Illariy.

Here the inclusion of Aymara structurally mirrors the Quechua lines that precede it by using the language to lay claim to a corresponding Indigenous ethnolinguistic nation. Although the first lines of the opening music do not make any explicit mention of a Quechua ethnolinguistic nation, the use of Quechua in these two lines is meant to represent and refer to all Quechua-speaking peoples, who together constitute a singular, pan-Quechua-speaking ethnolinguistic nation. The inserted Aymara phrases perform the same pragmatic function by making an explicit reference to the Aymara ethnolinguistic nation in the Aymara language. Yet such inserted edits of placing another Indigenous language within the same radio space was not evenly distributed, as was noted by the continued lack of any use of Quechua or acknowledgement of a Quechua ethnolinguistic nation in the opening to the Aymara program, *Markasa Layku*. The opening for *Markasa Layku* reflects the program's longstanding commitment to the idea that the Aymara language contains sentiments, perspectives, and worldviews that can only be understood by Aymara speakers.

[Example 17]
Introduction to *Markasa Layku*
1. [In man's voice] *Jallalla Aymaramarka!*
   Long live the Aymara Nation!

2. [response from bigger crowd] *Jallalla!*
   Long live!

3. [in woman's voice] *Aymaranakaxa kakanakasqamwa chulqiptnwa.*
   Us Aymaras are strong and resilient like the gray hairs on our heads.

4. *Aymaranakaxa kañiwa ukhama willt'ata jani tukusiriptanwa.*
   Us Aymaras are like the *cañihua*[8] plant, which once planted never dies or ends.

5. [in man's voice] Pachamama Radio, *chuyumapa taypipacha*
   From the heart of Pachamama Radio

6. *ist'anisiphtawa Markas(a) Layku.*
   you are listening to Markasa Layku.

7. [in woman's voice] *Aruskipaphañani jach'ay Aymaramarkasa*
   We speak so that our great Aymara nation

8. *nayraru sartaña pataki*
   can advance forward

9. [in man's voice] *Markas(a) Layku!*
   For our nation/peoples!

From 2015 to 2017, producers at Pachamama Radio decided to experiment with having Quechua and Aymara simultaneously featured on a single program. To accomplish this, they decided to feature their sole trilingual producer, Walter Escobar. As the son of a cross-linguistic marriage between an Aymara-speaking father and Quechua-speaking mother, Walter grew up primarily speaking Aymara at home with both his mother and father. But growing up, Walter's mother would also frequently return to her natal, Quechua-speaking community, located on the Capachica peninsula. She took Walter and his siblings on these trips, and through this experience they learned to speak Quechua from interacting with their maternal grandparents. His trilingual upbringing of speaking Aymara at home and Quechua with his maternal grandparents helped develop his interest in Indigenous-language education and the possibility of using both lenguas maternas for mass media broadcasting.

Yet being multilingual does not mean that creating a bilingual, Quechua-Aymara program is a simple process. And despite Walter's linguistic abilities, he alongside other producers encountered different challenges in the process of creating a truly bilingual, pan-Indigenous, Quechua-Aymara linguistic space. The first attempt came in the form of a very short series of four-to-six-minute news announcements that were aired once in the morning and once in the evening. Titled *Willakuykuna-Yatiyawinaka*, these short news segments would present two to three stories of the previous day's news narrated in both Quechua and Aymara. While this was a bilingual show, the structure of these short news announcements was around a pattern of deliberate switches between Quechua and Aymara, thus signaling to listeners a switch in language and listening publics.

[Example 18]
From *Willakuykuna-Yatiyawinaka*, July 8, 2015
1. [enter music]

2. [male voice] En Pachamama Radio
   On Pachamama Radio

3. [female voice] <u>Willakuykuna</u>! *Yatiyawinaka*!
   Willakuykuna! Yatiyawinaka!

4. [male voice] Uniendo los pueblos originarios de Abya Yala!⁹
   Uniting the original communities of Abya Yala!

5. [music changes to Andean flutes and harps]

6. <u>Sumaq punchay yachun munasqay waqiy-panaykuna</u>!
   Good day those my brothers and sisters who are listening!

7. <u>Kaykunamin Willakuykuna</u>!
   This is Willakuykuna!

8. <u>Qhari yachachiqllata yuyarinchis</u> "Dia del Maestro" <u>nispa</u>,
   For the male teachers let us remember to wish them "Happy Teachers' Day"

9. <u>Yuyariyananchista warmi yachachiqta</u> "Dia de la Maestra" <u>nispa</u>.
   And for the women teachers let us also wish them "Happy Teachers' Day"

10. <u>Niyananchista chay soqta p'unchaypi</u>.
    And we say it on this the sixth day.

11. <u>Manan chayta ninchischu qhari warmi yurarisqa kanan</u>.
    And not only for the male teachers but for the female teachers as well [we wish them all].

12. <u>Hinaspapis mana chay p'unchay kunallachu yuyarinanchis</u>.
    And not only on this day will we remember [to honor them].

13. <u>Mana hinataq sapa p'unchay yuyarinanchis</u>,
    And also not on only one day, but on every day we will remember [to honor],

14. <u>yachachaqninchiskunata nispa hamut'ari waqiynchis yachachiq</u>
    Electorio Aguilar.
    our teachers, just like what our brother and teacher Electorio Aguilar says.

15. *Chachax yatichirinakiwa ampt'atasphkixa* "Dia del Maestro" *sasina*.
    For the male teacher we remember to say "Happy day of the teacher."

16. *Ampt'asaphjarakiñasawa warmi yatichirita* "Dia de la Maestra" *sasina*.
    And we also remember to wish to the women teachers "Happy day of the teacher."

17. *Arsusiphayani ukuru suqtaw (a)ruma.*
    And we say it on this sixth day.

18. *Janipi ukhax(a) amt'utakitixa.*
    Which should not be forgotten.

19. *Chachawarmiwa amtutayapaxa ukhatsa sap(a) uruwa ampt'usiphayasaxa.*
    We [instead] must remember [to honor] all of our male and female teachers like this.

20. *Janiwa ukurukikiti yatichanakanxa ur(u)paxa.*
    And not only on one day but [honor] our teachers every day.

21. *Amuyt'aniwa jilata yatichiri* Electorio Aguilar.
    [As is said] by our brother and teacher Electorio Aguilar.

[Followed by sound bite of interview with Electorio Aguilar in Spanish]

The clean divide between Quechua and Aymara spoken segments made *Willakuykuna-Yatiyawinaka* an example of multilingual programming through "coexisting monolingualisms" (Jaffe 2007). Even though *Willakuykuna-Yatiyawinaka* was technically a bilingual show, each code was clearly separated, sometimes with a musical interlude, which indicated a clear switch for listeners who might be expecting one language or another. Additionally, each part of the Quechua or Aymara segments also conformed to ideals of Indigenous linguistic purity, exemplifying the highest perceived standards of each language. Thus, in each change, Walter not only switched between Quechua and Aymara but also performed the ideal monolingual for each language.

Presenting Indigenous-language multilingualism as coexisting monolingualisms soon became the dominant structure for other Quechua-Aymara programming on the station. After starting *Willakuykuna-Yatiyawinaka*, the director of Pachamama decided to try to introduce some Quechua on *Markasa Layku* by bringing in a Quechua speaker named Nancy, who was once one of the hosts on *Pacha Illariy*. Together, Nancy and Walter would share the interactive space with Modesto Palomino, the senior and longtime Aymara-speaking cohost on *Markasa Layku*, making the formerly Aymara-language radio show a multilingual program that could reach all Indigenous-language communities, Quechua and Aymara speaking alike, across the altiplano. In this format, Nancy and Modesto represented the idealized monolingual for their respective Indigenous languages, with Walter serving as the interactional mediator between the two.

Yet unlike *Willakuykuna-Yatiayawinaka*, balancing the switching, transitions, and time on air between Quechua-speaking content covered by Nancy and Aymara talking points covered by Modesto was more of a challenge since these transitions were happening in real time. This was even more challenging because neither Nancy's discussions nor Modesto's discussions in their portions would be translated into the other language, thus causing breaks in listening continuity on what had otherwise been a long-standing, Aymara-language radio show. This made balancing the transitions between Quechua and Aymara on the show a complicated, interactional act.

Take for instance the following segment from the first few minutes of the program from 2016. For that particular episode, Nancy took the lead to greet her listening public. Once she was done with her opening greeting and pleasantries, she then turned to Walter, who acknowledged the completion of her turn by addressing her as *panay* Nancy or "sister Nancy" and then proceeded to speak in Aymara, marking a broader switch between Quechua and Aymara portions of the show.

[Example 19]

1. Nancy: Ahina kay kushan na(ña)ñaykuna-turaykuna.
   That is how things are my sisters and brothers.

2. Ahhh turachay Walter! Allinch'isillaykuy? Imanaylla?
   Ahhhh my brother Walter! Good afternoon? How are you?

3. Walter: Jallami panay Nancy! *Kunjamas siphtasa munata jilatanaka kullakanaka?*
   That is right sister Nancy! How are you all my beloved brothers and sisters?

4. *Arunt'asjaphañani.*
   We greet you.

Walter continued his segment in Aymara, and eventually turned the floor over to Modesto, who also continued the Aymara portion of the show until he ended his turn. This meant that it was now Walter's turn to lead the conversation. Walter responded by acknowledging in Aymara the end of Modesto's turn and then switched to speaking Quechua, which also changed his interlocutor from Modesto to Nancy, and signaled a switch in listening publics on the show.

[Example 20]
1. Modesto: *Yati . . . yathjaphtaw, ist'asirinakaphtaw akiri wakichawi,*
    You know . . . you all already know that you are listening to this program,

2. *Markas(a) Layku! Jilata* Walter!
    Markasa Layku (About the [Aymara] people)! Brother Walter!

3. Walter: *Ukhamaw munata marakachirinaka*—hina(m)pas,
    That is it my beloved people—like this,

4. ahh . . . ñapakusunchis llapan runa masinchiskunata,
    ahh . . . we greet all people/neighbors,

5. llapan llaqta masinchiskunata,
    all our village neighbors,

6. llapan waynakunata, llapan sipaskunata.
    and all the young men and women.

Such switching between Quechua and Aymara portions within the same program reinforced both the boundedness of Quechua and Aymara ethnolinguistic publics as well as the incommensurability between them. Yet those boundaries were defined not only by a change in language but also by certain untranslatable differences that make each language and its linguistic practices unique and distinct. One area of communicative distinction that reinforced these differences could be found in the use of sibling kin terms. The use of sibling kin terms in greetings and forms of address is a common practice among those who are involved in Indigenous politics in the region, and it is used to signal solidarity between Indigenous individuals, indexing closeness and equality instead of hierarchy and social distance. Although many Indigenous puneños will generally use the Spanish terms *"hermano"* and *"hermana,"* the choice to use kin terms from an Indigenous language often reflects the speaker's full commitment to Indigenous political projects within the region. In Aymara, the terms behave similar to English or Spanish kin terms, where the terms for brother and sister are the same regardless of the gendered identity of the speaker and are only determined by the gender of the addressee.

Aymara kin terms:
jilata: brother
kullaka: sister

Quechua kin terms, on the other hand, are based on the gendered identity of both the addressee and the speaker. As such, there are four possible sibling kin terms that delineate different gendered combinations of speaker and addressee.

Quechua kin terms:
wayqi: male to male sibling pair
pana: male to female sibling pair
tura: female to male sibling pair
ñaña: female to female sibling pair

This difference in sibling kin terms in the flow of conversation marks one major site of translingual incommensurability between Quechua and Aymara, where gender in that moment becomes an important variable in defining the relationship between the participants present or referred to in each utterance. This also means that between the languages, there is no commensurate translation for the words "brother" or "sister." This lack of commensurability in the pragmatics of kin term usage reinforces the boundaries between linguistic communities and listening publics. And when used in public media, such as the interactions between individuals on a radio program, the selective deployment of these kin terms by the various hosts maintains the separation between the various listening publics engaging with the program. This kind of pragmatic work, for instance, can be seen below, taken from another episode of *Markasa Layku*.

[Example 21]
1. Nancy: <u>Ahina kay kushan—(ña)ñaykuna turaykuna</u>.
    That is how things are my sisters and brothers.

2. <u>Ahhh turachay</u> Walter! <u>Allinch'isillaykuy? Imanaylla?</u>
    Ahhhh my brother Walter! Are you well? How are you?

3. Walter: <u>Jallami panay</u> Nancy! *Kunjamas siphtasa munata jilatanaka kullakanaka?*
    That is right sister Nancy! How are you all my beloved brothers and sisters?

4. *Arunt'asjaphañani.*
    We greet you.

In this segment, Nancy is speaking in Quechua, while Walter is speaking in Aymara. And, within each of their turns, each speaker is also addressing a wider listening public, addressing their listeners as brothers and sisters. However, Nancy's way of addressing her brother and sisters who are listening to the show does not map neatly onto the same group of brothers and sisters that Walter is addressing in Aymara. This comes from the fact that Nancy's use of *ñañay* and *turay* is based on her own positionality as a female Quechua speaker, not only invoking a Quechua listening public but also establishing a specific relationship between her Quechua-speaking audience and herself. A similar type of effect emerges from *jilatanaka* and *kullakanaka*, where invoking the Aymara sibling terms in Aymara at that moment creates a listening space that is directed specifically for the Aymara-listening public, reaffirming the boundaries between Quechua and Aymara communities and nations throughout the region.

More interesting, however, are the linguistic decisions that Walter makes when addressing Nancy. When Walter takes over his turn, he switches his language to Aymara. Yet even within the stream of talk in Aymara, Walter acknowledges Nancy in Quechua with the interactionally appropriate kin term "*panay*." By doing this, Walter reinforces Nancy's position as a Quechua woman—one who has a specific relationship to him as a Quechua sister and therefore must be addressed as such. But by knowing how to use the correct term, Walter also positions himself as a Quechua speaker and someone who could also claim legitimate membership within the broader Quechua ethnolinguistic community.

Knowing how to correctly use each kin term also becomes another way that transitions between Quechua and Aymara segments are managed. Each kin term both signals a switch in attention for listening publics and serves as a form of interactional footing (Agha 2005; Goffman 1981) to establish oneself or another person as a member of a particular ethnolinguistic public and nation. Take, for example, the following turn-taking between Walter, Nancy, and Modesto from another episode of *Markasa Layku*. The topic at that moment was the cold front that had settled in the altiplano at the start of winter and cautioning people to take care of themselves and their animals to prevent getting sick. Walter introduced the topic first in Aymara, and then proceeded to talk about the same topic in Quechua. Nearing the end of his turn to speak, Walter signaled the switch into Aymara by addressing Modesto as *jilata* Modesto.

[Example 22]
1. Walter: Chayrayku, nuqanchis mana unqunanchispaq—
 And for that reason, we should not get sick—

2. kikin wawakunaman—
 the same for children as well—

3. Hinallataq kikin—kuraq runa masinchiskunaman
 And like this as well—for our older neighbors

4. qankunaqa—qhawarinkichis nispa nisunchis.
 for you all—pay attention and notify someone [if you are sick].

5. Ehh ... *jilata* Modesto ... *Masuruthpacha janilacha* ...
 Ehh ... brother Modesto ... from yesterday, correct ...

6. Modesto: *Jani jawichas untaskax—*
 [And] I won't even see my grandmother—

7. Walter: = *Jani jawichas untaskampi* =
 = Won't be seeing (your) grandmother =

8. Modesto: = [laughing] *Janiwa jilata* =
 = No brother =

9.   *Anu usuntallaxa wakisirikit—*
               [And] it's not good that the dogs are getting sick—

Through saying "*jilata* Modesto," Walter not only switches to Aymara but also establishes Modesto's membership within a broader Aymara public along with himself. Once Modesto finished, Walter once more picked up the responsibility of transitioning from Aymara to Quechua, opening the interactional space for Nancy to speak. This transition was marked by him addressing Nancy using the correct kin term of "*panachay* Nancy," to which she responds using the correct kin term of "*turachay* Walter."

[**Example 23**]
1. Walter: *Ukhamaw jilata-kullakanaka.* Panachay Nancy—
   And that is how it is brothers and sisters. Sister Nancy—

2. Nancy: = Ahinapuni chiqaqa =
   = And it's the same always =

3. Walter: = Allinraqchu kashan =
   = Are you not well =

4. Nancy: = allinraq kashani—allinraq allinraq =
   = I am good—good, good =

5.   Imaraykuchus anchaytapuni—
           For this reason always—

6.   Qan nishanki hinapas turachay Walter kay—
           Just as you said Brother Walter this—

7.   Ehh . . . qurahampi unukunata u(hay) hakusunchis.
           Ehh . . . we are going to take medicinal teas.

In carefully using the linguistically correct kin terms for both Modesto and Nancy, Walter reinforces the differences in the roles between his two cohosts and the populations that they are representing. Not using *kullaka* for Nancy or *wayqiy* for Modesto signals how Nancy and Modesto belong to two separate and distinctive linguistic communities. The fact that Walter and his multilingual proficiency is mediating the interaction also places Walter in the unique position as the ideal multilingual.

Instead of being read as a hybrid Quechua-Aymara figure, Walter in his performance upholds the divide between Quechua and Aymara as completely separate codes. This performance also presents Walter as the perfect multilingual puneño through his embodied fluency of Quechua, Aymara, and Spanish as bounded, discrete, linguistic codes.

Having Quechua and Aymara on the air at the same time was a short-lived experiment at Pachamama. Its end was precipitated by Nancy taking another job to produce her own Quechua radio show in Cusco. Soon after her departure from Pachamama, Walter was also offered a job to lead the new Aymara-based news program *Jiwasanaka* on the national television channel, TVPerú. Both their departures ended any continued effort for Quechua-Aymara programming on *Markasa Layku* or any other similar program on Pachamama Radio. Nevertheless, this short stint also elicited strong reactions from listeners and other producers at Pachamama, who had opinions about including another Indigenous language on any of the Indigenous-language shows.

One such response came from one of the episodes where Nancy and Walter were absent, leaving Modesto in charge of conducting the program. That day, Modesto and his guest were talking about the significance of *Markasa Layku* and the importance the show had for Aymara-speaking communities. In this discussion, Modesto exclaimed that *Markasa Layku* was first and foremost designed for the Aymara nation. During this show, I was sitting with Roberto, listening with him in his producer's booth. When Modesto made that comment, I asked Roberto if he agreed with Modesto's comment. He agreed, noting that while there were good intentions behind bringing Nancy to speak Quechua on *Markasa Layku*, having Nancy on the show detracted from the main purpose of the program. For Roberto, having Quechua on the show *"no alcanza bien,"* or does not go well, with Aymara because the language, speaking practices, and associated values and worldviews for Quechua speakers are ultimately different from those of Aymara speakers. In this comment, linguistic differences between Quechua and Aymara went deeper than the differences between their grammatical structures. Both languages had to be kept separate because they each communicated a specific set of values and worldviews that only made sense to their respective speakers. Quechua and Aymara, therefore, do not go well together on a single show. Yet this also means that Quechua- and Aymara-speaking and listening publics do not mesh together as well, with any attempt to include the two creating an acoustic, cultural, and cognitive dissonance.

From the Altiplano to the Nation: Extending the Boundaries of Indigenous Language Use

Within the realm of Indigenous language maintenance, revitalization, and reclamation, there are several reasons why institutions are seen as important social actors for such projects. Institutions often have financial resources to back these projects and the ability to scale them for larger audiences and demographics. Institutions and their associated practices also lend an air of legitimacy and expertise, two qualities that are often sought after with the hope of bolstering the visibility, importance, and authenticity of Indigenous and minority voices. Lastly, institutions do not exist by themselves, but instead within a broader political network. Their situatedness within such networks ensures their visibility and lends additional authority to the work they do, especially if the other institutional bodies associated with this work are connected with the state or other establishments of prestige and power.

The presence and increasing dominance of institutionally sanctioned and privileged versions of Quechua and Aymara within Puno are the result of a combination of these factors. Some, like Pachamama Radio and *Los Andes*, are independent organizations that are not connected to any governmental body. Others, like IEB-funded programs at schools, are backed by the state at the regional and national level. But as institutions they all work in similar ways by setting the standards for Indigenous language use and regimenting those standards and other kinds of differences. For all three cases discussed in this chapter, the regimentation of Indigenous-language use and communicative practices was embedded within a larger ideological and discursive project around mobilizing the language of ethnolinguistic difference as the primary form of inter-Indigenous differentiation in the region. Such practices shift the conversation around Indigenous identity away from localized and place-derived ways of reckoning inter-Indigenous difference and toward unifying and essentializing the differences between Quechua and Aymara speakers through their shared language and linguistic heritage. But the stakes of these kinds of practices, and the work that institutions do to accomplish these goals, do not end with introducing a new sense of ethnolinguistic membership among Quechua- and Aymara-speaking puneños. Like other Indigenous groups, Quechuas and Aymaras are also members within stateless nations—communities that for Quechua- and Aymara-speaking puneños are neither recognized by the Peruvian state nor confined to the boundaries within the nation.[10] Instead, developing and circulating the language of indigeneity, and with it the political awareness that comes from identifying as an Indigenous individual within a larger corporate ethnic Indigenous community, are necessary acts in the overall politicization of indigeneity for other rights and forms of recognition (Postero 2017). Having puneños see themselves as Quechuas and Aymaras is not only for cultural pride; these new forms of social and political alignment are also critical in the fight to address the wrongdoings that have affected these communities, whether they be the historical denial of Indigenous languages and linguistic practices or the right to protect and control natural resources, from water to mining.

Institutionalized Indigenous linguistic practices become the vehicle to promote this kind of discursive awareness of Indigenous membership within otherwise stateless Quechua and Aymara nations (Swinehart and Graber 2012). But these institutionalized linguistic practices can also contradict, transform, and obscure other ways of being an Indigenous language speaker and individual that are also important to Quechua- and Aymara-speaking communities across Puno. Because processes of ethnolinguistic differentiation are often accompanied with synchronous processes of social and linguistic purification, institutions introduce new kinds of boundaries that often challenge other ways of understanding and scaling these differences. The promotion and relative prestige of institutionally backed linguistic practices also contributes to the devaluation of everyday Quechua and Aymara communicative and interactive practices such that these modes of engaging with and across Quechua and Aymara's linguistic boundaries do not conform to preferred bounded and purified ways of speaking both languages and performing a Quechua or Aymara ethnic Indigenous identity. Through this, institutions and their linguistic practices set new linguistic and cultural standards for the region for Quechua and Aymara as languages and ethnic identities, shaping conversations and discursive practices in how inter-Indigenous identity should be managed. These ideologized discourses shift the focus away from kinship-based modes of recognizing difference and delegitimize the place and function of other forms of linguistic and social boundary crossing. And in some institutional practices, gender differences that include the creation of specific female figures become important symbolic actors in establishing what language use should look like in this new ideological landscape of inter-Indigenous language contact and social difference in the region.

CHAPTER 4

Mythical Mothers and the Reinvention of Indigenous Contact

Every year on November 5, puneños of all ages gather on the shores of Lake Titicaca in the predawn hours, bundled with their warmest blankets, food, and pocket change in hopes of reserving a prime location and unobstructed view. When the first few families arrive, it is still dark outside, the only light emanating from the streetlights that automatically dim as the sunlight begins to creep over the horizon. The air smells a bit smoky—the remnants of small wood-burning fires that are still used in urban homes within the regional capital. Vendors soon line the streets, claiming specific areas on the sidewalks and the main avenue where they will sell food, drinks, and other items to the slowly gathering crowds, while also hoping to not miss out on the approaching festivities and spectacle. The first vendors who arrive are those selling breakfast fare for the early risers: pushcarts carrying empanadas, *salteñas*, and warm cereal beverages made of quinoa, *cañiwa*, and maca mixed with milk and sugar. As the morning progresses, these vendors give way to those selling *chicharrón, ceviche, choclo con queso,* and *lomo saltado con chuño y queso frito*,[1] and others selling wide-brimmed hats, visors, and umbrellas to provide the necessary shade cover from Puno's high-desert sun that reaches its highest intensity by the middle of the day.

As the early dawn transitions into the morning, the crowds multiply, with families gathering together and filling in the sidewalks of the avenues that connect the main boardwalk on Lake Titicaca's marina to Puno's central soccer pitch and stadium. As the air gets warmer, the smell begins to change—it is a long-running joke among puneños that Lake Titicaca is the *desague* (sewer) for Puno, which becomes less funny as the daytime sun continues to warm the water and all the unwanted contents lying at the bottom of the lake by the city. Children and teenagers, already enjoying the day off from school, eagerly wait for the start of the main event. Some impatiently hope to fill the time by buying snacks and treats from the various vendors, needling their parents to buy them ice creams, *raspadillas*, fried chicken with french fries, or other kinds of street food delicacies that they would otherwise never be allowed to eat at home.

Finally, well past the middle of the morning, the anxious and restless crowd begins to settle, staring off into the lake. In the quiet distance drums can be heard. Soon after, small silhouettes of boats appear, with the drums and sounds of a conch shell getting louder and more audible with each passing moment. Members of the crowd carefully jostle each other to get a better glimpse of the boats that are coming from the direction of the Uros—the floating islands made of *totora* reeds in Lake Titicaca. Small children climb atop the shoulders of family members, describing everything that they see to their older family members below. In the meantime, the sound of drums and Andean flutes become more audible. With each moment, as the musical notes become clearer, families and individuals who have waited by the docks since the morning's wee hours get ready to finally witness the long-anticipated event.

Within minutes of hearing the loud music, three large boats made of totora reeds arrive at the docks at the main wharf in Lake Titicaca. The music of Andean panpipes and drums cue hundreds of local puneño middle-school- and high-school-age students, dressed in popularized Inka attire, to get in their formations and begin dancing. As the students line up around the docks and dance to the music, a young couple—a husband-and-wife pair—slowly disembark the largest of the three totora boats (figure 8) onto the shores to be received by a *yatiri*, a local shaman and Andean priest. As they disembark the boat and meet with the yatiri, the crowd, a multigenerational, multilingual, and multiethnic group, lets out a loud cheer. After hours of waiting, they are now celebrating their first glimpse of the arrival of Manqu Qhapaq and Mama Uqllu—the mythical founding couple of Puno, the altiplano, and the Inka empire.

FIGURE 8 The arrival of Manqu Qhapaq and Mama Uqllu. Credit: Sandhya Krittika Narayanan (author).

In this chapter, I analyze the annual reenactment of the arrival of the mythical couple, Manqu Qhapaq and Mama Uqllu, performed and celebrated every year on the anniversary of the founding of the city of Puno. Based on the origin myth for the founding of Indigenous civilization in the altiplano, the annual reenactment of the arrival of Manqu Qhapaq and Mama Uqllu publicly celebrates the Indigenous roots of the region, centering Puno as an Indigenous space through ritual performance. In this way, the ritualized performance of the arrival and celebration of Manqu Qhapaq and Mama Uqllu is a kind of invented tradition (Hobsbawm and Ranger 1983) that today is part of the calendar of festivals and celebrations that define the cultural and historical heritage of Puno and the altiplano. Yet unlike other kinds of celebrations in the city or region, which either attend to the cultural practices of present-day communities, commemorate specific historic events, or venerate specific religious icons, the celebration of Manqu Qhapaq and Mama Uqllu celebrates the mythical, deep historic past of Puno. Through this annual celebration, which culminates in the reenactment of the arrival of the mythical couple, puneños not only celebrate and promote the mythical origins of their region but also cement these mythologies in relation to a specific view of Indigenous cultural and linguistic continuity from the deep mythical past into the present. Such a reformulation is also gendered, where the origin and continuity of Indigenous linguistic and cultural diversity is refracted onto the gender differences embodied by the mythical couple. Such a process not only creates an additional layer of significance for puneños but also reproduces gendered norms and expectations from these mythologized discourses, recentering particular views of women as mothers and wives in the founding and perpetuation of linguistic difference and inter-Indigenous diversity in the region and across the Andes.

Indigenous Authenticity, Language, and Folkloric Reinvention

Ritualistic plays have a long history in the Andes, tracing back to pre-Columbian traditions where ritualistic play acting was staged on certain feast days for religious purposes (Cadena 2000; Mannheim 1984; Mendoza 2000). These practices, like other forms of Indigenous religious and cultural expression, were suppressed after the Spanish conquest and were regarded as subversive to Catholic doctrine. By the end of the eighteenth century, aspects of ritualistic play were taken up by Spanish criollos and mestizos to celebrate and folkloricize pre-Hispanic Andean heritage and cultivate their own distinct identity as Andean elites. Such practices were revived once more at the turn of the twentieth century, almost a century after Peru declared its independence in 1821 (Cadena 2000).[2] It was during this time that a new modern, intellectual, and nationalistic sensibility emerged across various Latin American republics from Mexico to Bolivia (Kuenzli 2013). These efforts redefined the national character, heritage, culture, and racio-ethnic roots through appropriating and refashioning Indigenous practices, languages, and pre-Hispanic identities. In Peru, these practices were realized through the activities of early twentieth-century *cusqueño* elites, who sought to valorize pre-Hispanic, Inkaic traditions in order to elevate the prominence and influence of Andean elite culture and society in creating a unique Peruvian national identity (Cadena 1998, 2000). As such, the *indigenismo* and *neoindige-*

nismo movements of the early to mid-twentieth century initiated a period of artistic, creative, intellectual, and political expression that was centered on highlighting and celebrating a specific form of Indigenous identity, culture, and linguistic practices as part of the national heritage and cultural bedrock of Peru.[3] Within these social movements, ritual play and performance once again emerged as a central tenet of celebrating and promoting the significance of Indigenous, Inkaic culture and history in the founding of the nation and in cementing the image of the Inka as a symbol of Peru.

Ritual plays around Indigenous themes continue today and are often prominently featured in materials produced by PromPerú, the promotional arm of the national Ministry of Tourism. The most famous of these is the Inti Raymi celebration in Cusco, performed every June after the winter solstice (June 21st). The performance's form and structure still hearken back to its origins as a reinvented practice created by criollo and mestizo elites from Cusco in the early twentieth century. Yet the elevation of such performances also reconfigured a new set of relationships between race, indigeneity, and language as part of a broader national project around mestizaje (Wade 2016), reformulating racial and ethnic mixture in relation to a longer process of acculturation toward European cultural and linguistic practices. In this view, racial and ethnic mixture, which constitutes a mestizo or "mixed" identity, becomes the default racial category of national belonging and citizenship, and the racio-ethnic benchmark that justifies the exclusion and denial of equal treatment for populations who are interpreted to have not fully embraced the signs and lifestyles associated with the default racio-ethnic category (Canessa 2012b). For Indigenous populations and communities in the Andean highlands, therefore, the denial of a mestizo identity and racialization of indigeneity in everyday interactions is based not only on whether the individual speaks an Indigenous language, but also on their dress, the foods that they eat, and if they continue to live in rural areas (Huayhua 2014).

Although mestizaje in some ways rejects the continued maintenance of signs of indigeneity, the elevation and privileging of the racial category is also based on specific kinds of pre-Hispanic Indigenous histories and heritages, which together form a pre-Hispanic link that creates a kind of continuity between the nation and its Indigenous past. During the indigenismo and neoindigenismo movements, redefining mestizo identity as the national identity of Peru was enacted through selectively celebrating Inka cultural traditions, practices, and histories. As the last great empire of the Andes prior to the Spanish conquest, the Inka empire was already valued within national discourses and rhetoric as laying the foundation for subsequent processes of Europeanization and modernization that accompanied the Spanish conquest, and later, the Wars of Independence (Mendez 1996). Thus, in Peru, the interest and reinvention of Indigenous cultural practices was focused on the legacy of the Inkas, discursively positioning them as the predecessors and forebears of the modern mestizo nation. But this selective valorization and reinvention of Inkaic history as part of Peru's national narrative did not extend to contemporary Indigenous communities or forms of Indigenous identity and expression. As a result, modern-day Indigenous populations and their practices were excluded from discourses of *mestizaje*, perpetuating ongoing forms of racialization and discrimination.

This focus on the Inka throughout the varied history of Indigenous cultural revival and reinvention also had linguistic consequences. As Mannheim (1984, 1992) noted, the first wave of this cultural revival and interest in pre-Hispanic Indigenous culture in the late seventeenth century through the mid-eighteenth century was accompanied by a renewed interest in Indigenous linguistic practices. As such, cusqueño elites during the late colonial period ushered in a Quechua literary renaissance. Yet this Quechua was a highly stylized, syncretic variety of the language that was largely influenced through the overlay of Spanish discursive and rhetorical structures.[4] This restructured form of Quechua eventually came to be known as *Qapaq Simi* (lit. "high tongue") and was the variety used by cusqueño elites during the late colonial period to mythologize and dramatize the lives of the Inka ruling family and nobility in plays like *Ollantay*. Though public celebrations for Qapaq Simi would eventually fall out of favor following the Tupac Amaru II uprising in the late eighteenth century, the highly stylized linguistic register would be re-adopted by early twentieth-century indigenistas in Cusco. As Marisol de la Cadena (2000) notes, the revalorization of Qapaq Simi in public celebration of Inkaic history and in intellectual discussions on the language, culture, and traditions of the pre-Hispanic past all contributed to the preferential celebration of linguistic and cultural practices that were ideologized as representative of a pre-contact past associated with Inka nobility and elites. Together, these histories ensured that Qapaq Simi, a Spanish-inflected variety of Quechua, would become the only acceptable version of Quechua. In addition to initiating the reinvention of Inka traditions, the indigenismo movements of the early twentieth century also saw the creation of the High Academy of Quechua in Cusco to study and promote the use of Qapaq Simi.

Such linguistic reformulations continue to shape the kinds of ideological interpretations and expectations surrounding Indigenous language use and indigeneity in the Andes (Coronel-Molina 2008). Like the elevation of the Inka as the legitimate Indigenous heritage within the nation, the elevation of a Qapaq Simi Quechua enabled the continued marginalization of contemporary Indigenous populations and their ways of speaking. This applies not only to other Quechua-speaking communities across the Andes but also to other Andean Indigenous communities, such as Aymara-speaking communities, whose linguistic and cultural identity are excluded from the mystique and image of the Inka. Kuenzli (2013) describes this challenge in relation to the first attempts to valorize Indigenous heritage in early twentieth-century Bolivia, where liberal politicians who wanted to advocate for greater Indigenous rights were confronted with the challenge of how to present Indigenous, and especially Aymara, histories and traditional practices as compatible with emerging ideas around Bolivia's national identity at the time. Despite the successes that accompanied the discovery of the archaeological ruins of Tiwanaku outside of La Paz, which became a symbol of Bolivia's Indigenous heritage and greatness that predated the arrival of the Inca from Peru, public sentiment did not accept the legitimacy nor contributions of Aymara communities in the highlands following their involvement in the civil war of 1899. Reframing the indigeneity of Aymara communities thus as something in the distant past that was first transformed through Inka conquest, and later Spanish colonialism, became a way to reposition the legitimacy of highland Indigenous communities as part of Bolivia's national narrative. To support these efforts, Liberal Party activists went to Indigenous highland Aymara-speaking communities outside of La Paz to teach them how to speak Quechua in order to stage plays depicting curated Inka histories in the region. In these plays, Aymara-speaking community members were also tasked with inhabiting the role of Inkas, producing performances that revised the history of local communities as having been at one point associated with the glory and acceptable indigeneity of the Inka empire and civilization. In addition to obscuring local linguistic traditions and cultural histories, these plays and other related activities reinforced ideas of a legitimate Indigenous identity and citizenship within Bolivia as being associated with the Quechua-linguistic practices of the Inka. The similarities between these projects and the activities pursued by the indigenistas of the early twentieth century in Peru demonstrate how to this day, legitimate performances of indigeneity that do not conflict with or challenge narratives of the nation-state are rooted within the mythology surrounding the Inka and the valorization of Quechua linguistic practices that are specifically associated with a distinct and ancient pre-contact past.

This legacy of reinvented Indigenous traditions by indigenista and neoindigenista intellectuals, however, also continues to exist as an ideological and political double-edged sword for Indigenous communities across the Andes. On the one hand, the historical elevation and promotion of Inkaic cultural traditions and a specific form of Quechua has a marginalizing effect that erases other forms of Indigenous linguistic and cultural heritage and diversity. At the same time, the invention and popularization of such projects also provides the space for Indigenous communities to negotiate some form of recognition and political legitimacy. For instance, despite having their own cultural and linguistic differences marginalized by participating in Quechua-language ritualistic plays, Kuenzli (2013) also notes that participation in these performances provided Indigenous Aymara-speaking communities in the highlands surrounding La Paz the opportunity to claim their own legitimate citizenship in relation to the state.

Ritual play and public performance of Indigenous histories therefore are an uneven landscape, still enmeshed in the paradoxes that have both enabled and limited the kinds of performances that occur, and are rooted in a neocolonial acceptance of certain kinds of Indigenous expression that place specific social constraints on how Indigenous communities choose to participate in performing and promoting their own unique

Indigenous cultural identities and histories. The annual reenactment of the arrival of Manqu Qhapaq and Mama Uqllu is caught in this same set of tensions. As a public, ritual performance, its popularity in the region emerged from settler-colonial practices that have reinvented local Indigenous Andean traditions in the altiplano. Yet the performance, and the ways in which it has been reformulated, provide Indigenous puneños the space to also establish the cultural and linguistic legacies of their region in ways that are legible to non-puneños within Peru and abroad.

From an Origin Story to the Origins of an Empire: Reinventing a Myth and the Place of the Altiplano

In the altiplano and Puno, the dominant myth that explains the origin of humanity and civilization is the story of the arrival of Manqu Qhapaq and Mama Uqllu. According to the most common telling of the myth, this brother-sister, husband-wife pair were born out of the waters of Lake Titicaca as the "son of the Sun" and the "daughter of the Moon." Together they arrived on the shores of Lake Titicaca and from there traveled north toward more fertile lands to found the capital for their future grand empire and civilization. However, prior to moving northward, the couple first civilized the peoples living around Lake Titicaca and across the altiplano. In discussing the myth with Señor Abelardo, he told me that before the arrival of Manqu Qhapaq and Mama Uqllu, the people of the region were not human and were feral, closer to animals. Their deities helped turn them into "people" by teaching them how to live according to honoring the earth, the cosmos, and setting up a good society.

This emphasis is telling, in that part of the myth involves each member of the mythical pair initiating and introducing practices that are foundational to Andean notions of personhood and kinship. Manqu Qhapaq, for instance, is said to have introduced agriculture and animal domestication. Mama Uqllu is said to have introduced the art of cultivating crops as well as the art of spinning, dyeing, and weaving animal fibers, such as the wool from alpacas and vicuñas. Together, they both introduced to the people the practice of venerating celestial bodies like the sun and the moon and instilling the practice of reciprocity with pachamama (Mother

Earth) and the apus (mountain deities). Although the mythical pair were not the first humans to arrive to the altiplano, they were certainly the first people who helped the other first humans become runa or jaqi, real humans and people, by engaging in practices that constitute Indigenous personhood.

Knowing these particulars within the origin myth becomes more significant in relation to the contexts in which the myth is invoked. Traditionally, the reenactment of the myth is part of a longer tradition of ritualistic play that has been practiced by communities that bordered the shores of Lake Titicaca. Many older puneños in their seventies and eighties, such as my neighbors and the elderly parents of my friends and acquaintances who grew up in communities that bordered the shores of Lake Titicaca, would still remember how their community leaders would stage the arrival of the mythical pair as an annual celebration for that community. One notable example was recounted to me by an elderly puneño, the father of one of the women who worked in Mercado de San Ignacio, who came from a community outside of Juli, located on the southern shores of Lake Titicaca. He mentioned that when he was a child, the annual reenactment was a much simpler event that began with choosing two young adults from the community to play the mythical pair. Everyone in the community would wake up before sunrise to witness the performance in the tidal inlets of the lake. A local yatiri would welcome the crowd and announce the arrival of the mythical couple and commemorate the event with an alpaca sacrifice that would be offered to pachamama. The rest of the alpaca would then be cooked and distributed to everyone present as part of a communal feast. Yet during this time, many forms of Indigenous celebrations were sanctioned by the church and local authorities, requiring these celebrations to be conducted in a much simpler and clandestine manner.

In spite of the secrecy associated with the play, the celebration of the mythical pair's arrival was traditionally celebrated within the first couple of weeks of November, which coincides with the start of the planting season. The correlation between the arrival of the mythical couple and fertility and productivity is mentioned in the original myth, where Manqu Qhapaq is credited for introducing agriculture to the humans of the altiplano. In these smaller, older celebrations, part of the ritual performance includes a ceremonial first breaking of the earth with a traditional Andean hoe, completed by Manqu Qhapaq. This is followed by Mama Uqllu planting a seed and sprinkling some of the water from Lake Titicaca over it to make it grow. Because of this, the myth was part of a larger ritual that celebrated the first planting for the year along with commemorating the mythical couple who introduced these practices to the altiplano.

During my time in Puno, I was told about various communities that continued to host this kind of celebration as a small, community-centered ritual and celebration to mark the start of the planting season. However, such celebrations were overshadowed by the larger reenactment and celebration that was staged on November 5 each year in the center of Puno. While the smaller, community-centered celebrations celebrate the cycle of reproduction and fertility, the November 5 celebrations showcase the extent to which the celebration has undergone different layers of revision. The significance of the date is that November 5 is celebrated as the anniversary of the founding of Puno in the late sixteenth century. Unlike the grassroots celebrations that were conducted by local communities, the November 5 reenactment is managed, promoted, and controlled by the Federación de Foklór (Federation of Folklore) in Puno—the primary institutional arm that manages the production and promotion of all things "folkloric," Indigenous, or traditional for the entire Department of Puno. Like the resurgence of other Indigenous ritual plays in the Andes, the decision to celebrate the founding of Puno with the reenactment of Manqu Qhapaq and Mama Uqllu was not made by local Indigenous leaders, but instead by a small group of puneño elites who were still living in the region in the 1960s, establishing a new relationship between the traditional Indigenous origin story of the altiplano with the colonial founding of the city.[5]

Because of this legacy, the myth's ending has also been modified to describe the final destination of the mythical couple, stating that when they moved up north, they specifically moved to the fertile valleys of the Sacred Valley, eventually founding the city of Cusco and the Inka empire. In this revision, Manqu Qhapaq becomes the first Inka, with Mama Uqllu becoming the first *Quya* or queen consort. But by making this change, the revised myth positions the altiplano as an important region in the founding of the Inka empire, and in establishing an Andean pre-Hispanic civilization. Such a revision underscores the significance of the altiplano in the development of humanity and human civilization in the region, elevating Puno's otherwise peripheral status to being historically and culturally on par with Cusco's cultural achievements. This revised significance is often articulated in the promotion of the founding myth and the reenactment that it inspires through the placement of markers throughout the city that highlight the historic and cultural heritage of Puno. For instance, in the neighborhoods located just above the Plaza de Armas is a statue of Manqu Qhapaq pointing north toward Cusco, with a sign indicating that he was the first Inka located at its base. Additionally, there is a sidewalk mosaic on one of the main tourist streets in the center of the city, bearing the caption *Cuna del Imperio Inka* (Cradle of the Inka Empire). Together, these markers serve as material reminders that reinforce the mythical origin of the Inka empire as having first come from the altiplano.

Inventing the Gendered Origins of Linguistic Diversity in the Altiplano

Since the early 1980s, the Federación de Foklór has come to be primarily run by first- and second-generation Quechua- and Aymara-speaking migrants. Because of this, the Federación is regarded as one institutional arm that works directly with rural, Quechua- and Aymara-speaking communities, with the aim of promoting Puno, both as a city and a region, as a place that is rooted in Indigenous multilingualism and multiethnic diversity. Since this time, and through the interest of stakeholders who have closer connections with Quechua- and Aymara-speaking kin and communities, the original myth of Manqu Qhapaq and Mama Uqllu underwent another revision. Unlike the kinds of cultural revisions inspired by earlier indigenista movements of the twentieth century, which sought to position contemporary mestizo society as the natural heirs of the Inka, this revision instead reflected and projected backward in time the origins of Indigenous linguistic and cultural diversity in the region. With this, the myth was once more revised as a way to draw attention to Puno's identity as a linguistic and inter-Indigenous ethnic meeting point.

Yet this latest revision that encompassed the origins of linguistic diversity and difference in the region was also a gendered one, producing a new mythologized origin of linguistic difference that aligned each present-day Indigenous language with each member of the mythical couple. Manqu Qhapaq, being the first Inka, was also recast as the first Quechua speaker, where through him and his descendants in the Inka empire, Quechua spread throughout the Andes. Mama Uqllu is portrayed as the first Aymara speaker, where to this day, many puneños will reverently refer to her as the "mother of all Aymaras." It is through her, and a specific line of her descendants, that Aymara was first introduced into the region, where it remained primarily in the altiplano. Through this narrative revision, then, Quechua and Aymara as languages and distinct populations of speakers originated in Puno and the altiplano. And, because Aymara speakers were descendants of Mama Uqllu, she became a particularly significant public figure for Quechuas and Aymaras alike across Puno. So much so that of the two characters, Mama Uqllu became the figure that puneños attending the annual reenactment and following the festivities and hype for the annual celebration paid more attention to when determining if the annual reenactment was a success.

These revisions that reconnect the basic myth to Indigenous linguistic and cultural diversity in the region have also contributed to restructuring the staging of the annual reenactments and shaping audience expectations and evaluation of the performance. As the first Inka and first Quechua speaker, Manqu Qhapaq is expected to perform his speech in Quechua, and ideally the most pristine version of Quechua that might represent a pre-contact variety that is absent of any influence with Spanish or Aymara. As the mother of all Aymaras, Mama Uqllu is also expected to speak perfect Aymara, and within her speech, reflect the original Aymara that is free of contact or influence from both Spanish and Quechua. These expectations of authenticity were also coupled with expectations and idealizations of phenotypic racialized features that each figure was meant to embody. Both Manqu Qhapaq and Mama Uqllu were expected to appear like the most perfect forms of an original Andean Indigenous individual, whose phenotypic features have not been corrupted through the sexual encounters and sexualized histories brought on by colonialism. This meant that both members of the mythical pair had to have dark coppertone skin, with long black hair and sturdy build. Manqu Qhapaq had to be tall and muscular. Mama Uqllu had to be sturdily built and reflect the fact that she was created to withstand the harsh climate of the altiplano and the physical labor demands associated with agriculture and herding animals. As one of my puneña friends told me, "Mama Uqllu needs to know the feeling of dirt under her nails," a statement that recognizes not only Mama Uqllu's symbolic role in fertility and productivity but also the significance and importance of Indigenous women doing physical labor and contributing equally to the survival and sustainability of the Andean family and society.

Searches for actors to play each role since the '80s have largely focused on finding individuals who fit these linguistic and phenotypical attributes. Yet in my time speaking with former Federación employees, former and current actors, and everyday puneños, it soon became clear that of the two characters, most of the excitement and curiosity was primarily reserved for the individual chosen to play Mama Uqllu. For the role of Manqu Qhapaq, the expectations associated with the actor seemed fairly simple. Most puneños and organizers I spoke with seemed content as long as the individual actor met the basic linguistic and physical requirements and expectations of the mythical figure. If the individual chosen to play the leading male role also had extensive acting experience, that was an additional bonus. But the choice for Mama Uqllu came with a few extra requirements that covered not only her linguistic background and look but also moral qualities and characteristics. This meant that the actress chosen to play Mama Uqllu had to speak perfect Aymara, have the physical qualities expected of the founding mother and demigoddess, and represent the ideal Indigenous Andean woman and the ideal Indigenous wife. In sum, Mama Uqllu had to embody and represent the authentic Indigenous woman, which included being free of vices, being a symbol of purity and chastity, and being able to perform and communicate her love and pride for the traditional lifeways of the altiplano. As one of my neighbors in Chucuito, a three-time former Mama Uqllu in the early 1990s, told me, "Being Mama Uqllu means being known as the perfect puneña."

Even within the performance, Mama Uqllu also seemed to capture more of the audience's interest and scrutiny. Right at the beginning of the performance, when the mythical couple steps out of the lake and boards a cart that carries them to the central stadium, Mama Uqllu is expected to carry an item in her hands. Whatever she holds is then taken as a sign for the fortunes for the upcoming year. If she holds potatoes in her basket during her procession, it means that everyone would receive a good harvest for the year. Corn symbolizes wealth and money. And a basket full of coca leaves represented good health. This interest in Mama Uqllu and her relevance and importance for the altiplano would also continue into her speech. For instance, memories of past Mama Uqllu speeches recall her talking about loving the land, taking care of the environment, and exhorting puneños to never lose sight of who they are as puneños and to never forget their love for Puno, the altiplano, and the region's Indigenous cultural and linguistic roots and identity. Such messages are often contrasted by Manqu Qhapaq's speeches, which have typically focused on maintaining traditional values and relationships with the world, and the importance of a good, fair government that he as the first Inka, and his descendants, will establish.

Scaling the Myth: From the Altiplano to the World

Although the arrival of Manqu Qhapaq and Mama Uqllu is a highly visible public event, it is nevertheless one that is mostly attended by local puneños. Compared to similar versions of public displays of indigeneity, such as the Inti Raymi celebrations in Cusco, the reenactment in Puno has neither the size nor the scale of what has become a globally recognized event and tourist attraction. Because of the relative success of the Inti Raymi celebrations in boosting tourism in Cusco and the Sacred Valley, many of the associates of the Federación felt that the annual reenactment and celebrations for the anniversary of Puno should strive to be a larger event in an attempt to draw a similar international tourist crowd. This, in turn, might elevate Puno's visibility as a tourist destination and as the premier cultural and folkloric hub in the nation. In order to achieve this scale in visibility, in 2015 the Federación decided to bring non-local actors who had more national recognition and would have a stronger platform to promote the event. This was largely done by hiring and giving much of the creative and directorial control to the Cusco-based actor named Nivardo, who was already recognized as playing the Inka in the Inti Raymi celebrations in Cusco. The choice to hire him also meant that the selection of Mama Uqllu was also drawn from a pool of more nationally recognized actresses, who would have the clout to help elevate the event in the region. But this choice also opened the possibility of not selecting a local woman to play the titular mythical mother. This turned out to be the case with Nivardo as the creative director for the event, where every year the list of potential actresses to play the founding mother of the region and the mother of all Aymaras were primarily non-Aymara-speaking, and potentially non-Indigenous actresses from Lima.

The choice to incorporate nonlocal actors and perspectives into the production of the reenactment of Manqu Qhapaq and Mama Uqllu was met with mixed responses. While some puneños that I spoke with, ranging from my neighbors to friends who worked in the markets and in the tourist industry, were unhappy that Manqu Qhapaq was not from Puno, others felt that Nivardo's cusqueño roots made him an appropriate outside choice. Having a non-puneña play Mama Uqllu was also received with a lot of skepticism, where many of these same friends and acquaintances expressed a concern that only an Aymara-speaking puneña who was born and bred in Puno and in the altiplano could truly capture the essence of the mythical mother. Regardless of these varying conversations, the introduction, performance, and reception of these nonlocal performers as the mythical founding couple in the region reflected diverse competing perspectives on Indigenous language use and inter-Indigenous difference in the region. Moreover, the differences between the actual performances and the ways in which each performance was evaluated also refracted how gender differences, and in particular perceptions around the role and portrayal of Indigenous women, play out in the mythical staging of linguistic diversity and inter-Indigenous difference in Puno and across the Andes.

Reframing Quechua as the Language of the Inkas

As the main male protagonist playing Manqu Qhapaq, Nivardo was expected to perform his role as the first Inka by speaking only in Quechua. As someone who had played the role of the Inka emperor in the annual

Inti Raymi celebrations, he was more than familiar with the process of embodying the persona of a mythical, Inkaic leader, and performing his role in Quechua. But because of this background, and his roots in Cusco, he also performed his role using a variety of Quechua that was largely inaccessible to most Quechua-speaking puneños. While performing this kind of Quechua technically met the expectations of what Manqu Qhapaq should sound like, the structure and tone of his speeches and performance further distinguished it as linguistically outside of the altiplano. This distancing not only reaffirmed Nivardo's performance as the authentic standard of what Quechua should sound like according to many of the Quechua-speaking puneños I knew, but also established a new kind of benchmark for the kind of Quechua that should always be used in such public performances.

Building on his clout and reputation, Nivardo's speeches ultimately recreated what is now considered to be part of the standard repertoire of Inka emperor speeches—a genre that was not established by Indigenous Quechua-speaking individuals, but rather invented by criollo and mestizo indigenist elites and intellectuals who framed Indigenous ways and pre-Hispanic perspectives around romanticized visions of the Inka empire. These elements are evident in Manqu Qhapaq's main speech in 2016 addressing his puneño public, which features ideologized elements of Indigenous Andean cosmology, such as venerating the apus and pachamama, and a reminder to never forget the sacredness embedded within the land and landscape.

[Example 24]
Manqu Qhapaq's 2016 Speech
1. Apukuna, wawa(n)kuna!
   To the Apus, and their children!

2. Inkakunaq yupaychanan.
   Those venerated by the Inkas.

3. Mama Quyawan kushka
   With my queen, Mama Quya

4. hamaut'awan—
   (and) with this learned man—

5. kay hatun ayllumanta,
   from this grand place,

6. Qullasuyu ayllumanta.
   from Qullasuyu.

7. Mamallay!
   My mother! [to Pachamama]

8. Allinchayki—
   I salute you—

9. Llaqtaykiman chay hamusqayku chay may(q)manta.
   We have come to your province from far away.

10. qhawarinitaq simuyuyuta.
    and I see a land with the leaves of the quinoa plant.

11. Hinaqtinmi
    In this manner

12. Pachamama riqch'ari(n)
    Pachamama will begin to wake up

13. Mama Quchataq
    and the Mother Lake (Titicaca)

14. sunqunchispi tiya(n).
    will live in our own hearts.

15. Kushkataq
    And together

16. qhawanayuqkuspa!
    we will watch and care for one another!

17. Kay willka aylluman chayamuyku.
    To this sacred land we have come.

18. Wawaykuna!
    My children!

19. Qallarichun
    Begin

20. hatun q'uchurikuy!
    a great celebration of joy!

Similar themes are found in Nivardo's reprisal in the role of Manqu Qhapaq the following year, which included additional elements that are widely seen as mainstream signs of Indigenous Andean authenticity, such as the spiritual importance of coca leaves, and that the sources of strength for all Andean peoples are rooted in the maintenance and adherence to Indigenous lifeways and connections with the apus, pachamama, and the spiritual and medicinal properties of the coca leaf plant.

[Example 25]
Manqu Qhapaq's 2017 Speech
1. Willka Mama Coca
   Sacred Mama Coca

2. Apukuna yupaychanan
   The venerated Apus

3. Inkakuna quyawan,
   with the Queen of the Inkas,

4. Qanmi kanki
   You are

5. Runakuna kallpan.
   the force of the people.

6. Runakuna yuyaymi
   The knowledge of the people

7. Amapuni hayk'aqpas chinkaychu.
   Never ever will you all lose this yourself.

8. Qullasuyumarka mantapacha
   From this land of Qullasuyu

9. Tiqsimuyun uyarichun.
   That the entire world hears this.

10. <u>Kawsayninchista</u>
    Of our way of life

11. <u>Kay willka Cocapaq</u>
    For which this coca leaf is sacred as well

12. <u>Llamillarichun sapanqa chakrapi</u>
    it will begin to grow and flower in each field

13. <u>Uywanchiskunataq mirarichun</u>
    that with our spirits it will reproduce itself

14. <u>Runakunataq</u>
    and the people

15. <u>Sumataq q'ancharichun sapa p'unchaw.</u>
    that with each day they begin to become more resplendent.

16. <u>Willkaq Mama Coca</u>
    Sacred Mama Coca

17. <u>Amapuni hayk'aqpas ch'inkaychu.</u>
    that you never lose.

18. <u>Runakunaq kallpan</u>
    the strength of the people

19. <u>Inkaykunaq yupaychanan</u>
    venerated by the Inkas

20. <u>Mamalla</u>
    only you my Mother

21. *Jallalla Punumarka!*
    Hail the province of Puno!

22. *Jallalla Qullasuyumarka!*
    Hail the province of Qullasuyu!

Per the standard ideologized expectations, Nivardo's Quechua in both his speeches did not contain any Spanish or Aymara, with the exception of "*Jallalla Punumarka! Jallalla Qullasuyumarka!*," performed as a gesture to acknowledge the Aymara-speaking presence in the audience and region. But Nivardo's Quechua performance also meets a growing awareness that a performance containing good and proper Quechua is also achieved through incorporating elements that are now the cornerstone of a hyper-purist form of Quechua that is promoted in language educational institutions and associated with Cusco as the epicenter of Quechua cultural and linguistic authority.

One primary way that Nivardo performs this hyper-purism is through the use of calqued lexical items so as to avoid the use of a Spanish lexical alternative. This can be seen in the following line, where Nivardo uses the calqued word *hamaut'a* to refer to a ritual priest.

(Manqu Qhapaq's 2016 Speech, Lines 3–4)
Mama Quyawan kushka **hamaut'awan**—
With my queen, Mama Quya (and) with this **learned man**—

In the context of the performance, Nivardo was explicitly referring to the presence and importance of the ritual priest. Normally across the altiplano, ritual priests are either referred to as *chamán* (shaman), or *yatiri*. While both words are used by Quechua and Aymara speakers, yatiri is of Aymara origin and primarily used by Aymara speakers. Chamán is of neither Quechua nor Aymara origin, yet it is used by speakers of both backgrounds to also refer to a ritualistic priest. The choice to use *hamaut'a*, a word of Quechua origin that historically refers to the kind of role that priests occupied in pre-Hispanic Andean society, avoids the kinds of ideological threats to linguistic purism that the other two more commonly used phrases might present. Yet in the process, the choice to use hamaut'a also presented Quechua-speaking audience members with a word that they may not be familiar with at all, enhancing the distancing effect of Nivardo's assumed persona and elevating the performance as something close to what an authentic, pre-contact Inka and pre-contact Quechua speaker might have spoken like.

These kinds of hyper-purist choices were present throughout both of Nivardo's speeches in 2016 and 2017 (table 1) and are part of a longer legacy of purification practices associated with colonial-era translations of Quechua (Durston 2007) and with language purification practices associated with the High Academy of Quechua in Cusco (Coronel-Molina 2008). This linguistic "purism" also carries into the discursive and poetic features present across Nivardo's speeches for both years, which also enhance the social and temporal distance between Nivardo's embodiment of Manqu Qhapaq and the everyday puneños he is addressing. These discursive features include repetition (i.e., repeatedly addressing *Willka Mama Coca*), parallelism (i.e., *Runakuna kallpan, Runakuna yuyaymi*, "or the strength of the people, the knowledge of the people"), and direct affirmative repetition (i.e., *Qanmi kanki*, or "you, you are"). Such purisms are also found in more subtle aspects of the morphology of Quechua, which enhance the poetic and discursive effects of his speech.

One frequent example of using a morpheme that otherwise would not be commonly found in puneño Quechua is the verbal morpheme *-chu* (table 2). When added to the verbal root, it gives the meaning of an authoritative directive, with the implication of having a kind of social force that will be realized and achieved by the intended addressee. Typically, Quechua-speaking puneños do not use *-chu* to communicate a directive. Often, this use of *-chu* implies that there is a significant social difference between addresser and addressee to be able to wield the social force to compel another person to accomplish that act. Directives in puneño Quechua are socially dependent and can only felicitously be used by individuals in positions of higher respect, such as directives between parents and children. However, directives of this nature tend to remain in the infinitive form of the verb. For instance, it is common to hear Quechua-speaking puneño parents instructing their children to come to them using the infinitive verb "*hamuy*" (to come or "come"). In the contexts that I heard parents use the directive morpheme *-chu*, its use often connoted a sense of urgency or importance, or it was used to pragmatically convey a warning associated with the directed action being requested. For instance, if the child did not immediately perform the directed task, such as come at their parent's initial directive ("hamuy"), then the parent would repeat the directive with the addition of the *-chu*, which metapragmatically commands the child to immediately tend to what their parent was asking them to do, or else. Nivardo's use of *-chu*, therefore, is marked when compared to how Quechua-speaking puneños perform these directives in their day-to-day interactions. But, when

TABLE 1 Lexical Purisms in Manqu Qhapaq's Speeches

Speech Year	Line Number	Purist Lexical Item Used	Meaning/Gloss
2016	2	yupaychanan	"The venerated"
2016	8	allinchayki	"I salute you"
2017	32	llamillarichun	"Begin to flower/ bloom (directive)"
2017	35	q'ancharichun	"Be resplendent (directive)"

TABLE 2 Directives in Manqu Qhapaq's Speeches

Speech Year	Line Number	Lexical Item	Meaning/Gloss
2016	19	qallari**chun**	"Begin"
2017	29	uyari**chun**	"Listen"
2017	32	llamillari**chun**	"Begin to flower or bloom"
2017	33	mirari**chun**	"Begin to reproduce (animals)"
2017	35	q'anchari**chun**	"Begin being resplendent"

considered within the discursive space of an official speech made by the Inka, Nivardo's use of *-chu* reinforces the believability of him voicing the role of the first Inka, while also reproducing romanticized notions of Inkaic regal power. In this sense, the use of *-chu* is received as a felicitous performative and directive that conforms with the reinvented image of Inkaic power and authority. This reception also extends Nivardo's believability as the Inka beyond his Quechua-speaking audience by aligning his performance to nonlocal expectations of how the mythical Inka rulers spoke and behaved.

Although the majority of attendees for the annual reenactment were primarily local puneños, Nivardo's linguistic performance interpolated a broader set of ratified listeners who extended beyond the boundaries and listening expectations of Quechua- and Aymara-speaking puneños. And to a certain degree such a broader audience was present as ratified listeners for his performance. During both the 2016 and 2017 performances, for instance, sections of the central soccer arena included small pockets of European tourists and tourists from neighboring Latin American countries like Chile, Argentina, and Brazil. The central ritual ceremony for the reenactment was also broadcast regionally and on the national television station, TVPerú. In this light, Nivardo's performance did not only have to be acceptable according to local expectations of the Inka. His performance also had to be legible and recognized as adhering to ideologized expectations of Inkaic grandeur and power by a broader audience who have little to no background on the specific details of the significance of the performance within the altiplano. These linguistic choices when reproduced by Quechua-speaking puneños in their everyday interactions might be interpreted as odd, overly formal, unintelligible, or socially infelicitous. But as the embodiment of the first Inka, Nivardo's use of these purist lexical alternatives and implementation of hyper-purified discursive framing devices distinguishes him and his character from a typical Quechua-speaking puneño, elevating the role and social prestige of the titular character, and the Quechua that he speaks.

Regardless of their opinion about hiring a nonlocal Manqu Qhapaq to perform in their local annual tradition, the one aspect that all of my Quechua-speaking interlocutors, and even some of the Aymara-speaking ones, could agree on was that Nivardo's Quechua sounded exactly like what they thought that the Quechua of Inka should sound like. Furthermore, these same interlocutors generally agreed that the Quechua that was spoken in the performance adhered to the basic stipulation for any actor playing the titular male lead—that their Quechua be the most perfect form of the language. Nivardo's Quechua in his speeches maintained the indexical associations between how Manqu Qhapaq should be performed and what he should sound like. The performance, furthermore, set a new standard for audience expectations of what kind of Quechua the actor playing Manqu Qhapaq should use when performing the mythical founding figure of the altiplano. Even though Manqu Qhapaq was the founding figure of the altiplano, his Quechua could not sound like he was from the altiplano.

Yet despite these assertions, it is still important to note that the structure and characteristics of Manqu Qhapaq's performance were originally conceived by non-Indigenous individuals in the altiplano. Manqu Qhapaq, as performed in the reenactment celebrating the founding of Puno, is a reinvented version of a traditional mythical figure that was central to life for smaller, Indigenous communities around Lake Titicaca. His Quechua was not just the Quechua from Cusco but a highly modified one that has, ironically, been shaped and modified by Spanish speakers and Spanish colonial institutions. Regardless of these contradictions, the role of Manqu Qhapaq is not only significant in establishing the origin of the peoples and cultures of the altiplano and connecting the founding of the Inka empire and spread of Quechua with Puno. The role is also a gendered performance, and one that establishes the divisions and expectations associated with Indigenous Andean men. These gendered ideologies become more pronounced in the portrayal and reception of Mama Uqllu, where the indexical associations between language, gender, and Indigenous ethnic identity become sites of controversy and discursive contestation when actresses chosen to play the mythical mother fail to live up to audience expectations and ideologies of Aymara womanhood and Indigenous femininity in the altiplano.

Nonlocal Mama Uqllus and the Challenges of Modeling Ideal Indigenous Femininity

Of the two members of the founding original couple of the altiplano, the characterization and portrayal of Mama Uqllu was accompanied by more scrutiny and more expectations than that of Manqu Qhapaq. These expectations encompassed both her performance as the original and best speaker of Aymara as well as her significance as the original, ideal Indigenous woman of the altiplano. But such assumptions become fraught with the introduction of nonlocal actresses to play Mama Uqllu. The choice to select a nonlocal actress to play Mama Uqllu was largely made by Nivardo as part of his contract to play Manqu Qhapaq and serve as creative director for the event. As a nationally renowned actor, Nivardo was highly connected to various actors, and acting collectives and groups across Peru, with the majority of these organizations being located in Lima. Because of his national reputation, Nivardo decided that as part of his directorial responsibilities that came along with playing the role of Manqu Qhapaq, he would also have full control for selecting the actress to play Mama Uqllu. This resulted in him choosing Lima-based actresses to play the titular female lead for both 2016 and 2017. When I once briefly spoke with him about his decision to select *limeña* actresses to play the role of Mama Uqllu, he justified the decision on the grounds that limeña actresses had the necessary acting training and overall professional seriousness to properly carry out the role. And as actresses based out the national capital, these women would also have some national fame that would elevate the importance of the performance at the national, and potentially international, level.

This latter part was something that members of the Federación de Folklor and other puneños also reflected on when discussing Nivardo's executive decision to select the next Mama Uqllu from a pool of actresses he knew who were primarily born and raised in Lima. These members and officials all noted that having a nonlocal actress play Mama Uqllu detracted from the event and its uniquely puneño roots, in that actresses (and actors) who were from the region and knew the region thus knew how to inhabit the role in a way that both showed their love and pride for the altiplano. However, these same officials also conceded that if the ultimate plan was to elevate the fame and visibility of the annual reenactment so that it achieves the same level of national and international fame that the Inti Raymi celebration enjoys (and a subsequent boost to the local tourist industry), then having a nonlocal Mama Uqllu is probably a necessary component for achieving those goals. This aspect also resonated with younger puneños, like my neighbors' children and grandchildren or the teenage daughters of market vendors, who had some familiarity with actresses chosen to play Mama Uqllu during those years and were excited that a relatively famous actress was coming all the way to Puno to perform in their humble local reenactment. These kinds of comments highlight how collaborating with actors outside of Puno could have the potential to bring more attention to the region, which typically is portrayed as a peripheral high-altitude region. But in doing this, the performance and local ritual risked losing its significance and connection with puneños by also potentially choosing an actress who had no connection to either Puno or the altiplano, nor any knowledge or speaking proficiency in Aymara.

In the end, the fact that both nonlocal actresses did not know how to speak Aymara like a puneña resulted in an onslaught of criticism and backlash against the performance each of those years. Public commentators on local radio stations, including those on Pachamama Radio, for instance, criticized the Federación for their decision to allow actresses with no knowledge of Aymara to even participate in the event, let alone play the founding mother of all Aymaras and mother of the altiplano. Even my casual conversations with friends and acquaintances following the event each year also revealed how dismayed folks were that the Federación could even allow someone who did not know Aymara to step on stage as Mama Uqllu, citing the fact that there were plenty of beautiful and qualified local Aymara-speaking girls with an interest in acting who would have done a much better job of playing the mythical mother. These criticisms were not unfounded. In both 2016 and 2017, the local actor playing the main yatiri in the annual reenactment was tasked with coming up with the basic script for the actresses in Spanish along with Nivardo, which would then be translated into Aymara. This fact is important for two reasons. First, the co-authorship behind Mama Uqllu's main speech and script highlights how outside perspectives, and the ideologized understanding of Andean Indigenous mythologies and folklore, shaped the construction of Mama Uqllu's speech, making it a hybrid text that included the overlay of a non-Indigenous ideologization of pre-Hispanic mythological figures associated with the Inka. This hybridization is also reflected in the translation practices associated with the text, which, after first being written in Spanish, was then translated into Aymara. Thus, not only were the concepts and content contained in Mama Uqllu's speech drawn from non-Indigenous perspectives and influences, but the structure of her text was also framed through the discursive techniques and practices around Spanish. In some ways, this act of translating from Spanish to Aymara was thought to help ensure that Mama Uqllu's speech remained a linguistically pure text. But such translational practices also detracted from the speech's authenticity, ensuring that it would not be legible to local Aymara-speaking puneños.

In addition to co-authoring and translating Mama Uqllu's script, the actor playing the yatiri was also responsible for teaching and coaching each actress in proper pronunciation practices so that her speech would feel authentic and acceptable to all puneños, Aymara and Quechua speakers alike. However, the actresses selected to play the part of

Mama Uqllu only arrived for rehearsals and practices a few days before each performance, leaving only a finite amount of time for each non-Aymara-speaking actress to master and memorize a speech in Aymara and perform it convincingly to meet the listening expectations of her broader puneño audience. It was then seen as only natural by many puneños that these nonlocal, non-Aymara-speaking actresses would make mistakes in their performance and fail to properly capture the essence of Mama Uqllu. This fact was actually expected by many of my interlocutors in the weeks leading up to each performance, who all agreed that there was no possible way for a non-Aymara-speaking actress to perfectly master the Aymara language and embody the role of Mama Uqllu. Much of this came from a broader ideologization that Aymara is a difficult language to speak, and that only a native speaker born and brought up on Aymara soil could ever truly command the language. These kinds of statements were shared not only by my Aymara-speaking friends but also by my Quechua-speaking friends, who likened the difficulty of mastering Aymara pronunciation and phonetics to the difficulties that are associated with speaking English. It came as no surprise then to many of my Aymara-speaking friends, acquaintances, and interlocutors when Mama Uqllu's annual speech not only had egregious mistakes in Aymara but was also sometimes unintelligible. This became an issue when replaying the recording of the event with some of my Aymara-speaking friends who attended the performance with me and noted the difficulty that they had in fully understanding what each actress was trying to say in her expected speech. Translating her speeches, therefore, was a challenging process that ultimately produced a basic interpretation of what might have been the original communicative intention for each actress, becoming an act of interpretive accommodation that more reflected the generosity of my interlocutors for trying to make sense of each speech and less on each actress's ability to adequately convey that message in Aymara.[6] Nonetheless, with the help of my interlocutors like Señor Abelardo and Señora Marcela, we were able to attempt an approximate interpretation and translation of what each Mama Uqllu might have been trying to say in their annual speech.

The first nonlocal Mama Uqllu to be placed under puneños' listening scrutiny was a woman named Estefany, who assumed the role in

2016. Even though she had no roots with the area, she ended up being viewed by many puneños as a moderately believable Mama Uqllu, which stemmed from the fact that she made sure to take a few extra days to meet with Federación officials and get to know the region so that she could properly inhabit her character. Like Manqu Qhapaq's speech, Estefany's 2016 Mama Uqllu speech included themes that are generally recognized as necessary components in reinvented ritual plays depicting pre-Hispanic Andean peoples and folklore.

[Example 26]
Mama Uqllu's 2016 Speech
1. *Chachanaka! Warmichaka!*
   Men! Women!

2. *Nayra pachaq jatunaka*
   From before of those ancient mountains

3. *Jumanakaruwa aynuka awatanxa*
   (that) you all to plow the lands and herd domesticated animals

4. *Pachamama taykasaxa—*
   this earth is our mother—

5. *Jumanakaxa—*
   (For) you all—

6. *wiñay pacha y warmanta*
   a land for eternity and [untranslatable]

7. *Jilat kullakanaka*
   Brothers and sisters

8. *takenisa—*
   all of us—

9. *sarañani*
   we go

10. *kuputaqiru*
    on the proper path

11. *Jawilla, jawilla*⁷—
    [incantation to bring in the good spirits]

12. *Jawilla, jawilla!*
    [incantation to bring in the good spirits]

Included in Estefany's speech were expected themes such as the explicit mention of traditional Andean practices such as love of the land and reverence for Mother Earth. As an Aymara woman from the altiplano, Estefany was also expected to mention her pride in her people and send a message that resonated with Indigenous Aymara-speaking puneños, and Indigenous communities more generally, across the altiplano. However, because Estefany was not an Aymara speaker and did not have enough time to properly learn Aymara in the days leading up to her performance, her speech the day of contained several mistakes that made it difficult for Aymara listeners to fully understand (table 3).

The following year a new Mama Uqllu was selected by the name of Nidia. Like the previous year's actress, Nidia was another nonlocal actress, raised and based in Lima. But unlike Estefany, Nidia had some extended family who still lived on the Quechua-speaking peninsula of Capachica on Lake Titicaca. This extended familial connection signaled to may puneños that Nivardo had taken to heart their concerns from the previous year and sought to find an actress who had some connection to Puno and the altiplano. Even though Nidia's family did not come from an Aymara-speaking province, some direct kin-relationship with Capachica as a region that is located directly on Lake Titicaca meant that she had some basic understanding of the relationship between Mama Uqllu and the lake. And even though Nidia's roots in Puno made aspects of her selection more acceptable for many puneños, her lack of Aymara knowledge exacerbated existing complaints of not finding an appropriate and suitable actress to play the mother of all Aymaras. The biggest source of these complaints came from Nidia's performance, which resulted in a speech that was almost entirely unintelligible to every Aymara speaker present at the performance and those listening to its broadcast that year. As noted in the translations, the majority of her speech posed some difficulties for my Aymara interlocutors like Señor Abelardo and Señora Marcela, who gave their best approximations of what Nidia might have said.

TABLE 3 Errors and Commentaries on Mama Uqllu's Speech

Line Number	Error	Approximate Interpretation of Intended Meaning	Metalinguistic Commentary on Approximate Interpretation
1	Chachanaka! Warmi-**chaka**!	Men! Women!	Should have used the suffixing plural morpheme -*naka*.
3	Jumanakaruwa aynuka awatanxa	(that) you all to plow the lands and herd domesticated animals	More appropriate to say "*jumanakawa aynuqa awatiphtwa.*"
6	wiñay pacha **y warmanta**	a land for eternity and (unintelligible)	Use of the Spanish conjunction "*y*" for "and" is not appropriate. Could not interpret "*warmanta.*"
7	**Jilat** kullakanaka	Brothers and sisters	More appropriate to say "*jilatanaka, kullakanaka.*"
8	ta**k**enisa	all of us	More correct to say "*taqinisa*" with the uvular voiceless stop [q] to match intended meaning.
10	kuputakiru	On the proper path	More correct to say "*kupu thaqiru*" with the voiceless uvular stop [q] and the voiceless aspirated alveolar stop [th] to match the intended meaning.

[Example 27]
Mama Uqllu's 2017 Speech

1. *Uywinakasanxa*
    With the animals

2. *Unata umapa*
    And of the water

3. *Ajayanka*
    The spirits

4. *Umanchawketa—*
    Has taught/showed us—

5. *Thakinakasasa*
   [to] our path

6. *Ika uñan chiriwampi mirapana*
   [untranslatable] That those who will be leading us are watching

7. *mirant'aña*
   and they believe

8. *Ika jaqa uka samxa umaxapa*
   [untranslatable]

9. *Julichaqmaya*
   From Juli

10. [inaudible] —*kama unchjakispi kutipanxa*
    [inaudible] —to return to

11. *Taknakakapis*
    [untranslatable]

12. *Pachamama horakisa,*
    The time of Pachamama,

13. *Halpanamkapa wayrampi chikanchansita*
    With the earth and the wind

14. *Uyspuspa jallaw—*
    [untranslatable]

15. *Takinakama—*
    [untranslatable]

16. *Uñasiañthxa—*
    [untranslatable]

17. *Cholqin choqjañani.*
    To produce potatoes.

18. *Qullasuyumarka,*
    In the Province of Qullasuyu,

19. *Apuqulluna*
    Of the mountain beings

20. *Pawatina*
    [untranslatable]

21. *Paltixskta*
    That is may never be lacking

The process of transcribing and translating the Mama Uqllu speeches performed by both Estefany and Nidia required my Aymara-speaking interlocutors to ultimately guess not only what each actress said in Aymara, but also what they could have possibly intended to mean within the length of their discourse. This process, which often was frustrating for speakers and listeners like Señor Abelardo and Señora Marcela, who were both very quick to declare that neither performance was Aymara at all, was also an insightful ethnographic moment. Their reactions to the process of guessing and accommodating Estefany's and Nidia's speeches reflect their own personal experiences of linguistic accommodation, similar to the kinds of accommodative practices that they encounter when communicating with non-Aymara speakers across Puno. Additionally, the kinds of interpretations that they produced when listening to both speeches, and the conversations with them that ensued, also reflect a broader ideologized consensus of what should be included in a proper Mama Uqllu speech, based on more successful speeches of actresses playing the role in the past. This process of guessing and accommodating any kind of interpretation was slightly easier for Estefany's performance, where, although her manner of delivery and overall content of the speech was odd, Señor Abelardo and Señora Marcela could both somewhat figure out what she might have been trying to say. Doing this exact same process for Nidia's performance, however, proved to be more challenging, where both Señor Abelardo and Señora Marcela felt that there was nothing sensible within her speech.

Overall, puneños, Quechua- and Aymara-speaking alike, were adamant that the performances of both Mama Uqllus fell far below the standards and expectations of what made a good Mama Uqllu. Language was always the primary source of complaints, where the fact that neither actress knew Aymara was already seen as a strike against their authenticity, which devalued their overall performance. Yet it was not simply that neither actress knew Aymara, it was also that in their attempts to perform their speeches they could not get rid of a Spanish-inflected Aymara in their performances, making them sound like Spanish speakers who maintained their Spanish accents while trying to pronounce Aymara words and sentences. For a role that privileged Aymara linguistic purity and authenticity, having the audible influence of Spanish violated the basic expectations of actors portraying and voicing Mama Uqllu. In other words, instead of believably animating what the original Mama Uqllu might have sounded like, both actresses instead sounded like a typical Spanish speaker trying to learn how to speak and perform Aymara for the first time.

These evaluations and reactions to their linguistic performances were also extended to other aspects of the actresses' interpretations and portrayals of Mama Uqllu. Various evaluations provided by many of my friends and acquaintances of both Quechua- and Aymara-speaking backgrounds in the days following the annual reenactment drew attention to the fact that neither actress was able to embody the qualities that defined the ideal Indigenous woman of the altiplano. For instance, several of my friends commented on how both the actresses' performances and interpretations of Mama Uqllu lacked the proper speech qualities and affective stances that were ideologized as defining characteristics of an Aymara woman, and Indigenous women from the altiplano. Typically, Indigenous puneñas are thought to be more forceful, rebellious, and overall much stronger than Indigenous women found in other parts of the Andes. As Señor Abelardo once told me, the women in Puno are *bravas*, a term that not only means "bold" but carries additional connotations of toughness that gives puneña women an independent streak or edge over other Indigenous Andean women, who, when compared to puneñas, are depicted as demure and docile. Of these, Aymara-speaking women are also stereotypically viewed as more resilient than Quechua-speaking women—a view that is shared (for better or worse) by many of the Quechua- and Aymara-speaking market women I came to know. This kind of toughness is often linked to the idea that Aymara-speaking women are tougher businesswomen. But it is also used to rationalize why Aymara-speaking women might appear to be more engaged in activism and politics. Such assertions of toughness, however, are all ideologized indexical associations between the phonetic qualities of Aymara and the qualities that characterize an Aymara speaker, and how those connections contrast against the phonetic properties of Quechua and those indexical linkages with the characteristics and personality differences of Quechua speakers. Quechua, with its tonal modulations and open syllable structure, is often perceived to sound sweeter than Aymara. Yet this sweetness is also extended to Quechua speakers, who are not only seen as sweeter but also milder, quieter, and more obsequious in personality and temperament. When compared to Quechua, Aymara sounds rougher, a perceptual evaluation that is possibly due to phonotactic rules in the language that produce vowel deletions and consonant clusters, which are absent in Quechua.[8] Yet this roughness is then extended to the qualities that define Aymara speakers, who are also positioned as rougher, tougher, and more brava than their Quechua-speaking counterparts.

Although a mythical divine mother, Mama Uqllu was also an Aymara speaker, and the first Aymara-speaking woman of the altiplano. Therefore, it was expected that every actress playing Mama Uqllu captured these core essential qualities of being an Indigenous puneña of the altiplano, and particularly, replicating how contemporary Aymara-speaking women should behave. This means that Mama Uqllu's speech was expected to be performed clearly, where the actress playing the mythic mother was expected to speak to her public directly without any kind of floral or poetic embellishments or without any kind of tonal variation. Similar to how Aymara women are perceived throughout the altiplano, Mama Uqllu is expected to be the model that established the direct, confident, and sometimes blunt ways that Aymara women are thought to, and often prided for, speaking in. This directness is also indexically linked to qualities such as strength and authority. But such strength and authority have to be physically embodied and effectively performed through speaking directly to the crowd in an equally strong, clear, and authoritative voice.

The failings that were then attributed to both performances of Mama Uqllu were not only because neither actress knew Aymara (or even Quechua) but also because they lacked this broader knowledge and understanding of the qualities and core essential features that define ideologized perceptions of Indigenous femininity in the altiplano. This deficiency prevented them from being able to capture the essential qualities that define Indigenous women in Puno, and in particular, establish the difference between Indigenous Aymara-speaking women from Quechua-speaking ones. Of the two, Estefany was generally considered to have performed slightly better because she delivered her speech in a loud and strong voice. During her performance, her body posture was tall and strong, and she maintained a consistent tone for most of her speech, fluctuating only a little bit between high and low tones where changes in her intonation were used for dramatic effect. Conversely, Nidia's performance the following year was regarded as a significantly worse performance because it did not match expectations of how Indigenous Aymara women, or the ideal Indigenous puneña, should present herself in public. In addition to not properly learning Aymara, her performance was interpreted as weak—evaluations that were rooted in the fact that her speech was marred with long pauses placed awkwardly in the middle of phrases. Her voice quality was also problematic; she frequently modulated her voice that often could only be heard as an inaudible hush or whisper at the end of each phrase, qualities that were the antithesis of speaking with confidence and authority. Instead of speaking with a clear voice, her voice wavered, exacerbating perceptions that her voice, and performance, was soft and weak. And while she was addressing her audience, her body was bent, and her head pointed down toward the ground, eventually kneeling on the ground in a submissive position, providing additional evidence to support critiquing her performance as being weak and inappropriate for Mama Uqllu. These performative choices all contradicted expectations of how a queen and wife of the Inka should behave. But they also violated basic qualities that are recognized characteristics of Indigenous puneña women.

For many of my friends and acquaintances, as well as several disappointed comments from audience members who sat next to me during Nidia's performance in 2017, the portrayal of Mama Uqllu was seen as weak and submissive—two qualities that no one in Puno would ever associate with an Indigenous Aymara puneña. While Nidia spoke, I heard loud complaints from those sitting around me, heckling her by saying, "*No escucha*" (Can't hear you), and loudly commenting among themselves that Nidia's voice was too soft for the role, and that she misrepresented the character of Aymara women, and Indigenous women of the altiplano more generally. Yet these critiques relating to the weak linguistic performance of Nidia (and to a lesser degree Estefany) were also extended outward to their physical appearance, which also became another strike against both actresses and bolstered the general perception that both actresses were weak, ineffective, and ultimately poor choices to represent puneña women and Mama Uqllu. As professional actresses based in Lima, both women were slim and light skinned. Though discourses around the racialization of colorism is not always as extensively discussed in Puno or Peru as in other places in Latin America such as Brazil (Roth-Gordon 2017), lighter complexion and thinner builds are prized physical qualities associated with an ideal femininity, racializing the ideal woman in Peru as a non-Indigenous, non-Afro-Peruvian mestiza. These standards contradict with how dark skin and, more importantly, bigger and muscular bodies are valued among Indigenous communities. As Andrew Canessa (2012a) notes, body fat and having an abundance of these bodily substances not only is a sign of health but also reflects a capacity to work and signals the overall strength and wellness of the individual.

Estefany and Nidia, as slim and fair-complexioned Lima-based actresses, embody the physical qualities and racialized expectations of mestizaje, conforming to idealized standards of femininity within the nation. Yet in Puno and the high Andes, their bodies become a site of racial contention, unearthing long-held practices of marginalization that targeted and racialized not only Indigenous linguistic practices but also Indigenous female bodies. Not having these physical attributes was interpreted by my Quechua- and Aymara-speaking friends to reflect the fact that neither actress (nor the version of Mama Uqllu they were representing) had the necessary physical experience or preparation to engage in manual labor associated with farming, herding, and bearing and raising children in the high Andes. Instead, both Estefany's and Nidia's slim figures made their weakness more apparent and were sometimes even the butt of jokes that also reinforced how inappropriate both female choices were to portray and represent Indigenous women of the altiplano. This was especially true for Madelina, one of my Aymara-speaking friends. An older Aymara-speaking woman from the province of Moho with a sharp wit and sharper tongue if you crossed her, she enjoyed making jokes at the expense of both actresses in the days and weeks following the performance. After the 2016 performance, she commented that the Mama Uqllu was so thin that she has cooked and eaten *tallarin* (linguine) that was thicker and heavier. Similarly, after the 2017 performance, she joked that the Mama Uqllu chosen was so small that all it would take was one small and gentle breeze from Lake Titicaca to blow her off the totora boat—a joke she animated while blowing a small coca leaf off the palm of her hand.

Not being able to speak Aymara is only part of a larger critique that was directed against these nonlocal Mama Uqllus. But this lack of linguistic knowledge was also ideologically linked to other physical and performative failures that doomed these actresses' reception in Puno. Threading through the various critiques, complaints, and even jokes is an implicit underlying connection between Indigenous linguistic and communicative practices in the altiplano and discourses surrounding Indigenous identity and femininity in the region. Being a good Indigenous woman of the altiplano is based on knowing one of the Indigenous languages in the region perfectly, where the intrinsic knowledge that is within each language enables the development and cultivation of other puneña qualities. Yet it is not enough to just be a good Indigenous woman. Instead, actresses had to become the ideal Indigenous woman of the altiplano, where success was measured by one's ability to properly capture the essence of all Indigenous women in the region through a single linguistic performance.

Inventing the Ideal Puneña Woman

Ritual performances as ideologized practices provide the opportunity to create a new narrative and telling of a place and its people, allowing participants and audience members to jointly construct alternative interpretations of their own histories, as well as their broader significance. For the arrival of Manqu Qhapaq and Mama Uqllu, the myth in its current form does more than simply celebrate the arrival of the first founding humans of the region. It establishes a mythical origin story for the founding of linguistic and Indigenous ethnic diversity and difference as well. Although the myth and reenactment are set in the mythical past, the versions of Quechua and Aymara used in these performances are modern creations and are thus inventions in their own right (Makoni and

Pennycook 2007), with each version of Quechua and Aymara as used in the performance being modern ideological artifacts that are the product of colonial contact and influence. Despite such contradictions, invented and reinvented versions of traditions create a space for local organizations to promote a specific narrative of their origins, and in the process draw attention to the special qualities and characteristics that make each region in the Andes a unique manifestation of Indigenous heritage that is different from its neighbors.

For Puno and puneños, embracing such reinvented origins of Indigenous linguistic and ethnic diversity in the region provides the opportunity to promote their distinct social, historical, and cultural significance on a regional, national, and global level. In this reinvention, puneños also replicate and reinforce specific ideological connections between gender, language use, Indigenous identity, and indigeneity in the altiplano. Through this, the relationship and divide between men and women and between Indigenous masculinity and femininity become even more apparent through the formalization of the roles and mythology of Manqu Qhapaq and Mama Uqllu in representing the entire region. As the mythical Indigenous founding pair of the altiplano and the Andes, Manqu Qhapaq and Mama Uqllu replicate how each Indigenous gendered embodied performance is legitimized, and idealized, by and through their mastery of a pure, pre-contact, idealized Indigenous language and linguistic variety. Additionally, as an interlinguistic couple, and per the current-day celebration of the myth, they are the first and original interlinguistic couple of the region, where each member maintains the boundaries between their linguistic varieties and languages in spite of their union, thus upholding a broader ideal across the altiplano of presenting Quechua and Aymara as bounded languages that correspond to bounded groups.

Puno therefore is home to close contact and unions between Quechua and Aymara speakers, a precedent first established by the mythical couple themselves. Yet such intimacy of contact does not have to blur or erase the boundaries between the languages or their corresponding populations. Instead, each member of this gendered ideal is also implicitly understood to uphold these differences between languages and speakers, modeling these ethnolinguistic differences for all puneños. And within the scope of the narrative and myth, each member of the mythical couple embodies the incommensurable difference between Quechua and Aymara and bequeathes these differences to their descendant populations. Yet in addition to modeling and upholding the symbolic lines that separate Quechua speakers from Aymara speakers, and Indigenous, ethnic Quechuas from Aymaras, the annual reenactment also reflects how mythologies on the origin of Indigenous linguistic and ethnic difference are also an origin story of the first models of ideal gendered relationships and qualities in the region. But unlike the equal treatment afforded to representing Quechua and Aymara in other institutionalized language practices, here the mythologization of gender differences finds itself on unequal footing, especially in regard to the expectations placed on the performances and representations of Mama Uqllu. And it is here that Mama Uqllu's framing as the mother of all Aymaras becomes most significant. Unlike Manqu Qhapaq, who eventually becomes the first Inka, and thus becomes a figure who is revered and can be claimed by a larger Andean, Indigenous population, the recognition of Mama Uqllu as a significant mythical figure does not extend beyond the altiplano. Her framing as an Aymara speaker also fully emplaces her as a central figure to the altiplano, home to both her descendants, Quechuas and Aymaras. Her strength of character and force of will are qualities that are most closely linked to being an Aymara-speaking woman but are also shared by all puneños and Indigenous individuals of the altiplano, woman and man, Quechua and Aymara speaking alike. And although she is married to a Quechua-speaking man, she, in her performance and her mythologized life, maintained the boundaries between Quechua and Aymara in her descendants by practicing and modeling an idealized pure form of Aymara that distinguishes her speech from the speech of her husband.

In this way, Mama Uqllu not only becomes the embodiment of a female ground zero for Indigenous ethnic authenticity and legitimacy in the region but also becomes the original Indigenous woman of the altiplano, and by extension, the most ideal and perfect Indigenous female representation from the region. Through the annual performance, the ways in which the character is discussed and interpreted by both Quechua- and Aymara-speaking puneños, and the reception of the performances made by local and nonlocal actresses, both good and bad, emphasize how Mama Uqllu is not only the founding mother in the region but also an idealized Indigenous female figure. This view establishes other frames to understand and evaluate Indigenous ethnic and linguistic legitimacy and authenticity in the region for both men and women. Moreover, such a view also enshrines the specific place that women and Indigenous femininity have in managing the perpetuation of ethnolinguistic Indigenous difference, and the expectations associated with performing and maintaining a true puneño Indigenous linguistic and cultural identity for future generations to come.

CHAPTER 5

Fairest in the Land

The Pageantry of Linguistic Variation and Diverse Female Bodies

In the materials published by PromPerú, the promotional arm of the national Ministry of Tourism, each departmental designation of Peru is advertised with a specific epithet as a way to draw the interest of national and international tourists, thus stimulating the national economy and capitalizing on aspects of national diversity in ways that serve the state. Puno's title is *Capital Foklórico Peruano* (the Folkloric Capital of Peru). The title largely refers to the maintenance of Indigenous and mestizo cultural practices like music, dance, costume, and other performative genres. For their part, these practices have withstood otherwise discriminatory policies by the state since the colonial conquest of the region. However, what is not explicitly mentioned in this title is the diversity of performative genres labeled as "traditional" or "pre-modern" in the region, and how these differences are maintained down to the community level. Notably, this preservation of hyperlocal Indigenous performative genres emphasizes how Indigenous forms of identity are in some ways still tied to community-specific practices that include dress, dance, and music in addition to language.

The significance of these differences, however, is not lost to puneños especially in relation to projects around cultural revitalization and maintenance in the region. Within the calendar of public performances that display the range and diversity of Indigenous performative arts across the altiplano, publicly staged competitions that take place within the regional capital of Puno have become one popular forum to promote and celebrate the maintenance of local traditions and practices in the region. During mid- to late August, for instance, such forms of Indigenous performative expression are distilled into an all-day showcase and competition of *sikurris*, the traditional ritual music that is sung and played on Andean panpipes and drums, which are usually performed during important ritual and religious feast days.[1] The competition of sikurris draws teams from various communities across the linguistically and culturally distinct provinces within the altiplano, primarily consisting of men playing instruments and singing traditional songs while accompanied by teams of women performing the traditional dances to the music. Their performances are evaluated by a specific team of judges and by everyday puneños in the audience, who over the years have built up their own expectations of judging the authenticity of the songs, dance, and dress associated with each community. Yet competitions like the Concurso de Sikurris are not about the differences between Quechuas or Aymaras. Instead, these competitions are moments that reinforce the enduring importance of Indigenous diversity beyond ethnolinguistic categories, and locating that variation as autochthonous to a named place or community.

The performance and celebration of hyperlocal diversity takes on a new level of visibility six months later during the festivities of the Virgen de la Candelaria, or "the Virgin of the Candlelight." Typically celebrated for two weeks around the end of January and beginning of February, the Virgen de la Candelaria is the central celebration for the patron saint of Puno. Today it is one of the largest celebrations in Peru, known throughout the country and across the Andes for both its intensity and the amount of money that families spend on sponsoring groups to perform during the entire celebration. For two weeks, the small regional capital of Puno is bursting at its seams as both the pious and the partiers crowd the streets to dance and celebrate for Puno's patron saint. The celebration attracts puneños from across the altiplano who participate in the various dance groups. It also attracts an even larger puneño diaspora of second- and third-generation migrants who live in Arequipa, Lima, and abroad. During my fieldwork in Puno, the festivities had become a spectacle at such a large scale that many of the main dancing events were recorded and broadcast on TVPerú, making it one of the few times that the peripherality of Puno takes center stage in the national consciousness.[2]

Part of the spectacle that has made the Virgen de la Candelaria celebrations famous is the diversity of dances that are traditional to the Peruvian and Bolivian altiplano. One of the more popular sites within this array of performances, and perennial audience favorites, is the showcase of the *danzas mestizos* (mestizo dances).[3] This colorful spectacle famously includes elaborate masks for dances like La Morenada, Diablada, and Waka Waka, with equally intricate dresses for women. Younger puneños gravitate toward dances like Caporales that allows young men and women to perform a sensuousness that is also heightened with sartorial details carefully sequined into boots, hats, and dresses.[4] Yet equally dizzying are the *danzas autóctonas* (authochthonous dances), the parade of dance teams hailing from individual communities across the altiplano performing the traditional local dances and songs associated with carnavales (figure 9). Like the competition of sikurris, the danzas autóctonas are valued precisely because of the diversity of Indigenous representation that is communicated across various scales. At the national level and from the perspective of viewers in Lima, the variations

FIGURE 9 The *Ayarachis de Cuyo-Cuyo*, the traditional danza autóctona for the community of Cuyo-Cuyo. Credit: Sandhya Krittika Narayanan (author).

in dance, dress, and music are read as folkloric differences in an otherwise undifferentiated mass of Indigenous Andean communities that make up the altiplano. But for puneños, the community performances, marked by other signs of authenticity such as song repertoires (and the languages they are performed in), clothes, and dance steps, reinforce the importance of place-based modes of identification in the region, and how those identities are reinforced through differences in celebratory and ritual practices. In this sense, the danzas autóctonas showcase and reinforce the importance of community-based autochthony, and the various symbolic mediums that communicate inter-Indigenous difference and diversity in the region.

Across the Andes, public performances like the Concurso de Sikurris or the danzas autóctonas remain an important site to promote and negotiate Indigenous identity and shifting forms of indigeneity in relation to the state (Mendoza 2000, 2008; Van Vleet 2005). Yet while such performances are often approached in relation to the recognition of Indigenous identities within national discourses, they are often less frequently discussed in terms of how they complicate these discourses through presenting competing visions of indigeneity, highlighting the degree to which those manifestations of unique Indigenous identities are maintained at much smaller, local scales. This contrast is critical toward understanding the popularization of Indigenous public performances as nationalized spectacles that can be consumed by a broader audience both in Peru and abroad. The support of organizations and institutions like the Federación de Foklór de Puno ensure that Puno's Indigenous cultural vitality is known nationally through acquiring permissions to broadcast these events on the national TV station. Yet the differences in viewing perspectives matter in how these kinds of publicized celebrations are received. To the casual coastal viewer in Lima, these celebrations might appear as folkloric, bright, and colorful, interpreting the differences in dress and music as superficial variations of a single Andean Indigeneity. But for puneños participating in or observing these performances and festivities, each difference stands out as a testament to the persistence of a more localized form of distinct Indigenous identities, reinscribing how the autochthony of named places remains an important focal point in understanding inter-Indigenous difference in the region that transcends beyond ethnolinguistic identifiers like Quechua and Aymara.

With every rhythmically coordinated step of the instrumentalists, to every turn and flare of the skirt, these performances also magnify the importance of gendered roles and gendered divisions in upholding these hyperlocal differences that are central to defining inter-Indigenous differences in the altiplano. Whether it be the gender division present in the sikurris or each locally specific presentation of each danza autóctona, Indigenous public performances demonstrate how gender differences and the specific roles, responsibilities, and the symbolic importance attributed to each gender identity remain a cornerstone for shaping ideas about Indigenous identities and difference in the region. With the exception of a few dances that are explicitly gendered as male,[5] dances and ritual public performances include the participation of both men and women. Even the male-dominated sikurri performances are not complete without a group of female dancers accompanying them. Having representation between both men and women in these ritual dances thus reinforces ideological—and today, romanticized—ideas around Andean gender complementarity. Yet similar to the unequal scrutiny placed on evaluations of the performance of Mama Uqllu, public performances and celebrations of Indigenous differences and hyperlocal cultural and linguistic identity are also not applied equally to male and female performers, resulting in women bearing more of the ideological load as the primary caretakers of Indigenous linguistic knowledge and cultural traditions.

While most public performances of puneño indigeneity are based on the visible participation of men and women, there is one particular set of public performance that is only open to women—Indigenous beauty pageants.[6] This chapter looks at performances and evaluations of contestants in Indigenous beauty pageants, highlighting how the participation, performances, and evaluations of young Indigenous puneña women in these staged competitions of Indigenous identity and authenticity in Puno reinforce and uphold the role of young women as the primary caretakers of an Indigenous authenticity that is rooted in the maintenance of purified, hyperlocal differences and expressions of Quechua and Aymara indigeneity. Indigenous beauty pageants, like other examples of beauty pageants around the world, offer young women the chance to perform and embody competing and conflicting perspectives on the defining qualities and essences of a community or nation. Through these public performances, beauty pageant contestants inscribe these debates and discussions onto their bodies, having these contrasting ideas recognized through their performances on the stage, which are then read and evaluated by judges and audience members alike. Success within the pageant space, therefore, is a jointly constructed interaction between contestants' performance of Indigenous altiplano linguistic and cultural fidelity and judges' and onlookers' reception of those performances.

While the end goal of such competitions is to select a winner who best represents the ideals of Indigenous femininity in the altiplano, the performances by all the contestants collectively reflect the role that women are expected to inhabit as guardians and keepers of inter-Indigenous linguistic and cultural knowledge for future generations of puneños. At the same time, beauty pageant contestants do not represent the average Indigenous puneña. Instead, contestants, their performances, and how those performances are received reproduce emerging discourses around idealized forms of Indigenous femininity. In this way, pageants offer an opportunity to consider how contestants are also evaluated and oriented toward the future of hyperlocal, inter-Indigenous differences in the altiplano, and the role that these young women will play in upholding those distinctions.

Indigenous Beauty and Femininity Across the Altiplano

Beauty pageants are experimental battlegrounds where ideologies around womanhood and feminine ideals intersect with nationalist projects, socioeconomic and class-based aspirations, racializing aesthetics, and competing standards of cultural and national authenticity (Banet-Weiser 1999). The flexibility of the genre has allowed for its global proliferation, creating a space for participants to enact different visions of womanhood in relation to their cultural or national context, and exercise varying forms of agency that reflect diverse values, priorities, and ideologies for contestants, event organizers, and viewers (Billings 2014; Gustafson 2006; Rogers 1998; Schackt 2005). The historical contours of Indigenous beauty pageants in the Andes highlight these often conflicting and contradictory views and practices. The first Indigenous-focused beauty pageants emerged in the early to mid-twentieth century as a product of the neoindigenista intellectual movement that emerged in Cusco (Cadena 2000). These early beauty pageants were created as part of racializing projects that focused on racial purity and phenotypic integrity for Indigenous Andean women, reinforcing the relationship between women and the racialization of Indigenous populations in the Andes. These early iterations of Indigenous-centered beauty pageants contrast sharply against the present-day popularization of the event, which across the Andes today is primarily centered on celebrating Indigenous identity, unity, and autochthony and seen as part of a broader project aimed at promoting cultural and language revitalization efforts.[7]

In the altiplano, beauty pageants are often organized with special holidays and events, such as patron saint festivals or the anniversary of the founding of a particular province and municipality within the Department of Puno. As such, one can find locally run Indigenous-centered beauty pageants throughout the year, drawing in a small pool of contestants from a local community, and a slightly larger audience who are all of that community. Across these various beauty pageants, the format and general expectations are very similar. Contestants must be young women, usually between eighteen and twenty-four years old, must have grown up within that particular province or municipality, and must still have their family residing there. Typically contestants are young women who are unmarried, though they may have a child of their own. Young women must present themselves in the most traditional and authentic dress of that particular locale, answer questions that reflect their knowledge of that specific place, correctly perform the traditional dance of their region (figure 10), and most importantly, address the judges and audience members in the correct linguistic variety that is associated with that particular locale.

On a local level, beauty pageants are one kind of gender-specific public spectacle that reinforces the cultural and linguistic distinctiveness of a specific province or district. Even provinces and districts that speak the same Indigenous language (either Quechua or Aymara) are nevertheless composed of different performances as young women perform specific dances, wear specific clothes, and are careful to speak only a specific linguistic variety that can be identified with a bounded community or place pertaining to that geographic designation. Audience members expect these details to be performed, and they are also an important social

FIGURE 10 A beauty pageant contestant performing the traditional dance of her community. Credit: Sandhya Krittika Narayanan (author).

actor in the evaluation and legitimization of Indigenous female authenticity in these beauty pageants. Some of this can be seen in the reaction to a contestant's inability to correctly answer a question about their specific region, where an unprepared young contestant is immediately met with jeers and boos from the crowd. Such negative reactions become more amplified when a contestant is also unable to talk about their region and, worse, is unable to do this in their locally specific linguistic variety. For instance, in one smaller local pageant, held in the Quechua-speaking district of Macusani, one unfortunate candidate struggled to introduce herself in Quechua, eliciting boos from the audience. Those reactions continued when she incorrectly named the various communities that were included within Macusani and Carabaya, provoking more angry and disappointed reactions from the crowd. Similarly, in another beauty pageant contest held in Illave, one contestant was booed for her inability to speak Aymara, where the almost exclusive reliance on Spanish in her speech and introduction to the audience identified her as a youth who had spent most of her life primarily in the urbanized commercial center of Juliaca. The role and importance of the audience in these competitions highlight how the curation and regimentation of Indigenous female authenticity is part of a larger, co-constructed set of standards. Judges, who are often language and cultural professionals and experts, bear some of this responsibility and are backed by various forms of institutional expertise. However, the audience also plays an important role in determining what Indigenous female authenticity and excellence looks like. As such, their reactions have the potential to recognize the validity of a pageant contestant's performance. In doing so, they also reproduce the boundaries that constitute membership within those communities and the identities that they inscribe.

Belleza del Altiplano: Competing to be the Ideal Indigenous Woman of the Altiplano

Locally organized beauty pageants create the ideological framework that privileges the maintenance of signs that reproduce forms of inter-Indigenous difference and distinction. Such regimes of valuing and evaluating local emblems of inter-Indigenous differences come to the fore during larger, regional-wide competitions that provide a platform for contestants from across the altiplano. In this vein, the largest pageant space that allows for comparison and evaluation of the maintenance of inter-Indigenous cultural and linguistic differences is found in the staging of the biannual *Belleza del Altiplano* (Beauty of the Altiplano).[8] The event is traditionally organized prior to the official festivities associated with the Virgen de la Candelaria. Doing this ensures that the winner of the pageant would be featured in the competition of the danzas autóctonas, where past winners typically wear their winning sash as they dance in their community's team. Sharing the same season as the festivities of the Virgen de la Candelaria also makes the beauty pageant as one celebration in what has now become a month of smaller festivities and spectacles that culminate in the patron virgin celebration. And like these other festivities, the Belleza del Altiplano not only reinforces the diversity of linguistic and cultural traditions found across the Department of Puno, but also focuses those distinctions and the significance they bring to constituting inter-Indigenous difference through evaluating female performances and female bodies.[9]

Like other more Indigenous-focused celebrations associated with the Catholic celebration, the Belleza del Altiplano only started in the late 2000s. Its creation coincided with the promotion of other kinds of celebrations of Indigenous difference in Puno around the same time, such as the competition of sikurris in August and the inclusion of the danzas autóctonas as part of the Virgen de la Candelaria celebrations. Its appearance during this decade situates the event as another example of Indigenous cultural and linguistic revitalization and political reclamation within Puno. Moreover, the social zeitgeist at the time that spurred the creation and institutionalization of all these events also emerged to elevate and legitimize Indigenous cultural and linguistic expression among a younger generation of puneños, who more than ever before were seen as growing up without any connection to their Indigenous roots and identities.

These were themes that became apparent during my conversations with René, the founder and main organizer and producer of the Belleza del Altiplano. René was a Quechua-speaking, queer-identifying puneño in his forties who was part of the first wave of Indigenous migrants to live and be brought up within Puno. He and his parents migrated from the Quechua-speaking province in Azangaro in the '80s, and like other Indigenous puneños, René spent his youth growing up between Puno and Azangaro. His parents eventually returned to their natal province, but René stayed in the city and built a reputation as someone interested in preserving Indigenous traditions around the altiplano. In particular, René was interested in preserving the art of traditional textiles and weaving, collecting the unique clothing traditions from every province and district across the Department of Puno to be housed in his textile museum. During his travels and excursions to various communities to collect valuable heirloom textiles and dresses, René also noticed how the younger generation of Indigenous puneños, and especially the younger generation of women, were losing touch with the traditions and practices of their mothers and grandmothers. Concerned about this loss and rupture in the transmission of traditional knowledge between generations of women, René started the Belleza del Altiplano to encourage and empower young Indigenous women across Puno to remain connected and take interest in their Indigenous heritage and in maintaining their traditional, hyperlocal Indigenous practices. In particular, Renée wanted young Indigenous women to not reject learning their traditional knowledge and practices, and not lose touch with knowing how to act and present themselves in ways that reflect their unique community and locale-based traditions, which included maintaining their proficiency in their local Indigenous linguistic and communicative practices.

Although the Belleza del Altiplano was founded and motivated by the desire to revalorize and maintain the diversity of Indigenous linguistic and cultural traditions across the altiplano, the event is nevertheless a modern spectacle, tinged with priorities and practices that highlight how the politicized aspects of Indigenous cultural vitality and revalorization in the region intersect with more modern visions of the future of Indigenous heritage and identity. This was partly reflected in the pageant's focus on the aesthetics of Indigenous femininity, which sought to highlight and recontextualize the value and beauty of Indigenous feminine traditions for a modern audience. This emphasis also blends into ideas of how women are expected to present themselves on the stage and in the competitive world of beauty pageants, melding a combination of traditional authenticity with modern sensibilities and ideological stances of how idealized forms of Indigenous femininity should be exhibited and performed. And like other kinds of modern pageants, the Belleza del Altiplano also privileged certain qualities that straddled the line between traditional Indigenous authenticity and visions of modern womanhood, such as confidence, poise, and love and pride in being an Indigenous puneña from the altiplano.

These criteria together inform how contestants are evaluated. Within the Belleza de Altiplano competition, contestants are expected to wear and showcase three different outfits: the traditional garb of daily wear, more formal dress associated with occupying positions of leadership, and festive wear and dress that is worn when they dance and perform their traditional songs. Costumes are meant to be authentic and are evaluated for their use of traditional all-natural materials like wool, alpaca fibers, and cotton. During the competition, contestants are also expected to display their community-specific traditional attire across the stage, embodying a level of comfort and ease with wearing their traditional garb that one might expect with supermodels strutting the latest haute couture fashions down a runway. According to René, it is during these fashion presentations that contestants are judged for poise and confidence, qualities that reflect these women's affinity for wearing traditional clothing associated with their distinct Indigenous community and identity, signaling how immersed they are in their local, Indigenous heritage and traditional practices.

Confidence and poise also guide the expectations of how young women are expected to speak and address the audience during the competition. Like smaller, locally organized beauty pageants, contestants in the Belleza del Altiplano are expected to speak in the specific provincial or local linguistic variety of Quechua and Aymara, indexing their Indigenous authenticity and their rootedness in their community. The use of each contestant's specific regional Indigenous linguistic variety is primarily judged during the opening introduction that each contestant is expected to make. These introductions, appearing during the first round of the competition associated with wearing one's traditional daily attire, is the primary space where linguistic fluency and authenticity is judged. During this opening introduction, contestants are given three to four minutes to tell the audience who they are, where they are from, what they are wearing, and which community and specific group of Indigenous individuals they are representing—all in their local Indigenous linguistic variety. According to René, although judges are expected to evaluate speeches so that they uphold ideas around Indigenous linguistic purity that include the absence of Spanish and another Indigenous language in these speeches, he also noted that judges are instructed to also evaluate the overall performance and delivery of the speeches in relation to how confident and composed each contestant appeared on stage. Receiving a higher score means that contestants who are able to communicate in their local Indigenous linguistic variety correctly are also equally successful in convincing judges and the audience of their validity as cultural and linguistic ambassadors for their specific community or province.

These kinds of evaluative expectations were also mirrored by the composition of judges recruited to evaluate contestants in this event. The Belleza del Altiplano competition that I attended in 2017, for instance, consisted of four judges, who had in some capacity served as a judge in the competition in previous years. To judge and evaluate the authenticity of dances, René had invited a professor of folkloric dance performance from the Universidad Nacional del Altiplano (National University of the Altiplano). A Quechua-speaking former Belleza del Altiplano, and an older Aymara-speaking Señorita Campesina[10] were also invited to evaluate the linguistic performances and delivery by each contestant. Lastly, a former Miss Puno winner, who fit the mold of a typical Western beauty pageant winner, was invited to evaluate contestants on their poise, grace, and confidence, determining if each Belleza competitor was beauty queen material. As such, the composition of the judges' panel highlights the balance between traditional and modern revisionist perspectives of traditional Indigenous feminine aesthetics. Judges, like a former Miss Puno winner, bring in contemporary perspectives and an evaluative lens on how female beauty should be properly performed. And although the judges selected to rate linguistic and dancing performances might appear at first glance to be chosen to evaluate the level of traditionality represented in each contestant's performance, those readings of an authentic Indigenous tradition cannot be separated from more recent discourses around ethnolinguistic distinction and historical discourses around an idealized feminine indigeneity.[11]

Purity and Poise: Performing Indigenous Language Proficiency

One fundamental criterion of a successful Indigenous beauty pageant contestant in the Belleza del Altiplano competition is the expectation that contestants will speak their heritage Indigenous language during their introduction to the crowds. During such introductions, judges and audience members evaluate to what degree the speaker is able to command their heritage lengua materna with a certain degree of ideologized linguistic purity that includes limiting the amount of Spanish loans in their speech, not including the other Indigenous language in their performance, and performing a variety that accurately represents the contestant's speech community. Balancing all of these expectations, however, was also a tall task for all contestants, where the emphasis on upholding ideals of ethnolinguistic purity conflicts with the actual realities of speaking in ways that also maintain hyperlocal differences between communities. For instance, it is not uncommon across Quechua- and

Aymara-speaking communities to find the incorporation and syncretization of loans from other languages within that community's local set of repertoires. Yet these locally recognized ways of speaking that include loans from other linguistic varieties conflict with the increasing push to promote linguistically pure versions of Quechua and Aymara across the Department of Puno.

This was a problem for one of the three Aymara-speaking contestants of the evening, Vicky Cruz from Platería. An Aymara-speaking province located in what is largely seen and regarded as the *zona Aymara* south of Puno, Vicky Cruz came onto the stage addressing the judges and audience in the prototypical formal forms of address now largely associated with Indigenous language use in formal settings. While Platería is recognized as an Aymara-speaking area, and is ethnically identified as Indigenous Aymara, its proximity to Puno and Quechua-speaking areas contributes to the high frequency of Spanish found in local residents' communicative repertoires as well as the potential for there to also be some Quechua loans. This proximity is also compounded by the fact that many residents from Platería often travel daily into Puno, which also intensifies the contact that speakers have with Spanish and Quechua and increases the likelihood for linguistic elements from both languages to enter into the Aymara variety that is spoken from this area. This was certainly true of Vicky's speech during her introduction.

[Example 28]
Vicky Cruz from Platería (Aymara)
1. *Jilatanaka, kullakanaka,*
   Brothers, sisters,

2. *sumakiw jupana.*
   may you all be well.

3. *Nax sutixa*
   My name is

4. *Vicki Gracela Asqui Cruz.*
   Vicki Gracela Asqui Cruz.

5. *Nayax jutawtwa*
   I come from

6. *kha*—comunidad Camaqani,
   that—the community of Camaqani,

7. distrito Plateria,
   district of Plateria,

8. provincia de Puno.
   in the Province of Puno.

9. <u>kunam</u> *sixa*,
   Right now, I am going to tell you,

10. *tiburu uchasiñawi*.
    [about how] we place ourselves.

11. *Ma* comunidad*xa yuntatw lurata*.
    A community where they work with plows.

12. *Ma* <u>liqlla</u>—mutl(i) color.
    A shawl—that is multicolored.

13. *Ukhat jutiwa ma kuna*,
    And there are other things,

14. *Ukhat . . . wak'ampi*,
    like . . . this belt,

15. *pollerampi*.
    and traditional skirt.

16. *Mirqi polleritampi*.
    And this old/used skirts.

17. *Ukhampi—*
    with these—

18. *ukha . . .* comunidad—
    in this . . . community—

19. *ukhamphtwa*.
    they are like this.

20. *Ukhasti*.
    And therefore.

21. *Luraphtwa*,
    we make,

22. Lana*w* . . .
    wool . . .

23. *uwesat luraphtwa*,
    and made from sheep,

24. *payeta*.
    textile.

25. *ukhat* payeta*sti lurajaphtwa*,
    And from this textile we make,

26. *polleritanaka*.
    skirts.

27. Gracias.
    Thank you.

The general structure and order of elements in Vicky's speech is representative of the genre of introduction speeches found in Indigenous beauty pageants across the altiplano. Vicky first introduced herself and spoke about where she was from. She then started to talk about what she was wearing and connected who she was and her performance to her home region. In going through this speech, however, Vicky had to rely on Spanish, either by relying on whole phrases to describe her community or by including syncretized Spanish loans, such as the word *"payeta"* which is an Aymara-inflected version of the Spanish term *"bayeta."* Her speech also included elements that for some in the audience, and perhaps for the judges as well, could have been interpreted as Quechua loans. For instance, her use of *kunam* to mean "now" or "at this moment" contrasts against expected Aymara equivalents such as *ichuru* (today) or *ichaqa* (now), which are both terms that are acceptable within purist versions of Aymara. The lack of fidelity to a purist version of Aymara could also be interpreted with the presence of a bivalent term like *liqlla*, which, while used by many Aymara women to mean "shawl," is nevertheless marked in more linguistic purist contexts where the term *"awayu"* is considered more appropriate.

Linguistic purity, however, is not solely valued for its association with upholding Indigenous cultural and linguistic authenticity. Within the scope of beauty pageants, the ability to perform such linguistic purism is also indexically linked with a contestant's poise and confidence, qualities that are not only important for the winner of Belleza del Altiplano but also an important quality for the ideal Indigenous woman from the altiplano. By not stumbling through one's speech in either Indigenous language, contestants are able to convince the judges and the audience not only that they are comfortable with speaking their Indigenous lengua materna, but also that they are able to demonstrate this self-confidence in identifying with their Indigenous heritage through how they command and perform their lengua materna in front of an audience. René and the judges privileging performances that are read as confident, however, does not necessarily mean that contestants who are fluent and perhaps even dominant in their Indigenous lengua materna have the stage presence to convey this confidence. In one of my conversations with René prior to competition, he mentioned to me that it was not good enough for any girl from the countryside who speaks their language and practices their traditions to win the Belleza del Altiplano. For René, the winner had to be able to demonstrate this comfort with their Indigenous heritage by addressing the public in perfect Quechua or Aymara with a level of confidence and composure.

During the 2017 Belleza, for instance, there were many contestants whom René had personally recruited to participate in the competition. His selection of these women came from seeing them participate at their respective local Indigenous beauty pageant competitions. After seeing them speak either Quechua or Aymara fluently, he would encourage them to participate in his larger regional competition. Yet his expectations of the performances from his selected favorites would sometimes fall short, resulting in many Quechua- and Aymara-speaking contestants fumbling their performance because of nerves. One such recruit was a young woman named Marcelina Mamani, a Quechua-speaking contestant from the Quechua-speaking province of San Antonio de Esquilache. Having grown up primarily in her provincial hometown, Marcelina was comfortable with speaking Quechua on a conversational level. This comfort and fluency were absent from her speech on the day of the competition, which resulted in the judges evaluating her as not fluent in

Quechua, and by extension, lacking the necessary poise and confidence expected of any Belleza winner.

[Example 29]
Marcelina Mamani from San Antonio de Esquilache (Quechua)
1. Imanaylla kashankis . . . kay munay tuta?
   How are all of you . . . this beautiful evening?

2. [Clears her throat] turaykuna ñañaykuna
   Brothers and sisters

3. ñuqa hamushqani . . .
   I have come . . .

4. haqay distrito . . .
   from that far away district . . .

5. de San Antonio de Es . . . Esquilache llaqtamanta.
   from San Antonio of Es . . . of [the district] of Esquilache.

6. Sutinmitaqmin Marcelina Mamani Ticona . . .
   My name is Marcelina Mamani Ticona . . .

7. ñuqa . . . [clears throat]
   I . . .

8. kunan tuta riqsarishita munaykis . . .
   tonight I want you all to get to know . . .

9. haqay sumaq llaqtayman . . . llaqtayta.
   from a beautiful far away town . . . town.

10. Haqay sumaq llaqtaypi kashan . . .
    In that distant beautiful community there is . . .

11. mmm . . . pikuña puna . . . tarukakuna . . .
    mmm . . . [who?] high altitudes . . . deer . . .

12. haqay sumaq q'uni unu.
    over there is the beautiful hot springs.

13. qamkuna . . . puririwaqchis chaqaykama.
    all . . . can travel together over there.

14. ña ririkamawaqchis turaykuna ñañaykuna.
    We could all go there together with me brothers and sisters.

15. Kunan tuta chayta riqsichikuyta munanchis.
    Tonight you all would like to get to know about that.

16. Ancha munasqa turaykuna ñañaykuna.
    My wonderful brothers and sisters.

17. Hinallataqmin . . . kashan . . . haqay . . . unay . . .
    And therefore . . . there is . . . over there . . . over there . . .

18. mina San Antonio nisqapi.
    a mine called San Antonio.

19. Chay . . . haqay sumaq llaqtaymin . . . tiyarikurqan . . .
    That . . . over there [in] that beautiful community . . . resided . . .

20. kunan presidentenchis . . .
    the current president . . .

21. Pedro Pablo . . . Kuczynski . . .
    Pedro Pablo . . . Kuczynski . . .

22. Qamkuna tapurikunkischa . . . imanasqataq tiyarikurqan, nisqa.
    You all may ask . . . what is there, you may say.

23. Tiyarikurqan . . .
    Over there, there resides . . .

24. tatan haqaypi . . . hampiqkurqan.
    over there . . . medicinal/curing properties.

25. Chaymantataq . . .
    And also/thereafter . . .

26. [clears throat] kashallantaq . . .
    what is found there . . .

27. haqay . . . llaqtaypi . . . sumaq mikhunakuna . . .
    in that distant . . . community . . . is good food . . .

28. uywa . . .
    animals . . .

29. <u>chikuna puna ... uywa tinkaykuna</u> ...
    [untranslateable] high altitudes ... and animals meeting ...

30. <u>chayatam sinchikuyta munarqaykis kunan tuta</u>.
    this and much more if you like this evening.

31. Gracias.
    Thank you.

When chatting with René after the competition about how each contestant fared, he noted that Marcelina's speech came off as unnatural and staged and did not convince the judges of her fluency or knowledge of Quechua. For one thing, Marcelina spoke with many pauses, creating stretches of silence that made it seem like she was trying to remember a speech that she had memorized. These pauses were even more palpable when she also came to the end of a sentence or statement, which, for René and the judges, made it seem like she was searching for something to say to fill the time. A similar kind of evaluation was also applied to the moments of grammatical correction, like she did in the phrase "*haqay sumaq llaqtayman ... llaqtayta*." To René, and even to my other Quechua-speaking interlocutors like Señora Fidelia when I played the recording of these performances for them, these mistakes made it seem like Marcelina was not comfortable with speaking Quechua in public more generally. Additionally, these mistakes were exacerbated by her physical performance, where Marcelina did not speak clearly into the microphone and did not address the judges and audience directly. Further compounding her underwhelming performance, she only looked at the ground or off to the side while speaking. Despite her background as a Quechua speaker, and indeed being someone who spoke Quechua in her everyday life with her family and within her community, she was evaluated as not being confident in her knowledge of Quechua. As a result, she was not judged as possessing the poise and confidence that was expected for a Belleza del Altiplano winner.

The process of reading and interpreting poise, composure, and confidence onto contestants' performances extended to participants who also might have initially appeared as the most virtuosic in their linguistic and cultural knowledge. This was the case for Yessica Quispe, a young Aymara-speaking woman from the noted Aymara-speaking region of Juli, located on the shores of Lake Titicaca on the southernmost part of the zona Aymara. Another one of René's recruits, Yessica established her linguistic and cultural fluency and competence by addressing both the judges and audience in what is now regarded as a formal and proper variety of Aymara. Such formality also aligns with broader expectations puneños have about the Aymara that is spoken around Juli, which, of the Aymara varieties spoken in Puno, is typically considered to be one of the best, if not also the most ideologically pure, authentic, and closely aligned with the best Aymara that is spoken in La Paz, Bolivia. Some of these associations and expectations for the Aymara spoken in Juli come from the region's historical connections as a seat of power for the powerful Lupaca state and kingdom that emerged in the region after the fall of Tiwanaku. The significance of Juli was maintained even after the region's incorporation into Qullusuyu in the Inka state. Moreover, its importance as an Indigenous political and religious center was recognized by the Spanish, resulting in the city being chosen as one of the first places in the altiplano and Andes where the Catholic missionaries established a church following the Spanish colonial conquest in the region.

These sentiments and ideologized associations between Juli, its role in shaping the history of the region, and the quality of Aymara that is spoken there are widely known by both Quechua- and Aymara-speaking puneños, thus setting a high bar for Yessica's introduction and performance. True to these associations, Yessica's introductory speech initially demonstrated her mastery of the Aymara from Juli, aptly demonstrating in her speech a command of morphologically complex words and grammatically complex sentences. The level of confidence in her speech, however, diminishes when Yessica eventually stumbles in her delivery, producing pauses and fillers in her performance. In the end, the strong opening to Yessica's speech slowly lost its coherence, pegging her as lacking the confidence and ability to speak and command a pure version of Aymara.

[Example 30]
Yessica Quispe from Juli (Aymara)
1. *Waliki[12] jilatanaka, kullakanaka. Akha utasana juntasiphañani takpachampi*
   Greetings brothers and sisters. In this house we all come together

2. *Kamisaraki sasina.*
   and I greet you by saying "Kamisaraki."

3. *Anchitanxa nayaxa kuntaniwtwa khaysa Juli markatuqita*
   In this moment I have come from that village/province called Juli

4. *Nayana sutixasti Yessica Maribel Quispe Caceres—*
   My name is Yessica Maribel Quispe Caceres—

5. *Ukhamaw jutaniwayta khaysa* comunidad
   Therefore I come from that community

6. *jach'a jaqi qilqanixa uksatuqita,*[13]
   To the judges,

7. *ist'atasiwniwtwa kunjatiqja sap(a)uru*
   You all will hear how everyday life is like

8. *nayaxa—*
   I—

9. *uthjastwa—*
   I live—

10. *uhhmm . . . nisktwa yaputuqiro uwiwatuqiro jai ukham pacha.*
    uhhmm . . . thinking about the crops and the animals in these lands.

11. *Yat'aphtawa taqini—*
    And as is widely known—

12. *khaya* campa*chawa nayaxa sap(a)uru uthjastwa.*
    I live in that country area every day.

13. *Nistuta sapauru*
    For this everyday

14. *uhh . . . uywaxa watiri jay ukama mistwa.*
    uhh . . . I am there caring/herding the animals.

15. *Ukhamaraki,*
    And for this reason,

16. *jumanakaru anchitax khapharakiw mamawata aruma urasana Juli markatuqiro*
    I say to you all now this evening on behalf of the people and province of Juli

17. wisita*niphma.*
    [you all] should visit.

18. *Wali sumawan nanakana—*
    We are good people—

19. *manq'anaxa . . .*
    eat [the typical food we eat] . . .

20. *Ukhamaraki quta . . . qawayana . . . wali suma*
    And like this the lake . . . and the shores . . . they are really nice

21. *uuu . . . ah . . . uthjaphaytu—*
    uuu . . . ah . . . we have—

22. *ya . . . uh . . .*
    Yes . . . uh . . .

23. templos . . . coloniales . . . *unjitayñawa—*
    colonial . . . churches . . . one can see—

24. *wakisirirakiwa—*
    like this [it is good to consider]—

25. *jiwasataki.*
    for you and me both.

26. *Ukchakispa warmixaxa.*
    This is all as a woman [I can say].

27. *yius pagara . . . ist'aniw* [inaudible].
    Thank you[14] . . . listen [inaudible].

As one of René's own personal recruits, René was certain that Yessica's background as a young Aymara-speaking woman immersed in her linguistic and cultural tradition would shine through at the Belleza del Altiplano competition. Indeed, the opening portions of Yessica's speech uphold this expectation, where Yessica communicates the special history of Juli through a hyper-purist version of Aymara. However, her performance was interpreted as lacking in confidence and poise when she lost track of her planned speech, resulting in long pauses where she was searching for the next thing to say, which resulted in her losing some of her discursive coherence, and rushing to finish her time on stage and quickly make her exit. Although she ended up being one of the finalists and stronger contenders for the Belleza competition, these mistakes in her speech did cost her the crown, revealing faults in Yessica's ability to present her knowledge and legitimacy as an Indigenous linguistic and cultural ambassador of Juli.

Affective Evaluations: Indigenous Legitimacy, Pride, and Love

In addition to demonstrating one's composure, poise, and confidence when presenting themselves as the contestants and Quechua- and Aymara-speaking representatives, winners and finalists also had to effectively communicate their love and pride for their local Indigenous identity and a deep affection and pride for being an Indigenous puneña. According to René, being proud and having love for one's Indigenous background is primarily signaled by the inclusion of a broader message or vision in each contestant's speech. That message or vision can, for instance, be interpreted through carefully including details that are emblematic of a contestant's community. Such details enable contestants to perform a very specific kind of strategic essentialism (Bucholtz 2003; Wee 2018). In doubling down on the specifics of their place and home region, contestants perform how these lifelong connections have helped them cultivate a unique love for their natal community and background. Additionally, having some intrinsic pride in one's Indigenous background could also shine through a performance if the contestant mobilizes their personal connections with their Indigenous heritage and community into a broader message of Indigenous revalorization for all Indigenous, Quechua- and Aymara-speaking puneños. Because cultivating and demonstrating love and pride in one's Indigenous heritage was an important evaluative metric for the Belleza competition, speeches and performances that did not necessarily reproduce ideologically pure versions of either Quechua or Aymara were sometimes overlooked in favor of performances that included messages of pride and encouragement for the younger generations to also embrace their Indigenous heritage and locally specific linguistic and cultural practices.

In the 2017 Belleza del Altiplano, the role and significance of performing one's love and pride in being an Indigenous puneña was especially important when comparing two contestants from the same provincial region of Puno, Cuyo-Cuyo. Located in the northernmost part of the Department of Puno in what is known as the *ceja de selva* ("eyebrow of the jungle"), Cuyo-Cuyo is a Quechua-speaking area that is the gateway from the Andes to the lowland Amazonian regions. Historically, culturally, and linguistically, the region is regarded throughout the altiplano as being home to some of the most ancient traditional cultural practices and a very old form of Quechua that is different from other Quechua-speaking areas of the Andes. When Quechua-speaking puneños spoke of Cuyo-Cuyo, they sometimes mentioned how people from the community represented older versions of Indigenous traditions and Quechua-speaking practices that predated the arrival of the Inka. Moreover, the community's location in the ceja de selva has also influenced discourses that characterize the place and its people as being relatively untouched by the consequences of Spanish contact, enabling *cuyu-cuyeños* to maintain a kind of cultural and linguistic purity that is not found in any other community in the Department of Puno. In addition to being a stronghold for ancient linguistic and cultural traditions within Puno and the altiplano, Cuyo-Cuyo is also seen as being home to some of the most attractive and beautiful women in the altiplano. I have heard Quechua- and Aymara-speaking puneños, both men and women, who note that the women from Cuyo-Cuyo are particularly beautiful and maintain their beauty even through their old age. In these metacommentaries, ideas around female Indigenous beauty in Cuyo-Cuyo are linked to how the versions of Quechua spoken in Cuyo-Cuyo are also considered particularly pretty and sweet. This sweetness is heightened by the aesthetics of dress, textile, and dance traditions native to Cuyo-Cuyo. These discourses and commentaries highlight how conceptions around beauty in speech, region, cultural practices, and women are connected to each other through fractal recursivity (Irvine and Gal 2000), indexically linking qualities like sweetness and beauty onto the Quechua of Cuyo-Cuyo and scaling those same qualities onto other practices and people associated with the place.

The fact that the winner of the 2017 Belleza competition was from Cuyo-Cuyo might have been influenced by these widely held discourses about the distinct uniqueness of Cuyo-Cuyo's local Indigenous identity. But this decision was also enabled by the fact that there were two entries from Cuyo-Cuyo during the 2017 Belleza. Having two competitors from Cuyo-Cuyo offered the judges and audience members the chance to compare both contestants against each other and evaluate each of them against metadiscursive commentaries pervasive throughout Puno about the qualities and characteristics that defined Indigenous identities, and especially Indigenous women from Cuyo-Cuyo. Moreover, having two contestants from the same region provided an important opportunity to see which contestant was more skilled in communicating their love and pride for being from Cuyo-Cuyo and identifying as an Indigenous woman from the altiplano.

The first contestant was a young woman named Maribel Phaye. Maribel's Quechua performance reflected a kind of Quechua linguistic purism that aligned with ideologized expectations of how Quechua speakers from Cuyo-Cuyo spoke. Yet, despite her fluency, Maribel also seemed to stumble in several places across her speech, creating the impression that she was not only somewhat uncomfortable addressing the crowd in Quechua, but also slightly inauthentic.

[Example 31]
Maribel Phaye from Cuyo-Cuyo
1. Imanaylla wayqi-panaykuna, allillanchu?
   How are you my brothers and sisters, are you well?

2. Kay tutapiqa hatun ñapakuynita aparimushaykichis.
   This evening I salute all of you.

3. Qalan—qalantitichisman.
   Every—to everyone.

4. Llapan[15] . . .
   To all . . .

5. Llapan tiqsimuyuntinman . . .
   To all the world . . .

6. Llapan umalliqman.
   To all the (elected) authorities.

7. Llapan ... Lla ñawinchariqman ...
   To all ... To all the professionals (in attendance) ...

8. Llapan ... akllariqman.
   To all ... the judges.

9. Hinallataq ...
   Like this as well ...

10. Llapan tinkuriqman.
    To all those in attendance.

11. Kay hatun atipanakuy tutapi ...
    This great competition tonight ...

12. Kay hatun atipanakuy tutapi ...
    This great competition tonight ...

13. Miss Andina suticharisqapi.
    Called Miss Andina.

14. ñuqa kashani ... Sandia—Cuyo Cuyo llaqtamanta(q).
    I am here ... From Sandia—from the village of Cuyo-Cuyo.

15. Estan chaytapim Punu ayllu suticharisqa.
    That is here in the Department of Puno.

16. Sutiytaqmin Maribel Garcina Phaye.
    My name is Maribel Garcina Phaye.

17. wataytaqmin karishan ...
    my age is ...

18. isqay chunka- isqa[ni]yuq.
    Twenty-two.

19. ñuqa hamurishani kay p'achaywan.
    I have come here with these clothes of mine.

20. Kay p'achawaytaymi ñuqa ... ñuqayku utalizayku haqay llaqaypi ...
    My clothes ... we use in my community ...

21. Cuyo Cuyo ... Cuyo Cuyo llaqta nirisqapi.
    Cuyo-Cuyo ... in the village of Cuyo-Cuyo.

22. <u>Kay monterata ñuqayku apayu</u>,
    This montera [hat] I have brought,

23. <u>yana monterata rikumushankichis hina</u>.
    And see [for yourselves] how black this montera is.

24. Kay phuñuqchata apan . . .
    [It is] adorned with ribbons . . .

25. <u>Kay akhuñata apan</u> . . .
    [It is] adorned with a veil . . .

26. <u>Kay montera maymanta hamurin</u>.
    This <u>montera</u> from where it comes.

27. <u>Kay monteraqa hamurin</u>.
    This <u>montera</u> comes from there [Cuyo-Cuyo].

28. <u>Suticharisqa nisqamanta huk urqumanta hamurishan kayta</u>.
    It is said that this [<u>montera</u>] comes from the mountain.

29. <u>Chay urqutaqpi taririkun</u>.
    It can be found in that mountain.

30. <u>Punalaqi hinarisqapi</u>.
    Like in Puno.

31. <u>Chay urqu sutintaqmin</u> . . .
    And the name of that mountain is . . .

32. <u>T'aplanesqa chaymantan hamurin kay monteraqa</u>.
    T'aplanesqa and therefore from there comes this montera.

33. <u>Kay</u> . . . <u>kay</u> comercio <u>chukutaqmin kashan</u> . . .
    This . . . this <u>chuku</u> is [from] the market . . .

34. <u>chayqa chirita parata atahawanku</u>.
    It can protect me from the cold and rain.

35. <u>Hina chakrata puririnku</u>.
    Like this (the people of Cuyo-Cuyo) walk in the fields.

36. <u>Hin</u> . . . <u>hinay</u> . . . <u>hinay maykunapi puririnku chaykunapi</u>.
    Like this . . . like . . . like this in all parts in these ways the people walk.

37. <u>Chaymantataqmin</u> . . . <u>kay</u> hora<u>na nisqa kashan</u>.
    And next as well there is . . . at this hour as I mentioned.

38. <u>Taytay ñay(w)paq pachaqan mana tarirkuchu.</u>
    You do not find the traditional clothes of the past [as often].

39. Chumpa<u>pis</u> ni casaca <u>nisqapis</u>.
    There were no sweaters or jackets [back then].

40. <u>Chaymanta kay murana nirisqa(n)</u>
    Next, (I have) here this embroidered sweater

41. <u>Kay puka murana nirisqa kashan</u>—
    This red embroidered sweater that is—

42. Casaca andina <u>nirisqa kashan</u>.
    Also called the Andean jacket.

43. <u>Chay patanmanta mikhay</u> chaliku <u>nirisqa kashan</u>.
    On top of this there is this vest called <u>mikhay</u>.

44. <u>Chaymantaqmin kay lliqlla</u> . . .
    And also this shawl . . .

45. <u>Kay lliqllatapis ñuqayku awariyku</u>.
    This shawl as well we [from Cuyo-Cuyo] weave.

46. <u>Chaytataqmin atahariwanku hina paramanta hina chirimanta atahariwanku.</u>
    And this as well protects me equally from the rain as well as from the cold.

47. <u>Chaymantataqmin kay ch'umpi nirisqa kashan kay rikumushawan-kichis</u>.
    And like this as well there is this belt that you all can see as well.

48. <u>Kay cinturapi ñuqayku chayta apariniyku</u>.
    On the waist we put this belt.

49. <u>Kaymantataqmin kay p'istu nirisqa</u>—
    And here as well this is something called an overcoat—

50. <u>Kay pi'stuka nirisqa kashan</u>.
    This here is was is called an overcoat.

51. Chayqa en . . . falda uhh . . . falda nirisqamantan cha(ymanta)taq apariyku.
    Therefore in . . . skirt uhh . . . what they call a skirt as well I am wearing.

52. Kay phulqu nirisqa taqmin chakipi apashani.
    These booties as well I wear on my feet.

53. Chaytaqmin . . .
    And like this as well . . .

54. zapatuta nirita munan.
    These beautiful shoes.

55. Chay phulqutaqmin ruwarisqa kashan.
    These booties are also handmade.

56. Llamaqaramanta ruwarisqa kashan.
    They are made from the hide of the llama.

57. Haqay Cuyo-Cuyo llaqta nisqapi.
    from that village called Cuyo-Cuyo.

58. Kunantaqmin chakrata ñuqa puririsaq.
    And right now, I go to the field [with this dress].

59. Ahinata ñuqayku chakrata puriririyku.
    Like this we walk through the fields [in our dresses].

60. [drops shawl and opens up coca leaves to offer on stage]

61. ñuqa kunan kaypi ki'intuykurikusaq chakra puririnaypaq . . .
    Now I am going to offer (these coca leaves) to go to the fields . . .

62. Apu . . . Ch'uchu, Llaqtapata, Chuqichambi!
    And to the Apu . . . to [Apu] Ch'uchu, [Apu] Llaqtapata, and [Apu] Chuquichambi!

63. Mama Lloja Calballo, ama kunankaparapis parachunchu, parapis suquwachunchu.
    And to Mama Lloja Calballo, now that it does not rain, and that I don't get wet.

64. Ratu <u>chakrayta ruwankumusaq</u>.
    Quickly in a moment, I will work the fields.

In the days following the Belleza competition, I chatted with René to ask how he and the judges rated Maribel's performance. In our conversation, René noted that Maribel was definitely immersed in her Cuyo-Cuyo Indigenous heritage and Quechua language. With the exception of a few moments, her Quechua did not rely on Spanish as a replacement for common lexical words. And even the few times that her speech did contain some examples of Spanish loans, those examples were syncretized into her Quechua through the correct phonological and morphological changes that make them part of Quechua linguistic practices in Cuyo-Cuyo and across the altiplano. Yet these factors that might have made Maribel seem knowledgeable in performing her Indigenous linguistic and cultural background also made her somewhat off-putting to both René and the judges. René noted that Maribel spoke in a way that felt too formal ("*llena de formalidades*"), which made her seem too distant, impersonable, and unrelatable as a contestant. Some of this formality and impersonability for René came from the fact that Maribel really only talked about herself and what she was wearing. Her focus on herself meant that she had no time in the speech to try to reach out and connect with a larger audience or speak to a broader, imagined set of potential listeners. For René, the absence of any such broader message coupled with the heightened formality of her speech made Maribel seem cold, formal, and distant from her audience.

Part of that formality could be interpreted as referring to the content of Maribel's speech, which did not convey her love for Cuyo-Cuyo in any direct statement. But some of this formality, and by extension impersonability, came from how Maribel delivered her opening salvos to the judges and audience. Unlike some of the other contestants from the evening, Maribel rarely modulated her voice, coming off as very serious to René and the other judges. But this seriousness and formality was also interpreted from the discursive choices that she included in her speech. Like any kind of formal speech, Maribel employed moments of repetition, repeating that the evening was a great evening for competition (lines 11–12), stressing where her traditional *montera* was from (lines

26–27), and also stressing that the way she is dressed is not only how she lives her daily life but also how all women from Cuyo-Cuyo walk through the world and live their daily lives (lines 35–36). Maribel's speech also repeatedly used specific discourse markers, such as *kaymantaqmin* ("and here as well") and *chaymantaqmin* ("and next as well" or "and also next"). These discourse markers are often found in speeches that one might hear from a politician or a teacher, who use these markers as rhetorical devices to carefully enumerate their points to strengthen their argument. Similar to a political orator carefully outlining their vision to creating a better society, Maribel carefully used these similar discourse markers to create a formal speech that communicated in detail how her body and clothes were an authentic embodiment and representation of Cuyo-Cuyo indigeneity.

Maribel's lexical choices also reinforced the sentiment that her speech was really formal and did not adequately demonstrate her sincere love for Cuyo-Cuyo that René had instructed the judges to look for and evaluate. In several instances, Maribel chose hyper-purist lexical alternatives to commonly used Spanish lexical loans, such as the alternatives for professionals (*ñawinchariq*, line 7), judges (*akllariq*, line 8), and audience members (*tinkuriq*, line 10) in attendance. The choice to use these hyper-pure Quechua calques of Spanish lexical loans and concepts was also mirrored in her almost exclusive maintenance of SOV (subject-object-verb) word order. Though Quechua (and Aymara) are both recognized as having a standard SOV word order, this grammatical status today is also imbued with additional ideological stakes, where the maintenance of SOV in spoken Quechua is a mark of linguistic purity and the absence of change in spite of long-term language contact with Spanish.[16] However, what these discursive preferences for SOV exclude is the fact that in Quechua and Aymara conversations, verbs can appear in sentence medial positions.[17] Maribel may have carefully sought to perform Quechua in a way that conformed to idealized expectations of what a good and pure Quechua should sound like. But in the process, her adherence to this kind of linguistic and discursive purity made her sound too formal and less like a typical woman from the region that you might have a conversation with.

Maribel's introductory speech, more than a personal performance of who she was, was a formal performance. That formality was established in her opening address to the judges and audience and continued through the end of her speech, where she shifted the interactional footing of her speech, abruptly ending her direct address to the audience and instead reenacting a play replete with a performative ritual offering of coca leaves to the mountains and deities, and a closing line to her monologue indicating her intention to go back to her work in the fields. These switches in her interactional footing made it seem like Maribel was performing an elaborate monologue that could have appeared from a play written about Indigenous life in Cuyo-Cuyo. Yet for René and the judges, these performative choices moments made Maribel seem distant, cold, and, for René in particular, *soberada* (snooty or arrogant). These were not qualities that either a Belleza champion or even an ideal woman of the altiplano should embody, where the ideal woman should be down-to-earth and have a connection with her community and all those around her.

For René and the judges, the best display of love and pride in one's heritage came from the other contestant from Cuyo-Cuyo that evening, Monica Yanapa. In René's mind, not only was Monica's performance radically different from Maribel's, but she also stood apart from the other contestants in being the most convincing and sincere in performing her love and commitment to promoting her Indigenous cultural and linguistic heritage on the competition stage and in her everyday life. These evaluations, in addition to Monica's grace modeling the different fashions from Cuyo-Cuyo, and beautifully performing Cuyo-Cuyo's venerated ritual dance tradition, the Ayarachis de Cuyo-Cuyo, helped her ultimately secure the crown and win the Belleza competition for the evening.

[Example 32]
Monica Yanapa from Cuyo-Cuyo (Quechua)
1. Allin, allin.
   Good, good.

2. Ñapakuyniyta apamuykichis,
   I bring my salutations to all of you,

3. ñapanpikichisman.
   and I greet all of you.

4. Ñuqaqta suti, Monica Yurley Yanapa Ramos.
   My name is Monica Yurley Yanapa Ramos.

5. <u>Chunka-isqun wataniyuq kani</u>.
   I am eighteen years old.

6. <u>Ñuqa hamushani huk unay llaqtamanta</u>.
   I have come from a village that is far away.

7. <u>Maychus imaymana t'ikakuna kan</u>.
   Where there are all types of flowers.

8. <u>Maychus, hampiq qorakuna</u>,
   Where, medicinal plants fill the mountains,

9. <u>unumanta—q'uni unuhampi</u>.
   that come from the water—hot medicinal waters.

10. Aguas . . . termos medicinales <u>nisqata</u>.
    These are called hot thermal waters [hot thermal springs].

11. <u>Chaymantapis, hatun apu urqukuna</u>.
    And also there, there are large sacred mountains.

12. <u>Chaypi, kinri patapatakuna</u>.
    There, in the mountains are terraces.

13. <u>Chay</u> . . . <u>chay ruwasqan</u> . . . <u>ñawpa runakuna</u> . . .
    That . . . that they were made . . . the ancestors of the past . . .

14. <u>Chaymantapis</u> . . .
    And next is . . .

15. <u>ima munay kay</u> . . .
    how beautiful [this] . . .

16. <u>churakusqay</u>.
    [the way] I have dressed myself.

17. <u>Chaqaypi sapa p'unchay churakuyku</u>.
    Like this in my community I dress myself like this.

18. <u>Imaymana kay montera</u>,
    Take this montera [for instance],

19. <u>Kay, t'ikakuna chaymanta kanmi</u>.
    These, flowers that are from there after all.

20. <u>Kay ajuñakuna nuqayku rurasquy—ruwasqayku.</u>
    This montera we have ma—have made.

21. <u>Hukmanta huk,</u>
    And from the other ones,

22. <u>Kay, kay chukuyku,</u>
    This, this veil,

23. <u>kay lliqllayku ñuqayku</u> tejes<u>qayku.</u>
    This shawl we wove ourselves

24. <u>Qamkunapis,</u>
    You all,

25. <u>sipaskuna,</u>
    young women,

26. <u>qamkuna ruwas—</u>
    you all make—

27. <u>ruwanaykichis.</u>
    You all should make these things.

28. <u>Ama chinkachunchu chay.</u>
    You cannot lose it [the tradition].

29. <u>Hinaspapis kay chalecoy,</u>
    Like this my vest of mine

30. <u>kay chukuy,</u>
    this veil of mine

31. <u>kay p'istuy,</u>
    this jacket [of sheep wool] of mine

32. <u>ima munay!</u>
    how beautiful they are!

33. <u>Kay phulquy,</u>
    These booties of mine,

34. <u>munay.</u>
    are also beautiful.

35. <u>Chaymin llaqtay Cuyo-Cuyo</u>!
    That is my community of Cuyo-Cuyo!

In relistening to Monica's speech, Renée noted that she made some small mistakes such as misconjugating verbs (lines 20; 26–37). However, these moments did not threaten Monica's claim to Quechua fluency nor her connection to her community. Instead, her speech felt natural and reflected how she normally would speak Quechua with other people from Cuyo-Cuyo. Her message and structure of her speech was also simple and direct, focusing on building a connection with her audience through strategically using her pauses and shorter phrases to highlight the unique history, geography, and culture of Cuyo-Cuyo. Most importantly, Monica's introductory speech contained a broader message and imperative for all young women to never forget the Indigenous traditions and practices that are central to their Indigenous heritage. Including this kind of message changed Monica's footing over the course of the speech. Though her speech initially was framed as a performer speaking directly to the judges and to the audience present in the auditorium that day, her message of empowerment shifted her alignments to a broader imagined set of Indigenous listeners, urging them to take initiative and immerse themselves in their Indigenous heritage, communities, and linguistic and cultural practices.

Monica was the only contestant to include a broader message that underscores the importance of knowing and maintaining one's Indigenous cultural and linguistic traditions. And in doing this, Monica was able to perform her love and pride in her Indigenous heritage and identity, highlighting how her love and commitment to Cuyo-Cuyo can be scaled to encompass a love for, pride in, and commitment toward all Indigenous cultures, languages, and traditional practices across the altiplano and Andes. Being able to successfully deliver her introduction on stage already meant that she was confident, poised, and comfortable with performing her Indigenous heritage and identity in front of others. But through her speech, she also established her authority and authenticity as a true native daughter of Cuyo-Cuyo. Finally, in being selected as the winner of the Belleza competition that evening, Monica was also officially recognized as the ideal Indigenous woman of the altiplano.

The Problems of Being Too Perfect: Failing to Perform the Authentic Puneña

As a beauty pageant focused on celebrating the unique identities and female bodies that constitute indigeneity in the altiplano, all contestants in the Belleza del Altiplano competition were expected to align their performances with the signs that lend to the enfigurement of the ideal Indigenous puneña. This requirement superficially might seem like the easiest to fulfill. After all, if contestants performed their community-specific Indigenous practices, linguistic varieties, and identities that were located in the altiplano, then by extension they would be interpreted by judges and audiences as having performed in a way that conformed with idealizations of the perfect Indigenous puneña. Yet in an era where young puneñas, and Indigenous puneño youth more generally, are opting to learn their heritage Indigenous language from institutions, the ability to present a linguistic performance that is authentic to speech practices in the altiplano is not necessarily a guarantee. This also means that contestants, recognizing that judges value performances that are linguistically pure, may also modify or alter their introductory speeches in ways that reflect how Quechua and Aymara are taught within these institutions. But in doing so, contestants also introduce linguistic and communicative elements that are distinctly not puneña. Linguistic performances that are too perfect, both in linguistic composition and in the manner of delivery, become performatively salient for not capturing the distinct essence of puneña femininity—a subcategory of the figure of Indigenous female personhood that frames the ideal Indigenous woman of the altiplano as having a beauty and grace that is balanced with strength of character, assertiveness in spirit, and a directness in her speech. These are qualities that define Indigenous femininity, beginning with Mama Uqllu. More importantly, they are qualities that are shared (albeit to different degrees) by Quechua- and Aymara-speaking puneñas alike.

This issue of being too perfect, where a contestant runs the risk of being seen as inauthentic to the identities and experiences of Indigenous women in the altiplano, directly affected the evaluations for Adelina Pacco. Representing the Quechua-speaking district and community of Coasa, Adelina had many of the qualities that, on paper, René and the other judges felt would set her up as a particularly strong contender for the Belleza crown. She was beautiful; had stage presence, confidence, and poise; was knowledgeable about her community; and generally seemed to possess a love and pride for her heritage and identity as an Indigenous woman from Coasa. These qualities certainly helped how Adelina fared in the competition, whereby the end of the night she was named a runner-up to Monica's winning performance. However, one major critique that René and the other judges leveled against her performance was how the Quechua she used in her introduction speech did not sound like it came from any Quechua-speaking community in the altiplano.

[Example 33]
Adelina Pacco from Coasa (Quechua)
1. Ave Maria <u>purisima</u>.[18]
    Ave Maria [and her purity].

2. <u>Kay pipas, ñuqay pipas, mana kanqachu</u>,
    Whoever is here, with me as well, and those who are not here with me,

3. <u>chay llaqtamasi ñuqari(k)i kanqa</u>.
    will be like our community friends.

4. <u>Qam ripunkiyaña chaypas</u>,
    even though you may leave,

5. <u>uyarikunqachu</u>,
    you all will listen,

6. <u>puñenopas kaykita</u>.
    about Puno.

7. <u>Punumantasqani, Punumantasqa hamuni ahina ñañay</u>.
    I am from Puno, and from Puno I come like this my sisters.

8. Mamita Candelaria <u>sutichayamanta</u>,
    In the name of the Virgin of Candlelight,

9. <u>qallariqamusaq</u>.
    I am going to begin.

10. <u>ñapakuyniwan, yuyaychaykunawan</u>,
    I greet all of you with my speech,

11. ahinayata tukuchaykumushasaq [inaudible].
    and like it [my speech], I will end [inaudible].

12. Imanaylla kapushawankichis ayllu masikuna?
    How are all of you friends and neighbors?

13. Imanaylla kapushawankichis ayllu masikuna?
    How are all of you friends and neighbors?

14. Allillanchu kashankichis?
    You all are well?

15. Qaliqllachu? Kusiskallachu?
    Healthy? Happy?

16. Muna(s)qachu kay sumaq ch'isikuypi.
    Beloved audience tonight is a beautiful night.

17. ñuqapis ancha kusiska chaymurqamuni.
    I also have arrived very happy.

18. Sunquypas imanayllatataq, "potokuq potokuq" nispara nishawan.
    My heart as well is beating with a "potokuq potokuq."

19. ñuqa hamushani kay hatun ñañ (ay)kuyman, llapa Coasa [inaudible]—
    I have come on this great road for my sisters, for all of Coasa [inaudible]—

20. visitapi turismo, k'aya nichisikiwipi.
    and visit for tourism, [untranslatable].

21. Coasa llact(a)paq, pimanta, sutimanta, ñapakaykamu(y)kichis.
    For the village of Coasa, for whom, in the name of, I salute all of you.

22. Chaymantapis, chayachakamu(y)kichis huk hatun qhapaq ñan,
    After all, for you all I made a grand journey [here],

23. sapanqa muyunqachispa [inaudible]
    and for each every single one of us going around [inaudible]

24. Ancha sumaq umalliq nin,
    as a great leader said,

25. llactanchis michik kuraq turay hamaut'a,
    the leader who is our teacher and older brother for our people,

26. Juan Luque Mamani,[19]
    Juan Luque Mamani,

27. ancha munasta llaqta kamachi(chi)qkuna—
    beloved by all the authorities of the villages—

28. kay hatun felizmanta.
    of this great festival.

29. Ahinallataq, huchuychaq aylluskunamanta,
    like this, for the small communities,

30. kay sumaq sipas atipanakuy,
    this competition of beautiful young women,

31. qhari, warmi, akllatytakuna.
    men, women, the selected competitors.

32. Chaymantapis,
    And after this as well,

33. ñuqa pachata illariykurqani.
    I was born at this twilight hour.

34. Haqay—ñuqa hampacha illariymurqani Coasa llaqtaypi.
    [From] there—I from a young age was born in the village of Coasa.

35. Haqay charango, mandolina, chilladora rasqakuna nirqampi.
    There where the men who play the charango, mandolin, and chilladora.

36. Qhari, wayna wakapunachiqkuna ayllumpi.
    Men, young male cowherders in the village.

37. Chaymantapis
    And as well

38. kuraq turayku, Nestor Enriquez Rodríguez Willpachura.[20]
    our big brother, Nestor Enriquez Rodríguez Willpachura.

39. Chaypaq patachanmi,
    In addition to this,

40. llaqtamasinmi, kanchamasinmi kashayanmi.
    The neighbors and kinsmen [from Coasa] are here.

41. Coasamantasqani, Coasamantasqa hamuni.
    I am from Coasa, I have come from Cosa.

42. ñuqa pachaqallariq kani.
    I am going to begin.

43. Mama killa[inaudible] kunapi, munayta k'acharinkusqayku
    In this night with Mother Moon [inaudible], we are going to dress ourselves beautifully.

44. Hinallataq, awichinapas, kay . . .
    And like as well, for the grandparents, this . . .

45. haqay masi phaway(kachaqa)hasqa [inaudible]—
    my fellow kinsmen from there who traveled across [inaudible]—

46. (q)uchuñapuni pacha kusikuymanta.
    [untranslatable] this is the time to be happy.

47. Tata mamaypis, ancha kusiska suyamurirqanku.
    My parents as well are really happy and waiting [here].

48. Chay punchaytaqmi kasqa, isqay chunka soqtayuq,
    Today is the twenty-sixth day,

49. [audience shouting]

50. Illapachayuq uchayta,
    and with thunder,

51. [audience shouting "hora"]

52. ñuqaq wataykaqmi isqay chunka hukniyuq.
    I am twenty-one.

53. ñuqay kay . . . ñuqa rimamusqaykichis pachaykuymanta.
    I am here . . . I will speak with all of you about my land.

54. Qhawarichakichis hinapas ima sumaq montera qhawkankichis.
    As we can see like this how beautiful is this hat for you all to see.

Adelina's performance at that moment was cut short, as René and the judges in the front signaled her to end things quickly. This meant that she had to end her speech and not say everything she had originally planned in order to convince René and the judges that she could be a potential Belleza winner. Like Marcelina's performance, Adelina's performance disappointed René in a few ways. First, as a young woman from Coasa, Adelina was pretty and sweet, and matched several other discourses across the altiplano that also describe the women from Coasa as being sweet and naturally pretty. For instance, when I discussed the competitors with Señora Fidelia in the days following the competition, she also agreed with Adelina's final place as runner-up for the Belleza crown, saying, "Oh, the girls from Coasa are really very pretty and beautiful." From previous experiences, René also knew that Adelina spoke Quechua and was comfortable conversing with her family and kinsmen in her local Quechua variety. However, this aspect of her linguistic knowledge did not come through that evening, resulting in a performance that did not reflect how a true woman from Coasa should speak.

In this vein, part of the problem with Adelina's speech was its length and discursive structure. In addition to it being too long, it meandered in different directions, focusing too much time on recognizing elected officials or commenting on the evening and not enough on who she is and the region that she is from—things that she mentioned over halfway through her time on stage (line 41). This longer format to Adelina's speech, and the fact that it seemed to be almost too formally structured, was a sign to René that the speech was memorized, and also a script that she had written with the help of a trained expert in Quechua. This formality could be noted not only in the structure and content of the overall speech (which was cut short), but also in how each line was constructed with selecting hyper-purist lexical alternatives instead of more colloquial variants or syncretized Spanish loans (line 8, line 13) and the use of repetition and parallel structures (lines 7, 41, and 54).

What amplified these mistakes was also Adelina's delivery, which René said he and all the judges noted was performed like she was singing (*"como si fuera cantando"*), regularly modulating her pitch between high and low tones that gave a rhythm and some basic tuning to everything she communicated. Her sing-song approach to her speech became even more noticeable because Adelina did not stand still while speaking to her public. Instead, she was constantly moving from side to side, coordinating the lightness of her steps with the high and low tonal changes of her speech. Though this way of speaking might have been coached by a tutor or teacher with institutionalized training and expertise in a more standardized form of Quechua, her performance contradicted general expectations of how puneña women, regardless of if they are Quechua speaking or Aymara speaking, are expected to communicate in the altiplano.

Typically, puneños characterize how they talk as being *directo* (direct), *seco* (dry), and *tosco* (rough). At times during our post-competition conversations and review of the contestants and their performances, René echoed these remarks, saying that a true Quechua puneña must sound seco and tosco. Included in this list is the qualifier *frio* (cold), indicating to some degree that these qualities are embodied in the speech practices of puneños because they match the landscape and the environmental demands of living in the altiplano, which is also a colder, drier, and rougher climate and environment to be in. Some Quechua speakers I knew would also comment that these qualities in the different varieties of puneño Quechua were also a product of being in contact with Aymara-speaking communities; the years of close proximity with Aymara speakers in Puno changed the basic aesthetic properties of Puno Quechua such that it shared many of those same qualities found in Aymara. During my fieldwork, I was often told by my Quechua-speaking interlocutors that not only was the Quechua spoken in Cusco or Ayacucho the best, but it was also the sweetest and most beautiful sounding Quechua. By contrast, the Quechua of Puno is rough and not as pleasant sounding as the other Quechua varieties spoken in Peru.

In our conversation after the competition, René echoed many of these sentiments, saying that Adelina's performance was too *dulce* (sweet) and therefore sounded inauthentic to how Quechua is spoken both in Coasa and across Puno and the altiplano. Yet this sweetness also betrayed the main qualities of puneña Indigenous femininity that the Belleza competition was designed to highlight and celebrate: the strength, toughness, and resilience of Indigenous women of the altiplano. True, Indigenous women from the altiplano may not speak as sweetly as their peers across the Peruvian Andes. But by speaking in ways that are less pretty and more direct, rough, and dry, Indigenous puneñas also embody and personify those speech qualities in their everyday lives, making women who are tougher, more direct, and more resilient.

For René and the other judges, Adelina's performance completely rejected the qualities and characteristics that defined puneña indigeneity in

Coasa and across the altiplano with her hyper-perfect speech. While she might have performed aspects of an Indigenous female identity, it did not speak to the qualities and characteristics that define Indigenous women from Coasa, or from the altiplano more generally. This failure in Adelina's performance also highlights a deeper, underlying tension within institutionalized competitions and performances of Indigenous authenticity for Indigenous puneña femininity. Formally organized performances like the Belleza del Altiplano competition, complete with the backing and sponsorship of other noted regional institutions like Pachamama Radio or the Federación de Folklór, may feel the need to align their own practices of promoting Indigenous identities in the altiplano in ways that conform with national or global expectations of what Quechua and Aymara speakers and Indigenous communities should be like. This is certainly the case with participating in practices that contribute to promoting and upholding a distinct ethnolinguistic boundary between Quechuas and Aymaras. Yet the comments and reactions toward Adelina's performance also highlight a different set of sensibilities that recognize the importance of maintaining and promoting forms of Indigenous identity and inter-Indigenous differences in the altiplano beyond discourses of Indigenous ethnolinguistic difference between Quechuas and Aymaras. Furthermore, such differences extend beyond those between languages and can only be legible and understood through the embodied practices of people from these communities, such as the performances by young women in beauty pageants and other kinds of public spectacles and events.

In this regard, linguistic perfection can be interpreted as upholding ideologies of ethnolinguistic difference, while aligning Quechua- and Aymara-speaking contestants with linguistic ideals spoken in ideologized centers of Indigenous linguistic purism. Yet by adhering too closely to such standards, contestants run the risk of betraying their commitment to the linguistic and cultural practices that make the altiplano distinct and unique. To be puneña and from the altiplano means to have a deep understanding of these differences that together establish and reproduce inter-Indigenous differences that transcend Indigenous ethnolinguistic labels. And to be crowned winner of Belleza del Altiplano signals not only the full embodiment of this understanding, but also performing and demonstrating it for all to admire and celebrate.

Beauty Pageants and Indigenous Female Futures

Beauty pageants, in all their variations, serve different purposes. At their basest, fundamental level, they are competitions that reproduce and celebrate specific configurations of signs and values that compose an ideal womanhood and femininity. At the same time, these signs semiotically connect to other gendered and nongendered values and ideologized expectations of ideal subjecthood, personhood, and citizenry within each context. The intersection between such ideologized expectations and the public spectacle of female bodies is in some ways not surprising. Instead, the focus on female bodies[21] homes in on the reproductive potential of women in upholding and maintaining such expectations for the future. Through participating in such contests, women are evaluated for their ability to not only perform ideals of femininity but also perform their capacity to reproduce such gendered norms and their associated indexical values in the future by fulfilling their capacity to have and raise children.

The contestants who compete in Indigenous beauty pageants, and especially in the Belleza del Altiplano competition, are not simply competing to reproduce ideas of Indigenous authenticity and purity. Their presence in these competitive genres also contributes to the reinforcement of a new set of ideological parameters that constitute Indigenous identity, authenticity, and, more importantly, inter-Indigenous difference in the altiplano. The confluence of these varying, and sometimes contradictory, ideological points of view are in many ways modern and new, departing from previous ideals of inter-Indigenous difference as well as models and conceptions of indigeneity as were once understood by contestants' grandmothers and mothers. Yet for contestants, this contradiction does not conflict with the basic goals of participating in such competitions. Instead, beauty pageant competitions frame traditional conceptions and modes of understanding Indigenous identity and inter-Indigenous difference within a more modern ideological ground and carry such new modern configurations into the future through imparting these expectations onto the next generation of Indigenous puneños.

The young Belleza contestants were all women who had and maintained close connections with their Indigenous communities. At the same time, they were young women who had all engaged in some form of higher education, taking institutional or vocational courses in Juliaca, or enrolling in the local university in Puno and majoring in education, anthropology, or sociology. And yet, when I talked with René about the importance and value of these beauty pageants, he very confidently remarked, "You see these girls. All of them leave their homes and come to the city to study and become professionals. But they will also go on to be mothers and raise children. And we have to make sure that these girls know how to maintain our traditions and languages when they raise their own children." For René, the judges, audience members, and even some of the contestants themselves, competitions like the Belleza del Altiplano offer the opportunity to showcase and model the ideal Indigenous woman of the future, who, through participating and perhaps even winning these competitions, will be able to promote such ideals for the next generation of puneños through their role as mothers and wives. Being the ideal Indigenous woman of the future does not mean moving away from tradition. Instead, as these contestants highlight, it requires these young women to deftly integrate, balance, and perform their knowledge and expertise of authentic traditions with equally authentic local linguistic practices and make them legible within modern genres and for modern, global audiences. At the end of the night, only one contestant is crowned the winner. But her victory also becomes an important link in reinforcing and maintaining the configuration of signs and indexical features that constitute the ideal Indigenous puneña of the future.

Conclusion

The Gendered Indigenous Voice in a Global World

In the early years of my fieldwork, Lima was abuzz with the publication of the photographer Mario Testino's latest collection. A world-famous fashion photographer, Peru's native son had traveled abroad and earned his renown in the world of high-fashion photography, capturing the latest designs in haute couture from the fashion world's most famous houses. Eventually, his celebrity status was further established by directing fashion shoots that were featured in elite fashion magazines such as American *Vogue* and *Vanity Fair*. By the early 2000s, Testino had already cemented his place as one of Peru's most successful native sons.

Between 2007 and 2012, Testino returned to his roots, capturing the fashions of his native homeland. But his artistic vision took a specific focus—concentrating on the intricate diversity of dress and customs associated with Andean Indigenous individuals. Taking inspiration from Martin Chambi, the early twentieth-century Peruvian photographer of Indigenous, Quechua-speaking heritage famous for his black-and-white photographs of Machu Picchu and Indigenous Andean life, Testino framed his collection, *Alta Moda*, as a series of portraits that highlighted the varied sartorial designs and dresses that are regarded as being iconic of traditional Andean Indigenous lifeways and practices.[1] Following a similar genre of portraiture that Chambi used in capturing images of

Indigenous individuals in the Andean highlands, Testino's *Alta Moda* combined contemporary fashion aesthetics associated with the world of high fashion and haute couture along with the highly focused and intimate study of Andean Indigenous individuals through their fashions.

Testino's *Alta Moda* launched as a museum exhibit in his eponymous museum, Museo Mario Testino (MATE), in Lima in late 2013, followed immediately by the publication of the collection into a book. Although by 2014 the exhibit had already expanded and traveled internationally and was presented in cities like New York and Dallas in the United States, the collection and the press remarks from the original opening could be seen everywhere in Lima, celebrating not only the meticulous research Testino conducted in conceptualizing the photo shoot, but also the international renown and fame that the Peruvian photographer, and his Peruvian Andean Indigenous subjects, were also receiving from the international fashion and art world. Part of the exhibit's appeal nationally and internationally came from Testino's use of his signature style of portraiture that captures the personality and warmth of his photographic subjects. But the exhibit's popularity also stemmed from how the exhibit and collection focused on physical and visual aspects of Andean indigeneity that reproduced romanticized views and discourses of Andean Indigenous otherness. In this way, *Alta Moda* reproduced what María Elena García (2022) calls the "settler-colonial sublime"—presenting and elevating Indigenous Andean sartorial practices while simultaneously obscuring the appropriation of such practices within a settler-colonial and globalized capitalist framework.[2] While his collection photographed both men and women, the publicity for the event and the image selected for the book jacket featured an Indigenous woman from the southern Andes wearing a traditional dress associated with springtime festivities like carnavales from the community of Espinar, in the Department of Cusco.

Images of Indigenous peoples, Andean or otherwise, are now mass-circulated, consumable objects at a global level. Such images have circulated across the globe since colonialism (Poole 1997), feeding and cultivating the global imagination of what constitutes an Indigenous Andean individual, subject, and citizen. While those contours might highlight different ideological trends and foundations that have shaped various visual incarnations of Indigenous Andean figures of personhood, Testino's *Alta Moda* highlights how certain genres of capturing and framing Andean indigeneity nevertheless persist through today. Like Chambi, Testino's images reproduce specific ideas about Andean indigeneity, captured through carefully staged scenes and on Indigenous bodies. But the decision to prominently feature the female Indigenous body on press releases for the exhibit and the book also reflects modern discussions and twentieth-century trends that place racial differences and Indigenous authenticity in orbit with social, cultural, and political projects associated with Indigenous women and their bodies (Barrig 2001; Cadena 2002).

These highly circulated images of Andean Indigenous individuals, therefore, have a certain level of ubiquity that makes their indigeneity legible and recognizable at a global level. Yet such images carry a kind of fixity that limits other possibilities of understanding and negotiating Andean indigeneity. Moreover, such images reproduce specific tropes and narratives around indigeneity and Andean Indigenous identity, highlighting Indigenous cosmologies and worldviews in ways that are decontextualized from their day-to-day lived experiences. The narrowness of these tropes becomes more salient when the central figures of these images of Andean indigeneity are Andean Indigenous women—visually immortalized in ways that emphasize not only the indelible links and associations between indigeneity and traditionality but also how female bodies are the primary bearers of those indexical connections.[3] Additionally, they are also images that literally frame indigeneity and forms of Indigenous identity in very specific ways, obscuring other possible ways to interpret or conceptualize what these terms and ways of living might signify for those who reside within diverse Indigenous communities across the Andes. While these images uphold certain connections between Andean Indigenous femininity and Indigenous traditionalism, they do so through a subtle erasure of Andean inter-Indigenous difference, eliding the complex ways that those differences and diversity are both understood as well as inscribed and embodied through the daily communicative and social practices of Indigenous Andean individuals, women and men alike.

In many ways the lives, experiences, and communicative practices of Indigenous puneñas featured in this book counteract these dominant narratives, fleshing out the complexity of being an Indigenous puneña and the role that they play in shaping and negotiating ideologized understandings around Indigenous linguistic praxis and inter-Indigenous difference in Puno. Whether it be narratives on the experiences of being brides and wives or the experiences of market women, these unique perspectives, specific to the linguistic and social histories of Indigenous multilingualism and inter-Indigenous interactions and relationships, emphasize how Indigenous women in Puno have always found ways to navigate across various linguistic and social boundaries of difference. And through these years of interaction and social negotiation, these women have also created niche spaces to cultivate important social networks that define their identity and belonging. Whether it be the networks that Indigenous puneña market women spend a lifetime building and accumulating or the more subtle, quiet, symbolic transformations and social embedding that Indigenous puneña brides and wives undergo in their husbands' communities, these practices and their processes demonstrate how Indigenous puneñas manage linguistic and social multiplicity and difference to establish their membership within various communities across the altiplano.

Yet these narratives and examples are countered with other ones, such as the reinvention and annual reenactment of Mama Uqllu or the performances and evaluations associated with Belleza del Altiplano contestants, which reveal the extent to which even local initiatives aimed at promoting and celebrating Indigenous puneño heritage and social diversity are not immune from the same kinds of tropes and images of Andean indigeneity that are present in the artistic gaze of photographers like Mario Testino, and circulated and consumed by a wider global audience. Both the scrutiny and expectations around the linguistic performance of Mama Uqllu and the promise of a new future for Indigenous puneña identity represented by beauty pageant competitors highlight how these recently ideologized figures of Indigenous puneña personhood are evaluated in relation to shifting ideological expectations that align inter-Indigenous linguistic and social differences along ethnolinguistic ideologized boundaries. The specific qualities of Indigenous puneña womanhood and personhood that each of these female Indigenous figures invoke bear certain similarities with nonlocal, globalized tropes of Indigenous femininity. Like Testino's images of Indigenous female tradition, Mama Uqllu and beauty pageant contestants also frame their performances in relation to the enduring importance of a pre-modern, pre-contact traditionality. Although these subfigures are reframed to explicitly reflect histories of inter-Indigenous difference, the legitimacy of their performances are nonetheless measured and evaluated to the degree to which the Indigenous puneñas (and even non-Indigenous, non-puneñas) performing these subfigures are able to reproduce globally circulated signs and values of a traditional Indigeneity.

As I have shown in this book, these four subfigures of Indigenous wives and brides, Indigenous market women, portrayals of Mama Uqllu, and Indigenous beauty pageant contestants, collectively contribute to a broader ideologized figure of Indigenous puneña personhood. Together, these four subfigures represent not only the range of social and cultural practices that shape Indigenous puneña identity but also the range of linguistic and communicative practices, including transitions and fluidity in multilingual practices and forms of hyper-purist and hyperlocal performances of linguistic authenticity. This spectrum of linguistic, communicative, and cultural practices and social forms, embodied and exemplified by, and through, the daily lived practices and specialized performances of Indigenous puneñas, highlights the competing and often contradictory perspectives on inter-Indigenous contact and processes of Indigenous differentiation. Being puneño means that one has to negotiate between practices that foster fluid or flexible linguistic boundaries in order to allow instance of communicative and social transformations and accommodation, alongside other ideologized practices and discourses that emphasize the boundedness not only between Indigenous linguistic varieties but also those that define hyperlocal social identities and inter-Indigenous differences. The contrast that emerges between these opposing sets of practices and discourses that characterize puneño indigeneity, and the fact that they are regimented and evaluated on Indigenous puneñas, mirrors what I have described elsewhere as intersecting scalar regimes of Indigenous femininity (Narayanan 2022b). Like the figure Indigenous puneña personhood, Andean Indigenous femininity is also a composite matrix of different ideologized scalar regimes. This means that Indigenous women's subjectivities are shaped through different comparative frameworks along racial, gendered, and linguistic axes. Similarly, these contrasting features and practices of Indigenous puneña personhood also reflect competing ideologized scales of evaluating puneño Indigeneity and inter-Indigenous difference.

These scalar evaluative frameworks, therefore, impact and affect the ways that Indigenous puneña women are racialized and gendered by Indigenous puneños, and also by non-Indigenous audiences. These evaluative frameworks also interact with contrasting ideologies around Indigenous linguistic expertise and speakerhood, establishing new evaluative frameworks to measure and legitimate Indigenous linguistic expertise and knowledge, while also erasing, obscuring, or devaluing other forms of Indigenous linguistic and communicative knowledge and practices. The four subfigures of Indigenous puneña personhood described in this book exemplify these differences, where certain figures such as Mama Uqllu and beauty pageant contestants are ideologized to perform privileged versions of Indigenous multilingual knowledge and expertise, making them more legitimate examples of Indigenous puneña female speakerhood in the Andes over other kinds of Indigenous puneña women like Indigenous market women. Yet these inequalities that compare and distinguish between specific types of female speakers are also ideologized further to encompass other kinds of hierarchies that legitimate and authenticate Indigenous speakerhood in Puno and the altiplano more generally. And these evaluations are also centered on gender differences as a primary axis of difference, where the inequalities in linguistic and communicative competence and expertise that separates certain subfigures of Indigenous puneña personhood from others are then reproduced and scaled outward to also encompass the stances that privilege Indigenous puneño men over women as more legitimate representatives of Indigenous language speakerhood, Indigenous ethnic identity, and inter-Indigenous ethnic difference.

Such inequalities, for instance, can be seen in the discrepancies between how Indigenous men and women are represented in public performances and spaces in Puno. Although I have focused on specific, privileged public performances of Indigenous puneña identity, it is important to note that these select domains for Indigenous female public performances pale in comparison to other public spaces that are largely dominated by men. Local politics at the departmental level highlight this discrepancy, where politicians in the region are primarily male. Female participation in local politics is noticeably less. Moreover, female politicians, like their female counterparts performing as Mama Uqllu or in beauty pageants, are scrutinized more closely if they are unable to demonstrate their fluency and knowledge of their lengua materna. Male candidates are often exempt from this same kind of public scrutiny, where the degree to which they can effectively command their lengua materna is often excused by puneños and not often considered as a deficiency or fault of these candidates.[4]

Such gendered differences also permeate into the basic intersubjective experience of ethnographic and linguistic fieldwork. During my time in Puno, it was rare for any male Quechua or Aymara speaker to feel that they were unqualified to speak their Indigenous linguistic variety, or express concerns that they somehow lacked the appropriate knowledge that they felt they needed to participate in an anthropological study of Quechua or Aymara linguistic practices in Puno conducted by a researcher from a U.S. academic institution. The same, however, was not true for many of the women I met, who often were very reluctant to participate in this study. Instead, they would suggest that I speak with their husbands, fathers, or brothers, who they felt would be better suited to help me with my research. These conversations and reactions highlight how such gendered discrepancies come to bear within basic interactions, even for those with whom I had become well acquainted during my fieldwork. Although these gendered discrepancies for self-evaluations of linguistic fluency should not be read as a cause or reason for why Quechua- and Aymara-speaking puneñas might be interpreted as less "authentically" Indigenous than Indigenous puneños, they nevertheless serve as another touchstone to understand the complex gendered dynamics that shape past histories and ongoing discussions of inter-Indigenous difference, Indigenous linguistic knowledge and praxis, and the practices and characterizations that constitute legitimate Indigenous speakerhood in the region. These differences in how people evaluate their indigeneity, Indigenous authenticity, and even Indigenous linguistic knowledge and proficiency, are not simply a product of gendered inequalities in the region. Instead, they are a product of a larger set of processes that involve the intersection of gender differences in histories of inter-Indigenous relationships, Indigenous multilingual communicative practices, and competing regimes of understanding and negotiating inter-Indigenous identity and social differences.

All these examples stress the importance of centering gender differences within any context of language contact, especially when considering the dynamics of linguistic and social contact between minoritized, Indigenous, or other kinds of subaltern groups. The description and analysis of the four subfigures of Indigenous puneña personhood, along with these other metalinguistic evaluations of the linguistic legitimacy and proficiencies of Indigenous puneño men and women, highlight how past and current understandings of Indigenous identity, of Quechua and Aymara as languages, and even who counts as a speaker of each, has always been and continues to be a gendered question that treats and evaluates men differently from women. These tensions are at the center of kinship practices that are founded on linguistic and social transformations, and important to encouraging diverse translinguistic repertoires and practices, which sustain the livelihood of Indigenous market women. But perceptions and evaluations of these linguistic and social practices, and the ways that they are also reflexively purified and idealized in Mama Uqllu and beauty pageant performances, brings to the fore how newer ideologized expectations around inter-Indigenous linguistic legitimacy and authenticity become meaningful when embodied by Quechua- and Aymara-speaking women.

Centering the Indigeneity of Contact

The building for the Unidad Nacional de Comunidades Aymaras (UNCA), the national political representative body for all Aymara-speaking communities across Peru, looks like other recently constructed buildings in Puno. Cement and brick exterior, with darkened windows to keep out the sun, UNCA's headquarters practically blends into its urban landscape. If it weren't for a tiny, handwritten sign above the main doorway, and a poem in Aymara painted on one of the outer walls of the building, it would be almost impossible to discern that the building was an official political headquarters, let alone a building dedicated for elected UNCA officers and representatives. But because the building happened to be on my walking route between Mercado de San Ignacio and Pachamama Radio, I regularly made it a point to pop in to see if I could casually catch up with any officer or representative who happened to be in Puno.

CONCLUSION   273

I was fortunate to become acquainted with two of UNCA's presidents during my time in Puno. During the early stages of my fieldwork, the president was a man named Mauro Cruz, who was UNCA's president from 2012 to 2016. During his tenure as UNCA's president, Mauro saw his office as the representative arm of all Aymara-speaking communities and the broader Aymara nation in Peru. As such, he not only spent most of his tenure traveling around the altiplano to hear the needs of different Aymara-speaking communities, but also made it a point to meet with government officials in Lima to advocate for the needs of Aymara-speaking communities in Peru and form alliances with other Aymara-nation representatives in Bolivia and Chile.

Whenever Mauro was back in town, I would try to catch up with him to get a sense about the kinds of political activities and projects he was spearheading on behalf of Aymara-speaking communities across Puno. One day I was curious if Mauro, on behalf of UNCA, ever engaged with Quechua-speaking communities or Quechua-speaking political organizations. At that point, I had seen enough of Puno and had walked up, down, and across the city and its ever-growing periphery. And yet in these ambulatory explorations, I had not once encountered a building or organization for Quechua-speaking communities that was similar in its mission and goals to UNCA. Was there a comparable organization to UNCA in Puno? Mauro acknowledged my confusion but also noted that even though Puno did not have a political organization representing its Quechua-speaking communities, it was not a point of concern since those kinds of organizations existed in other areas in Peru that were home to only Quechua-speaking communities, like Cuzco or Ayacucho. I then asked him, if such an organization were to exist in Puno, would he collaborate and engage with them, similar to how he does outreach with other Aymara leaders and representatives in Bolivia and Chile? After considering my question, Mauro stoically responded, "Quechuas and Aymaras are like oil and water. They can coexist, but they do not mix well."

When I first heard Mauro's response, I took it as a polite and diplomatic way of saying that Quechua- and Aymara-speaking groups, political organizations, and institutions do not mesh well, and that they can merely coexist without any kind of overlap or integration. Like oil and water, the two groups, and the languages that naturalize the boundedness of each group, are kept separate from each other by an impermeable boundary. Today the discursive landscape both within and outside of Puno is focused on the reification and naturalness of Indigenous ethnolinguistic boundaries like Quechua and Aymara. Linguistically, both languages as they are spoken in the altiplano have not undergone any significant grammatical changes to produce some kind of inter-language or mixed variety, despite the length and duration of contact that they have had with each other. Discussions and political projects in Puno and in Peru position each ethnolinguistic group as two radically different Indigenous Andean populations. And across various social scales and domains, the naturalness of a boundary between Quechua and Aymara is also discursively upheld, lending to not only the social force of these boundaries but also a kind of authority and legitimacy that can be associated with each ethnolinguistic label and designation.

Yet in spite of the perceived naturalness of these Indigenous ethnolinguistic differences, the stories, life histories, perspectives, and experiences in this book highlight the numerous ways that such boundaries not only have been traversed, but also have shifted over time across the altiplano. This simple fact presents a different account of Quechua and Aymara inter-Indigenous difference that cannot be reduced to basic coexistence. Instead, inter-Indigenous relationships in Puno have been shaped by complex interactions and dynamics, creating histories that demonstrate the crossing of various linguistic and social boundaries that constitute difference in the region, as well as moments of negotiation that allow puneños to play with these boundaries in distinct ways. Such forms of negotiation continue today, where, despite the dominance of discourses of ethnolinguistic difference, Quechua- and Aymara-speaking puneños are still confronted with the challenge of understanding and sorting out what Quechua or Aymara are linguistically, culturally, socially, and historically in ways that conform to larger movements around Andean Indigenous solidarity, while also reflecting the particular history of the altiplano.

Part of the goal of this book is to highlight the role that Indigenous women play in navigating these histories and ongoing ideological discussions and practices around inter-Indigenous linguistic and social difference in the region. But another goal is to also draw out what inter-Indigenous contact and interactions and relationships look like from the perspectives of Indigenous puneños themselves, especially as they continue to rationalize and reexamine their own Indigenous ancestries and histories of contact with other groups and communities in the altiplano. Contact and interactions between Indigenous groups is not new, where inter-Indigenous difference was negotiated in various ways in the past that was meaningful to Andean Indigenous practices of understanding personhood, kinship, and difference more generally. But it is also not a relic of the past, where contact remains an important and critical piece that informs newer discursive projects that reframe inter-Indigenous multiplicity and diversity in ways that allow the linguistic and social complexity of the altiplano to be legible on a larger social and global scale. Language is a part of this process. It is mobilized in certain ways to help reify the boundaries between Indigenous, ethnic Quechuas and Aymaras. But equally important is also the language that is used to convey such differences, which figures into how puneños advocate for their own representation and legitimacy, and influence how they evaluate their place in this shifting linguistic and political landscape.

Indigenous Languages and Their Speakers: Who and What Counts?

What does it mean to be a Quechua or Aymara speaker in Puno today? What does being a speaker of these Indigenous languages look and sound like? And more importantly, who counts as a speaker of Quechua and Aymara in a zone where those linguistic and social boundaries have not been universally fixed, apparent, or consistently recognized by Indigenous Quechua- and Aymara-speaking puneños? Versions of these questions informed my initial entry into Puno and shaped my interactions and conversations with my interlocutors and friends. These questions also guided how I tried to make sense of the contradictions and moments of overlap between how my interlocutors thought about these Indigenous languages and ethnolinguistic social categories, and how they practiced their lenguas maternas in their everyday interactions. Yet even when removed from the dry, sunny days; cold nights; and hustle and bustle of Puno's busy, narrow streets and plazas, these questions still stick with me and continue to inform my own constant interrogation and understanding of what it means to be an Indigenous speaker in Puno, regardless of gender identity or one's lengua materna. This book is a product of that reflexive meditation on these questions in order to understand how Indigenous puneños navigate their linguistic and social histories, and the ways that those accounts and understandings are also in flux, transforming in response to new social pressures and discursive constructions around indigeneity that they hear as puneños and as Indigenous citizens. Yet I am also keenly aware that these questions cannot be absolutely answered over the scope of this or any book. And that is because these questions, and the kinds of responses that they have elicited, are also in a state of ideological change. Such changes can potentially produce different perspectives on Indigenous language use and inter-Indigenous identity in the future, which in turn can also influence how these Indigenous languages and lenguas maternas will be spoken, practiced, and understood by future generations.

In spite of these ongoing shifts, these questions that I opened this section with remain important for this book for two reasons. First, these questions, and especially the ability to ethnographically ask them, are not constants or social facts that can be universally applied to all ethnographic contexts of language contact and inter-Indigenous multilingualism. The fact that such questions could be asked within Puno today reflects the extent to which this kind of ideological transformation has taken place among Quechua and Aymara speakers. Second, even though such questions can be asked in Puno, it also does not mean that this kind of ideological change is equally represented in the discursive practices and Indigenous communicative repertoires of all Indigenous puneños, reminding us that such ideological and discursive awareness is highly situational (Irvine 2022). In other words, answering these questions and participating in the discursive practices associated with them are not things that every speaker is able to do. Instead, the ability to recognize and respond to such questions are kinds of knowledge that vary across age, residence, and gender. It also means that the ability to answer such questions, and the ways that those answers either align or contradict with Quechua- and Aymara-speaking puneños' communicative practices, are ideologically positioned perspectives that are not equally available for all

Indigenous puneños. Such variation speaks to competing ideological regimes that manage what Quechua and Aymara are as linguistic varieties, all the while also regimenting who, and what, is an ethnic, Indigenous Quechua or Aymara within Puno and the altiplano. Like other kinds of language ideological projects of making and maintaining boundaries, the work of purifying and defining the boundaries of Quechua and Aymara linguistically intersects with other kinds of acts of negotiation to determine what Quechua and Aymara mean as cultural, social, and historical facts. Unpacking how the terms "Quechua" and "Aymara" are invoked across these various social and discursive scales is an emerging ideological project in the region.[5] It is a scalar project that requires a specific kind of access and perspective to understand what these terms encompass and what is at stake by using them (Gal and Irvine 2019; Irvine 2016). Even to use them to measure and rank other puneños as being more or less "Quechua" and "Aymara," or a proficient or poor speaker of Quechua or Aymara, reflects a specific kind of positionality.[6] But this positionality is also connected to a specific set of perspectives, and positioned interests, that influence reflexive commentaries and evaluations of individuals along these categories.

This process of scaling who gets to be recognized as a legitimate speaker of Quechua and Aymara, and who gets counted as an ethnic, Indigenous Quechua and Aymara, is additionally fraught in Puno because of its histories of contact that have complicated the boundaries between languages and speakers. But the complexity of these processes is also shaped by how the semiotic relationships between language and inter-Indigenous difference are also shifting and changing. Questions around who and what counts as a Quechua or Aymara speaker represents for puneños an awareness about these terms as distinct languages, resulting in a recalibration of the relationship between language, linguistic proficiency, Indigenous identity, and Indigenous difference. This ethnography captures a small snapshot of what this process looks like. However, what is important to remember is that such processes are ever evolving, creating new regimes and points of contention that will continue to shape the landscape of how a Quechua or Aymara in Puno should be and sound like. Through this shift, new evaluative frameworks for who counts as a speaker of each language will continue to emerge in ways that magnify not only differences in educational access and professional positionality, but also gender differences within the region.

Underlying all of these changes is a larger, unresolved question about the state of Quechua and Aymara as ideologically constructed and objectified languages within our globalized world. Quechua and Aymara's "language" status today is undeniable. Within intellectual and academic discourses, both varieties are established languages that have deeper histories in different language families. And the presence of such discourses within the broader ideological landscape of Puno has also introduced another term that has also impacted discussions and understandings around Quechua and Aymara speakerhood and linguistic difference: *idioma*. Unlike lengua, idioma carries all of the connotations of a named, bounded, grammatically distinct language. Idioma, when used by Indigenous puneños and non-puneños alike, is often reserved for more globally recognized languages, like Spanish or English. Idioma also refers to the formal recognition and treatment of languages as distinct abstract, bounded grammatical systems. Having idioma thus applied as a categorical descriptor for Quechua and Aymara not only positions these Indigenous ways of speaking as formal, bounded, and abstract grammatical systems, but also confers upon them a level of linguistic legitimacy and recognition that extends beyond Puno and Peru. Talking about Quechua and Aymara as idiomas elevates these Indigenous varieties into linguistic objects that can be discussed, politicized, and recruited into discourses around language rights and Indigenous-language maintenance and revitalization. The ideological effects that come from labeling Quechua and Aymara as idiomas also allows these languages as they are conceptualized and ideologized today to be projected into the past, creating associations that make Quechua as it is spoken today the "language of the Inkas" and present-day forms and grammatical descriptions of Aymara as the "language of Tiwanaku."

Yet these alternative forms of linguistic labeling and their ideological outcomes are also a continuation of the coloniality of language. And here, this linguistic coloniality extends to the ways that Quechua and Aymara are discursively imagined as homogenous, bounded, and immutable idiomas such that they are radically different from the Quechua and Aymara repertoires that Indigenous puneños would identify as their lenguas maternas. Unlike the term "idioma," lengua materna evokes additional intimacies that situate these modes of communication within spheres of domesticity such as the hearth and home. Such indexical associations accentuate the gendered connotations of the phrase, connecting linguistic heritage with mothers and maternal figures, the individuals most closely aligned with the responsibilities of maintaining the transmission and reproduction of locally specific Indigenous linguistic and cultural knowledge. But as lenguas maternas, the legitimacy of these communicative practices and repertoires does not extend beyond the hearth and home, in spite of the advances created by Indigenous language institutions (Godenzzi [1997] 2012; Hornberger 2014; Luykx, García Rivera, and Julca Guerrero 2016) and Indigenous media practices (Swinehart 2012; Villarreal 2017).

Thus, the questions of who counts and what counts as a speaker of Quechua or Aymara depends on if these terms are assumed to refer to intimate communicative repertoires that define an individual's lengua materna or are interpreted to refer to more formally recognized and institutionally backed idiomas. Both orientations toward understanding Quechua and Aymara result in significant differences in how puneños think about and describe their linguistic heritage and qualify their linguistic knowledge. If Quechua and Aymara are discussed in relation to a speaker's lengua materna, my friends, acquaintances, and interlocutors felt more comfortable discussing their linguistic knowledge and speaking their unique lengua materna during interviews and conversations. But without that framing, speakers instead assumed I was asking about their knowledge of Quechua or Aymara as idiomas, requesting that they elaborate on the grammatical features that make each language unique and distinct. And in that framing, my speakers were often more uncertain of how they should, or even could, answer my queries. Unlike a lengua materna, idioma carries additional connotations of formal linguistic knowledge that is regimented and standardized. Claiming to know Quechua or Aymara as an idioma means knowing how to read and write both languages, and to have one's linguistic knowledge certified by other experts. And while a lengua materna is acquired through daily socialization practices, an idioma can only be acquired and realized through formal institutional means. Knowing Quechua and Aymara as idiomas means that speakers can only have access to this knowledge through public domains that are distinct from the domestic, communal, and more social spaces that cultivate a variety of lenguas maternas. Such differences matter, directly affecting how Quechua and Aymara speakers get counted, recognized, or even valued. Moreover, these differences also reveal how the politics of who gets counted and recognized as a speaker are inseparable from the kinds of linguistic objects that are counted to begin with. Together, the politics, policies, and practices associated with counting and legitimating linguistic varieties and their speakers impact the maintenance of Indigenous linguistic knowledge and the future of Indigenous multilingual practices in the region.

Embracing a Pan-Andean Indigeneity in the New Year

Across the Andes, the arrival of the Andean New Year on June 21 has now become an important celebration of Indigenous heritage, cosmology, autochthony, and recognition. In the southern hemisphere the date marks the winter solstice, signaling the shift in seasons when the landscape moves out of the coldest period of the year toward warmer suns that will allow for the cultivation of crops and the reproductive fecundity of livestock. The significance of this time of year was not missed by Spanish colonial missionaries who instituted the celebration of San Juan de Bautista (Saint John the Baptist) on June 24—a celebration that across Puno commemorates the coldest night of the year. The celebration typically features the lighting of a large bonfire in the center of communities in the dead cold of an Andean winter's night. For much of the twentieth century, celebrating the Andean New Year was often performed quietly, a subversive celebration of Andean Indigenous customs that would soon be followed by the more public celebrations of the night of San Juan. Yet with the increasing push toward revitalizing Andean Indigenous political, cultural, and linguistic sovereignty, the celebration of the Andean New Year has now become an official event across the Department of Puno, with smaller celebrations organized by local, provincial municipalities, and a larger celebration organized by the Federación de Foklór in the regional capital of Puno. Like other productions staged by the Federación, the celebration of the Andean New Year is also a regimented event arranged by the expertise of local authorities to contain elements

CONCLUSION

that are recognized as the epitome of traditional, pre-contact, Andean Indigenous cultural and religious practices.

Because of this, the ritual celebration is a piecing together of various traditions found across the altiplano that are associated with the Andean New Year and with other kinds of Indigenous celebrations. Central to the celebration is the construction of a ritual fire to make an offering to Pachamama (Mother Earth). Depending on the year, the event can also include the sacrificial offering of an alpaca. Traditionalism also extends to the clothes that people wear to the event, which largely consists of textiles made of alpaca fibers, and wearing the traditional *ojotas* or tire-rubber sandals. The event would take place in the early morning hours, before the sun rose over Lake Titicaca. For hours, attendees, who are mostly municipal officials and some local residents interested in the event, will wait patiently in the frigid Andean winter temperatures, waiting to see the first rays of sunlight rise over the horizon above Lake Titicaca, thus marking the new year and the beginning of another revolution around the sun.

Since I started conducting research and fieldwork in Puno in 2014, I became accustomed to waking up early to watch the ritual in Chucuito. As an Aymara-speaking community, the ceremony was primarily conducted in Aymara and performed by a local Aymara-speaking yatiri. But in 2017 I decided to attend the Andean New Year ritual celebrations in the regional capital of Puno, wondering if aspects of the performance might be different from what I had previously seen. While the 2017 performance had many of the same basic elements as the celebration in Chucuito, the ritual also incorporated performances and speeches in both Quechua and Aymara, reflecting the shared Indigenous linguistic heritage of Puno.

Most of the main incantations and ritual invocations were conducted in Aymara, performed by the same Aymara-speaking yatiri who also played the role of the principal yatiri in the annual reenactment of Manqu Qhapaq and Mama Uqllu. Quechua was mostly incorporated as smaller asides in the yatiri's speech, utilizing some commonly heard phrases that were also present in the staging and performance of the arrival of the mythical couple. But right before the sun was about to rise over Lake Titicaca, a small change was incorporated into the program. Señora Evangelina, one of the longtime female workers and coordinators at the Federación de Folklór, was given the opportunity to speak during the annual ritual. In the days following the ritual, I would recount the sequence of events of the ritual with some of my interlocutors like Señora Marcela, Señora Fidelia, and Señor Abelardo. In these conversations, all of them expressed some surprise when I mentioned that Señora Evangelina gave a small speech during the ritual. My interlocutors' surprise at the mention of this novelty stemmed from the fact that in these kinds of rituals, women do not have active roles, often standing silently in the background as assistants to the principal yatiri. Señora Evangelina's speech within the ritual therefore added a modern twist to a practice that otherwise restricted any kind of speaking responsibility to men.

[Example 34]
1. De todos los pueblos,
   From all the villages,

2. de todas las culturas,
   from all the cultures,

3. nos encontramos en este momento.
   we all come together to meet each other in this moment.

4. Un momento más sagrado de recibimiento,
   A most sacred moment for receiving,

5. del nuevo año.
   the new year.

6. <u>Tata Inti, Mamay Phaxsi.</u>
   Father Sun. Mother Moon.

7. <u>Quta Mama. Pachamama.</u>
   Mother Lake [Titicaca]. Mother Earth.

8. <u>Qanrayku kaypi llapan huñurusqa kashayku.</u>
   For you all we have all gathered together here like this.

9. <u>Kusisqa sunquwan,</u>
   With happy hearts,

10. <u>sumaq sunquwan,</u>
    with good hearts,

CONCLUSION 283

11. <u>kunan suyakuyku</u>.
    today we wait [for you].

12. <u>Hawan tupaspa kunan sumaq watapi</u>.
    [untranslateable] to meet today on this beautiful [new] year.

13. <u>Sumaq yuyaychaspa</u>,
    For the good knowledge,

14. <u>sumaq kawsaypaq</u>.
    for a good life.

15.   = Yatiri: *jallalla jallalla jallalla jallalla* =

16. <u>Pachamama, ñapachiwayku</u>,
    Mother Earth, we salute you,

17. <u>ñañykita sumaqta</u>,
    your path is good,

18. <u>sumaqta ari</u>.
    it is beautiful.

19. <u>Uywachiwayku</u>,
    Take care of us,

20. <u>Yachaynikiwa(n), allinta</u>.
    With your knowledge, is good.

21. <u>Pachamama</u>,
    Mother Earth,

22. te agradecemos por muchas alegrías,
    we thank you for the many happinesses,

23. por muchas bendiciones,
    for [your] many blessings,

24. por las familias,
    for the families,

25. por los niños,
    for the children,

26. por las madres,
    for the mothers,

27. por los padres, los ancianos,
    for the fathers, the elders,

28. por todos, los que existen.
    for all, who exist.

Presented in a combination of Quechua and Spanish, Señora Evangelina's speech departed from standards of what might be considered acceptable in institutionalized Indigenous rituals and public performances. And given the spiritual significance of the early morning ceremony celebrating the Andean New Year, Señora Evangelina's speech takes on additional salience for going against the expected norms of proper ritual linguistic practices that bar the use of Spanish, and any non-purist version of Quechua or Aymara. Nevertheless, Señora Evangelina's performance also captures the linguistic and communicative essence of being a puneña today. Through combining her knowledge of Quechua and Spanish in a ritual that is shared by all Indigenous puneños, Señora Evangelina was able to pragmatically communicate the connections and solidarities that unite all Indigenous communities, cultures, and heritages present in Puno and the altiplano. Her speech was not directed to only Quechua or Aymara speakers. Instead it was performed for the benefit of all peoples who trace their belonging and identity to Puno and the altiplano, thus utilizing her different linguistic repertoires to reach out and speak to as broad of an audience as possible, and not solely limiting her message to only other Quechua speakers like herself.

To be an Indigenous puneño means navigating such contradictions, such as the tension between being different and distinct, while also sharing a broader set of cultural practices. Yet these differences are also made more meaningful by the different roles that men and women play in such ideological and discursive negotiations, as well as the different kinds of expectations and practices most closely associated with each Indigenous gendered subjectivity. As this book has carefully shown, Indigenous identity, Indigenous linguistic difference, and gender are intimately linked, forming a close relationship that adjusts itself even with the introduction of new ideological orientations toward gender, Indigenous identity and difference, and Indigenous linguistic praxis. On the winter solstice and Andean New Year, a day of renewal and continuity, those relationships were reproduced through the performances enacted by ritual specialists and other participants. But even in this ritual space, the introduction of small changes such as the inclusion of Señora Evangelina and her linguistic repertoires opened the door for new alignments between Indigenous linguistic authority, Indigenous identity, and gender to take hold, commemorating the dawn of a new year and signaling a potentially new vision of Indigenous puneño identity for the future to come.

Notes

Introduction

1. The one other time that any attempt of documenting Indigenous ethnic differences on the national census was in 1961, which included questions regarding cultural practices, dress, and language of Indigenous communities across the highlands.
2. The term "Inka" has been more commonly spelled with the *c*, as seen in English-language textbooks as "Inca" and "Inca Empire." The use of the *c*, however, comes from a colonial orthographic practice as first written by Spanish conquistadors and explorers. While the *c* follows the orthographic practices of Spanish colonial writers and conquerors, the use of the *k* aligns with the phonemic inventory of Quechua, referring to the voiceless, unaspirated, velar stop. Considering the colonial associations with the orthographic spelling of Inca, and the phonetic and phonological significance associated with *k*, I will use the *k* in all places that typically have utilized the *c*. This decision also follows Mannheim's rationalization for the *k* over the *c*, which includes both the colonial origins of *c* and the fact that the *c* in colonial records and writings was also used to represent the unaspirated, uvular, voiceless stop [q].
3. The glorification of a pre-Hispanic Indigenous past and identity would subside within Peruvian national politics for the remainder of the nineteenth century. The resurgence of the glorification of an Inkaic Indigenous past as a key part of Peruvian racial and national identity would only reemerge in the early twentieth century during the indigenista movement that helped reshape discussions around Peru's Indigenous roots and heritage and Peru's racial identity as a nation of mestizos. This period also saw shifts in discussions around race that contributed to the dominance of ideas around mestizaje, where Andean intellectuals in the 1920s and 1930s began to interrogate and critique the biological

underpinnings of race and advocate for an epistemological shift to think of indigeneity and racial differences as based on moral, and later cultural, differences. As Marisol de la Cadena (1998) notes, however, these intellectual shifts created a "silent racism" that denounced biological racism against Indigenous populations while maintaining ideas of racial superiority between Indigenous Andean populations and Spanish-speaking intellectual and professional elites on the grounds of the cultural differences and perceived differences in morality and character between rural, pre-modern Indigenous individuals, and acculturated Spanish-speaking citizens.

4. The terms "Mandinga" or "Mandinka" are colloquially used to refer to people of Afro-Peruvian descent. The term is a reference to the ethnically and linguistically diverse populations originally from Mali, Senegal, and Guinea who were brought to Peru and other parts of Latin America as slaves.

5. Mestizaje as both a racial and national ideology of racial mixture and miscegenation is found across Latin America. However, what mestizaje refers to, and the specific historical circumstances that have guided the development of its racializing ideology in relation to nation-building projects, is also varied. In Peru in particular, Marisol de la Cadena (2005) notes that even the etymological development of mestizo and mestizaje is itself a conceptual hybrid, built on contradictory perspectives on the boundedness of racial and ethnic identities. Moreover, the invocation of mestizaje across Latin America and the Caribbean has also been observed to produce two diverging effects: one of national inclusion and another that reproduces and maintains social differences and forms of exclusion as a means to uphold a unifying nationalist ideology. As Peter Wade (2005) suggests, however, thinking of mestizaje as only either of these processes is too simplistic, arguing that in reality mestizaje is the intertwining of both these processes that in turn shapes embodied lived experiences of individuals and the ways that they rationalize and make sense of their racialized subjectivity.

6. During my time in Puno, there was talk of potentially revitalizing Uru. The subject of this revitalization will be the topic of future research.

7. The deep historical connections of Quechua-Aymara contact have been corroborated with more recent historical linguistic research, which cites a longer history of contact between Quechua and Aymara speakers in the Southern Peruvian Andes. See Adelaar (2012) for more detailed analysis of the different points of Quechua-Aymara contact in the linguistic changes that were the result of this contact.

8. While the origin of the name Quechua is unclear, it seems that it came from the word *qheshway*, or "valley," thus referring to the spoken variety of the people from the lowland valleys (Mannheim 1991). In my own interactions with Aymara speakers, I was told that Aymara is actually the contracted form of *jaya marra aru*, which means "speech of one millennium."

9. Both the indigenista and neoindigenista movements were intellectual, political, and cultural movements that sought to reframe the relationship between An-

dean indigeneity and Peruvian national racial and cultural identity. The details and vicissitudes of both movements and their consequences on the complicated relationship between race and culture, and especially the place of mestizaje and indigeneity in racial and ethnic identities in the nation, has been explored in greater detail by Marisol de la Cadena (2000). In summary, these movements emerged as a reactive project by Andean elites who wished to elevate the symbolic cultural and political significance of the Andean region vis-à-vis the cultural and political hegemony maintained by Europeanized coastal elites. The two movements differed in their relative approaches and engagement with Andean Indigenous populations and Andean indigeneity writ large. The indigenista movement was primarily focused on elevating the cultural significance of pre-Hispanic Andean Indigeneity, particularly the language, government, and civilizations associated with the Inka empire. The neoindigenistas extended this cultural focus on indigeneity to focus on mixture and acculturation that elevated processes of mestizaje and set the stage for later discourses that defined the racial character of Peru as being a nation of mestizos. Through this, both movements nonetheless perpetuated the continued marginalization and racialization against contemporary Andean Indigenous populations, considering them less legitimate than their pre-Hispanic forbears or incompatible with a modern nation of acculturated mestizos. Neither movement was explicitly about language. However, both movements operationalized specific ideological associations between language, race, indigeneity, and gender that continues to inform any analysis of Indigenous language use and indigeneity today. These associations will be explained in further detail in the remaining chapters in this book.
10. See Boesten (2014) for an alternative analysis of these processes through the lens of Judith Butler.
11. There is another zone of contact in the Department of Puno between Quechua- and Aymara-speaking communities between Taraco and Huancané that is also home to inter-Indigenous multilingual interactions (Moya 2013). However, during my preliminary visits, I noticed that these interactions were limited to market days, and the boundary that separated Taraco and Huancané as communities separated the languages spoken in each community, where Taraco was known as a Quechua-speaking community and Huancané an Aymara-speaking one.
12. UNCA stands for Unidad Nacional de Comunidades Aymaras, the representative organization for Aymara communities across the Department of Puno and Peru.
13. For more on linguistic life histories as a method, see Babel (2018) and Kroskrity (2021).

Chapter 1

1. For Señora Florencia, these complications became even more apparent when I finally was able to conduct a sociolinguistic interview with her, in which she had some difficulty answering my questions about her linguistic knowledge and competence (Narayanan 2023).

2. The placement of Todos los Santos celebrations on November 1 and 2 is not only a product of Spanish colonialism. This time of year has also been traditionally associated with venerating the dead even in pre-Hispanic times and can be seen in the names of the month in which these celebrations take place, which is *Ayamarka killa* in Quechua and *Ayamarka phaxsi* in Aymara. Ayamarka refers to the spaces associated with the dead and recently deceased.
3. A more detailed ethnographic account and analysis of the shifts in understanding place-based versus ethnolinguistic modes of identification and how they relate to locating and understanding differences in the altiplano can be found in Narayanan (forthcoming).
4. This kind of difference, however, can be seen across the altiplano, where communities that today may say that they speak the same "language" nevertheless have differences between them. The most notable example of this is the differences that are found within and across the two main Aymara-speaking regions within the altiplano: first, the southern Aymara provinces that begin in the regional capital of Puno and continue along the southern rim of the Lake Titicaca basin toward the border with Bolivia and, second, the northern Aymara provinces that are primarily Moho and Huancané, and Conima, which are often regarded as the locations of the sweetest or more pleasant-sounding Aymara in the region. However, similar kinds of variations can be found across the various Quechua-speaking provinces too, which highlights how such minute variations nevertheless are just as important as cross-linguistic differences in constituting inter-community and inter-Indigenous differences.
5. One issue in these cross-linguistic marriages that I could never fully get a response about was how individuals from different linguistic backgrounds met and got married. With the exception of women who primarily worked in the city of Puno, details about courtship were rarely shared with me, as several older women in their late fifties through late sixties would dismiss those questions or those details. This could have been because of my age, or rather, that those details and stories were not considered appropriate stories to share with me, who was so much younger than them. But from the few times that I was able to elicit details about the process of courtship, these details seemed to focus on one of two options. First, a woman's hand in marriage was something that was requested and agreed upon by the parents of families, where typically the boy's parents or elderly kinsmen would go to the girl's family and request their daughter's hand in marriage. The second way, which happened for some of the women in cross-linguistic marriages I came to know, occurred through introductions and encounters between couples would happen during *carnavale* celebrations. Typically the celebrations are open to non-community members to participate in the festivities. It is also a time for young people to meet, providing a space for courtship that is in line with the celebration of spring and fertility. These celebrations therefore provide an opportunity for new relationships to be formed and, in some cases, participate in unions through bride capture

(Van Vleet 2008). While these stories of meeting one's future spouse or partner in carnavales might bear some resemblance to modern, Western notions of love, courtship, and companionate marriage, it is also important to remember that for older puneños in their forties, fifties, sixties, and older, marriage is not always talked about in terms of love and courtship, and instead is regarded as just another step in shaping one's personhood and an important site in the reproduction of sociality across the Andes.

6. This aspect is important and differentiates the relationship between language and kinship in the altiplano from other cases of Indigenous multilingualism across the Americas. In a similar pattern of marital and linguistic exogamy, for instance, Janet Chernela describes how linguistically exogamous women in the Uaupés River region in the northwestern Brazilian Amazon are still able to provide some socialization to children in the various matrilects of the community, creating a unique community of practice where children are immersed in their patrilect yet are also aware of their mother's language and the boundaries between the two.

7. The ways that these narratives as warnings emerged during my many casual conversations with older puneña women in their fifties and sixties highlight the dialogic nature of performance, akin to Van Vleet's account of being warned about the dangers that are associated with traveling alone through the highlands (Mannheim and Van Vleet 1998). Normally, these warnings would emerge after being asked if I was married or single (at the time, single), which would then be followed by a longer conversation about the virtues of remaining single and all the problems that other young women my age have faced from impetuously coupling up with the first cute boy that showed interest in them. Other times, however, I would see this same contextual dialogicity emerge in the conversations between women, where a mother would be concerned about the boy her young daughter is dating, which would then elicit a range of narratives and cautionary tales that would work the anxious mother up even further.

8. At the time, this applied to individuals in their late twenties through mid-thirties, younger Indigenous puneños who were closer to my age, and who had also come to Puno to partake in different educational and economic opportunities that the city had to offer. Furthermore, as part of the younger generation of puneños starting families in the region, these cross-linguistic marriages not only took place between young men and women who met each other through work, school, or a mutual friend while living in Puno, but also were based on ideas of love, romance, and companionate marriages. Many of these couples were my peers and friends and would talk about their courtship through narratives that resemble Western notions of dating and forming a relationship based on love, respect, equality, and friendship before deciding to cohabitate together, start a family, and eventually get officially married. These younger, cross-linguistic marriages for Indigenous puneños, who were either younger members of Generation X or Millennials, were based on ideas of companion-

ate marriage and differed from those of older generations of women in cross-linguistic marriages that were not necessarily based on romantic visions of love and respect and instead something that was expected of young women and men once they had entered their early adulthood. These companionate relationships based on love and respect also seemed to create an equal partnership for young couples, which departs from the gendered asymmetries between men and women in previous generations of cross-linguistic marriages. This equality between men and women in younger, cross-linguistic marriages, therefore, could also play a role in changing how the maintenance of maternal versus paternal linguistic and cultural practices are practiced among the children and future generations of these relationships.

Chapter 2

1. While it was more popular to purchase goods from more permanent market associations, it was also equally common for puneños to purchase goods from solo vendors. Solo market vendors would typically only sell items in smaller quantities, making it more affordable for puneños who may not be inclined to purchase things in large amounts.
2. See Buechler and Buechler (1996) and Paulson (2002) for similar ethnographic descriptions of the expansive networking practices of Indigenous Andean market women.
3. The prosodic differences between Quechua and Aymara were often discussed as one of the primary differences between speakers. Aymara was noted for a lack of tonal inflection, which speakers would metalinguistically describe as being more "direct" and drier. The intonational highs and lows in Quechua, conversely, were often metalinguistically interpreted as sounding closer to singing a song, making the language seem more beautiful or poetic when compared to Aymara. One of my Aymara-speaking friends, for instance, used to joke that all Aymara men should learn enough Quechua to sing songs in the language, because Quechua made for a more beautiful language to woo and court a woman.
4. In some ways, the kinds of metalinguistic approximations for Quechua and Aymara provided by market women could share some resemblances with a mock register. These similarities, however, require further analysis. For more on mock registers, see Chun (2004), Hill (2008), Meek (2006), and Slobe (2018).
5. For more on listening repertoires and listening competence, see Slotta (2017).
6. I use interactional footing here to identify and describe the shifts in speaker alignments within an interaction (Goffman 1981), such as the change in alignment that Indigenous market vendors make such that the differences in their linguistic heritage with a customer does not prohibit a potential transaction or sale from going through.
7. Señora Celia worked as a healer, or *curandera*, and reader of fortunes on the side and maintained a dedicated clientele of women who sought out her spiritual healing services. She would often perform informal readings of coca

leaves for some of her customers who would come and see her in her market stall. But on her days off from the market, she would travel to various homes around Puno as a healer through guinea pig readings. According to Señora Celia, healing through a guinea pig involved placing the guinea pig on top of the areas on the body that was causing pain or problems for the individual. She would then kill the guinea pig and open it up to look at the organs and muscles and see if they had changed through the absorption of bad energies from the patient. She would then fix the injury within the dead guinea pig, stitch it back up, and place the stitched guinea pig back on the patient to transfer the healing energies into the human body, all the while chanting and praying to various saints and Jesus Christ. Although Indigenous puneños would seek out medical treatment from formal, modern medical clinics, these practices were nonetheless balanced through the services provided by *curanderos* like Señora Celia and their healing abilities through sympathetic guinea pig readings and repairs.

8. The emphatic ending of *-pe* is a common feature of Andean Spanish that is a product of Spanish contact with both Quechua and Aymara. In addition to asserting emphasis on a statement, its use at the end of sentences also provides a similar evidential effect by asserting the validity of a claim or statement being made. For more on discourse markers in Andean Spanish influenced by Quechua and Aymara contact, see Babel (2009) and Escobar (2011).

9. This kind of code-switching, which pragmatically shifts the interactional footing of speakers, is a common practice among older Indigenous puneños that warrants additional analysis in the future. In these conversations, the shifts in these kinds of narrative and conversational code-switching performs similar metapragmatic effects of voicing other people, or making a commentary on moral differences that have also been analyzed in Jane Hill's (1995) "The Voices of Don Gabriel." Also, these kinds of conversational code-switching also serve as boundary-making and social-distancing practices, similar to Meek (2014).

10. During my time in Puno, it was common to hear puneños from all walks of life discuss the power and evils that come from envy and jealousy perpetuated through gossip and bad intentions. The role and power of envy in talk requires further analysis for future research in the region. For a comparable case in the Andes, see Van Vleet (2003, 2020). For a comparable case in the Middle East, see Hughes (2020).

Chapter 3

1. This kind of hyper-focus on the boundary between Quechua and Aymara contrasts with Karl Swinehart's (2012) analysis of Aymara regimentation practices in El Alto and La Paz, Bolivia, where practices to maintain a "pure Aymara" are focused primarily on the presence of Spanish loans and not on the percentage of shared lexical roots between Quechua and Aymara. As I argue in this chapter and throughout the book, this focus on Quechua and Aymara differences

is reflective of the longer history and visibility of Quechua-Aymara contact in Puno, which complicates how puneños align with discourses of indigeneity and seeing themselves as members within a broader ethnic, Indigenous collectivity.
2. For more on the nature of language in the altiplano, also see Narayanan (Forthcoming).
3. During this time, reading the news online was not at all a common practice for Indigenous puneños. Most puneños at this time did not have internet within their homes, requiring internet use to take place at local, public internet cafes. Even then, most puneños I knew did not use the internet to read up on the news and preferred to rely on reading headlines in newspapers from local newspaper stalls, listening to the news on the radio, or watching the national television channel for their nightly news program. This also applied to puneño youth at the time. While youth were certainly more comfortable with the internet, internet use was limited to social media activity on Facebook. News consumption for this group still relied on access to newspapers or watching the news on the national television station. This was also compounded by the fact that websites for newspapers at this time were minimal, not containing any additional features beyond the main headlines of the day. This meant that interest in columns like *Willakuy-Yatiyawinaka* could only be read through purchasing a physical copy of *Los Andes*.
4. In other areas, bilingual intercultural education is listed as EIB (*educación intercultural bilingue*); however, I will only refer to bilingual Indigenous language programs as IEB because that was the acronym that was consistently used throughout my time in Puno. Moreover, conversations around Indigenous language education programs and practices were colloquially referred to as IEB.
5. IES Maria Salesiana is a pseudonym for the school.
6. Pachamama Radio is not the first radio station to attempt Indigenous-language programming. The oldest in the region is *Onda Azul*, which is still affiliated with conservative factions in the Catholic Church. However, these early Indigenous-language productions were for the most part limited to religious programs and translating sermons and prayers in either Quechua or Aymara. Today *Onda Azul* does have some news programs offered in either language, but because of its associations with the Catholic Church, it is not considered an independent voice for the people like Pachamama Radio. There are also smaller organizations through the local university, UNCA (the political organization representing the Aymara nation in Puno), and IDECA (a cultural preservation organization) that also produce cultural and journalistic content in the Indigenous languages; these programs are broadcasted from Pachamama based on a weekly time that they have rented from the radio station.
7. *Cosmovisión* refers to a general worldview that encompasses the cosmological alignments and ecological beings.

8. Cañihua is another grain native to the Andean altiplano, similar to quinoa. It is typically roasted, ground, and made into a porridge for breakfast.
9. Abya Yala is one of the names given to the New World that is found in colonial-era documents and records.
10. This is especially true for Aymara activists in the region, who see the Aymara communities in Puno as forming the Peruvian side of a broader Aymara nation that extends into Bolivia and northern Chile. To this end, the primary representative body for all Aymara communities in Puno that also serves as the representative body for all Aymaras in Peru (which include the smaller number of Aymara communities in Moquegua and larger numbers of migrant Aymara neighborhoods and populations in Arequipa and Lima) is UNCA (*Unidad Nacional de Comunidades Aymaras*). The president of UNCA is voted in by representatives from Aymara-speaking districts and provinces within the Department of Puno. This president then liaises with the Peruvian national government and with designated Aymara leaders who represent their nations in Bolivia and Chile. UNCA's offices are located in the regional capital of Puno.

Chapter 4

1. These food items are commonly found sold from small street food vendors in Puno and across the altiplano and Andes more generally. Chicharrón is fried, spiced pork rinds, often served with boiled potatoes. Ceviche is a salted and brined fresh fish dish often served with *cancha de maíz*, or toasted corn kernels, which add a salty crunch. Choclo con queso is boiled Andean corn served with a slice of cheese. And lomo saltado con chuño y queso frito is a spicy beef dish served with boiled freeze-dried potatoes (chuño) and fried Andean cheese (*queso frito*).
2. Although Peruvian independence was officially declared on July 28, 1821, the Peruvian wars for independence was a longer series of military conflicts that occurred between 1809 and 1826.
3. In an endnote in the introduction, I described the basic differences between the indigenista and neoindigenista movements. Here, it is important to note that both movements were ultimately projects around defining the racial and cultural identity of the modern nation. Indigenous language use was a small part of this process. However, ideas around Indigenous language use for both projects nevertheless privileged a kind of purist, Spanish-overlaid register of Quechua that was distinct from the communicative practices of Indigenous Quechua-speaking communities across the Andes.
4. These changes to the syntactic structure and discursive practices associated with Quechua first began through colonial translation practices with the purpose of using Quechua for Catholic conversion and transmitting Christian doctrine. Both Mannheim (1991) and Durston (2007) highlight that this regrammaticalization of Quechua conformed to understandings of the grammatical

structures and rhetorical devices associated with Spanish, Latin, and Ancient Greek texts.
5. Unfortunately, I could not find any written record or history that documented the first November 5th performance or the beginnings of the performance of Manqu Qhapaq and Mama Uqllu as part of anniversary celebrations. All details about the first staging of the arrival of the mythical couple come from conversations with local officials at the Federación de Foklór in Puno, and whatever local puneños remember about the event.
6. Because of this issue, the transcription of Mama Uqllu's speeches for both years as well as their corresponding translations were the best approximation that my Aymara-speaking interlocutors could provide from relistening to the event. Approximations provided by my interlocutors, and in particular, those made by Señor Abelardo and Señora Marcela, who helped the most with trying to decipher and make sense of the speeches, are based on the kinds of things that they have grown accustomed to hearing in Mama Uqllu's speeches of the past. Thus, some of those expectations also have shaped the ways that my interlocutors have made sense of the Aymara utterances produced by both Mama Uqllus and the intended meaning that they were trying to convey.
7. According to my interlocutors and in conversation with the actor playing the *yatiri*, the word *"jawilla"* seems to function similar to an "amen" used at the end of Christian prayers.
8. Despite the typological similarities between Quechua and Aymara, the phonotactics between each language contribute to these perceptions of essentialized differences between speakers and their language. The morpho-phonetics of Aymara result in the deletion of vowels in unstressed syllables that produces such consonant clusters (Coler, Emlen, and Banegas-Flores 2022; Muysken 2012). This contrasts with Quechua, which maintains an open CV(C) syllable structure with no vowel deletion. The lack of deletion of unstressed vowels lends itself to the perception by speakers that Quechua is a more beautiful language because it sounds more like a song.

Chapter 5

1. The sikurri tradition is also one that is unique to the altiplano. The tradition of playing specific kinds of songs with rhythmic passes on drums and on the Andean panpipes is said to have originated in the province of Moho, the easternmost province within the Department of Puno that both borders Lake Titicaca and also forms the border with Bolivia. More specifically, the tradition is claimed to have originated within the district of Conima. This distinction has given *conimeños* and *moheños* a unique pride in being from the birthplace to the sikurri tradition that is today regarded as part of the unique folkloric character of Indigenous cultures and traditions in the altiplano. During the annual competition of the sikurris, groups from Moho and Conima as part of their song repertoires will insert a line declaring that they are the *cuna de los sikurris*

(cradle of the sikurris). Similarly, I have seen this line printed on the uniforms of groups from Conima, such as the back of the poncho that all members of that particular *comparsa*, or "group," wears for that year. The sikurri's origin in Conima and Moho also means that the tradition is today read as an Aymara tradition or artform—a view that I have heard echoed by Aymara-speaking puneños, and especially by Indigenous migrants and non-Indigenous residents in larger cosmopolitan cities in Peru like Arequipa and Lima. While the tradition and rituals associated with the sikurris might be more closely aligned with the history and traditions of a few Aymara-speaking communities, the tradition is practiced across both Quechua- and Aymara-speaking communities across the altiplano, where each community has maintained their own repertoire of songs over the generations. Although the annual competition of sikurris does feature a small imbalance in the number of groups from Aymara-speaking provinces versus Quechua-speaking provinces, that imbalance is primarily due to the fact that Conima and Moho tend to send multiple groups each year to compete, while other provinces and districts may only send one or two groups to represent their specific locality.
2. During the times that I would visit friends in Lima, the Candelaria was always one of the few more positive associations that limeños had with the region. As noted in the introduction, most limeños do not have a positive view of Puno or the altiplano and are often unaware of the linguistic and cultural diversity of the region, or dismiss the region as an impoverished, Andean rural backwater. Televising the performances by puneños during the two-week Candelaria period is the only time that residents along coastal cities like Lima get an alternative glimpse of life in Puno and the altiplano.
3. Naming this genre of performances danzas mestizos draws attention to the diverse influences that can be found in these dances. While the majority of them are rooted within Andean dancing traditions in the highlands, such as the *tinkus*, *kullahuada*, and *llamerada*, some dances such as the recent adoption of the *saya* and the more traditional *La Morenada* and *El Rey Moreno* also highlight the histories of Afro-Peruvian slavery from the Andean lowlands and their intersection with highland culture. In this sense, danzas mestizos refers to the non-autochthonous nature of these dances, which through their repertoire and performance and dress do not represent a specific Andean Indigenous autochthonous community or hyperlocal set of practices. Instead, these are dances that have developed and emerged in conjunction with Catholicism and syncretism of Indigenous and Afro-Peruvian histories. However, while I was in Puno, there were two kinds of more specific Indigenous performances included in the *traje de luces*. The first is the inclusion of winning sikurri groups from the August competition of sikurris, with special attention provided to the *ayarachis* who typically come from the Quechua-speaking provinces like Lampa. The second are the *q'arapulis*, also known as the *qina-qina* (or as spelled in newspapers across the altiplano, *quena-*

quena), who typically come from the Aymara-speaking centers like Chucuito and Juli.

4. The incorporation of the caporales dance into the Virgen de la Candelaria celebrations is also fairly recent. Today, this has created a rivalry between the festivities in Puno and the celebration of carnavales in Oruruo in Bolivia, to see which Indigenous altiplano celebration is the larger spectacle. Although puneños and Bolivians will argue and debate as to whether or not the traje de luces dances are really puneño or Bolivian, I think it is best to think of these performances as part of a distinct altiplano identity that is not restricted or limited to national boundaries and borders. Given the porousness between Puno and Bolivia, and the frequency and ease with which puneños will travel to Bolivia (and vice versa), it only makes sense that certain cultural forms and celebratory dances will be shared in the process. Moreover, prior to the wars for independence in the nineteenth century, Puno, La Paz, and Oruro were all part of a single Spanish Catholic administrative region known as Alto Peru, which also reinforces the longer histories of connection and exchange between communities in the altiplano.

5. Dances that are typically only gendered as male are usually dances that highlight or reflect specific Indigenous militaristic dances. These kinds of performance forms portraying fighters and warriors usually involve some play fighting and can include acts of strength or violence from throwing punches to the men whipping each other. One of the top-ranked danzas autóctonas groups in Puno that was a male-only warrior dance was the Unqaqus from Macusani in the province of Carabaya. This, however, is slowly changing, where some of these more militaristic danzas autóctonas are including young women. The push for female inclusion in some of these male-dominated performance genres can also be seen in how women are included in the male roles for dances that also have a female component. For instance, in the danzas mestizas dance, the caporales, the gender differences between male and female energies are sharply contrasted by dress and dance moves. Men wear flamboyant boots and cowboy hats and dance with high-energy choreography. But these groups can also include women, referred to as *machas*, who can participate in the male choreography while opting out of the hyper-feminine costuming that involves wearing heels, miniskirts, and long braids.

6. This chapter focuses on the performances of cisgender, heteronormative Indigenous femininity in Indigenous beauty pageants. However, it is important to recognize the presence and histories of nonbinary and queer Indigenous individuals in the Andes and how they today find ways to perform their gender identity, sexuality, and indigeneity. The organizer of the Belleza competition, René, identifies as a queer Indigenous man and is active in the small but strong queer Indigenous community in Puno. Depending on his own schedule as well as the availability of financial support and resources, he has organized a pag-

eant for queer Indigenous men dressed in Indigenous drag. How Indigenous language use, gender identity, and sexuality intersect among members of this community requires further research and is something I hope to do with my future, ongoing research in Puno.

7. The popularization of Indigenous beauty pageants is not only limited to the Andes; it is also recognized as key in promoting Indigenous cultural authenticity and vitality throughout the Americas. These contests also often intersect with the aims and goals of language-revitalization projects, thus centering ideas of authenticity in and through linguistic authenticity and purity (Wroblewski 2014).

8. There is a smaller competition that evaluates inter-Indigenous difference and authenticity at the Miss Belleza de Foklórica that also takes place in the weeks leading up to the Virgen de la Candelaria celebrations. This competition is split between representing the danzas mestizas and danzas autóctonas. However, this competition is not framed around evaluating Indigenous authenticity through language and cultural authenticity, nor are the contestants in the danzas autóctonas competition given as much space or priority in the competition. Because of this, the Belleza del Altiplano is the only pan-altiplano competition that is solely focused on celebrating inter-Indigenous difference and cultural and linguistic vitality. However, because of the scale of the competition, where René was the primary organizer doing most of the heavy lifting and organizational work for the competition, the event was only held once every two years. For René, this timing was more manageable for raising the funds, securing sponsors and judges, and drumming up support and recruiting potential contestants.

9. The Belleza del Altiplano is an open competition, where any eligible woman may sign up to participate and pay the nominal entrance fee of twenty soles. Eligibility is determined by age and by not winning or placing as a runner-up in previous years. Interestingly, eligibility was not restricted to only residents. This was done so that girls who were from these regional provinces, but who were primarily living in Puno or Juliaca for school, could still participate in the contest on the grounds that they maintained their Indigenous roots and heritage with their natal communities. Because of the open nature of the entry, it is highly common that not all provinces and municipalities are represented equally within the scope of the competition, sometimes producing an imbalance in linguistic representation in the competition as well as sometimes duplicating representation of candidates from the same region. According to René, he and the judges work hard to make sure that in their judging they try to account for these imbalances in producing a round of finalists that have some parity between Quechua- and Aymara-speaking contestants. In the Belleza competition that I attended in 2017, there were a total of twelve contestants: three from Aymara-speaking backgrounds and nine from Quechua-speaking backgrounds.

10. The Señorita Campesina competition was one of the older Indigenous beauty pageants organized by criollo and mestizo elites in the mid-twentieth century in Puno. It was an example of a racializing project of distinguishing Indigenous and mestizo identities as a way to catalog national racial progress during the neoindigenista movement that concluded in the mid-twentieth century (Cadena 2000). Thus, even though the focus of these contests was on Indigenous women, they were neither run nor organized by Indigenous actors, nor did they allow much space for Indigenous female agency, which is centered in more contemporary Indigenous beauty pageants.

11. For the 2017 Belleza del Altiplano competition, I was unable to get a chance to speak directly with the contestants or the judges. Based on past years, with some accusations of cheating or unfair judging, René did not want anyone talking with the judges before, during, or after the competition, including me. Similarly, that year he wanted to ensure that there was order backstage, and he also did not want noncompetitors backstage speaking with the contestants. These decisions he implemented were to ensure that there was no drama or chaos backstage and that the competition occurred without any hitches. I therefore solicited evaluations of each contestant's performances by discussing and replaying the performances with friends like Señora Fidelia and Señora Marcela, who had attended the event in years past but could not accompany me that year. But many evaluations and perspectives from the judges came from René, who had seen their evaluations and also discussed their decision-making process with all of them during and immediately after the competition. René did promise to show me the handwritten notes from the judges so that we could go over their comments together. Unfortunately, in the aftermath of the competition, René lost those forms and papers. Nevertheless, he remembered clearly how each contestant was judged as I replayed for him each of the performances from that evening, combining his own insight as a pageant organizer for many years with the comments and evaluations made by the judges. Although I was not able to speak directly with the contestants before and during the competition, the few that I did meet, combined with post-competition conversations with Señoras Fidelia and Marcela and with René, draw attention to the kinds of linguistic performances that resonate with puneños' ideas around the ideal Indigenous puneña. This suggests that these kinds of discourses extend beyond the Belleza competition and seep into the evaluations and performances found in other locally run Indigenous beauty pageants across the Department of Puno. Moreover, considering that this competition has been run since the early 2000s, and that most contestants are young women whom René had personally recruited to compete, René's comments are also based on how he has seen these young women perform in other contexts and how his comments from the competition in past years go on to inform the next iteration of performances from pageant contestants.

12. This is a colloquial greeting that means "are you good?" and is heard commonly throughout Puno. In an opening, it translates to "greetings."
13. On the original recording, this line was slightly inaudible. Based on my conversations with Señor Abelardo and other Aymara speakers who helped make out the transcription, the line *jach'a jaqi qilqanixa uktsatuqita* seems to be addressing literally "the great people who are writing," which would imply the judges who are present and writing down notes.
14. This commonly heard phrase is a calque of the Spanish phrase *que Dios [te] pagara*, or "may God pay you," which is understood and used colloquially as expressing gratitude even though the ideologized correct form to express gratitude in Aymara is said to be *paysuma*.
15. This transcription of *llapan*, or "all" with the palatal liquid seems to be a Cuyo-Cuyo variant of the glide [j] that is found in Cusco. Therefore, while the contestant said "llapan," in Cusco the pronunciation would be *yapan*.
16. Along with being a point of discussion in ideological discourses connected with Quechua linguistic purity and authority, SOV sentence structures are also a noted feature of Andean Spanish. The prevalence of SOV structures in the Spanish spoken across the Andes is explained as a result of long-term language contact between Spanish and Quechua and Spanish and Aymara, where Spanish syntactic structures grammatically converge to mirror the clausal and sentence structures of both SOV languages (Escobar 2011; Ocampo and Klee 1995). In addition to being a consequence of Spanish contact with Quechua and Aymara in the Andes, this variety of Spanish is also ideologically stigmatized speech practice among Indigenous Andean bilingual speakers, highlighting the influence of Quechua and Aymara in producing a nonstandard, and therefore less correct, version of Spanish than what is spoken by non-Indigenous, Spanish monolinguals.
17. The different indexical readings of word order are not only restricted to Quechua and Aymara. See Jennifer Jackson's (2013) analysis of the indexical associations for Malagasy syntax and the implications of using more formal versus informal syntactic word orders in the *kabary* genre of political oratory.
18. Using this greeting in the opening also indexes traditional greetings during the colonial period.
19. At the time of this research, Juan Luque Mamani was the president of the Department of Puno. Being president of a regional department is similar to being a state-level or provincial governor.
20. The mayor of Coasa during this time.
21. This does not exclude the ways that queer and trans communities have also utilized the beauty pageant genre as a space to contest gendered norms, and within that, contest the normative associations between gender and citizenry. See Besnier (2002) for an analysis of these practices that subverts the link between gender and citizenship in Tonga, and Kulick (1998) for a similar ethnographic approach to queer communities in Brazil.

Conclusion

1. Between 2007 and 2012, Testino conducted research with the costume archive at the Filigrinas Peruanas, one of the largest dance associations in Cusco that has housed and preserved the traditional handwoven costumes associated with dances and ritual festivities from communities across the Department of Cusco. As inspiration for the staging of his portraits, Testino also worked with the Archivo Fotográfico Martin Chambi in Cusco. Even though the exhibit was framed around Indigenous Andean handwoven textiles and fashions, which Testino likened to the amount of detail, attention, and care that is imbued into Parisian haute couture fashions, it is important to note that the exhibit only featured fashions and traditional dresses from the Cusco region.
2. The *Alta Moda* exhibit also featured designs from John Galliano's fall/winter 2005 haute couture collection for Dior that Testino also photographed. This 2005 collection also highlights the settler-colonial sublime of Andean Indigenous and traditional practices, where the collection and show included a specific section of dresses that were directly inspired and touched on the traditional dress and designs of festive wear and costumes of Andean *cholas* from the Peruvian and Bolivian altiplano.
3. Nell Haynes's (2013) discussion of *cholitas luchadoras* in La Paz, Bolivia, also touches on these same connections between the global recognition of the image of female indigeneity and their connection with Indigenous identity and traditionalism. In this vein, the cholitas luchadoras subvert and challenge gendered and racial expectations of traditional, Indigenous femininity, through their participation in *lucha libre*-style wrestling matches and the global attention that they get through these kinds of public performances.
4. This inequality was the case for the president of the Department of Puno from 2014 to 2018, Juan Luque Mamani. Even though Mamani campaigned as an Indigenous Quechua puneño, he normally would not speak Quechua and was known to not be fluent in his lengua materna. This linguistic fault, however, was typically excused by many Quechua-speaking puneños I knew, who still recognized him as a representative of their Quechua puneño identity despite the fact that he was neither fluent nor comfortable speaking in his lengua materna and primarily campaigned in Spanish.
5. See Blommaert (2007) and Blommaert, Westinen, and Leppänen (2015) for further discussion on sociolinguistic scales. For a more comprehensive discussion of scale as a discursive, ideological practice, see Carr and Lempert (2016).
6. For a similar case of this kind of ideological scaling of speakers along the lines of proficiency and knowledge, see Meek (2014, 2016) in relation to the drawing of boundaries around ideal speakers of Kaska and how such idealizations get counted and statistically represented at community-level language-revitalization projects and larger governmental and institutional forms of documenting Indigenous language speakers.

Bibliography

Adelaar, Willem F. H. 2012. "Modeling Convergence: Towards a Reconstruction of the History of Quechuan–Aymaran Interaction." *Lingua* 122 (5): 461–69. https://doi.org/10.1016/j.lingua.2011.10.001.
Adelaar, Willem F. H., and Pieter Muysken. 2004. *The Languages of the Andes*. Cambridge: Cambridge University Press.
Agha, Asif. 2005. "Voice, Footing, Enregisterment." *Journal of Linguistic Anthropology* 15 (1): 38–59. https://doi.org/10.1525/jlin.2005.15.1.38.
Agha, Asif. 2006. *Language and Social Relations*. Cambridge: Cambridge University Press.
Agha, Asif. 2011. "Large and Small Scale Forms of Personhood." In Mediatized Communication in Complex Societies, special issue, *Language & Communication* 31 (3): 171–80. https://doi.org/10.1016/j.langcom.2011.02.006.
Aikhenvald, Alexandra Y. 2010. *Language Contact in Amazonia*. Oxford: Oxford University Press.
Alcalde, M. Cristina. 2022. "Coloniality, Belonging, and Indigeneity in Peruvian Migration Narratives." *Latin American and Caribbean Ethnic Studies* 17 (1): 58–77. https://doi.org/10.1080/17442222.2020.1805846.
Alderman, Jonathan. 2021. "House Personhood in Rural Andean Bolivia." *Anuac* 10 (2): 129–54. https://doi.org/10.7340/anuac2239-625X-4550.
Allen, Catherine J. 2002. *The Hold Life Has: Coca and Cultural Identity in an Andean Community*. Washington, DC: Smithsonian.
Arispe-Bazán, Diego. 2023. "The Racial Politics of Queer, Urban, Second Generation Indigenous Lima Locals." In *Ethnographic Insights on Latin America and the Caribean*, edited by Melanie A. Medeiros and Jennifer R. Guzmán, 149–60. Toronto: University of Toronto Press.

Babb, Florence E. 1998. *Between Field and Cooking Pot: The Political Economy of Marketwomen in Peru.* Austin: University of Texas Press.
Babb, Florence E. 2018. *Women's Place in the Andes: Engaging Decolonial Feminist Anthropology.* Berkeley: University of California Press.
Babel, Anna M. 2009. "Dizque, Evidentiality, and Stance in Valley Spanish." *Language in Society* 38 (4): 487–511. https://doi.org/10.1017/S0047404509990236.
Babel, Anna M. 2018. *Between the Andes and the Amazon: Language and Social Meaning in Bolivia.* Tucson: University of Arizona Press.
Babel, Anna M. 2022. "The Sweet Land: Manufacturing 'Tradition' in Small-Town Bolivia." *Journal of Linguistic Anthropology* 32 (1): 4–27. https://doi.org/10.1111/jola.12303.
Back, Michele, and Virginia Zavala, eds. 2018. *Racialization and Language: Interdisciplinary Perspectives from Perú.* New York: Routledge.
Ball, Christopher. 2014. "Linguistic Subjectivity in Ecologies of Amazonian Language Change." In *Iberian Imperialism and Language Evolution in Latin America*, edited by Salikoko S. Mufwene. Chicago: University of Chicago Press.
Banet-Weiser, Sarah. 1999. *The Most Beautiful Girl in the World: Beauty Pageants and National Identity.* Berkeley: University of California Press.
Barrig, Maruja. 2001. *El mundo al revés: Imágenes de la mujer indígena.* Buenos Aires, Argentina: CLACSO-Consejo Latinoamericano de Ciencias Sociales.
Besnier, Niko. 2002. "Transgenderism, Locality, and the Miss Galaxy Beauty Pageant in Tonga." *American Ethnologist* 29 (3): 534–66.
Bilaniuk, Laada. 2005. *Contested Tongues: Language Politics and Cultural Correction in Ukraine.* Ithaca, NY: Cornell University Press.
Billings, Sabrina J. 2014. *Language, Globalisation and the Making of a Tanzanian Beauty Queen.* Bristol, UK: Multilingual Matters.
Blommaert, Jan. 2007. "Sociolinguistic Scales." *Intercultural Pragmatics* 4 (1): 1–19. https://doi.org/10.1515/IP.2007.001.
Blommaert, Jan, Elina Westinen, and Sirpa Leppänen. 2015. "Further Notes on Sociolinguistic Scales." *Intercultural Pragmatics* 12 (1): 119–27. https://doi.org/10.1515/ip-2015-0005.
Boesten, Jelke. 2014. "Inequality, Normative Violence, and Livable Life: Judith Butler and Peruvian Reality." In *Peru in Theory*, edited by P. Drinot, 217–43. New York: Palgrave Macmillan.
Bolin, Inge. 2006. *Growing Up in a Culture of Respect: Child Rearing in Highland Peru.* Austin: University of Texas Press.
Bourdieu, Pierre. 1991. *Language and Symbolic Power.* Edited by John B. Thompson. Translated by Gino Raymond and Matthew Adamson. Cambridge, MA: Harvard University Press.
Bouysse-Cassagne, Thérèse. 1986. "Urco and Uma: Aymara Concepts of Space." In *Anthropological History of Andean Polities*, edited by Nathan Wachtel, Jacques Revel, and John V. Murra, 201–27. Cambridge: Cambridge University Press.

Bucholtz, Mary. 2003. "Sociolinguistic Nostalgia and the Authentication of Identity." *Journal of Sociolinguistics* 7 (3): 398–416. https://doi.org/10.1111/1467-9481.00232.

Buechler, Hans C., and Judith-Maria Buechler. 1996. *The World of Sofía Velazquez: The Autobiography of a Bolivian Market Vendor*. New York: Columbia University Press.

Cadena, Marisol de la. 1995. "'Women Are More Indian': Ethnicity and Gender in a Community Near Cuzco." In *Ethnicity, Markets, and Migration in the Andes: At the Crossroads of History and Anthropology*, edited by Brooke Larson, Olivia Harris, and Enrique Tandeter, 329–47. Durham, NC: Duke University Press.

Cadena, Marisol de la. 1998. "Silent Racism and Intellectual Superiority in Peru." *Bulletin of Latin American Research* 17 (2): 143–64.

Cadena, Marisol de la. 2000. *Indigenous Mestizos: The Politics of Race and Culture in Cuzco, Peru, 1919–1991*. Durham, NC: Duke University Press.

Cadena, Marisol de la. 2002. "The Racial-Moral Politics of Place: Mestizas and Intellectuals in Turn-of-the-Century Peru." In *Gender's Place: Feminist Anthropologies of Latin America*, edited by Rosario Montoya, Lessie Jo Frazier, and Janise Hurtig, 1st ed., 155–75. New York: Palgrave Macmillan.

Cadena, Marisol de la. 2005. "Are Mestizos Hybrids? The Conceptual Politics of Andean Identities." *Journal of Latin American Studies* 37 (2): 259–84. https://doi.org/10.1017/S0022216X05009004.

Cadena, Marisol de la. 2015. *Earth Beings Ecologies of Practice Across Andean Worlds*. Durham, NC: Duke University Press.

Campbell, Lyle. 1995. "The Quechumaran Hypothesis and Lessons for Distant Genetic Comparison." *Diachronica* 12 (2): 157–200. https://doi.org/10.1075/dia.12.2.02cam.

Canessa, Andrew. 2006. "Todos Somos Indígenas: Towards a New Language of National Political Identity." *Bulletin of Latin American Research* 25 (2): 241–63. https://doi.org/10.1111/j.0261-3050.2006.00162.x.

Canessa, Andrew. 2012a. *Intimate Indigeneities: Race, Sex, and History in the Small Spaces of Andean Life*. Durham, NC: Duke University Press.

Canessa, Andrew. 2012b. "New Indigenous Citizenship in Bolivia: Challenging the Liberal Model of the State and Its Subjects." *Latin American and Caribbean Ethnic Studies* 7 (2): 201–21. https://doi.org/10.1080/17442222.2012.686335.

Canessa, Andrew. 2014. "Conflict, Claim and Contradiction in the New 'Indigenous' State of Bolivia." *Critique of Anthropology* 34 (2): 153–73. https://doi.org/10.1177/0308275X13519275.

Carr, E. Summerson, and Brooke Fisher. 2016. "Interscaling Awe, De-Escalating Disaster." In *Scale: Discourse and Dimensions of Social Life*, edited by E. Summerson Carr and Michael Lempert, 1st ed., 133–56. Oakland: University of California Press.

Carr, E. Summerson, and Michael Lempert. 2016. *Scale: Discourse and Dimensions of Social Life*. Oakland: University of California Press.

Carsten, Janet. 1995. "The Substance of Kinship and the Heat of the Hearth: Feeding, Personhood, and Relatedness Among Malays in Pulau Langkawi." *American Ethnologist* 22 (2): 223–41.

Carsten, Janet. 1997. *The Heat of the Hearth: The Process of Kinship in a Malay Fishing Community*. Oxford: Oxford University Press.

Carsten, Janet, ed. 2000. *Cultures of Relatedness: New Approaches to the Study of Kinship*. Cambridge: Cambridge University Press.

Carsten, Janet. 2004. *After Kinship*. Cambridge: Cambridge University Press.

Carter, W. E. 1977. "Trial Marriage in the Andes?" In *Andean Kinship and Marriage*, edited by Enrique Mayer and Ralph Bolton, 177–216. Washington, DC: American Anthropological Association.

Cerrón-Palomino, Rodolfo. 1994. *Quechumara: Estructuras Paralelas de Las Lenguas Quechua y Aimara*. Vol. 42. La Paz, Bolivia: Centro de Investigación y Promoción del Campesinado.

Chernela, Janet. 2004. "The Politics of Language Acquisition: Language Learning as Social Modeling in the Northwest Amazon." *Women and Language* 27 (1): 13–20.

Chun, Elaine W. 2004. "Ideologies of Legitimate Mockery: Margaret Cho's Revoicings of Mock Asian." *Pragmatics* 14 (2–3): 263–89. https://doi.org/10.1075/prag.14.2-3.10chu.

Coler, Matt. 2014. *A Grammar of Muylaq' Aymara: Aymara as Spoken in Southern Peru*. Leiden, Netherlands: Brill.

Coler, Matt, Nicholas Q. Emlen, and Edwin Banegas-Flores. 2022. "Vowel Deletion in Two Aymara Varieties." *Italian Journal of Linguistics* 32 (1): 151–74. https://doi.org/10.26346/1120-2726-152.

Collins, Jane L. 1986. "The Household and Relations of Production in Southern Peru." *Comparative Studies in Society and History* 28 (4): 651–71.

Coronel-Molina, Serafín M. 2008. "Language Ideologies of the High Academy of the Quechua Language in Cuzco, Peru." *Latin American and Caribbean Ethnic Studies* 3 (3): 319–40.

Cox Hall, Amy, M. Cristina Alcalde, and Florence E. Babb. 2022. "Revisiting Race and Ethnicity in Peru: Intersectional and Decolonizing Perspectives." *Latin American and Caribbean Ethnic Studies* 17 (1): 1–11. https://doi.org/10.1080/17442222.2021.1932050.

Cusicanqui, Silvia Rivera. 2010. "The Notion of 'Rights' and the Paradoxes of Postcolonial Modernity: Indigenous Peoples and Women in Bolivia." *Qui Parle* 18 (2): 29–54. https://doi.org/10.5250/quiparle.18.2.29.

Cusicanqui, Silvia Rivera. 2012. "Ch'ixinakax Utxiwa: A Reflection on the Practices and Discourses of Decolonization." *South Atlantic Quarterly* 111 (1): 95–109. https://doi.org/10.1215/00382876-1472612.

Dorian, Nancy C. 1994. "Purism vs. Compromise in Language Revitalization and Language Revival." *Language in Society* 23 (4): 479–94.

Drinot, P., ed. 2014. *Peru in Theory*. New York: Palgrave Macmillan.

Durston, Alan. 2007. *Pastoral Quechua: The History of Christian Translation in Colonial Peru, 1550–1650*. Notre Dame, IN: University of Notre Dame Press.
Eckert, Penelope. 2008. "Variation and the Indexical Field." *Journal of Sociolinguistics* 12 (4): 453–76. https://doi.org/10.1111/j.1467-9841.2008.00374.x.
Eckert, Penelope, and Sally McConnell-Ginet. 1992. "Think Practically and Look Locally: Language and Gender as Community-Based Practice." *Annual Review of Anthropology* 21:461–90.
Emlen, Nicholas Q. 2015. "Public Discourse and Community Formation in a Trilingual Matsigenka-Quechua-Spanish Frontier Community of Southern Peru." *Language in Society* 44 (5): 679–703. https://doi.org/10.1017/S0047404515000597.
Emlen, Nicholas Q. 2016. "Multilingualism in the Andes and Amazonia: A View from In-Between." *The Journal of Latin American and Caribbean Anthropology*, 22 (3): 556–77. https://doi.org/10.1111/jlca.12250.
Emlen, Nicholas Q. 2017. "Perspectives on the Quechua–Aymara Contact Relationship and the Lexicon and Phonology of Pre-Proto-Aymara." *International Journal of American Linguistics* 83 (2): 307–40. https://doi.org/10.1086/689911.
Emlen, Nicholas Q. 2020. *Language, Coffee, and Migration on an Andean-Amazonian Frontier*. Tucson: University of Arizona Press.
Epps, Patience. 2009. "Language Classification, Language Contact, and Amazonian Prehistory." *Language and Linguistics Compass* 3 (2): 581–606. https://doi.org/10.1111/j.1749-818X.2009.00126.x.
Epps, Patience, and Kristine Stenzel. 2013. *Upper Rio Negro: Cultural and Linguistic Interaction in Northwestern Amazonia*. Rio de Janeiro, Brazil: Museo do Indio-FUANI.
Errington, James Joseph. 1998. *Shifting Languages: Interaction and Identity in Javanese Indonesia*. Cambridge: Cambridge University Press.
Errington, James Joseph. 2008. *Linguistics in a Colonial World: A Story of Language, Meaning, and Power*. Malden, MA: Blackwell.
Escobar, Anna María. 2011. "Spanish in Contact with Quechua." In *The Handbook of Hispanic Sociolinguistics*, edited by Manuel Diaz-Campos, 321–52. Oxford, UK: John Wiley & Sons.
Ferguson, Jenanne. 2019. *Words Like Birds: Sakha Language Discourses and Practices in the City*. Lincoln: University of Nebraska Press.
Gal, Susan. 1993. "Diversity and Contestation in Linguistic Ideologies: German Speakers in Hungary." *Language in Society* 22 (3): 337–59.
Gal, Susan. 2006. "Contradictions of Standard Language in Europe: Implications for the Study of Practices and Publics." *Social Anthropology* 14 (2): 163–81. https://doi.org/10.1017/S0964028206002515.
Gal, Susan, and Judith T. Irvine. 2019. *Signs of Difference: Language and Ideology in Social Life*. Cambridge: Cambridge University Press. https://doi.org/10.1017/9781108649209.

García, María Elena. 2005. *Making Indigenous Citizens: Identities, Education, and Multicultural Development in Peru*. Stanford, CA: Stanford University Press.

García, María Elena. 2008. "Introduction: Indigenous Encounters in Contemporary Peru." *Latin American and Caribbean Ethnic Studies* 3 (3): 217–26. https://doi.org /10.1080/17442220802462287.

García, María Elena. 2022. "Devouring the Nation: Gastronomy and the Settler-Colonial Sublime in Peru." *Latin American and Caribbean Ethnic Studies* 17 (1): 99–126. https://doi.org/10.1080/17442222.2020.1854293.

García, Ofelia, and Li Wei. 2018. "Translanguaging." In *The Encyclopedia of Applied Linguistics*, 1–7. Hoboken, NJ: John Wiley & Sons.

Godenzzi, Juan Carlos. (1997) 2012. "Literacy and Modernization Among the Quechua Speaking Population of Peru." In *Indigenous Literacies in the Americas: Language Planning from the Bottom Up*, edited by Nancy H. Hornberger, 237–49. Berlin: Mouton de Gruyter.

Goffman, Erving. 1981. *Forms of Talk*. Philadelphia: University of Pennsylvania Press.

Goldstein, Paul S. 2005. *Andean Diaspora: The Tiwanaku Colonies and the Origins of South American Empire*. Gainesville: University Press of Florida.

Gustafson, Bret. 2006. "Spectacles of Autonomy and Crisis: Or, What Bulls and Beauty Queens Have to Do with Regionalism in Eastern Bolivia." *Journal of Latin American Anthropology; North Miami* 11 (2): 351–79.

Gustafson, Bret Darin. 2009. *New Languages of the State Indigenous Resurgence and the Politics of Knowledge in Bolivia*. Durham, NC: Duke University Press.

Hanks, William F. 2010. *Converting Words: Maya in the Age of the Cross*. Berkeley: University of California Press.

Harris, Olivia. 1995. "Ethnic Identity and Market Relations: Indians and Mestizos in the Andes." In *Ethnicity, Markets, and Migration in the Andes: At the Crossroads of History and Anthropology*, edited by Brooke Larson, Olivia Harris, and Enrique Tandeter, 351–90. Durham, NC: Duke University Press.

Harris, Olivia. 2000. *To Make the Earth Bear Fruit: Essays on Fertility, Work and Gender in Highland Bolivia*. London: Institute of Latin American Studies.

Harris, Olivia. 2008. "Alterities: Kinship and Gender." In *A Companion to Latin American Anthropology*, edited by Deborah Poole, 276–302. Oxford: Blackwell. https://doi.org/10.1002/9781444301328.ch14.

Hauck, Jan David. 2018. "The Origin of Language Among the Aché." *Language & Communication* 63 (November): 76–88. https://doi.org/10.1016/j.langcom.2018 .03.004.

Hauck, Jan David. 2022. "Grammaticalization, Language Contact, and the Emergence of a Hortative in Guaraché, a New Mixed Language in Paraguay." *Languages* 7 (3): 173. https://doi.org/10.3390/languages7030173.

Hauck, Jan David. 2023. "Language Otherwise: Linguistic Natures and the Ontological Challenge." *Journal of Linguistic Anthropology* 33 (1): 4–24. https://doi.org /10.1111/jola.12384.

Haynes, Nell. 2013. "Global Cholas: Reworking Tradition and Modernity in Bolivian Lucha Libre." *The Journal of Latin American and Caribbean Anthropology* 18 (3): 432–46. https://doi.org/10.1111/jlca.12040.
Heath, Shirley Brice, and Richard Laprade. 1982. "Castilian Colonization and Indigenous Languages: The Cases of Quechua and Aymara." In *Language Spread: Studies in Diffusion and Social Change*, edited by Robert L. Cooper, 118–47. Bloomington: Indiana University Press.
Hickman, John M., and William T. Stuart. 1977. "Descent, Alliance, and Moiety in Chucuito, Peru: An Explanatory Sketch of Aymara Social Organization." In *Andean Kinship and Marriage*, edited by Enrique Mayer and Ralph Bolton, 43–59. Washington, DC: American Anthropological Association.
Hill, Jane. 1995. "The Voices of Don Gabriel: Responsibility and Self in a Modern Mexicano Narrative." In *The Dialogic Emergence of Culture*, edited by Dennis Tedlock and Bruce Mannheim, 97–147. Urbana: University of Illinois Press.
Hill, Jane H. 2008. *The Everyday Language of White Racism*. Chichester, UK: Wiley-Blackwell.
Hill, Jane H., and Kenneth C. Hill. 1986. *Speaking Mexicano: Dynamics of Syncretic Language in Central Mexico*. Tucson: University of Arizona Press.
Hobsbawm, Eric J., and Terence O. Ranger, eds. 1983. *The Invention of Tradition*. Cambridge: Cambridge University Press.
Hornberger, Nancy H. 1988. "Language Ideology in Quechua Communities of Puno, Peru." *Anthropological Linguistics* 30 (2): 214–35.
Hornberger, Nancy H. (1997) 2012. "Quechua Literacy and Empowerment in Peru." In *Indigenous Literacies in the Americas: Language Planning from the Bottom Up*, edited by Nancy H. Hornberger, 215–36. Berlin: Mouton de Gruyter.
Hornberger, Nancy H. 2014. "'Until I Became a Professional, I Was Not, Consciously, Indigenous': One Intercultural Bilingual Educator's Trajectory in Indigenous Language Revitalization." *Journal of Language, Identity & Education* 13 (4): 283–99. https://doi.org/10.1080/15348458.2014.939028.
Huayhua, Margarita. 2014. "Racism and Social Interaction in a Southern Peruvian Combi." *Ethnic and Racial Studies* 37 (13): 2399–2417. https://doi.org/10.1080/01419870.2013.809129.
Huayhua, Margarita. 2018. "Building Differences: The (Re)Production of Hierarchical Relations Among Women in the Southern Andes." In *Authority, Hierarchy, and the Indigenous Languages of Latin America: Historical and Ethnographic Perspectives*, edited by Alan Durston and Bruce Mannheim, 207–46. South Bend, IN: University of Notre Dame Press.
Hughes, Geoffrey. 2020. "Envious Ethnography and the Ethnography of Envy in Anthropology's 'Orient': Towards a Theory of Envy." *Ethos* 48 (2): 192–211. https://doi.org/10.1111/etho.12375.
Irvine, Judith T. 1989. "When Talk Isn't Cheap: Language and Political Economy." *American Ethnologist* 16 (2): 248–67.

Irvine, Judith T. 2016. "Going Upscale: Scales and Scale-Climbing as Ideological Projects." In *Scale: Discourse and Dimensions of Social Life*, edited by E. Summerson Carr and Michael Lempert, 213–22. Oakland: University of California Press. https://doi.org/10.1525/luminos.15.

Irvine, Judith T. 2022. "Revisiting Theory and Method in Language Ideology Research." *Journal of Linguistic Anthropology* 32 (1): 222–36. https://doi.org/10.1111/jola.12335.

Irvine, Judith T., and Susan Gal. 2000. "Language Ideology and Linguistic Differentiation." In *Regimes of Language: Ideologies, Polities, and Identities*, edited by Paul Kroskrity, 35–83. Santa Fe, NM: New School of American Research Press.

Jackson, Jennifer. 2013. *Political Oratory and Cartooning: An Ethnography of Democratic Process in Madagascar*. Chichester, UK: John Wiley & Sons.

Jaffe, Alexandra. 2007. "Corsican on the Airwaves: Media Discourse in a Context of Minority Language Shift." In *Language in the Media: Representations, Identities, Ideologies*, edited by Sally A. Johnson and Astrid Ensslin. London: Continuum.

Jaffe, Alexandra. 2019. "Standardization(s) and Regimentation: Polynomic Orthodoxies and Potentials." In Problematizing Language Regimes, special issue, *Language & Communication* 66 (May): 6–19. https://doi.org/10.1016/j.langcom.2018.10.008.

Jakobson, Roman. 1960. "Linguistics and Poetics." In *Style in Language*, edited by Thomas A. Sebeok, 350–77. Cambridge, MA: MIT Press.

Janusek, John Wayne. 2004. *Identity and Power in the Ancient Andes: Tiwanaku Cities Through Time*. New York: Routledge.

Kroskrity, Paul V. 1993. *Language, History, and Identity: Ethnolinguistic Studies of the Arizona Tewa*. Tucson: University of Arizona Press.

Kroskrity, Paul V. 2000a. "Language Ideologies in the Expression and Representation of Arizona Tewa Ethnic Identity." In *Regimes of Language: Ideologies, Polities, and Identities*, edited by Paul Kroskrity, 329–59. Santa Fe, NM: New School of American Research Press.

Kroskrity, Paul V. 2000b. "Regimenting Languages: Language Ideological Perspectives." In *Regimes of Language: Ideologies, Polities, and Identities*, edited by Paul Kroskrity, 1–34. Santa Fe, NM: New School of American Research Press.

Kroskrity, Paul V., ed. 2000c. *Regimes of Language: Ideologies, Polities, and Identities*. Santa Fe, NM: School of American Research Press.

Kroskrity, Paul V. 2018. "On Recognizing Persistence in the Indigenous Language Ideologies of Multilingualism in Two Native American Communities." In Indigenous Multilingualisms, special edition, *Language & Communication* 62 (September): 133–44. https://doi.org/10.1016/j.langcom.2018.04.012.

Kroskrity, Paul V. 2021. "Articulating Lingual Life Histories and Language Ideological Assemblages: Indigenous Activists Within the North Fork Mono and Village of Tewa Communities." *Journal of Anthropological Research* 77 (1): 83–102. https://doi.org/10.1086/712263.

Kuenzli, E. Gabrielle. 2013. *Acting Inca: Identity and National Belonging in Early Twentieth-Century Bolivia*. Pittsburgh, PA: University of Pittsburgh Press.

Kulick, Don. 1998. *Travesti: Sex, Gender, and Culture Among Brazilian Transgendered Prostitutes*. Chicago: University of Chicago Press.

Larson, Brooke. 1995. "Andean Communities, Political Cultures, and Markets: The Changing Contours of a Field." In *Ethnicity, Markets, and Migration in the Andes: At the Crossroads of History and Anthropology*, edited by Brooke Larson, Olivia Harris, and Enrique Tandeter, 5–53. Durham, NC: Duke University Press.

Leinaweaver, Jessaca B. 2007. "On Moving Children: The Social Implications of Andean Child Circulation." *American Ethnologist* 34 (1): 163–80.

Leinaweaver, Jessaca B. 2008. *The Circulation of Children: Kinship, Adoption, and Morality in Andean Peru*. Latin America Otherwise. Durham, NC: Duke University Press.

Leinaweaver, Jessaca B. 2009. "Raising the Roof in the Transnational Andes: Building Houses, Forging Kinship." *The Journal of the Royal Anthropological Institute* 15 (4): 777–96. https://doi.org/10.2307/40541754.

Leinaweaver, Jessaca B. 2019. "Kinship, Households, and Sociality." In *The Andean World*, edited by Linda J. Seligmann and Kathleen S. Fine-Dare, 235–48. New York: Routledge. https://doi.org/10.4324/9781315621715-16.

Lucero, Jose Antonio. 2008. *Struggles of Voice: The Politics of Indigenous Representation in the Andes*. Pittsburgh, PA: University of Pittsburgh Press.

Lucy, John Arthur. 1993. "Reflexive Language and the Human Disciplines." In *Reflexive Language: Reported Speech and Metapragmatics*, edited by John Arthur Lucy, 9–32. Cambridge: Cambridge University Press.

Luykx, Aurolyn, Fernando García Rivera, and Félix Julca Guerrero. 2016. "Communicative Strategies Across Quechua Languages." *International Journal of the Sociology of Language* 2016 (240): 159–91. https://doi.org/10.1515/ijsl-2016-0018.

MacCormack, Sabine. 1991. *Religion in the Andes: Vision and Imagination in Early Colonial Peru*. Princeton, NJ: Princeton University Press.

Makoni, Sinfree, and Alastair Pennycook. 2005. "Disinventing and (Re)Constituting Languages." *Critical Inquiry in Language Studies* 2 (3): 137–56. https://doi.org/10.1207/s15427595cils0203_1.

Makoni, Sinfree, and Alastair Pennycook, eds. 2006. *Disinventing and Reconstituting Languages*. Clevedon, UK: Multilingual Matters.

Makoni, Sinfree, and Alastair Pennycook, eds. 2007. *Disinventing and Reconstituting Languages*. Clevedon, UK: Multilingual Matters. https://doi.org/10.21832/9781853599255.

Mangan, Jane E. 2005. *Trading Roles: Gender, Ethnicity, and the Urban Economy in Colonial Potosí*. Durham, NC: Duke University Press.

Mangan, Jane E. 2016. *Transatlantic Obligations: Creating the Bonds of Family in Conquest-Era Peru and Spain*. New York: Oxford University Press.

Mannheim, Bruce. 1984. "Una Nación Acorralada: Southern Peruvian Quechua Language Planning and Politics in Historical Perspective." *Language in Society* 13 (3): 291–309.

Mannheim, Bruce. 1991. *The Language of the Inka Since the European Invasion*. Austin: University of Texas Press.
Mannheim, Bruce. 1992. "The Inka Language in the Colonial World." *Colonial Latin American Review*, no. 1–2, 77–108. http://dx.doi.org.proxy.lib.umich.edu/10.1080/10609169208569790.
Mannheim, Bruce. 1999. "Iconicity." *Journal of Linguistic Anthropology* 9 (1–2): 107–10. https://doi.org/10.1525/jlin.1999.9.1-2.107.
Mannheim, Bruce. 2018. "Three Axes of Variability in Quechua." In *The Andean World*, edited by Linda J. Seligmann and Kathleen S. Fine-Dare. London: Routledge. https://doi.org/10.4324/9781315621715-33.
Mannheim, Bruce. 2022. "Mother Tongue, Father Tongue, Place Tongue: Twenty-First-Century Language Transmission and Language Survival in the Andes and Western Amazonia." *Journal of Anthropological Research* 78 (4): 407–19. https://doi.org/10.1086/721974.
Mannheim, Bruce, and Krista E. Van Vleet. 1998. "The Dialogics of Southern Quechua Narrative." *American Anthropologist* 100 (2): 326–46.
Maxwell, Keely. 2011. "Hearth and Household Economy in an Andean Village." *Human Organization* 70 (2): 189–99.
Maybury-Lewis, David., ed. 2002. *The Politics of Ethnicity: Indigenous Peoples in Latin American States*. Cambridge, MA: Harvard University David Rockefeller Center for Latin American Studies.
Mayer, Enrique. 2002. *The Articulated Peasant: Household Economies in the Andes*. Boulder, CO: Westview Press.
Mayer, Enrique, and Ralph Bolton. 1977. *Andean Kinship and Marriage*. Washington, DC: American Anthropological Association.
Meek, Barbra A. 2006. "And the Injun Goes 'How!': Representations of American Indian English in White Public Space." *Language in Society* 35 (1): 93–128. https://doi.org/10.1017/S0047404506060040.
Meek, Barbra A. 2014. "'She Can Do It in English Too': Acts of Intimacy and Boundary-Making in Language Revitalization." In Reconceptualizing Endangered Language Communities: Crossing Borders and Constructing Boundaries, edited by Paul Kroskrity and Netta Avineri, special edition, *Language & Communication* 38 (September): 73–82. https://doi.org/10.1016/j.langcom.2014.05.004.
Meek, Barbra A. 2016. "Shrinking Indigenous Language in the Yukon." In *Scale: Discourse and Dimensions of Social Life*, edited by E. Summerson Carr and Michael Lempert, 70–88. Oakland: University of California Press.
Meek, Barbra A., and Jacqueline Messing. 2007. "Framing Indigenous Languages as Secondary to Matrix Languages." *Anthropology & Education Quarterly* 38 (2): 99–118.
Mendez, Cecilia G. 1996. "Incas Si, Indios No: Notes on Peruvian Creole Nationalism and Its Contemporary Crisis." *Journal of Latin American Studies* 28 (1): 197–225.
Mendoza, Zoila S. 2000. *Shaping Society Through Dance: Mestizo Ritual Performance in the Peruvian Andes*. Chicago: University of Chicago Press.

Mendoza, Zoila S. 2008. *Creating Our Own: Folklore, Performance, and Identity in Cuzco, Peru*. Durham, NC: Duke University Press.

Milroy, James. 2001. "Language Ideologies and the Consequences of Standardization." *Journal of Sociolinguistics* 5 (4): 530–55. https://doi.org/10.1111/1467-9481.00163.

Minks, Amanda. 2010. "Socializing Heteroglossia Among Miskitu Children on the Caribbean Coast of Nicaragua." *Pragmatics* 20 (4): 495–522. https://doi.org/10.1075/prag.20.4.02min.

Mintz, Sidney W., and Eric R. Wolf. 1950. "An Analysis of Ritual Co-Parenthood (Compadrazgo)." *Southwestern Journal of Anthropology* 6 (4): 341–68.

Moya, Cristina. 2013. "Evolved Priors for Ethnolinguistic Categorization: A Case Study from the Quechua–Aymara Boundary in the Peruvian Altiplano." *Evolution and Human Behavior* 34 (4): 265–72. https://doi.org/10.1016/j.evolhumbehav.2013.03.004.

Mufwene, Salikoko S., ed. 2014. *Iberian Imperialism and Language Evolution in Latin America*. Chicago: University of Chicago Press.

Mumford, Jeremy Ravi. 2012. *Vertical Empire: The General Resettlement of Indians in the Colonial Andes*. Durham, NC: Duke University Press.

Murra, John V. 1995. "Did Tribute and Markets Prevail in the Andes Before the European Invasion?" In *Ethnicity, Markets, and Migration in the Andes: At the Crossroads of History and Anthropology*, edited by Brooke Larson, Olivia Harris, and Enrique Tandeter, 57–72. Durham, NC: Duke University Press.

Muysken, Pieter Cornelis. 2012. "Modeling Quechua-Aymara Relationship: Structural Features, Sociolinguistic Scenarios and Possible Archaeological Evidence." In *Archaeology and Language in the Andes: A Cross-Disciplinary Exploration of Prehistory*, edited by Paul Heggarty and David Beresford-Jones, 85–110. Proceedings of the British Academy. Oxford: British Academy.

Narayanan, Sandhya Krittika. 2022a. "Contact." *Feminist Anthropology* 3 (2): 220–26. https://doi.org/10.1002/fea2.12079.

Narayanan, Sandhya Krittika. 2022b. "'Ni Paisana, Ni Jacinta': Language and the Scaling of Indigenous Femininity in Peru." *Signs and Society* 10 (3): 314–33. https://doi.org/10.1086/721736.

Narayanan, Sandhya Krittika. 2023a. "Language and the Emplacement of Indigenous Citizenship in Peru." In *Ethnographic Insights on Latin America and the Caribbean*, edited by Melanie A. Medeiros and Jennifer R. Guzmán, 111–22. Toronto: University of Toronto Press.

Narayanan, Sandhya Krittika. 2023b. "Under One Roof: Material Changes and Familial Estrangement in Puno, Peru." *Journal of Material Culture* 28 (1): 155–71. https://doi.org/10.1177/13591835221088515.

Narayanan, Sandhya Krittika. Forthcoming. "Shifting Linguistic Geographies: When Ideologies of 'Language' Collide with Histories of Language Contact in the Altiplano." In *Southern Epistemologies: Knowledge, Wisdom and Understanding in the Andes and Western Amazon*, edited by H. C. Barrett, M. Cepek, P. Quintanilla, E. Fabiano, and E. Machery. Chicago: HAU Press.

Needham, Rodney. 1971. "Remarks on the Analysis of Kinship and Marriage." In *Rethinking Kinship and Marriage*, edited by Rodney Needham, 1–34. London: Tavistock Publications.

Ocampo, Francisco, and Carol Klee. 1995. "Spanish OV/VO Word-Order Variation in Spanish-Quechua Bilingual Speakers." In *Spanish in Four Continents: Studies in Language Contact and Bilingualism*, edited by Carmen Silva-Corvalan, 71–82. Washington, DC: Georgetown University Press.

Ochs, Elinor, and B. Schieffelin. 1984. "Language Acquisition and Socialization: Three Developmental Stories and Their Implications." In *Culture Theory: Essays on Mind, Self, and Emotion*, edited by R. A. Shweder and Robert A. LeVine, 276–320. Cambridge: Cambridge University Press.

Ødegaard, Cecilie Vindal. 2010. *Mobility, Markets and Indigenous Socialities: Contemporary Migration in the Peruvian Andes*. Farnham, UK: Ashgate.

Paerregaard, Karsten. 1998. "The Dark Side of the Moon: Conceptual and Methodological Problems in Studying Rural and Urban Worlds in Peru." *American Anthropologist* 100 (2): 397–408. https://doi.org/10.1525/aa.1998.100.2.397.

Paugh, Amy L. 2012. *Playing with Languages: Children and Change in a Caribbean Village*. New York: Berghahn Books.

Paulson, Susan. 2002. "Placing Gender and Ethnicity on the Bodies of Indigenous Women and the Work of Intellectuals." In *Gender's Place: Feminist Anthropologies of Latin America*, edited by Rosario Montoya, Lessie Jo Frazier, and Janise Hurtig, 1st ed., 135–54. New York: Palgrave Macmillan.

Pennycook, Alastair, and Sinfree Makoni. 2020. *Innovations and Challenges in Applied Linguistics from the Global South*. Milton Park, UK: Routledge.

Poole, Deborah. 1997. *Vision, Race, and Modernity: A Visual Economy of the Andean Image World*. Princeton, NJ: Princeton University Press.

Poole, Deborah. 2016. "Mestizaje as Ethical Disposition: Indigenous Rights in the Neoliberal State." *Latin American and Caribbean Ethnic Studies* 11 (3): 287–304. https://doi.org/10.1080/17442222.2016.1219082.

Portocarrero, Gonzalo. 1993. *Racismo y mestizaje*. Lima, Peru: Sur Casa de Estudios del Socialismo.

Postero, Nancy. 2017. *The Indigenous State: Race, Politics, and Performance in Plurinational Bolivia*. Oakland: University of California Press.

Quijano, Aníbal. 2000. "Coloniality of Power and Eurocentrism in Latin America." *International Sociology* 15 (2): 215–32. https://doi.org/10.1177/0268580900015002005.

Quijano, Aníbal. 2007. "Coloniality and Modernity/Rationality." *Cultural Studies* 21 (2–3): 168–78. https://doi.org/10.1080/09502380601164353.

Rappaport, Joanne. 2014. *The Disappearing Mestizo: Configuring Difference in the Colonial New Kingdom of Granada*. Durham, NC: Duke University Press.

Reyes, Angela. 2021. "Postcolonial Semiotics." *Annual Review of Anthropology* 50:291–307. https://doi.org/10.1146/annurev-anthro-101819-110253.

Rogers, Mark. 1998. "Spectacular Bodies: Folklorization and the Politics of Identity in Ecuadorian Beauty Pageants." *Journal of Latin American Anthropology* 3 (2): 54–85. https://doi.org/10.1525/jlca.1998.3.2.54.

Rosa, Jonathan, and Nelson Flores. 2017. "Unsettling Race and Language: Toward a Raciolinguistic Perspective." *Language in Society* 46 (5): 621–47. https://doi.org/10.1017/S0047404517000562.

Roth-Gordon, Jennifer. 2017. *Race and the Brazilian Body: Blackness, Whiteness, and Everyday Language in Rio de Janeiro*. Oakland: University of California Press.

Salas Carreño, Guillermo. 2016. "Places Are Kin: Food, Cohabitation, and Sociality in the Southern Peruvian Andes." *Anthropological Quarterly* 89 (3): 813–40. https://doi.org/10.1353/anq.2016.0048.

Salas Carreño, Guillermo. 2019. *Lugares parientes: Comida, cohabitación y mundos andinos*. Lima, Peru: Fondo Editorial de la PUCP.

Schackt, Jon. 2005. "Mayahood Through Beauty: Indian Beauty Pageants in Guatemala." *Bulletin of Latin American Research* 24 (3): 269–87.

Seligmann, Linda J. 1993. "Between Worlds of Exchange: Ethnicity Among Peruvian Market Women." *Cultural Anthropology* 8 (2): 187–213.

Seligmann, Linda J. 2004a. *Peruvian Street Lives: Culture, Power, and Economy Among Market Women of Cuzco*. Urbana: University of Illinois Press.

Seligmann, Linda J. 2004b. "The Art of Expressive Exchange: The Mediation of Quechua Identity in the Marketplace." In *Quechua Verbal Artistry: The Inscription of Andean Voices*, edited by Guillermo Delgado and John M. Schechter, 123–44. Bonn, Germany: Shaker Verlag.

Shulist, Sarah. 2018. *Transforming Indigeneity: Urbanization and Language Revitalization in the Brazilian Amazon*. Toronto: University of Toronto Press.

Sillar, Bill. 2012. "Accounting for the Spread of Quechua and Aymara Between Cuzco and Lake Titicaca." In *Archaeology and Language in the Andes: A Cross-Disciplinary Exploration of Prehistory*, edited by Paul Heggarty and David Beresford-Jones, 295–320. Oxford: British Academy.

Silverblatt, Irene. 1987. *Moon, Sun, and Witches: Gender Ideologies and Class in Inca and Colonial Peru*. Princeton, NJ: Princeton University Press.

Silverstein, Michael. 2000. "Whorfianism and the Linguistic Imagination of Nationality." In *Regimes of Language: Ideologies, Polities, and Identities*, edited by Paul Kroskrity, 85–138. Santa Fe, NM: New School of American Research Press.

Singer, Ruth. 2023. *Indigenous Multilingualism at Warruwi: Cultivating Linguistic Diversity in an Australian Community*. London: Routledge.

Slobe, Tyanna. 2018. "Style, Stance, and Social Meaning in Mock White Girl." *Language in Society* 47 (4): 541–67. https://doi.org/10.1017/S004740451800060X.

Slotta, James. 2017. "Can the Subaltern Listen? Self-Determination and the Provisioning of Expertise in Papua New Guinea." *American Ethnologist* 44 (2): 328–40. https://doi.org/10.1111/amet.12482.

Spedding, Alison. 1994. "Open Castilian, Closed Aymara? Bilingual Women in the Yungas of La Paz (Bolivia)." In *Bilingual Women: Anthropological Approaches to Second-Language Use*, edited by Pauline Burton, Ketaki Kushari Dyson, and Shirley Ardener, 30–43. Oxford: Berg.

Stanish, Charles. 2003. *Ancient Titicaca: The Evolution of Complex Society in Southern Peru and Northern Bolivia*. Berkeley: University of California Press.

Stenzel, Kristine, and Nicholas Williams. 2021. "Toward an Interactional Approach to Multilingualism: Ideologies and Practices in the Northwest Amazon." *Language & Communication* 80 (September): 136–64. https://doi.org/10.1016/j.langcom.2021.05.010.

Swinehart, Karl. 2018. "Gender, Class, Race, and Region in 'Bilingual' Bolivia." *Signs and Society* 6 (3): 607–21. https://doi.org/10.1086/699668.

Swinehart, Karl F. 2012. "Metadiscursive Regime and Register Formation on Aymara Radio." In *Languages and Publics in Stateless Nations*, edited by Karl F. Swinehart and Kathryn Graber, special edition, *Language & Communication* 32 (2): 102–13. https://doi.org/10.1016/j.langcom.2011.05.004.

Swinehart, Karl F., and Kathryn Graber. 2012. "Tongue-Tied Territories: Languages and Publics in Stateless Nations." In *Languages and Publics in Stateless Nations*, edited by Karl F. Swinehart and Kathryn Graber, special edition, *Language & Communication* 32 (2): 95–97. https://doi.org/10.1016/j.langcom.2011.05.007.

Thomason, Sarah Grey. 2001. *Language Contact*. Edinburgh: Edinburgh University Press.

Tschopik, Harry. 1951. *The Aymara of Chucuito, Peru*. Anthropological Papers of the American Museum of Natural History: v. 44, pt. 2. New York: American Museum of Natural History.

Tucker, Joshua. 2019. *Making Music Indigenous: Popular Music in the Peruvian Andes*. Chicago: University of Chicago Press. https://doi.org/10.7208/9780226607474.

Valdivia, Carmen. 2020. "Toward a Decolonial Feminist Research on Indigeneity in Contemporary Peru." *Transmodernity* 9 (5). https://doi.org/10.5070/T495051215.

Van Vleet, Krista. 2002. "The Intimacies of Power: Rethinking Violence and Affinity in the Bolivian Andes." *American Ethnologist* 29 (3): 567–601.

Van Vleet, Krista. 2003. "Partial Theories: On Gossip, Envy and Ethnography in the Andes." *Ethnography* 4 (4): 491–519. https://doi.org/10.1177/146613810344001.

Van Vleet, Krista. 2005. "Dancing on the Borderlands: Girls (Re)Fashioning National Belonging in the Andes." In *Natives Making Nation: Gender, Indigeneity, and the State in the Andes*, edited by Andrew Canessa, 107–29. Tucson: University of Arizona Press.

Van Vleet, Krista. 2008. *Performing Kinship: Narrative, Gender, and the Intimacies of Power in the Andes*. Austin: University of Texas Press.

Van Vleet, Krista. 2020. "Maledictive Language: Gossip and Rumor." In *The International Encyclopedia of Linguistic Anthropology*, 1–8. Hoboken, NJ: John Wiley & Sons. https://doi.org/10.1002/9781118786093.iela0245.

Vázquez, Mario C. 1961. *Hacienda, peonaje y servidumbre en los Andes Peruanos.* Lima, Peru: Editorial Estudios Andinos.

Veronelli, Gabriela. 2015. "The Coloniality of Language: Race, Expressivity, Power, and the Darker Side of Modernity." *Wagadu: A Journal of Transnational Women's & Gender Studies* 13 (1).

Vilaça, Aparecida. 2016. *Praying and Preying: Christianity in Indigenous Amazonia.* Berkeley: University of California Press. https://doi.org/10.1525/9780520963849.

Villarreal, Gabriela Zamorano. 2017. *Indigenous Media and Political Imaginaries in Contemporary Bolivia.* Lincoln: University of Nebraska Press.

Vogel, Sara, and Ofelia García. 2022. "Translanguaging." In *Oxford Research Encyclopedia of Education*, edited by William T. Pink. Oxford: Oxford University Press.

Wade, Peter. 2005. "Rethinking 'Mestizaje': Ideology and Lived Experience." *Journal of Latin American Studies* 37 (2): 239–57.

Wade, Peter. 2008. "Race in Latin America." In *A Companion to Latin American Anthropology*, edited by Deborah Poole, 175–92. Chichester, UK: Blackwell Publishing.

Wade, Peter. 2016. "Mestizaje, Multiculturalism, Liberalism, and Violence." *Latin American and Caribbean Ethnic Studies* 11 (3): 323–43. https://doi.org/10.1080/17442222.2016.1214368.

Warren, Kay B., and Jean E. Jackson. 2002. *Indigenous Movements, Self-Representation, and the State in Latin America.* 1st ed. Austin: University of Texas Press.

Wee, Lionel. 2018. "Essentialism and Language Rights." In *The Multilingual Citizen: Towards a Politics of Language for Agency and Change*, edited by Lisa Lim, Christopher Stroud, and Lionel Wee, 40–64. Bristol, UK: Multilingual Matters.

Weismantel, Mary. 1995. "Making Kin: Kinship Theory and Zumbagua Adoptions." *American Ethnologist* 22 (4): 685–704.

Weismantel, Mary. 2001. *Cholas and Pishtacos: Stories of Race and Sex in the Andes.* Chicago: University of Chicago Press.

Weismantel, Mary, and Stephen F. Eisenman. 1998. "Race in the Andes: Global Movements and Popular Ontologies." *Bulletin of Latin American Research* 17 (2): 121–42.

Woolard, Kathryn. 1998. "Introduction: Language Ideology as a Field of Inquiry." In *Language Ideologies: Practice and Theory*, edited by Bambi B. Schieffelin, Kathryn Ann Woolard, and Paul V. Kroskrity, 1–47. New York: Oxford University Press.

Wroblewski, Michael. 2014. "Public Indigeneity, Language Revitalization, and Intercultural Planning in a Native Amazonian Beauty Pageant." *American Anthropologist* 116 (1): 65–80. https://doi.org/10.1111/aman.12067.

Yannakakis, Yanna. 2012. "Introduction: How Did They Talk to One Another? Language Use and Communication in Multilingual New Spain." *Ethnohistory* 59 (4): 667–74. https://doi.org/10.1215/00141801-1642698.

Zavala, Virginia. 2014. "What Is Quechua Literacy for? Ideological Dilemmas in Intercultural Bilingual Education in the Peruvian Andes." In *Educating in Language and Literacy Diversity: Mobile Selves*, edited by Mastin Prinsloo and Christopher Stroud, 45–72. New York: Palgrave Macmillan.

Zavala, Virginia, and Roberto Zariquiey. 2009. "'I Segregate You Because Your Lack of Education Offends Me': An Approach to Racist Discourse in Contemporary Peru." In *Racism and Discourse in Latin America*, edited by Teun A. van Dijk, translated by Elisa Barquin and Alexandra Hibbett, 259–90. Lanham, MD: Lexington Books/Rowman & Littlefield.

Zuidema, R. Tom. 1977. "The Inka Kinship System: A New Theoretical View." In *Andean Kinship and Marriage*, edited by Enrique Mayer and Ralph Bolton, 240–81. Washington, DC: American Anthropological Association.

Index

Abya Yala, 165, 295n9
accommodation, among Indigenous market women, 97–106, 109, 128, 131
activism, political: of Aymara-speaking women, 210; through Pachamama Radio, 157
actors, in ritual plays: Aymara-speaking women as, 212; casting, 190-1; criticism of performances, 202-204; linguistic performances of, 202; local, 190-91; as Mama Uqllu, 190–91, 201–14, 255; as Manqu Qhapaq, 193-201; non-local, 191-92
Afro-Peruvian populations, 10–11, 297n3; racial terms for, 288n4
agriculture: Mama Uqllu and, 185–87; Manqu Qhapaq and, 186; origins of, 186
Allen, Catherine, 14
Alta Moda (Testino), 265–67, 302n2
altiplano: Aymara language in, 16, 20; beauty pageants in, 227; *Belleza del Altiplano*, 229–33; in Bolivia, 19; extended boundaries of Indigenous language use, 176–78; geography of, 19–20; ideal puneña women in, 217; Indigenous femininity in, 214–15; Indigenous identity in, 5; Indigenous languages in, 292n4; Indigenous women in, 41–42; inter-Indigenous contact in, 19–28; kinship in, 49–54, 293n6; Lake Titicaca region, 19–20; linguistic diversity in, 23, 190–93; Mama Uqllu in, 181, 193–95; Manqu Qhapaq in, 181, 193–95; marriage preferences in, 58–60; multilingualism in, 20–21, 23–24, 26–27, 88–95; neutral language of, 131; origin myths in, 187–90; pan-Andean indigeneity in, 283; public performances in, 222; Quechua language in, 20; *sikurris* in, 298n1; social life in, 89; street markets in, 88–95; temperatures of, 19–20. *See also* Aymara-speaking women; Quechua-speaking women
Amaru, Tupac, II, uprising led by, 182–83
Amazon basin region: biodiversity of, 10; Indigenous language from, 8; inter-Indigenous languages in, 15

Andean culture: cosmology in, 193; elite, 180–81; Indigenous authenticity of, 180; kinship in, 185; personhood in, 185; priests in, 197; redefinition of, 180; reverence for Mother Earth in, 206; ritual plays in, 180–85. *See also* Mama Uqllu; Manqu Qhapaq

Andean region: ethnolinguistic groups in, 140; indigeneity in, 28–34, 291n9; *indigenista* movement and, 31, 290n9, 297n3; Indigenous identity in, 12–19, 29; Indigenous radio practices in, 161–62; Indigenous women in, 32; kinship in, 49–54, 57–60; language in, 28–34; multilingualism in, 88–95; music in, 103; *neoindigenista* movement and, 31, 99, 290n9, 297n3; New Year celebrations in, 282–87; orthographic practices in, 137–38; pan-Indigenous mobilizations in, 12; personhood in, 57–58; Peruvian national identity and, 182–83; puneña women in, 217; ritualistic plays in, 182; San Juan de Bautista celebration, 282; street markets in, 88–95; Tupac Amaru III uprising in, 184–85; women in, 28–34. *See also* altiplano; *specific countries*

Los Andes (newspaper), 141-46, 174

Arequipa, Peru, 9, 68; street markets in, 126

Ashaninka language, 8, 10

attire, costumes and: in *Belleza del Altiplano*, 229–30; for New Year celebrations, 281

authenticity: in *Belleza del Altiplano*, 229–30; Indigenous beauty pageants and, 224, 226-27, 264, 299n8; of Indigenous identity, 180–85; of puneña women, 216–17, 254–62

authority, of Aymara-speaking women, 211

autochthony: hyperlocal forms of, 61; Indigenous, 157

autonomy, of Indigenous market women, 96–97, 99

Ayarachis de Cuyo-Cuyo, 251

Aymara culture, 3; in Puno, 4–5; Unidad Nacional de Comunidades Aymaras, 272–74, 294n6, 295n10

Aymara language, use of: in altiplano, 16, 20; in beauty pageants, 226-27; in *Belleza del Altiplano*, 230, 232–35, 239, 243; bilingual education in, 148–52, 155–56; in Bolivia, 273; boundaries of, 277; bounded readership and, 140–46; in Chile, 273; colonial legacy and, 140; communicative practices for, 37–38; community-specific speech practices, 61–62; cultural meaning of, 275–80; diagrammatic signs in, 135; differences with Quechua language, 7–12, 48–49, 125, 136; differences with Spanish language, 125, 136; ethnographic approaches to, 5; as ethnolinguistic category, 18; gendered associations in, 6–7; ideology of, 27; *idiomas* and, 135–36; Indigeneity of, 12; among Indigenous market women, 99–102, 107–10, 113–17, 124–25, 131; lack of tonal inflection in, 292n3; in Lake Titicaca region, 48; linguistic boundaries with Quechua language, 137; as linguistic variety, 27–28; literacy and, 142–48; Mama Uqllu and, 189–91; in media production, 142; morphological linguistic mix with, 125–26, 132–33; naming of, 26; in New Year celebrations, 281–84; objectification of, 278; orthographic practices in, 137–38; on Pachamama Radio, 157, 164, 167, 173; in popular culture, 6; for professionals, 4; in public performances, 39–40; in Puno, 16; purified form of, 148–52; as rougher-sounding language, 211; scalar evaluative frameworks for,

INDEX

277; semiotic differences with, 155; in shared sound spaces, 161–74; Spanish language influences on, 293n8; status of, 278; in street markets, 86–87, 93–94, 98, 100, 109–10; symbolic capital of, 122; Unidad Nacional de Comunidades Aymaras, 272–74, 294n6, 295n10; *zona Aymara*, 136–37. *See also* Aymara-speaking women; code-switching/mixing; *specific topics*

Aymara people: as ethnic category, 6; as stateless, 175. *See also* Aymara culture

Aymara-speaking women: authority of, 211; directness of, 211; gender roles and, 5; ideal puneña women as, 216–17; methodological approach to, 35–40; non-local Mama Uqllus, 214; political activism of, 211. *See also* Indigenous market women

beauty ideals, in *Belleza del Altiplano*, 231, 263

Beauty of the Altiplano. *See Belleza del Altiplano*

beauty pageants: in altiplano, 225; audiences for, 227; Aymara language in, 226; conceptual approach to, 223–24; as cultural construction, 224; female bodies and, 263; flexibility of, 224; gender-specificity of, 225–26; historical contours of, 224–25; history of, 224–25; Indigenous authenticity and, 224, 226, 263, 299n8; Indigenous female future and, 263–64; Indigenous femininity and, 224–27, 298n6; introduction speeches in, 230; judges in, 227; LGBTQ populations in, 301n21; local, 228; Miss Belleza de Foklórica, 299n8; popularization of, 299n7; as racializing project, 225; Señorita Campesina, 299n8; Spanish-speaking women in, 226–27; traditional dances in, 227

Belleza del Altiplano (Beauty of the Altiplano): attire and costumes in, 229–30; Aymara language use in, 230, 232–35, 239, 243; beauty ideals in, 229, 263; Catholic celebrations and, 228; cultural diversity and, 227–29; cultural traditions in, 242, 254; Cuyo-Cuyo contestants, 243–55, 301n15; eligibility criteria for, 299n9; evaluations of contestants, 229-31, 242–55; female empowerment through, 229–31; formality of language in, 249–50; goals of, 231; hyperlocal differences in, 233–34; Indigenous authenticity and, 231–32; Indigenous femininity and, 231; Indigenous pride in, 242–55; judges for, 230–31, 249, 251, 300n11; language proficiency in, 231–42; linguistic diversity and, 229–30; linguistic fluency in, 232, 235; local organization of, 229, 232, 298n6; Quechua language use in, 232–33, 235–39, 245; recruitment of contestants for, 232–33, 235–36; repetition in, 250; themes for, 230; traditional dances in, 253; Virgen de la Candelaria, 227

bilingual education, Indigenous: in Aymara language, 148–52, 155–56; classes in, 148–49; IEB programs, 147–56, 294n4; IES schools, 147–48; learning terms, 153–54; pedagogical method in, 148–52; in Peruvian schools, 147; in Quechua language, 152–56; through Spanish, 147–55; worksheets for, 152

bilingual intercultural education programs (IEB programs), 147–55, 294n4

bilingualism: among Andean Indigenous women, 32; in street markets, 103. *See also* bilingual education

biodiversity, of Amazon basin region, 10

bold toughness. *See bravas*

Bolivia, Republic of: altiplano in, 19; Aymara language use in, 273; Civil War of 1899, 183; gender in, 59; Indigenous citizens in, 13; Indigenous heritage in, 183; kinship, 59; national identity for, 183; plurilingualism in, 12; Plurinational State of, 160
bravas (bold toughness), 210–11
Brazil, colorism in, 213

Cadena, Marisol de la, 11, 182, 288n3, 288n5, 289n9
Canessa, Andrew, 13, 213
Carsten, Janet, 52
Catholic Church, Catholicism and: *Belleza del Altiplano* and, 228; conversion of Quechua persons, 295n4
Chambi, Martin, 265–67, 302n1
Chernela, Janet, 291n6
children: adoption and fostering of, 52–53; kinship practices and, 52–53; language socialization for, 63–67; *qullasuyeños*, 77
Chile, Aymara language use in, 273
Chipaya language, 21
Chucuito, 56–57
Civil War of 1899, in Bolivia, 183
Coasa, Peru, Quechua-speaking women in, 256–62
code-switching/mixing, between Aymara and Quechua languages, 48, 293n9; ethnolinguistic groups and, 138; among Indigenous market women, 97–98, 107, 122, 128; on Pachamama Radio, 164–66, 167-68, 171–72
colonialism, colonization and: Aymara language influenced by, 140–41; Indigenous languages and, 17; language frameworks influenced by, 25–26; literacy influenced by, 140–41; in Puno, 136-37; Quechua language influenced by, 140–41; *repartimiento* regulation, 23; settler-colonial hegemony, 15; settler-colonial sublime, 266; Spanish, 11; Todos Los Santos celebration and, 290n2. *See also specific topics*
coloniality of language, 17, 27
coloniality of power, 11
colorism: in Brazil, 213; in Peru, 213
community-specific speech/language practices: for Aymara speakers, 61–62; kinship and h practices and, 62; marriage and, 62–63; for Quechua speakers, 61–62; social identity and, 62
compadres, 50
Concurso de Sikurris, 222, 224
cooperative street markets, 93, 129–30
creativity, of Indigenous market women, 101, 125
criollas (white women), 122
cross-linguistic dynamics, between ethnolinguistic groups, 141
cross-linguistic marriages, 64–65, 69, 290n5, 291n8; female alienation in, 68; kinship and, 66–67, 77; *lengua materna* and, 77–78; linguistic exogamy in, 67; linguistic tension, 66; maternal linguistic heritage, 66–68; puneños and, 71–74, 76–77; *qullasuyeños* in, 77; in Qullasuyu, 77
Cruz, Mauro, 273–74
Cruz, Vicky, 232–34
Cusco (Cuzco), Peru, 9, 20, 69; High Academy of Quechua in, 198; Indigenous market women in, 122; Inti Raymi celebrations in, 191–92; ritual plays in, 181; tourism in, 192
Cusicanqui, Silvia Rivera, 33
Cuyo-Cuyo region, in Puno: Ayarachis de Cuyo-Cuyo, 251; *Belleza del Altiplano* contestants, 243–55, 301n15

dances, traditional: Ayarachis de Cuyo-Cuyo, 251; in beauty pageants, 225; in *Belleza del Altiplano*, 251; danza

autóctona, 221–22; *danza mestizos*, 221–22, 297n3, 298n5; Diablada, 221; gendering of, 223, 298n5; Indigenous identity and, 222; La Morenada, 221; as public performance, 221–23; *sikurris* and, 222–24; during Virgen de la Candelaria, 298n4; Waka Waka, 221
danza autóctona, 221–22
danzas mestizos (mestizo dances), 221–22, 297n3, 299n5
decolonization, among Indigenous populations, 17
Diablada dance, 221

Ecuador, pan-Indigenous mobilizations in, 12
Emlen, Nicholas, 21
Escobar, Walter, 164
ethnic diversity, ideal puneña women and, 215
ethnolinguistic groups, 157–58; in Andean region, 140; code-mixing/switching among, 141; generations of, 140; histories of cross-linguistic dynamics and, 141; ideology of, 140, 262–63; language contact and, 141; language modeling among, 142; language purism among, 140–42; linguistic boundaries between, 140–42; linguistic purism and, 141–42; multilingualism and, 141; naturalness of, 274; puneña women and, 217; in Puno, 138–39; social boundaries between, 140–41. See also Aymara language; Quechua language; Spanish language
Evangelical Protestant Christianity, 3

Federación de Foklór (Federation of Folklore), 187–99, 202, 222; Indigenous identity and, 262; New Year celebrations and, 280
femininity, Indigenous, 29; in altiplano region, 212–13; beauty pageants and, 224–27, 298n6; *Belleza del Altiplano* and, 229; construction of, 30; Mama Uqllu as ideal, 201–14; for puneña women, 261–62; racialization of, 213–14; scalar evaluative frameworks for, 269–70. See also gender roles
food, feeding practices and, 55
friendships, between Indigenous market women, 125–33

Galliano, John, 302n2
García, María Elena, 266
gender, gender practices and: Aymara language and, 6–7; beauty pageants and, 225–26; in Bolivia, 59; complementarity, 58; indigeneity and, 5; *indigenista* movement and, 31; kinship and, 57–60, 62–63; language contact and, 272; *lenguas maternas* and, 6; linguistic diversity and, 188–91; *neoindigenista* movement and, 31; in Puno, 35–40; Quechua language and, 6–7; in street markets, 87, 95–100; traditional dances and, 223, 298n5
gender identity, 60
gender roles: for Aymara-speaking women, 5; for Quechua-speaking women, 5. See also femininity
genealogies, for Indigenous languages, 60–69
Guaraché language, 15

Haynes, Neil, 302n3
hierarchies, racial, 5
High Academy of Quechua, 198
Hill, Jane, 293n9
horizontal kinship networks, 51–52, 57
huayno (traditional folk song), 100
husband-wife relationships, kinship practices and, 50

idealized languages. See *idiomas*
IDECA, 294n6

identity, identity formation and: gender, 60; racialized, 5. *See also* Indigenous identity; national identity

ideology: of Aymara language, 27; of ethnolinguistic groups, 138-140, 262–63; in ideals for puneña women, 214–15; Indigenous language and, 8; language, 15, 24–27; of Quechua language, 27

idiomas (idealized languages), 278-279

"I don't understand." *See mana entiendkichu*

IEB programs. *See* bilingual intercultural education programs

IES schools. *See* Institute of Education Sciences schools

imagery, images and, of Indigenous people: *Alta Moda*, 265–67, 302n2; consumption by global audiences, 270; history of, 268; indigeneity and, 269; Indigenous identity and, 269; narratives in, 269; reproduction of tropes in, 269; Testino and, 267–70

indigeneity: in Andes region, 28–34, 291n9; of Aymara language, 12; of contact, 274–77; formalization of, 33; gender and, 5; in images of Indigenous people, 267-68; kinship relationships and, 13–14; pan-Andean, 280–85; politicization of, 175; of Quechua language, 12; relationships of reciprocity and, 13–14; Unidad Nacional de Comunidades Aymaras and, 272–73, 294n6, 295n10

indigenismo movement, 180–81

indigenista movement, 31, 288n9, 295n3

Indigenous culture, identity and: beauty pageants as element of, 224; in *Belleza del Altiplano*, 244, 256; in Bolivia, 185; documentation of differences between, 7–12; national historic erasure of, 9–11; public performances and, 221–22; puneño youths and, 257; in Puno, 4–5, 224; reinvention of, 184; revival of, 184; tropes about, 269. *See also specific topics*

Indigenous identity: in altiplano, 5; in Andes region, 12–19, 29; authenticity of, 180–85; construction of personhood and, 19; through dances, 222; ethnographic approaches to, 13, 18–19; evaluation of, 28–29; Federación de Foklór and, 262; formal recognition of, 8; imagery of, 267; Indigenous language as influence on, 17–18; inter-Indigenous differences and, 14–15; local modes of, 14; Pachamama Radio and, 262; politics of ethnicity and, 33; pride in, 242–55; in Puno, 5, 18; social movements for, 12–13. *See also* Indigenous culture

Indigenous languages, linguistic knowledge and: in altiplano, 290n4; in Amazon basin, 8; coloniality of, 17; community-specific, 61; ethnographic contexts for, 276; evaluation of speakers of, 275–80; genealogies for, 60–69; historical approach to, 5–6; ideological challenges with, 8; Indigenous identity shaped by, 17–18; institutionalization of, 175–76; language contact zones, 15–16; legitimacy of, 42; *lenguas maternas* and, 6; literacy and, 140–46; men and, 5; multilingualism and, 6, 21–22, 34; in Puno, 131; racial purity of, 31; revitalization of, 147; scalar evaluative frameworks for, 302n6; settler-colonial hegemony and, 15; social diversity and, 6; social identity influenced by, 61. *See also* Aymara language; Quechua language; *specific languages*

Indigenous market women, 93; accommodation among, 97–102, 109–12, 132; adaptability of, 101; autonomy of, 94–95, 97; Aymara language use among, 99–104, 107–10, 113–17, 125,

131; code-mixing among, 97–98, 106, 124, 128; code-switching/mixing languages among, 97–98, 106, 124, 128; communication with vendors, 83; communicative competence among, 113, 117; communicative practices among, 10–8, 124, 130–32; conversation circles among, 99; creativity of, 101, 125; *criollas* as clientele for, 122; in Cusco, 122; customer interactions with, 105; dress and uniforms for, 95–96; economic independence of, 94–95, 97; friendships among, 122–30; generational differences among, 130–31; goods for, 130–33; humor for, 125; *idiomas* among, 132–32; language competence among, 117, 121; language errors for, 106; language fluency among, 117–22; language mimicry among, 112; linguistic ecology for, 128; linguistic flexibility among, 197–102, 109–12, 135; linguistic knowledge among, 122; linguistic limitations among, 117–20; linguistic sources in, 123–24; listening competence among, 117, 122; *mana entiendkichu* ("I don't understand"), 124–25; in market cooperatives, 126–7; morphological linguistic mixes among, 124–25, 129–30; multilingualism among, 97–98, 111–17; non-native languages for, 99; in Puno, 38–39, 87, 131; Quechua language use among, 97–104, 113–17, 124; Quechua women naming Aymara women, 101; receptivity in interactions among, 102–22; reciprocity among, 122; sale phrases among, 105–6; sales and economic success for, 122–30; self-perceptions of, 120; Spanish language use among, 98, 104, 121, 129, 130; translanguaging among, 97–98, 126–27; trust among, 122; vendor interactions with, 109–10; verb conjugation among, 120. *See also specific markets*

Indigenous men: historical treatment of, 34; Indigenous women as unequal to, 272, 304n4. *See also specific topics*

Indigenous populations: colonial legacy for, 33; decolonization among, 17; displacement of, 23; *indigenista* movement, 31, 288n9, 295n3; *neoindigenista* movement, 31, 96, 288n9, 295n3; silent racism against, 287n3. *See also* Indigenous culture; Indigenous identity; Indigenous languages

Indigenous puneños, 19, 28; in capital cities, 36; personhood and, 41–42; in rural communities, 36; social identity and, 54–55; women as, 29

Indigenous radio practices: in Andean region, 158–59; Pachamama Radio, 38, 154–61; Radio Quispillaccta, 159

Indigenous rights, 13

Indigenous women: in altiplano, 41–42; in Andes region, 32; bilingualism among, 32; as *bravas*, 210–11; communicative socialization among, 63; in cross-linguistic marriages, 64–69; cultural legacy of, 274–75; femininity and, 29; historical treatment of, 34; as hyper-Indigenous, 32; idealized version of, 78–81; ideologization of, 29; inequality with Indigenous men, 270, 302n4; linguistic genealogies for, 60–69; maternal community for, 63–64; as object of conquest, 30; personhood for, 255–56, 272; in politics, 270–71; as puneños, 29; sexuality of, 30; as wives, 60–69, 75. *See also* Indigenous market women

INEI. *See* Instituto Nacional de Estadística e Informática

Inka Empire, 183, 287n2; kinship practices in, 50; Quechua linguistic practices in, 182-83, 192–200; Tawantinsuyu, 22

Inkas sí, indios no ("Inkas yes, not Indians"), 9–10
Secondary Education schools (IES schools), 147
institutionally-sanctioned literacy, 143
Instituto Nacional de Estadística e Informática (National Institute of Statistics and Information Technology) (INEI), 7
inter-Indigenous ethnic differences, 5
inter-Indigenous languages, 14–15
inter-Indigenous multilingualism, 26–27, 35–40, 276
Inti Raymi celebrations, 191–93

Jackson, Jennifer, 301n17
Jiwasanaka (radio program), 173
judges, for beauty pageants, 227; for *Belleza del Altiplano*, 230–31, 249, 251, 300n11
Juliaca, Peru, 68

kinship, kinship practices and: through adoption and fostering, 52–53; in altiplano, 49–54, 291n6; in Andean culture, 187; in Andean region, 49–54, 57–60; in Bolivian highlands, 59; children in, 52–53; in communities, 57; community-specific speech practices and, 62; *compadres*, 50, 52; cross-linguistic marriages and, 66–67, 77; definition of, 49; ethnographic analysis of, 50–51; familial relationships, 52; feeding practices and, 55; gender and, 57–60, 62–63; husband-wife relationships, 50; indigeneity and, 13–14; in Inka Empire, 50; linguistic transmission and, 49; after marriage, 59–60; with nature, 53–54; with nonhuman entities, 53; Pachamama Radio and, 169–70, 171-173; paternal, 75; scope of, 49–50; in urban areas, 69–78
Kjarka, Wila, 13

Lake Titicaca region, 19–20, 22, 38, 177–78; Aymara language in, 48; Mama Uqllu myth and, 185; Manqu Qhapaq myth, 185
language, linguistics and: in Andes region, 28–34; anthropology of, 24–25; boundary regimentation and, 24; child language socialization, 65–69; colonial framework for, 25–26; coloniality of language, 17, 27; formality of, 249–50; history of language naming, 24; ideologies, 15, 24–26; kinship and, 291n6; mimicry of, 112; ontological invention of, 25–26; in Puno, 49; purism, 138–39, 148–53. *See also* bilingualism; multilingualism; plurilingualism; trilingualism; *specific languages*; *specific topics*
language contact: ethnographic context for, 276; among ethnolinguistic groups, 137-138; gender differences and, 272; Indigenous language zones, 15–16
language purism, 138-139; Aymara language and, 148–52; among ethnic groups, 138–40
Leinaweaver, Jessaca, 52–53
lenguas maternas (mother tongues): conceptual meaning of, 278–79; cross-linguistic marriages and, 77–78; gendered expectations and, 69; gender-specificity of, 6; linguistic knowledge and, 6; literacy and, 141; maintenance of Indigenous linguistic heritage, 75–76; in shared sound spaces, 161–63. *See also* Aymara language; Quechua language
LGBTQ populations, in Indigenous beauty pageants, 301n21
Lima, Peru, 9; extended boundaries of Indigenous language use, 174–76; Museo Mario Testino, 266; street markets in, 126
linguistic diversity: in altiplano, 23, 189–91; *Belleza del Altiplano* and, 227–28;

gender origins of, 178–91; ideal
puneña women and, 215; in *Willakuy-
Yatiyawinaka*, 145-46
linguistic ecology, 131
linguistic flexibility, among Indigenous
market women, 97–102, 112–15,
131-32
linguistic fluency, in *Belleza del Altiplano*,
230, 235
linguistic syncretism, 127
listening competence, among Indigenous
market women, 99, 117
literacy, Indigenous languages and: access
to literacy training, 141; Aymara language
and, 141–46; bounded readership
and, 140–46; colonial legacy of,
140–41; institutionally-sanctioned,
143; *lenguas maternas* and, 141; in
newspapers, 141–45; normalization
of, 142; promotion of, 141; Quechua
language and, 141–46
local beauty pageants, 225; *Belleza del
Altiplano*, 227, 230

male market vendors, 83; listening competence
among, 99
males, male gender roles and: dances and,
223; Indigenous linguistic knowledge
of, 5; paternal communities, 64
Mamani, Juan Luque, 301n19, 302n4
Mamani, Marcelina, 235–38
Mama Uqllu, 44, 296n5, 296n6; actor
portrayals of, 190–91, 201–14, ;
agriculture and, 185–87; in altiplano,
179, 191–92; annual celebration of, 179,
187; arrival of, 179, 185, 187; Aymara
language and, 189–90; Aymaraspeaking
women as, 214; casting
actors for, 202–3; celestial context for,
186; criticism of performances, 206,
209– 214;Federación de Foklór and,
202; ideal Indigenous femininity and,
200–14; as ideal puneña women, 215–
17; Lake Titicaca and, 185; linguistic
performances of, 205; local actor
portrayals of, 190–91; metalinguistic
commentary and, 207; non-local actor
portrayals of, 201–14; origin myth for,
179, 185–88; Puno and, 179; repetition
structures for, 260–61; in ritual plays,
192; scripts for, 205–9; speeches by,
205–9; as symbol of purity, 191; transcription
of speeches, 209
mana entiendkichu ("I don't understand"),
124–25
Mangan, Jane, 93
Manqu Qhapaq, 44, 296n5; actor representation
of, 192–201; agriculture and,
186; in altiplano, 179, 191–93; annual
celebration of, 179, 187; arrival of, 179,
185, 187; celestial context for, 185; ideal
puneña women and, 216; Lake Titicaca
and, 185; origin myth for, 179, 185–88;
Puno and, 179; in ritual plays, 192;
statue for, 188
Markasa Layku (radio show), 158–59,
162–63, 169–72
market association networks, 89–94
markets. *See* market vendors; street markets;
specific markets
market spaces. *See* street markets
market vendors, markets and: multilingualism
among, 36; purchase of
goods between, 292n1; vendor-client
relationships, 106. *See also* Indigenous
market women; male market vendors
marriage, marriages and: in altiplano,
58–60; community-specific speech
practices and, 62–63; cross-linguistic,
64–69; Indigenous wives, 60–69, 75,
78–81; kinship after, 59–60; *lengua
materna* and, 80; otherness of women
as result of, 60; patrilocality and, 58;
separation from community after, 59–
60; traditional Indigenous wife, 78–81.
See also husband-wife relationships

MATE. *See* Museo Mario Testino
maternal community, 63–64; linguistic heritage of, 66–68, 74
maternal figures. *See* Mama Uqllu
Matsigenka language, 10
media production, media and: Aymara language use in, 138; Pachamama Radio, 38, 156–61; public performances in, 221; Quechua language use in, 140; of ritual plays, 200
Mendez, Cecilia, 9
Mercado Bellavista, 103–4
Mercado de San Ignacio, 39, 83, 123, 146. *See also* Indigenous market women; male market vendors
mestizaje identity: historical exclusion, 7–8; as national identity for Peru, 11, 288n5; racial discourse on, 10–11
mestizo dances. *See danzas mestizos*
Mestizo identity: *danza mestizos*, 221–22, 297n3, 298n5
metadiscursive regimes, 137
migrant workers, in street markets, 85
mimicry, of language, 112
Miss Belleza de Foklórica pageant, 299n8
monolingualism, on Pachamama Radio, 166
Morales, Evo, 13, 160
La Morenada dance, 221
morphemes, in ritual plays, 198–199
morphological linguistic mixes, of Aymara/Quechua/Spanish, 124–25, 130–31
mosaic multilingualism, 22–23
Mother Earth. *See* Pachamama
mother tongues. *See lenguas maternas*
moto (speech impediment), 110
multilingualism: in altiplano region, 20–21, 23–24, 26–27, 90–95; communicative practices and, 271; cultural identity in, 24; Indigenous languages and, 6, 21–22, 34; among Indigenous market women, 97–102, 114–20; inter-Indigenous, 26–27, 35–40, 276; mosaic, 22–23; on Pachamama Radio, 166–68, 175; in Puno, 35–40; in street markets, 36, 86–95, 97, 102; translanguaging and, 97–98; in *Willakuy-Yatiyawinaka*, 164–67
Museo Mario Testino (MATE), 266
music: in Andean region, 103; *huaynos*, 103; *sikurris*, 220–22, 296n1

national census, in Peru, 7, 287n1
national identity, for Bolivia, 183
nature, kinship with, 53–54
neoindigenismo movement, 181–82
neoindigenista movement, 31, 96, 288n9, 295n3
newspapers, Indigenous language: *Los Andes*, 141, 174; Indigenous literacy and, 140–44; separation of languages in, 145; Spanish translations for, 142–44; trilingual, 141–43; *Willakuy-Yatiyawinaka*, 141–45
New Year celebrations, in Andean region: Aymara language use in, 281–84; Federación de Foklór and, 281; pan-Andean indigeneity and, 280–85; San Juan de Bautista celebration, 289; traditional dress, 281; yatiri speech, 281

origin myths: for Mama Uqllu, 179, 185–88; about Manqu Qhapaq, 179, 185–88
orthographic practices: in Andean region, 135–36; in Aymara language, 135–36; in Puno, 135–36; in Quechua language, 135–36; of Spanish colonial writers, 287n2

Pacco, Adelina, 256–62
Pacha Illariy (radio show), 158, 162, 166–67
Pachamama (Mother Earth), 281
Pachamama Radio, 38, 156, 294n6; Aymara language use on, 157, 164,

167, 173; founding of, 157; goals and purpose of, 157–58, 162; Indigenous identity and, 262; Indigenous unification through, 158; *Jiwasanaka*, 173; kin terms on, 168–69, 171–73; language-switching on, 164–66, 168, 171–72; *Markasa Layku*, 158–59, 163–64, 169–73; monolingualism programming, 166; multilingualism on, 166–68, 173; *Pacha Illariy*, 158, 162, 166–67; *Pedro Vilcapaza*, 160–61; political activism and, 160; Quechua folkloric traditions on, 159; Quechua language use on, 157, 164; as shared sound space, 161–74; trilingualism on, 164

Palomino, Modesto, 166–68, 172–73

pan-Andean indigeneity: in altiplano, 281; New Year celebrations and, 280–85; Pachamama offerings, 281

Paraguay, Guaraché language in, 15

parallelism, in ritual plays, 198

paternal communities, 64

paternal figures. *See* Manqu Qhapaq

paternal kin networks, 64

patrilocality, 58

pedagogical method, for Indigenous bilingual education, 148–52

Pedro Vilcapaza (radio serial), 160–61

personhood: in Andean culture, 185; in Andean region, 57–58; definition of, 41, 55; Indigenous identity and, 19; for Indigenous women, 255–56, 270. *See also* identity; social personhood

Peru: Afro-Peruvian populations in, 10–11, 288n4; colorism in, 213; extended boundaries of Indigenous language use, 174–76; geographic regions for, 10; *Inkas sí, indios no* ("Inkas yes, not Indians"), 9–10; Instituto Nacional de Estadística e Informática, 7; *mestizaje* identity in, 11, 288n5; as mestizo nation, 11; Ministry of Tourism in, 219; national census in, 7, 287n1; racial categories in, 5, 287n3, 288n5; rejection of historical Indigenous identity, 9–10; Wars of Independence in, 9, 295n2. *See also* altiplano; Lima, Peru; Puno, Peru; *specific topics*

Phaye, Maribel, 244–51

phrasebooks, in street markets, 91–92

Plaza de Armas, 135

plurilingualism, in Bolivia, 12

priests, in Andean culture, 197–198

PromPerú, 181, 219

public performances: in altiplano, 220; Aymara language use in, 39–40; in broadcast media, 221; dances as, 221–23; *danza mestizos*, 221–22, 297n3, 298n5; of Indigenous performative arts, 219–21; Quechua language use in, 39–40; of ritual plays, 184–85; *sikurris*, 220; Virgen de la Candelaria, 220–21. *See also* beauty pageants; ritual plays

puneña women, ideals for: in altiplano region, 215; in Andean region, 215; authenticity of, 255–63; Aymara-speaking women and, 216–17; ethnic diversity and, 215; ethnolinguistic differences, 217; failure to perform, 255–63; ideologized practices for, 214–15; Indigenous authenticity, 216–17; Indigenous femininity and, 261–62; legitimization of, 215; linguistic diversity for, 215; Mama Uqllu as, 215–17; Manqu Qhapaq and, 216; Quechua-speaking women and, 216; in ritual performances, 214–15

puneños: cross-linguistic marriages and, 71–74, 76–77; Federación de Foklór and, 187–88, 202; ideal puneña women, 214–17; Indigenous, 19, 28–29, 36; *lenguas maternas* among, 6; Pachamama Radio and, 156–61; Quechua language use, 243; women, 29; youth, 255

Puno, Peru: Aymara culture in, 4–5; *bravas* in, 210–11; colonial legacy of, 131; colorism in, 213; Cuyo-Cuyo region in, 243–55; ethnolinguistic groups in, 136–37; Federación de Foklór in, 187–88, 222, 262, 281; as Folkloric Capital of Peru, 219; founding myth for, 44; gender practices in, 35–40; Indigenous cultural vitality in, 222; Indigenous culture in, 4–5; Indigenous identity in, 5, 18; Indigenous languages in, 131; Indigenous market women in, 38–39, 87–88, 131; inter-Indigenous contact in, 19–28; inter-Indigenous ethnic differences in, 5; inter-Indigenous multilingualism in, 35–40; Lake Titicaca region and, 179; linguistic knowledge in, 49; Mama Uqllu and, 179; Manqu Qhapaq and, 179; market cooperatives in, 126; municipal buildings in, 135–36; orthographic practices in, 135–36; Plaza de Armas in, 135; professionals in, 4–5; Quechua culture in, 4–5; Quechua language use in, 261; Spanish language use in, 137; street markets in, 88–89, 126; Virgen de la Candelaria, 220–21; *zona Aymara* in, 136–37, 232; *zona Quechua* in, 136–37. *See also* Aymara language; Aymara-speaking women; Pachamama Radio; Quechua language; Quechua-speaking women

purism. *See* language purism

Putinapunco community, 21

Quechua, etymology of, 288n8

Quechua culture: High Academy of Quechua, 198; in Pachamama Radio, 159; in Puno, 4–5

Quechua language, use of: in altiplano, 20; in *Belleza del Altiplano*, 230–31, 235–39, 243; in bilingual education, 152–56; boundaries of, 277; bounded readership and, 140–46; colonial legacy and, 140–41; communicative practices for, 37; community-specific speech practices, 61–62; cultural meaning of, 275–80; in Cuyo-Cuyo, 243–55; diagrammatic signs in, 135; differences with Aymara language, 7–12, 48–49, 122, 133; differences with Spanish language, 122; ethnographic approaches to, 5; as ethnolinguistic category, 18; gendered associations in, 6–7; ideology of, 27; *idiomas* and, 132–33; Indigeneity of, 12; among Indigenous market women, 97–104, 113–17, 123–24; in Inka Empire, 184, 193–201; intonations in, 101; linguistic boundaries with Aymara language, 137; as linguistic variety, 27–28; literacy and, 140–46; in media production, 140; modeling standardized varieties of, 140; morphological linguistic mix with, 124–25, 129–30; naming of, 26; objectification of, 278; orthographic practices in, 135–36; on Pachamama Radio, 157, 164; in popular culture, 6; in public performances, 39–40; by puneños, 243; in Puno, 261; scalar evaluative frameworks for, 277; semiotic differences with, 155; in shared sound spaces, 161–74; SOV word order in, 250, 301n16; Spanish language influences on, 293n8; status of, 278; in street markets, 86–87, 90–91, 95, 97, 106–7; symbolic capital of, 122; *zona Quechua*, 136–37. *See also* code-switching/mixing; Quechua-speaking women; *specific topics*

Quechua people: Catholic conversion of, 295n4; as ethnic category, 6; Qapaq, 183; as stateless, 175

Quechua-speaking women: in Coasa, 256–62; gender roles and, 5; ideal

puneña women as, 216–17; methodological approach to, 40–45. *See also* Indigenous market women
Quijano, Anibal, 11
Quispe, Yessica, 239–42
qullasuyeños, 77
Qullasuyu, cross-linguistic marriages in, 77–78

race, racial categories and: beauty pageants and, 225; *mestizaje* identity, 7–8, 10–11; Mestizo identity, 181–82; in Peru, 5, 287n3
racial hierarchies, 5
racialized identity, 5; femininity as element of, 213–14
racism. *See* silent racism
Radio Quispillaccta, 159
reciprocity, among Indigenous market women, 122
repartimiento regulation, 23
repetition: in *Belleza del Altiplano*, 250, 260–61; in ritual plays, 198
Republic of Bolivia. *See* Bolivia
ritual plays: in Andean culture, 180–85; annual performance of, 179, 187; in Cusco, 181; ideal puneña women, 214–15; *indigenismo* movement, 181–82; Indigenous themes in, 181; Mama Uqllu in, 192; Manqu Qhapaq in, 192; Mestizo identity in, 181–82; morphemes in, 198–199; *neoindigenismo* movement, 181–82; parallelism in, 198; pre-Hispanic histories, 182; PromPerú, 181; public performance of, 184–85; in Quechua language, 182, 184; regional broadcasting of, 200; repetition in, 198; secrecy of, 186–87. *See also* Mama Uqllu; Manqu Qhapaq
rural areas, rural spaces: Indigenous puneños in, 36; inter-Indigenous multilingualism in, 35–40
Ruray, Sumaq, 72–74

Salesiana, Maria, 147–48
San Juan de Bautista celebration, 280
San Juan del Oro community, 21
scalar evaluative frameworks: for Aymara language, 277; for Indigenous femininity, 269–71; for Indigenous languages, 302n6; for Quechua language, 277
scripts, for ritual plays, for Mama Uqllu, 203–9
Seligmann, Linda, 122
Señorita Campesina pageant, 299 n8
settler-colonialism, language ideologies and, 15
settler-colonial sublime, 264
shared sound spaces: Aymara language use in, 161–74; *lenguas maternas* in, 161–62; Pachamama Radio as, 161–74; Quechua language use in, 161–74
Shipibo language, 8, 10
sikurris (traditional ritual music): in altiplano, 297n1; in Andean region, 222; competitions with, 220–222; Concurso de Sikurris, 220, 222; dances and, 220–22; public performances of, 220
silent racism, against Indigenous populations, 287n3
social identity, social personhood and: community-specific speech practices and, 62; formation of, 54; Indigenous languages as influence on, 61; Indigenous puneños and, 54–55; inter-Indigenous differences and, 54–55
social personhood, 54
SOV order. *See* subject-object-verb order
Spain, colonialism and, 11
Spanish language, use of: Aymara language influenced by, 293n8; in beauty pageants, 226–227; in bilingual education, 146–55; colonial context for, 131; differences with Aymara language, 123; differences with Quechua language, 123; *idiomas* and, 132–33; Indigenous

Spanish language, use of (*continued*)
bilingual education through, 147–56; for Indigenous market women, 99, 104, 121, 129, 130; in Indigenous newspapers, 143–45; linguistic syncretism and, 129; morphological linguistic mix with, 124–25, 129–30; orthographic practices of, 287n2; as primary language, 70; in Puno, 139; Quechua language influenced by, 293n8; in street markets, 86–87, 97, 106–7; symbolic capital of, 122

Spanish-speaking women, in beauty pageants, 226–27

speeches, in ritual plays: by Mama Uqllu, 205–209; transcription of, 209

speech impediment. *See moto*

street markets, market spaces and: in altiplano, 86–92; in Andean region, 86–92; in Arequipa, 127; Aymara language use in, 90–91, 95, 97, 106–7; bilingualism in, 102; communication with vendors in, 81; cooperative, 90, 126–27; currency issues in, 88; as gendered space, 92–97; gendering of, 85; intergenerational networks, 90–91; in Lima, 127; male market vendors, 83; market association networks, 87–91; market cooperatives, 90, 126–27; Mercado Bellavista, 102–3; Mercado de San Ignacio, 39, 81, 90, 93, 186; migrant workers in, 82; as multigenerational space, 93, 95; multilingualism in, 36, 84–93, 97, 102; phrasebooks in, 91–92; in Puno, 86–87, 126; Quechua language use in, 90–91, 95, 97, 106–7; receptivity in, 102–22; as self-sustaining economies, 106; social life in, 87; Spanish language use in, 97, 106–7. *See also* Indigenous market women; male market vendors; market vendors

subject-object-verb order (SOV order), in Quechua language, 250, 301n16

Swinehart, Karl, 293n1

Tawantinsuyu, 22
Testino, Mario, 268, 302n1; *Alta Moda*, 265–67, 304n2; Museo Mario Testino, 266; Peruvian heritage, 265
Tiwanaku empire, 22
Todos Los Santos celebration, 51, 290n2
tourism, in Peru: in Cusco, 191-92; Ministry of Tourism and, 219
traditional dances. *See* dances
traditional folk song. *See huayno*
traditional Indigenous wife, 78–79; *lengua materna* and, 81; linguistic transformation of, 80–81
traditional ritual music. *See sikurris*
translanguaging, among Indigenous market women, 97–98, 126–27
trilingualism: in newspapers, 140–43; on Pachamama Radio, 164
tropes, about Indigenous people and culture, 267
trust, among Indigenous market women, 122
Tucker, Joshua, 159

Unidad Nacional de Comunidades Aymaras (UNCA), 272–74, 294n6, 295n10
urban areas, urban spaces and: gendered linguistic genealogies in, 69–78; inter-Indigenous multilingualism in, 35–40
urban kinship, gendered linguistic genealogies and, 69–78
Uru language, 21

Vilcapaza, Pedro, 158
Villareal, Gabriela Zamorano, 160
Virgen de la Candelaria, 83–84, 297n2; *Belleza del Altiplano* and, 227; dances

during, 298n4; public performances of, 220–21

Wade, Peter, 288n5
Waka Waka dance, 221
Wars of Independence, in Peru, 9, 295n2
white women. *See criollas*
Willakuy-Yatiyawinaka (newspaper column), 141–43, 155, 294n3; Indigenous linguistic diversity in, 146
women: *criollas*, 122; ideal puneña women, 214–17; indigeneity in Andes region, 28–34; otherness of, 60; political activism of, 211. *See also* Aymara-speaking women; gender; Indigenous market women; Indigenous women; maternal community; Quechua-speaking women; Spanish-speaking women; *specific topics*
worksheets, for bilingual education, 152

Yanapa, Monica, 251–55
yatiri, speeches for, 281
youths, puneños and, 255
Yucatan Peninsula, language maintenance in, 16
Yucatec Maya language, 16

zona Aymara, in Puno, 136, 232
zona Quechua, in Puno, 136

About the Author

Sandhya Krittika Narayanan is an assistant professor of anthropology at the University of Nevada, Reno, where she also directs the Linguistic Anthropology Research Lab (LARL). Her research focuses on the Quechua-Aymara language contact and multilingualism in the Peruvian altiplano. Her work has been published in *Language and Communication, Signs and Society,* and *Gender and Language.*

Printed and bound by CPI Group (UK) Ltd, Croydon, CR0 4YY
25/11/2025

14779184-0005